SPSS/PC+ Advanced Statistics™ V2.0

for the IBM PC/XT/AT and PS/2

MARIJA J. NORUSIS/SPSS INC.

SPSS Inc.
444 N. Michigan Avenue
Chicago, Illinois 60611
312.329.3300

SPSS Europe B.V.
P.O. Box 115
4200 AC Gorinchem
The Netherlands
Tel. +31.1830.36711
Twx.: 21019 (SPSS NL)

For more information about the SPSS/PC+ Advanced Statistics™ V2.0 system and other software produced and distributed by SPSS Inc., please write or call

Marketing Department
SPSS Inc.
444 North Michigan Avenue
Chicago, IL 60611
312/329-3300

In Europe, please write or call

SPSS Europe B.V.
P.O. Box 115
4200 AC Gorinchem
The Netherlands
+31183036711
TWX: 21019 (SPSS nl)

Preface

SPSS/PC+ is a powerful software package for microcomputer data management and analysis. The Advanced Statistics option for SPSS/PC+ V2.0 is an add-on enhancement that enables you to perform sophisticated multivariate statistical analyses. The procedures in Advanced Statistics must be used with the SPSS/PC+ base system and are completely integrated into that system.

Advanced Statistics includes procedures for factor analysis, hierarchical log-linear analysis, cluster analysis (using two different algorithms), discriminant analysis, and multivariate analysis of variance, plus a new procedure for reliability analysis of additive scales. These procedures bring most of the power of mainframe statistical software to the personal computer. The algorithms and much of the programming are identical to those used in SPSS^X on mainframe computers. Although the size of the problems you can analyze may be limited by the amount of memory installed on your PC, statistical results you obtain from SPSS/PC+ will be as accurate as those computed on a mainframe.

SPSS/PC+ with Advanced Statistics will enable you to perform many analyses on your PC that were previously possible only on much larger machines. We hope that this new statistical power will make SPSS/PC+ an even more useful tool in your work.

Compatibility SPSS Inc. warrants that SPSS/PC+ and enhancements are designed for personal computers in the IBM PC and IBM PS/2™ lines with a 10MB or larger hard disk. These products also function on many closely IBM-compatible machines. Contact SPSS Inc. for details about specific IBM-compatible hardware.

Serial Numbers Your serial number is your identification number with SPSS Inc. You will need this serial number when you call SPSS Inc. for information regarding support, payment, a defective diskette, or an upgraded system.

The serial number can be found on the key diskette accompanying your system. If you are a Value Plus customer, it is on the diskette labeled U1. Before using the system, please copy this number to the **registration card.**

Registration Card STOP! Before continuing on, *fill out and send us your registration card.* Until we receive your registration card, you have an unregistered system. Even if you have previously sent a card to us, please fill out and return the card enclosed in your SPSS/PC+ Advanced Statistics package. Note: if your current order includes more than one SPSS/PC+ V2.0 product (SPSS/PC+, SPSS/PC+ Tables, SPSS/PC+ Trends, SPSS/PC+ Graphics, SPSS/PC+ Mapping, SPSS/PC+ Graph-in-the-Box, or SPSS/PC+ Advanced Statistics), you can return a single card.

Registering your system entitles you to

- Technical support on our customer hot-line.
- Favored customer status.
- *Keywords*—the SPSS user newsletter.
- New product announcements.

Of course, unregistered systems receive none of the above, so *don't put it off—send your registration card now!*

Replacement Policy Call the Micro Software Department at 312/329-3300 to report a defective diskette. You must provide us with the serial number of your system. SPSS Inc. will ship replacement diskettes the same day we receive notification from you. Please return the defective diskettes to the Micro Software Department, SPSS Inc., 444 North Michigan Avenue, Chicago, IL 60611.

Shipping List The shipping list for SPSS/PC+ V2.0 Advanced Statistics is on a separate sheet in the package.

Training Seminars SPSS Inc. provides both public and onsite training seminars for SPSS/PC+. There is a two-day introductory course to familiarize users with the basics of SPSS/PC+. In addition there is an advanced course, also two days, that deals with more sophisticated aspects of the program. Additional seminars treat specialized topics such as data entry, graphics, report writing, and time series analysis. All seminars feature hands-on workshops.

SPSS/PC+ seminars will be offered in major U.S. and European cities on a regular basis. For further information on these seminars or to schedule an onsite seminar, call the SPSS Inc. Training Department at 312/329-2400.

Additional Documentation Additional copies of all three SPSS/PC+ system manuals may be purchased separately. To order additional manuals, just fill out the enclosed Documentation Card and send it to

SPSS Inc.
Documentation Sales
444 N. Michigan Avenue
Chicago, IL 60611

Please be sure to include $3.00 for shipping and handling.

Techline The SPSS technical hot-line is available to registered customers of SPSS/PC+. Customers may call the Techline for assistance in using SPSS products or for installation help for one of the warranted hardware environments.

To reach a Techline consultant, call 312/329-3410, 9:00 a.m. to 5:00 p.m. (central time). Be prepared to identify yourself, your organization, and the serial number of your system. If a consultant is not available, an answering machine will take your message and a consultant will return the call as soon as possible. In either situation, be prepared to summarize your problem and the reason for the call.

We Want to Hear from You Your comments are important. So send us a letter and let us know about your experiences with SPSS products. We especially like to hear about new and interesting applications using the SPSS/PC+ system. Write to

SPSS Inc. Marketing Department
Attn: Micro Software Products Manager
444 N. Michigan Avenue
Chicago, IL 60611

Contents

Introduction

About This Manual

About This Manual

This manual documents the statistical procedures available in SPSS/PC+ Advanced Statistics™. The manual is organized similarly to the *SPSS/PC+* base manual in that there are different parts designed to meet the needs of different users. For those who have limited experience with statistics, statistical overviews are available. For those who are already familiar with statistical computing, a reference section presents the procedures in SPSS/PC+ Advanced Statistics without extensive examples. You are likely to find different parts of the manual most valuable as your experience with SPSS/PC+ grows.

To use SPSS/PC+ Advanced Statistics, you should be familiar with the SPSS/PC+ language as described in the *SPSS/PC+* manual. In addition, this manual assumes that you know how to run the SPSS/PC+ system and that you are familiar with basic data entry and manipulation. If you are unfamiliar with SPSS/PC+, consult the base manual for further information.

If you have just received SPSS/PC+ Advanced Statistics, you may want to turn first to the installation instructions in the Appendix. You need to install SPSS/PC+ Advanced Statistics only once, unless you remove it from your system. (You can, however, remove and reinstall portions of the SPSS/PC+ system: see the section on SPSS MANAGER in the *SPSS/PC+* manual.) Once you have installed SPSS/PC+ Advanced Statistics, you will need to authorize the key diskette to use the additional procedures. These instructions are also in the installation instructions in the Appendix.

The four basic parts to this manual are described below.

Statistics Guide. The Statistics Guide (Part B) contains overviews of the statistics and operations for the six procedures contained in SPSS/PC+ Advanced Statistics. The SPSS/PC+ input used to create the sample output in these chapters is shown to help you understand each procedure's operation.

Command Reference. The Command Reference (Part C) is a detailed reference to the syntax and operations of the six procedures contained in SPSS/PC+ Advanced Statistics. The individual procedures are presented in alphabetical order. For each procedure, the Command Reference provides complete syntax rules plus details of operations. A section on using DATA LIST to read matrix materials into those procedures that accept matrix input is also included.

Examples. The examples presented in Part D illustrate typical uses of the six analytical procedures contained in SPSS/PC+ Advanced Statistics. The annotated input and output are arranged not to imitate an interactive SPSS/PC+ session but to demonstrate a set of commands that carry out a complete data analysis task.

You may find that these examples, with their interpretative commentary, extend your understanding of the logic of SPSS/PC+ command structure.

Appendixes. Installing SPSS/PC+ Advanced Statistics describes the process of copying SPSS/PC+ Advanced Statistics onto your system. It also explains how to authorize your key diskette to allow you to use these procedures. Differences Between SPSS/PC and SPSS/PC+ describes changes in the procedures between SPSS/PC+ and earlier versions of SPSS/PC. Help for SPSS[X] Users is intended for users familiar with the SPSS[X] system. It documents the important differences between SPSS[X] and SPSS/PC+. This appendix is especially useful for people who are transferring jobs between SPSS[X] and SPSS/PC+.

Statistics Guide

Contents

Chapter 1   Predicting Cure and Credit: Discriminant Analysis

Gazing into crystal balls is not the exclusive domain of soothsayers. Judges, college admissions counselors, bankers, and many other professionals must foretell outcomes such as parole violation, success in college, and creditworthiness.

An intuitive strategy is to compare the characteristics of a potential student or credit applicant to those of cases whose success or failure is already known. Based on similarities and differences a prediction can be made. Often this is done subjectively, using only the experience and wisdom of the decision maker. However, as problems grow more complex and the consequences of bad decisions become more severe, a more objective procedure for predicting outcomes is often desirable.

Before considering statistical techniques, let's summarize the problem. Based on a collection of variables, such as yearly income, age, marital status, and total worth, we wish to distinguish among several mutually exclusive groups, such as good credit risks and bad credit risks. The available data are the values of the variables for cases whose group membership is known, that is, cases who have proven to be good or bad credit risks. We also wish to identify the variables that are important for distinguishing among the groups and to develop a procedure for predicting group membership for new cases whose group membership is undetermined.

Discriminant analysis, first introduced by Sir Ronald Fisher, is the statistical technique most commonly used to investigate this set of problems. The concept underlying discriminant analysis is fairly simple. Linear combinations of the independent, sometimes called predictor, variables are formed and serve as the basis for classifying cases into one of the groups.

For the linear discriminant function to be "optimal," that is, to provide a classification rule that minimizes the probability of misclassification, certain assumptions about the data must be met. Each group must be a sample from a multivariate normal population, and the population covariance matrices must all be equal. Section 1.42 discusses tests for violations of the assumptions and the performance of linear discriminant analysis when assumptions are violated.

Sections 1.2 through 1.34 cover the basics of discriminant analysis and the output from SPSS/PC+ DSCRIMINANT using a two-group example. Extending this type of analysis to include more than two groups is discussed beginning in Section 1.35.

1.1
INVESTIGATING RESPIRATORY DISTRESS SYNDROME

Respiratory Distress Syndrome (RDS) is one of the leading causes of death in premature infants. Although intensive research has failed to uncover its causes, a variety of physiological disturbances, such as insufficient oxygen uptake and high blood acidity, are characteristic of RDS. These are usually treated by administering oxygen and buffers to decrease acidity. However, a substantial proportion of RDS infants fail to survive.

P. K. J. van Vliet and J. M. Gupta (1973) studied 50 infants with a diagnosis of RDS based on clinical signs and symptoms and confirmed by chest x-ray. For each case they report the infant's outcome—whether the infant died or survived—as well as values for eight variables that might be predictors of outcome. Table 1.1 gives the SPSS/PC+ names and descriptions of these variables.

Table 1.1 Possible predictors of survival

Variable name	Description
SURVIVAL	Infant's outcome. Coded 1 if infant died, 2 if survived.
SEX	Infant's sex. Coded 0 for females, 1 for males.
APGAR	Score on the APGAR test, which measures infant's responsiveness. Scores range from 0 to 10.
AGE	The gestational age of the infant measured in weeks. Values of 36 to 38 are obtained for full-term infants.
TIME	Time, measured in minutes, that it took the infant to begin breathing spontaneously.
WEIGHT	Birthweight measured in kilograms.
PH	The acidity level of the blood, measured on a scale from 0 to 14.
TREATMNT	Type of buffer adminstered (buffer neutralizes acidity). Coded 1 for THAM, 0 for sodium carbonate.
RESP	Indicates whether respiratory therapy was initiated. Coded 0 for no, 1 for yes.

Some dichotomous variables such as SEX are included among the predictor variables. Although, as previously indicated, the linear discriminant function requires that the predictor variables have a multivariate normal distribution, the function has been shown to perform fairly well in a variety of other situations (see Section 1.42).

In this example, we will use discriminant analysis to determine whether the variables listed in Table 1.1 distinguish between infants who recover from RDS and those who do not. If high-risk infants can be identified early, special monitoring and treatment procedures may be instituted for them. It is also of interest to determine which variables contribute most to the separation of infants who survive from those who do not.

1.2
Selecting Cases for the Analysis

The first step in discriminant analysis is to select cases to be included in the computations. A case is excluded from the analysis if it contains missing information for the variable that defines the groups or for any of the predictor variables.

If many cases have missing values for at least one variable, the actual analysis will be based on a small subset of cases. This may be troublesome for two reasons. First, estimates based on small samples are usually quite variable. Second, if the cases with missing values differ from those without missing values, the resulting estimates may be too biased. For example, if highly educated people are more likely to provide information on the variables used in the analysis, selecting cases with complete data will result in a sample that is highly educated. Results obtained from such a sample might differ from those that would be obtained if people at all educational levels were included. Therefore, it is usually a good strategy to examine cases with missing values to see whether there is evidence that missing values are associated with some particular characteristics of the cases. If there are many missing values for some variables, you should consider the possibility of eliminating those variables from the analysis.

Figure 1.2 shows the entire SPSS/PC+ job and the output produced by DSCRIMINANT after all the data have been processed. The first line of the output indicates how many cases are eligible for inclusion. The second line indicates the number of cases excluded from analysis because of missing values for the predictor variables or the variable that defines the groups. In this example, two cases with missing values are excluded from the analysis. If you use the WEIGHT command, DSCRIMINANT prints the sum of the weights in each group and the actual number of cases.

Figure 1.2 Case summary

```
TITLE 'INFANT SURVIVAL EXAMPLE--2-GROUP DISCRIMINANT'.
DATA LIST /CASEID 1-2 SURVIVAL 4 TREATMNT 6 TIME 8-10(1)
 WEIGHT 12-15(3) APGAR 17-18 SEX 20 AGE 22-23 PH 33-35(2) RESP 37.
VARIABLE LABELS SURVIVAL 'INFANT SURVIVAL'
 TREATMNT 'TREATMNT ADMINISTERED'
 TIME 'TIME TO SPONTANEOUS RESPIRATION'
 WEIGHT 'BIRTHWEIGHT IN KILOGRAMS'
 APGAR 'APGAR SCORE'
 SEX 'SEX OF INFANT'
 PH 'PH LEVEL'
 RESP 'RESPIRATORY THERAPY'.
MISSING VALUES RESP(9).
VALUE LABELS TREATMNT 1'THAM' 0'SODIUM BICARBONATE'
 /SEX 0'FEMALE' 1'MALE' /RESP 1'YES' 0'NO' 9'NO ANSWER'
 /SURVIVAL 2'SURVIVE' 1'DIE'.
DSCRIMINANT GROUPS=SURVIVAL(1,2)
 /VARIABLES=TREATMNT TO RESP.
```

```
On groups defined by SURVIVAL  INFANT SURVIVAL

       50 (unweighted) cases were processed.
        2 of these were excluded from the analysis.
           0 had missing or out-of-range group codes.
           2 had at least one missing discriminating variable.
       48 (unweighted) cases will be used in the analysis.


Number of Cases by Group

                  Number of Cases
     SURVIVAL  Unweighted    Weighted  Label

            1          26        26.0  DIE
            2          22        22.0  SURVIVE

     Total          48        48.0
```

1.3 Analyzing Group Differences

Although the variables are interrelated and we will need to employ statistical techniques that incorporate these dependencies, it is often helpful to begin analyzing the differences between groups by examining univariate statistics.

Figure 1.3a contains the means for the eight independent variables for infants who died (Group 1) and who survived (Group 2), along with the corresponding standard deviations. The last row of each table, labeled "Total," contains the means and standard deviations calculated when all cases are combined into a single sample.

Figure 1.3a   Group means and standard deviations

```
DSCRIMINANT GROUPS=SURVIVAL(1,2)
 /VARIABLES=TREATMNT TO RESP
 /STATISTICS=1 2.
```

Group means

SURVIVAL	TREATMNT	TIME	WEIGHT	APGAR	SEX	AGE	PH	RESP
1	0.38462	2.88462	1.70950	5.50000	0.65385	32.38462	7.17962	0.65385
2	0.59091	2.31818	2.36091	6.31818	0.68182	34.63636	7.34636	0.27273
Total	0.47917	2.62500	2.00806	5.87500	0.66667	33.41667	7.25604	0.47917

Group Standard Deviations

SURVIVAL	TREATMNT	TIME	WEIGHT	APGAR	SEX	AGE	PH	RESP
1	0.49614	3.48513	0.51944	2.77489	0.48516	3.11226	0.08502	0.48516
2	0.50324	3.70503	0.62760	2.69720	0.47673	2.71759	0.60478	0.45584
Total	0.50485	3.56027	0.65353	2.74152	0.47639	3.12051	0.41751	0.50485

From Figure 1.3a you can see that 38% of the infants who died were treated with THAM, 65% were male, and 65% received respiratory therapy. (When a variable is coded 0 or 1, the mean of the variable is the proportion of cases with a value of 1.) Infants who died took longer to breathe spontaneously, weighed less, and had lower APGAR scores than infants who survived.

Figure 1.3b shows significance tests for the equality of group means for each variable. The F values and their significance, shown in columns 3 and 4, are the same as those calculated from a one-way analysis of variance with survival as the grouping variable. For example, the F value in Figure 1.3c, which is an analysis of variance table for WEIGHT from procedure ONEWAY, is 15.49, the same as shown for WEIGHT in Figure 1.3b. (When there are two groups, the F value is just the square of the t value from the two-sample t test.) The significance level is 0.0003. If the observed significance level is small (less than 0.05), the hypothesis that all group means are equal is rejected.

Figure 1.3b   Tests for univariate equality of group means

```
DSCRIMINANT GROUPS=SURVIVAL(1,2)
 /VARIABLES=TREATMNT TO RESP
 /STATISTICS=1 2 6.
```

Wilks' Lambda (U-statistic) and univariate F-ratio
with   1 and   46 degrees of freedom

Variable	Wilks' Lambda	F	Significance
TREATMNT	0.95766	2.034	0.1606
TIME	0.99358	.2971	0.5883
WEIGHT	0.74810	15.49	0.0003
APGAR	0.97742	1.063	0.3080
SEX	0.99913	.4024D-01	0.8419
AGE	0.86798	6.997	0.0111
PH	0.95956	1.939	0.1705
RESP	0.85551	7.769	0.0077

Figure 1.3c   ONEWAY analysis of variance table for WEIGHT

```
ONEWAY WEIGHT BY SURVIVAL(1,2)
 /OPTIONS=2.
```

- - - - - - - - - - - - - - - O N E W A Y - - - - - - - - - - - - - - -

	Variable	WEIGHT	BIRTHWEIGHT IN KILOGRAMS
	By Variable	SURVIVAL	INFANT SURVIVAL

Analysis of Variance

Source	D.F.	Sum of Squares	Mean Squares	F Ratio	F Prob.
Between Groups	1	5.0566	5.0566	15.4894	.0003
Within Groups	46	15.0171	.3265		
Total	47	20.0737			

1.4
Wilks' Lambda

Another statistic displayed in Figure 1.3b is Wilks' lambda, sometimes called the U statistic (see Section 1.17). When variables are considered individually, lambda is the ratio of the within-groups sum of squares to the total sum of squares. For example, Figure 1.3c shows the sums of squares for variable WEIGHT. The ratio of the within-groups sum of squares (15.02) to the total sum of squares (20.07) is 0.748, the value for Wilks' lambda for WEIGHT in Figure 1.3b.

A lambda of 1 occurs when all observed group means are equal. Values close to 0 occur when within-groups variability is small compared to the total variability, that is, when most of the total variability is attributable to differences between the means of the groups. Thus, large values of lambda indicate that group means do not appear to be different, while small values indicate that group means do appear to be different. From Figure 1.3b, WEIGHT, AGE, and RESP are the variables whose means are most different for survivors and nonsurvivors.

1.5
Correlations

Since interdependencies among the variables affect most multivariate analyses, it is worth examining the correlation matrix of the predictor variables. Figure 1.5a is the pooled within-groups correlation matrix. WEIGHT and AGE have the largest correlation coefficient, 0.84. This is to be expected, since weight increases with gestational age. Section 1.19 discusses some of the possible consequences of including highly correlated variables in the analysis.

A *pooled within-groups* correlation matrix is obtained by averaging the separate covariance matrices for all groups and then computing the correlation matrix. A *total* correlation matrix is obtained when all cases are treated as if they are from a single sample.

Figure 1.5a   Pooled within-groups correlation matrix

```
DSCRIMINANT GROUPS=SURVIVAL(1,2)
 /VARIABLES=TREATMNT TO RESP
 /STATISTICS=1 2 6 4.
```

```
Pooled Within-Groups Correlation Matrix


              TREATMNT  TIME     WEIGHT   APGAR    SEX      AGE      PH       RESP

   TREATMNT   1.00000
   TIME        .01841  1.00000
   WEIGHT      .09091  -.21244  1.00000
   APGAR      -.03394  -.50152   .22161  1.00000
   SEX        -.03637  -.12982   .19500  -.02098  1.00000
   AGE         .05749  -.20066   .84040   .36329  -.00129  1.00000
   PH         -.08307   .09102   .12436  -.03156   .00205  1.00000
   RESP       -.00774  -.06994  -.02394   .16123   .26732  -.06828   .03770  1.00000

Correlations which cannot be computed are printed as '.'
```

The total and pooled within-groups correlation matrices can be quite different. For example, Figure 1.5b shows a plot of two hypothetical variables for three groups. When each group is considered individually, the correlation coefficient is close to 0. Averaging, or pooling, these individual estimates also results in a coefficient close to 0. However, the correlation coefficient computed for all cases combined (total) is 0.97, since groups with larger X values also have larger Y values.

Figure 1.5b   Hypothetical variable plot for three groups

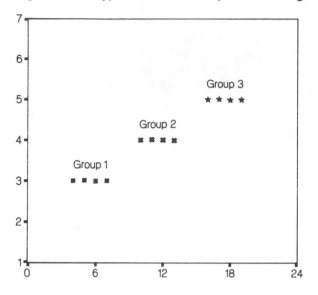

1.6
Estimating the Coefficients

Descriptive statistics and univariate tests of significance provide basic information about the distributions of the variables in the groups and help identify some differences among the groups. However, in discriminant analysis and other multivariate statistical procedures, the emphasis is on analyzing the variables together, not one at a time. By considering the variables simultaneously, we are able to incorporate important information about their relationships.

In discriminant analysis, a linear combination of the independent variables is formed and serves as the basis for assigning cases to groups. Thus, information contained in multiple independent variables is summarized in a single index. For example, by finding a weighted average of variables such as age, weight, and APGAR score, you can obtain a score that distinguishes infants who survive from those who do not. In discriminant analysis, the weights are estimated so that they result in the "best" separation between the groups.

The linear discriminant equation

$$D = B_0 + B_1X_1 + B_2X_2 + \ldots + B_pX_p$$ **Equation 1.6a**

is similar to the multiple linear regression equation. The X's are the values of the independent variables and the B's are coefficients estimated from the data. If a linear discriminant function is to distinguish infants who die from those who survive, the two groups must differ in their D values.

Therefore, the B's are chosen so that the values of the discriminant function differ as much as possible between the groups, or that for the discriminant scores the ratio

$$\frac{\text{between-groups sum of squares}}{\text{within-groups sum of squares}}$$ **Equation 1.6b**

is a maximum. Any other linear combination of the variables will have a smaller ratio.

The actual mechanics of computing the coefficients, especially if there are more than two groups, is somewhat involved (see Morrison, 1967; Tatsuoka, 1971).

The coefficients for the eight variables listed in Table 1.1 are shown in Figure 1.6. Small and large values are sometimes printed in scientific notation. For example, the number .006998343 might be printed as .6998343D−02.

Figure 1.6 Unstandardized discriminant function coefficients

```
DSCRIMINANT GROUPS=SURVIVAL(1,2)
 /VARIABLES=TREATMNT TO RESP
 /STATISTICS=1 2 6 4 11.
```

```
Unstandardized Canonical Discriminant Function Coefficients

              FUNC  1

TREATMNT      .4311545
TIME          .3671274D-01
WEIGHT       2.044035
APGAR         .1264302
SEX           .6998343D-02
AGE          -.2180711
PH            .4078705
RESP        -1.244539
(constant)   -.2309344
```

1.7
Calculating the
Discriminant Score

Based on the coefficients in Figure 1.6, it is possible to calculate the discriminant score for each case. For example, Figure 1.7a contains the value of each variable for the first five cases in the data file. The discriminant score for Case 1 is obtained by multiplying the unstandardized coefficients by the values of the variables, summing these products, and adding the constant. For Case 1, the discriminant score is

$$D_1 = 0.431(1) + 0.0367(2) + 2.044(1.05) + 0.126(5) + 0.007(0)$$
$$- 0.218(28) + 0.408(7.09) - 1.244(0) - 0.231 = -0.16$$

Equation 1.7

Figure 1.7a Values of the variables for the first five cases

```
COMPUTE SCORE=.431*TREATMNT + .0367*TIME + 2.04*WEIGHT + .126*APGAR
            + .007*SEX - .218*AGE + .408*PH - 1.24*RESP - .231.
FORMAT SCORE(F6.3).
LIST CASES=5 /VARIABLES=TREATMNT TO RESP SURVIVAL SCORE
 /FORMAT=NUMBERED.
```

```
C TREATMNT TIME WEIGHT APGAR SEX AGE  PH RESP SURVIVAL  SCORE

1        1  2.0  1.050     5   0  28 7.09    0        1  -.166
2        1  2.0  1.175     4   0  28 7.11    1        1 -1.269
3        1   .5  1.230     7   0  29 7.24    9        1    .
4        1  4.0  1.310     4   1  29 7.13    1        1 -1.123
5        1   .5  1.500     8   1  32 7.23    1        1  -.973

Number of cases read =      5   Number of cases listed =       5
```

Figure 1.7b contains basic descriptive statistics for the discriminant scores in the two groups. The mean score for all cases combined is 0 and the pooled within-groups variance is 1. This is always true for discriminant scores calculated by SPSS/PC+.

Figure 1.7b Descriptive statistics from procedure MEANS

```
DSCRIMINANT GROUPS=SURVIVAL(1,2)
 /VARIABLES=TREATMNT TO RESP
 /SAVE=SCORES=DISCORE.
VARIABLE LABELS DISCORE1 'DISCRIMINANT SCORE'.
MEANS TABLES=DISCORE1 BY SURVIVAL
 /STATISTICS=1.
```

```
Summaries of    DISCORE1   DISCRIMINANT SCORE
By levels of    SURVIVAL   INFANT SURVIVAL

      Value  Label              Sum       Mean      Std Dev Sum of Sq   Cases

          1  DIE          -18.525394  -.7125152   .9055960 20.5026022      26
          2  SURVIVE       18.5253943  .8420634  1.1018901 25.4973978      22

Within Groups Total        0.00000000 0.00000000 1.0000000 46.0000000      48
```

1.8
Bayes' Rule

Using the discriminant score, it is possible to obtain a rule for classifying cases into one of the two groups. The technique used in SPSS/PC+ DSCRIMINANT is based on Bayes' rule. The probability that a case with a discriminant score of D belongs to group i is estimated by

$$P(G_i \mid D) = \frac{P(D \mid G_i) P(G_i)}{\sum_{i=1}^{g} P(D \mid G_i) P(G_i)}$$

Equation 1.8

Sections 1.9 through 1.11 describe the various components of this equation and their relationships.

1.9
Prior Probability

The *prior probability,* represented by $P(G_i)$, is an estimate of the likelihood that a case belongs to a particular group when no information about it is available. For example, if 30% of infants with RDS die, the probability that an infant with RDS will die is 0.3.

The prior probability can be estimated in several ways. If the sample is considered representative of the population, the observed proportions of cases in each group can serve as estimates of the prior probabilities. In this example, 26 out of 48 cases for whom all information is available, or 54%, belong to Group 1 (nonsurvivors), and 22 (46%) belong to Group 2 (survivors). The prior probability of belonging to Group 1, then, is 0.54, and the prior probability of belonging to Group 2 is 0.46.

Often samples are chosen so that they include a fixed number of observations per group. For example, if deaths from RDS were rare, say occurring once per 100 RDS births, even reasonably large samples of RDS births would result in a small number of cases in the nonsurvivor group. Therefore, an investigator might include the same number of survivors and nonsurvivors in the study. In such situations, the prior probability of group membership can be estimated from other sources, such as hospital discharge records.

When all groups are equally likely, or when no information about the probability of group membership is known, equal prior probabilities for all groups may be selected. Since each case must belong to one of the groups, the prior probabilities must sum to 1.

Although prior probabilities convey some information about the likelihood of group membership, they ignore the attributes of the particular case. For example, an infant who is known to be very sick based on various criteria is assigned the same probability of dying as is an infant known to be healthier.

1.10
Conditional Probability

To take advantage of the additional information available for a case in developing a classification scheme, we need to assess the likelihood of the additional information under different circumstances. For example, if the discriminant function scores are normally distributed for each of two groups and the parameters of the distributions can be estimated, it is possible to calculate the probability of obtaining a particular discriminant function value of D if the case is a member of Group 1 or Group 2.

This probability is called the *conditional probability* of D given the group and is denoted by $P(D \mid G_i)$. To calculate this probability, the case is assumed to belong to a particular group and the probability of the observed score given membership in the group is estimated.

1.11
Posterior Probability

The conditional probability of D given the group gives an idea of how likely the score is for members of a particular group. However, when group membership is unknown, what is really needed is an estimate of how likely membership in the various groups is, given the available information. This is called the *posterior probability* and is denoted by $P(G_i|D)$. It can be estimated from $P(D|G_i)$ and $P(G_i)$ using Bayes' rule. A case is classified, based on its discriminant score D, in the group for which the posterior probability is the largest. That is, it is assigned to the most likely group based on its discriminant score. (See Tatsuoka, 1971, for further information.)

1.12
Classification Output

Figure 1.12 is an excerpt from the SPSS/PC+ output that lists classification information for each case for a group of cases whose membership is known. The first column, labeled "Case Number," is the sequence number of the case in the file. The next column, "Mis Val," contains the number of variables with missing values for that case. Cases with missing values are not used in estimating the coefficients and are not included in the output shown in Figure 1.12 (note the absence of cases 3 and 28). However, those two cases with missing values could have been classified and included in the table by substituting group means for missing values. The third column (Sel) indicates whether a case has been excluded from the computations using the SELECT subcommand.

Figure 1.12 Classification output

```
DISCRIMINANT GROUPS=SURVIVAL(1,2)
 /VARIABLES=TREATMNT TO RESP
 /STATISTICS=1 2 6 4 11 14.
```

Case Number	Mis Val	Sel	Actual Group	Highest Probability Group P(D/G) P(G/D)	2nd Highest Group P(G/D)	Discrim Scores
1			1	1 0.5821 0.5873	2 0.4127	-0.1622
2			1	1 0.5776 0.8884	2 0.1116	-1.2695
4			1	1 0.6814 0.8637	2 0.1363	1.1230
5			1	1 0.7962 0.8334	2 0.1666	-0.9708
6			1	1 0.9080 0.7367	2 0.2633	-0.5970
7		**	1	2 0.4623 0.5164	1 0.4836	0.1070
8			1	1 0.8433 0.7112	2 0.2888	-0.5149
9			1	1 0.6581 0.8695	2 0.1305	-1.1551
10			1	1 0.4577 0.5134	2 0.4866	0.0302
11			1	1 0.6087 0.6017	2 0.3983	-0.2006
12			1	1 0.1722 0.9655	2 0.0345	-2.0775
13			1	1 0.1140 0.9750	2 0.0250	-2.2930
14			1	1 0.3430 0.9360	2 0.0640	-1.6607
15			1	1 0.7983 0.6923	2 0.3077	-0.4569
16			1	1 0.7008 0.6482	2 0.3518	-0.3283
17			1	1 0.2090 0.9593	2 0.0407	-1.9687
18			1	1 0.1128 0.9752	2 0.0248	-2.2982
19			1	1 0.4383 0.9178	2 0.0822	-1.4875
20		**	1	2 0.9418 0.7493	1 0.2507	0.7690
21			1	1 0.7384 0.6658	2 0.3342	-0.3786
22		**	1	2 0.5161 0.5495	1 0.4505	0.1927
23			1	1 0.5399 0.8967	2 0.1033	-1.3255
24			1	1 0.4409 0.5026	2 0.4974	0.0582
25		**	1	2 0.8126 0.8288	1 0.1712	1.0791
26			1	1 0.7050 0.6502	2 0.3498	-0.3339
27			1	1 0.5804 0.5864	2 0.4136	-0.1597
29		**	2	1 0.4595 0.5146	2 0.4854	0.0272
30			2	2 0.8552 0.7160	1 0.2840	0.6596
31			2	2 0.6172 0.6062	1 0.3938	0.3423
32			2	2 0.6928 0.6443	1 0.3557	0.4469
33			2	2 0.8887 0.8063	1 0.1937	0.9820
34			2	2 0.6169 0.8793	1 0.1207	1.3423
35			2	2 0.6823 0.8635	1 0.1365	1.2514
36			2	2 0.7755 0.6824	1 0.3176	0.5568
37			2	2 0.6368 0.8746	1 0.1254	1.3143
38			2	2 0.0874 0.9795	1 0.0205	2.5512
39			2	2 0.1236 0.9735	1 0.0265	2.3821
40			2	2 0.0181 0.9925	1 0.0075	3.2050
41			2	2 0.9033 0.7349	1 0.2651	0.7206
42		**	2	1 0.5613 0.8920	2 0.1080	-1.2934
43		**	2	1 0.5270 0.5560	2 0.4440	-0.0799
44		**	2	1 0.3851 0.9281	2 0.0719	-1.5810
45			2	2 0.5574 0.5735	1 0.4265	0.2553
46			2	2 0.7718 0.8401	1 0.1599	1.1321
47			2	2 0.6792 0.6377	1 0.3623	0.4286
48			2	2 0.9649 0.7819	1 0.2181	0.8861
49			2	2 0.5742 0.8891	1 0.1109	1.4040
50			2	2 0.4533 0.9148	1 0.0852	1.5920

For cases included in the computation of the discriminant function, actual group membership is known and can be compared to that predicted using the discriminant function. The group to which a case actually belongs is listed in the column labeled "Actual Group." The most-likely group for a case based on the discriminant analysis (the group with the largest posterior probability) is listed in the column labeled "Highest Group." Cases that are misclassified using the discriminant function are flagged with asterisks next to the actual group number.

The next value listed is the probability of a case's discriminant score, or one more extreme, if the case is a member of the most-likely group.

The larger posterior probabilities of membership in the two groups $P(G|D)$ follow in Figure 1.12. When there are only two groups, both probabilities are given since one is the highest and the other the second highest. The probabilities 0.5873 and 0.4127 sum to 1 since a case must be a member of one of the two groups.

1.13
Classification Summary

You can obtain the number of misclassified cases by counting the number of cases with asterisks in Figure 1.12. In this example, 9 cases out of 50 are classified incorrectly.

More detailed information on the results of the classification phase is available from the output in Figure 1.13, sometimes called the "Confusion Matrix." For each group, this output shows the numbers of correct and incorrect classifications. In this example only the cases with complete information for all predictor variables are included in the classification results table. Correctly classified cases appear on the diagonal of the table since the predicted and actual groups are the same. For example, of 26 cases in Group 1, 22 were predicted correctly to be members of Group 1 (84.6%), while 4 (15.4%) were assigned incorrectly to Group 2. Similarly, 18 out of 22 (81.8%) of the Group 2 cases were identified correctly, and 4 (18.2%) were misclassified. The overall percentage of cases classified correctly is 83.3% (40 out of 48).

Figure 1.13 Classification results

```
DSCRIMINANT GROUPS=SURVIVAL(1,2)
 /VARIABLES=TREATMNT TO RESP
 /STATISTICS=1 2 6 4 11 14 13.
```

Classification Results –				
Actual Group		No. of Cases	Predicted Group Membership 1	2
Group 1 DIE		26	22 84.6%	4 15.4%
Group 2 SURVIVE		22	4 18.2%	18 81.8%
Percent of "grouped" cases correctly classified: 83.33%				

1.14
Histograms of Discriminant Scores

To see how much the two groups overlap and to examine the distribution of the discriminant scores, it is often useful to plot the discriminant function scores for the groups. Figure 1.14a is a histogram of the scores for each group separately. Four symbols (either 1's or 2's) represent one case. (The number of cases represented by a symbol depends on the number of cases used in an analysis.) The row of 1's and 2's underneath the plot denote to which group scores are assigned. We note that four Group 1 cases fall into the Group 2 classification region, and four Group 2 cases fall into the Group 1 region.

The average score for a group is called the group centroid and is indicated on each plot as well as in Figure 1.14b. These values are the same as the means in

Figure 1.7b. On the average, infants who died have smaller discriminant function scores than infants who survived. The average value for Group 1 infants who died is −0.71, whereas the average value for those who survived is 0.84.

Figure 1.14a   Histograms of discriminant scores

```
DSCRIMINANT GROUPS=SURVIVAL(1,2)
 /VARIABLES=TREATMNT TO RESP
 /STATISTICS=1 2 6 4 11 14 13 16.
```

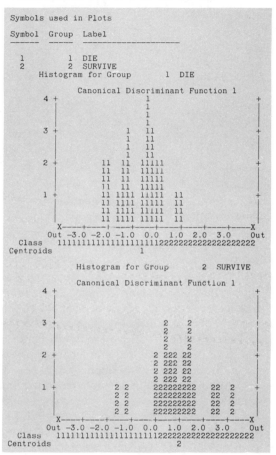

Figure 1.14b   Discriminant functions evaluated at group means

```
DSCRIMINANT GROUPS=SURVIVAL(1,2)
 /VARIABLES=TREATMNT TO RESP
 /STATISTICS=1 2 6 4 11 14 13 16.
```

```
Canonical Discriminant Functions evaluated at Group Means (Group Centroids)

    Group      FUNC   1

      1       -0.71252
      2        0.84206
```

The combined distribution of the scores for the two groups is shown in Figure 1.14c. Again four symbols represent a case, and you can see the amount of overlap between the two groups. For example, the interval with midpoint −1.25 has four cases, three from Group 1 and one from Group 2.

**Figure 1.14c All-groups stacked histogram
canonical discriminant function**

```
DSCRIMINANT GROUPS=SURVIVAL(1,2)
 /VARIABLES=TREATMNT TO RESP
 /STATISTICS=1 2 6 4 11 14 13 16 15.
```

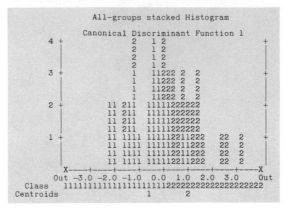

1.15
Estimating
Misclassification Rates

A model usually fits the sample from which it is derived better than it will fit another sample from the same population. Thus, the percentage of cases classified correctly by the discriminant function is an inflated estimate of the true performance in the population, just as R^2 is an overly optimistic estimate of a model's fit in regression.

There are several ways to obtain a better estimate of the true misclassification rate. If the sample is large enough to be randomly split into two parts, you can use one to derive the discriminant function and the other to test it. Since the same cases are not used for both estimating the function and testing it, the observed error rate in the "test" sample should better reflect the function's effectiveness. However, this method requires large sample sizes and does not make good use of all of the available information.

Another technique for obtaining an improved estimate of the misclassification rate is the "jackknife," sometimes called the leaving-one-out method. It involves leaving out each of the cases in turn, calculating the function based on the remaining n-1 cases, and then classifying the left-out case. Again, since the case which is being classified is not included in the calculation of the function, the observed (or apparent) misclassification rate is a less-biased estimate of the true one.

When one of the groups is much smaller than the other, a highly correct classification rate can occur even when most of the "minority" group cases are misclassified. The smaller group—adopters of a new product, diseased individuals, or parole violators—are, however, often of particular interest, and their correct classification is of paramount importance. The desired result is not to minimize the overall misclassification rate but to identify most cases of the smaller group. For example, by judging everyone to be disease-free in a cancer-screening program, the error rate will be very small, since few people actually have the disease. However, the results are useless since the goal is to identify the diseased individuals.

The result of different classification rules for identifying "minority" cases can be examined by ranking all cases on the value of their discriminant score, and determining how many "minority" cases are in the various deciles. If most of the cases of interest are at the extremes of the distribution, a good rule for identifying them can be obtained at the expense of increasing the number of misclassified cases from the larger group. If the intent of the discriminant analysis is to identify persons to receive promotional materials for a new product, or undergo further screening procedures, this is a fairly reasonable tactic. Unequal costs for misclassification can also be incorporated into the classification rule by adjusting the prior probabilities to reflect them. For further discussion see Lachenbruch (1975).

1.16
The Expected
Misclassification Rate

The percentage of cases classified correctly is often taken as an index of the effectiveness of the discriminant function. When evaluating this measure it is important to compare the observed misclassification rate to that expected by chance alone. For example, if there are two groups with equal prior probabilities, assigning cases to groups based on the outcome of a flip of a fair coin, that is, heads allocate to Group 1 and tails allocate to Group 2, results in an expected misclassification rate of 50%. A discriminant function with an observed misclassification rate of 50% is performing no better than chance. In fact, if the rate is based on the sample used for deriving the function, it is probably doing worse.

As the number of groups with equal prior probabilities increases, the percentage of cases that can be classified correctly by chance alone decreases. If there are 10 groups, only 10% of the cases would be expected to be classified correctly by chance. Observed misclassification rates should always be viewed in light of results expected by chance.

1.17
Other Discriminant
Function Statistics

The percentage of cases classified correctly is one indicator of the effectiveness of the discriminant function. Another indicator of effectiveness of the function is the actual discriminant scores in the groups. A "good" discriminant function is one that has much between-groups variability when compared to within-groups variability. In fact, the coefficients of the discriminant function are chosen so that the ratio of the between-groups sum of squares to the within-groups sum of squares is as large as possible. Any other linear combination of the predictor variables will have a smaller ratio.

Figure 1.17a   Analysis of variance table from MEANS for discriminant score

```
DSCRIMINANT GROUPS=SURVIVAL(1,2)
 /VARIABLES=TREATMNT TO RESP
 /SAVE=SCORES=DISCORE.
VARIABLE LABELS DISCORE1 'DISCRIMINANT SCORE'.
MEANS TABLES=DISCORE1 BY SURVIVAL
 /STATISTICS=1.
```

```
Criterion Variable DISCORE1


                            Analysis of Variance
                       Sum of              Mean
Source                 Squares     D.F.    Square        F       Sig.

Between Groups         28.7992      1      28.7992    28.7992   .0000
Within Groups          46.0000     46       1.0000

              Eta =  .6205    Eta Squared =  .3850
```

Figure 1.17a is an analysis of variance table from procedure MEANS using the discriminant scores as the dependent variable and the group variable as the independent or classification variable. Figure 1.17b shows a variety of statistics based on the analysis of variance table. For example the eigenvalue in Figure 1.17b is simply the ratio of the between-groups to within-groups sums of squares. Thus, from Figure 1.17a it is

$$\text{eigenvalue} = \frac{\text{between-groups ss}}{\text{within-groups ss}} = \frac{28.8}{46.0} = 0.626$$

Equation 1.17a

Large eigenvalues are associated with "good" functions. The next two entries in Figure 1.17b, percent of variance and cumulative percent are always 100 for the two-group situation. (See Section 1.38 for further explanation.)

Figure 1.17b   Canonical discriminant functions

```
DSCRIMINANT GROUPS=SURVIVAL(1,2)
  /VARIABLES=TREATMNT TO RESP.
```

				Canonical Discriminant Functions						
Function	Eigenvalue	Percent of Variance	Cumulative Percent	Canonical Correlation	: After : Function	Wilks' Lambda	Chi-squared	D.F.	Significance
					: 0	0.6149800	20.419	8	0.0089
1*	0.62607	100.00	100.00	0.6204998	:				

* marks the   1 canonical discriminant functions remaining in the analysis.

The *canonical correlation* is a measure of the degree of association between the discriminant scores and the groups. It is equivalent to eta from the oneway analysis of variance, in which the discriminant score is the dependent variable and group is the independent variable. Remember eta^2 is the ratio of the between-groups sum of squares to the total sum of squares and represents the proportion of the total variance attributable to differences among the groups. Thus, from Figure 1.17a, eta is

$$eta = \sqrt{\frac{28.8}{74.8}} = 0.620$$

Equation 1.17b

In the two-group situation, the canonical correlation is simply the usual Pearson correlation coefficient between the discriminant score and the group variable, which is coded 0 and 1.

For the two-group case, Wilks' lambda is the ratio of the within-groups sum of squares to the total sum of squares. It is the proportion of the total variance in the discriminant scores not explained by differences among groups (lambda plus eta^2 sum to 1.) From Figure 1.17a, lambda is

$$\lambda = \frac{46}{74.8} = 0.615$$

Equation 1.17c

As indicated in Section 1.38, small values of lambda are associated with functions that have much variability between groups and little variability within groups. A lambda of 1 occurs when the mean of the discriminant scores is the same in all groups and there is no between-groups variability.

A test of the null hypothesis that in the populations from which the samples are drawn there is no difference between the group means can be based on Wilks' lambda. Lambda is transformed to a variable which has approximately a chi-square distribution. Figure 1.17b shows that a lambda of 0.615 is transformed to a chi-square value of 20.42 with 8 degrees of freedom. The observed significance level is 0.0089. Thus, it appears unlikely that infants who die from RDS and those who survive have the same means on the discriminant function.

It is important to remember that even though Wilks' lambda may be statistically significant, it provides little information about the effectiveness of the discriminant function in classification. It only provides a test of the null hypothesis that the population means are equal. Small differences may be statistically significant but still not permit good discrimination among the groups. If the means and covariance matrices are equal, of course, discrimination is not possible.

1.18
Interpreting the Discriminant Function Coefficients

Table 1.18 contains the standardized and unstandardized discriminant function coefficients for the RDS example. The unstandardized coefficients are the multipliers of the variables when they are expressed in the original units. As in multiple regression, the standardized coefficients are used when the variables are standardized to a mean of 0 and a standard deviation of 1.

Table 1.18 Standardized and unstandardized discriminant function coefficients

Variable	Unstandardized	Standardized
TREATMNT	0.43115	0.21531
TIME	0.03671	0.13170
WEIGHT	2.04404	1.16789
APGAR	0.12643	0.34638
SEX	0.00700	0.00337
AGE	−0.21807	−0.64084
PH	0.40787	0.16862
RESP	−1.24454	−0.58743
(CONSTANT)	−0.23093	

The interpretation of the coefficients is also similar to that in multiple regression. Since the variables are correlated, it is not possible to assess the importance of an individual variable. The value of the coefficient for a particular variable depends on the other variables included in the function.

It is sometimes tempting to interpret the magnitudes of the coefficients as indicators of the relative importance of variables. Variables with large coefficients are thought to contribute more to the overall discriminant function. However, the magnitude of the unstandardized coefficients is not a good index of relative importance when the variables differ in the units in which they are measured. For example, the gestational age (variable AGE) is measured in weeks and ranges from 28 to 39 weeks, while the pH level ranges from 6.85 to 7.37. When the absolute values of the unstandardized coefficients are ranked from largest to smallest, age (−0.22) has a rank of 5. However, when the coefficients are standardized to adjust for the unequal means and standard deviations of the independent variables, the coefficient for age (−0.64) is the second largest.

The actual signs of the coefficients are arbitrary. The negative coefficients for age and respiratory therapy could just as well be positive if the signs of the other coefficients were reversed.

By looking at the groups of variables which have coefficients of different signs, we can determine which variable values result in large and small function values. For example, since respiratory therapy is usually initiated for infants who are in considerable distress, it is a bad omen for survival. Values of 1 for the RESP variable will decrease the function value. Infants who weigh more usually have better-developed lungs and are more likely to survive. Thus, larger weights increase the function. Large function values are associated with survival, while small function values are associated with death.

1.19
Function-Variable Correlations

Another way to assess the contribution of a variable to the discriminant function is to examine the correlations between the values of the function and the values of the variables. The computation of the coefficients is straightforward. For each case the value of the discriminant function is computed, and the Pearson correlation coefficients between it and the original variables are obtained.

Separate correlation matrices can be calculated for each group and the results combined to obtain a *pooled within-groups* correlation matrix like that in Figure 1.19. Or all of the cases can be considered together and a *total* correlation matrix calculated. The total correlation coefficients are larger than the corresponding within-groups correlations. However, the relative magnitudes will be similar. Variables with high total correlations will also have high pooled within-groups correlations.

Figure 1.19   Pooled within-groups correlations

```
Structure Matrix:

Pooled-within-groups correlations between discriminating variables
                                   and canonical discriminant functions
(Variables ordered by size of correlation within function)

               FUNC 1
WEIGHT        0.73338
RESP         -0.51940
AGE           0.49290
TREATMNT      0.26572
PH            0.25946
APGAR         0.19210
TIME         -0.10157
SEX           0.03738
```

Figure 1.19 indicates that variable WEIGHT has the highest correlation with the discriminant function. RESP has the second largest correlation in absolute value. The negative sign indicates that small function values are associated with the presence of respiratory therapy (coded 1) and larger values are associated with the absence of respiratory therapy. These results are similar to those obtained from the standardized coefficients.

However, if you compare Table 1.18 and Figure 1.19, you will notice that AGE, which has a negative standardized coefficient, is positively correlated with the discriminant function. Similarly, TIME, which has a positive standardized coefficient, has a negative correlation with the discriminant score. This occurs because WEIGHT and AGE, as expected, are highly correlated. The correlation coefficient is 0.84 from Figure 1.5a. Thus, the contribution of AGE and WEIGHT is shared and the individual coefficients are not meaningful. You should exercise care when attempting to interpret the coefficients, since correlations between variables affect the magnitudes and signs of the coefficients.

1.20
Fisher's Classification Function Coefficients

In Table 1.18, the linear discriminant function coefficients are those that maximize the ratio of between-groups to within-groups sum of squares. These coefficients are sometimes called the canonical discriminant function coefficients since they are identical to those obtained from canonical correlation analysis when maximally correlated linear combinations of the group membership variables and predictor variables are formed (see Tatsuoka, 1971).

Another set of coefficients, sometimes called Fisher's linear discriminant function coefficients or classification coefficients, can be used directly for classification. A set of coefficients is obtained for each group and a case is assigned to the group for which it has the largest discriminant score. The classification results are identical for both methods if all canonical discriminant functions are used (see Kshirsagar & Arseven, 1975; Green, 1979).

1.21
Relationship to Multiple Regression Analysis

Two-group linear discriminant analysis is closely related to multiple linear regression analysis. If the binary grouping variable is considered the dependent variable and the predictor variables are the independent variables, the multiple regression coefficients in Table 1.21 are obtained. Comparison of these coefficients to the discriminant function coefficients shows that the two sets of coefficients are proportional. The discriminant coefficients can be obtained by multiplying the regression coefficients by 4.04. The exact constant of proportionality varies from data set to data set, but the two sets of coefficients are always proportional. This is true only for two-group discriminant analysis.

Table 1.21 Regression and discriminant coefficients

Variable	B Regression	B Discriminant	Ratio
RESP	−0.3082	−1.2445	4.04
TIME	0.0091	0.0367	4.04
PH	0.1010	0.4079	4.04
TREATMNT	0.1068	0.4311	4.04
SEX	0.0017	0.0070	4.04
AGE	−0.0540	−0.2180	4.04
APGAR	0.0313	0.1264	4.04
WEIGHT	0.5062	2.0040	4.04

1.22 VARIABLE SELECTION METHODS

In many situations, discriminant analysis, like multiple regression analysis, is used as an exploratory tool. In order to arrive at a good model, a variety of potentially useful variables are included in the data set. It is not known in advance which of these variables are important for group separation and which are, more or less, extraneous. One of the desired end-products of the analysis is identification of the "good" predictor variables. All of the caveats for variable selection procedures in multiple regression (see the *SPSS/PC+* manual) apply to discriminant analysis as well.

The three most commonly used algorithms for variable selection—forward entry, stepwise selection, and backward elimination—are available in DSCRIMINANT. The principles are the same as in multiple regression. What differs are the actual criteria for variable selection. In the following example, only minimization of Wilks' lambda will be considered. Some others are discussed in Sections 1.30 through 1.34.

1.23 A Stepwise Selection Example

Since stepwise variable selection algorithms combine the features of forward selection and backward elimination, output from the stepwise method will be discussed. Remember that in a stepwise method the first variable included in the analysis has the largest acceptable value for the selection criterion. After the first variable is entered, the value of the criterion is reevaluated for all variables not in the model, and the variable with the largest acceptable criterion value is entered next. At this point, the variable entered first is reevaluated to determine whether it meets the removal criterion. If it does, it is removed from the model.

The next step is to examine the variables not in the equation for entry, followed by examination of the variables in the equation for removal. Variables are removed until none remain that meet the removal criterion. Variable selection terminates when no more variables meet entry or removal criteria.

1.24 Variable Selection Criteria

Figure 1.24 is output from the beginning of a stepwise variable selection job, listing the criteria in effect. As mentioned previously, several criteria are available for variable selection (see Section 1.22). This example uses minimization of Wilks' lambda. Thus, at each step the variable that results in the smallest Wilks' lambda for the discriminant function is selected for entry.

Each entry or removal of a variable is considered a step. The maximum number of steps permitted in an analysis is either twice the number of independent variables (the default) or a user-specified value.

Figure 1.24 Stepwise variable selection

```
DSCRIMINANT GROUPS=SURVIVAL(1,2)
 /VARIABLES=TREATMNT TO RESP
 /METHOD=WILKS.
```

```
Stepwise variable selection

    Selection rule:  Minimize Wilks' Lambda
    Maximum number of steps..................        16
    Minimum Tolerance Level.................   0.00100
    Minimum F to enter......................    1.0000
    Maximum F to remove.....................    1.0000
```

As in multiple regression, if there are independent variables that are linear combinations of other independent variables, a unique solution is not possible. To prevent computational difficulties the tolerance of a variable is checked before it is entered into a model. The tolerance is a measure of the degree of linear association between the independent variables. For the ith independent variable, it is $1 - R_i^2$, where R_i^2 is the squared multiple correlation coefficient when the ith independent variable is considered the dependent variable and the regression equation between it and the other independent variables is calculated. Small values for the tolerance indicate that the ith independent variable is almost a linear combination of the other independent variables. Variables with small tolerances (by default, less than 0.001) are not permitted to enter the analysis. Also, if entry of a variable would cause the tolerance of a variable already in the model to drop to an unacceptable level (0.001 by default), the variable is not entered. The smallest acceptable tolerance for a particular analysis is shown in Figure 1.24.

The significance of the change in Wilks' lambda when a variable is entered or removed from the model can be based on an F statistic. Either the actual value of F or its significance level can be used as the criterion for variable entry and removal. These two criteria are not necessarily equivalent since a fixed F value has different significance levels depending on the number of variables in the model at any step. The actual significance levels associated with the F-to-enter and F-to-remove statistics are not those usually obtained from the F distribution, since many variables are examined and the largest and smallest F values selected. The true significance level is difficult to compute since it depends on many factors, including the correlations between the independent variables.

1.25
The First Step

Before the stepwise selection algorithm begins, at Step 0, basic information about the variables is printed, as shown in Figure 1.25a. The tolerance and minimum tolerance are 1, since there are no variables in the model. (The tolerance is based only on the independent variables in the model. The minimum tolerance, which is the smallest tolerance for any variable in the equation if the variable under consideration is entered, is also based only on the variables in the equation.) The F-to-enter in Figure 1.25a is equal to the F test for equality of group means in Figure 1.3b. The univariate Wilks' lambda is also the same.

The WEIGHT variable has the smallest Wilks' lambda, and correspondingly the largest F-to-enter, so it is the first variable entered into the equation. When WEIGHT is entered, as shown in Figure 1.25b, the Wilks' lambda and corresponding F are the same as in Figures 1.3b and 1.25a. The degrees of freedom for the Wilks' lambda printed in Figure 1.25b are for its untransformed (not converted to an F) distribution.

After each step, SPSS/PC+ prints a table showing the variables in the model (see Figure 1.25c). When only one variable is in the model, this table contains no new information. The F-to-remove corresponds to that in Figure 1.25b since it represents the change in Wilks' lambda if WEIGHT is removed. The last column usually contains the value of Wilks' lambda if the variable is removed. However, since removal of WEIGHT results in a model with no variables, no value is printed at the first step.

Figure 1.25a Output at Step 0

```
DSCRIMINANT GROUPS=SURVIVAL(1,2)
  /VARIABLES=TREATMNT TO RESP
  /METHOD=WILKS
  /STATISTICS=5.
```

```
_____ Variables not in the analysis after step   0 _____

                     Minimum
Variable  Tolerance  Tolerance  F to enter  Wilks' Lambda

TREATMNT  1.0000000  1.0000000   2.0335      0.95766
TIME      1.0000000  1.0000000    .29713     0.99358
WEIGHT    1.0000000  1.0000000   15.489      0.74810
APGAR     1.0000000  1.0000000   1.0628      0.97742
SEX       1.0000000  1.0000000    .40245D-01 0.99913
AGE       1.0000000  1.0000000   6.9967      0.86798
PH        1.0000000  1.0000000   1.9388      0.95956
RESP      1.0000000  1.0000000   7.7693      0.85551
```

Figure 1.25b Summary statistics for Step 1

```
At step   1, WEIGHT    was included in the analysis.

                                 Degrees of Freedom  Signif.   Between Groups
Wilks' Lambda      0.74810        1      1    46.0
Equivalent F      15.4894         1      1    46.0    0.0003
```

Figure 1.25c Variables in the analysis after Step 1

```
_____ Variables in the analysis after step   1 _____

Variable  Tolerance  F to remove   Wilks' Lambda

WEIGHT    1.0000000   15.489
```

SPSS/PC+ also prints a test of differences between pairs of groups after each step. When there are only two groups, the *F* value printed is the same as that for Wilks' lambda for the overall model, as shown in Figures 1.25c and 1.25d.

Figure 1.25d *F* values and significance at Step 1

```
F statistics and significances between pairs of groups after step   1
Each F statistic has   1 and      46.0 degrees of freedom.

                    Group      1
                           DIE
   Group

       2  SURVIVE          15.489
                            0.0003
```

**1.26
Statistics for Variables Not in the Model**

Also printed at each step is a set of summary statistics for variables not yet in the model. From Figure 1.26, RESP is the variable which results in the smallest Wilks' lambda for the model if it is entered next. Note that the Wilks' lambda calculated is for the variables WEIGHT and RESP jointly. Its *F*-test is a multivariate significance test for group differences.

The *F* value for the change in Wilks' lambda when a variable is added to a model which contains p independent variables is

$$F_{change} = \left(\frac{n - g - p}{g - 1} \right) \left(\frac{(1 - \lambda_{p+1}/\lambda_p)}{\lambda_{p+1}/\lambda_p} \right)$$

Equation 1.26a

where n is the total number of cases, g is the number of groups, λ_p is Wilks' lambda before adding the variable, and λ_{p+1} is Wilks' lambda after inclusion.

If variable RESP is entered into the model containing variable WEIGHT, Wilks' lambda is 0.669. The lambda for WEIGHT alone is 0.748 (see Figure 1.25b). The F value for the change, called F-to-enter, is from Equation 1.26a:

$$F = \frac{(48 - 2 - 1)(1 - 0.669/0.748)}{(2 - 1)(0.669/0.748)} = 5.31 \qquad \text{Equation 1.26b}$$

This is the value for RESP in Figure 1.26.

Figure 1.26   Variables not in the analysis after Step 1

```
--------------- Variables not in the analysis after step   1 ---------------

                        Minimum
Variable  Tolerance   Tolerance   F to enter    Wilks' Lambda

TREATMNT  0.9917361   0.9917361    .84207          0.73435
TIME      0.9548707   0.9548707    .64894D-01      0.74702
APGAR     0.9508910   0.9508910    .19398D-01      0.74777
SEX       0.9619762   0.9619762    .24443          0.74406
AGE       0.2937327   0.2937327   1.0931           0.73035
PH        0.9845349   0.9845349    .60606          0.73816
RESP      0.9994270   0.9994270   5.3111           0.66912
```

1.27
The Second Step

Figure 1.27 shows the output when RESP is entered into the model. Wilks' lambda for the model is the same as Wilks' lambda for RESP in Figure 1.26. If WEIGHT is removed from the current model, leaving only RESP, the resulting Wilks' lambda is 0.855, the entry for WEIGHT in the second part of Figure 1.27. The F value associated with the change in lambda, F-to-remove, is 12.5, which is also printed in Figure 1.27.

$$F\text{-to-remove} = \frac{(48 - 2 - 1)(1 - 0.669/0.855)}{(1)(0.669/0.855)} = 12.5 \qquad \text{Equation 1.27}$$

Since the F-to-remove for all the variables in the model is larger than the default value of 1, none are removed.

Figure 1.27   RESP included in analysis at Step 2

```
At step   2, RESP       was included in the analysis.

                                    Degrees of Freedom   Signif.     Between Groups
Wilks' Lambda       0.66912           2     1     46.0
Equivalent F       11.1260                  2     45.0   0.0001


--------------- Variables in the analysis after step   2 ---------------


Variable  Tolerance   F to remove   Wilks' Lambda

WEIGHT    0.9994270   12.535         0.85551
RESP      0.9994270    5.3111        0.74810


--------------- Variables not in the analysis after step   2 ---------------

                        Minimum
Variable  Tolerance   Tolerance   F to enter    Wilks' Lambda

TREATMNT  0.9917051   0.9911962    .71594          0.65841
TIME      0.9492383   0.9492383    .53176D-02      0.66904
APGAR     0.9231403   0.9231403    .25589          0.66526
SEX       0.8879566   0.8879566    .19884D-01      0.66882
AGE       0.2914116   0.2914116   1.3783           0.64880
PH        0.9828797   0.9828797    .66764          0.65912


F statistics and significances between pairs of groups after step   2
Each F statistic has   2 and      45.0 degrees of freedom.
```

After WEIGHT and RESP have both been included in the model, the next variable that would result in the smallest Wilks' lambda if entered is AGE. Its F-to-enter is 1.38, and the resulting model lambda is 0.649. Thus, AGE is entered in Step 3.

1.28
The Last Step

After AGE is entered, all *F*-to-remove values are still greater than 1 so no variables are removed. All variables not in the model after Step 3 have *F*-to-enter values less than 1, so none are eligible for inclusion and variable selection stops (see Figure 1.28).

Figure 1.28   Output for Step 3

```
At step   3, AGE       was included in the analysis.

                                        Degrees of Freedom  Signif.   Between Groups
Wilks' Lambda          0.64880          3    1     46.0
Equivalent F           7.93913               3     44.0    0.0002


---------------- Variables in the analysis after step    3 ----------------


Variable  Tolerance  F to remove   Wilks' Lambda

WEIGHT    0.2926088   8.1466         0.76893
AGE       0.2914116   1.3783         0.66912
RESP      0.9915294   5.5307         0.73035


------------------ Variables not in the analysis after step    3 ----------------
                        Minimum
Variable  Tolerance   Tolerance   F to enter    Wilks' Lambda

TREATMNT  0.9904436   0.2907779    .61371         0.63967
TIME      0.9469645   0.2907135    .22714D-03     0.64880
APGAR     0.8055887   0.2543036    .92868         0.63509
SEX       0.8086141   0.2548962    .45854D-01     0.64811
PH        0.9482218   0.2778589    .34965         0.64357


F statistics and significances between pairs of groups after step   3
Each F statistic has   3 and      44.0 degrees of freedom.
```

1.29
Summary Tables

After the last step, SPSS/PC+ prints a summary table (see Figure 1.29). For each step this table lists the action taken (entry or removal) and the resulting Wilks' lambda and its significance level. Note that although inclusion of additional variables results in a decrease in Wilks' lambda, the observed significance level does not necessarily decrease since it depends both on the value of lambda and on the number of independent variables in the model.

Figure 1.29   Summary table

```
                              Summary Table

            Action      Vars  Wilks'
Step Entered Removed     In   Lambda   Sig.  Label
  1  WEIGHT              1    .74810   .0003  BIRTHWEIGHT IN KILOGRAMS
  2  RESP                2    .66912   .0001  RESPIRATORY LEVEL
  3  AGE                 3    .64880   .0002  GESTATION AGE
```

Table 1.29 shows the percentage of cases classified correctly at each step of the analysis. The model with variables WEIGHT, RESP, and AGE classifies almost 80% of the cases correctly, while the complete model with eight variables classifies 83% of the cases correctly. Including additional variables does not substantially improve classification. In fact, sometimes the percentage of cases classified correctly actually decreases if poor predictors are included in the model.

Table 1.29   Cases correctly classified by step

Variables included	Percent correctly classified
WEIGHT	68.00
WEIGHT, RESP	75.00
WEIGHT, RESP, AGE	79.17
All eight variables	83.33

1.30
Other Criteria for Variable Selection

In previous sections, variables were included in the model based on Wilks' lambda. At each step, the variable that resulted in the smallest Wilks' lambda was selected. Other criteria besides Wilks' lambda are sometimes used for variable selection.

1.31
Rao's V

Rao's V, also known as the Lawley-Hotelling trace, is defined as

$$V = (n - g) \sum_{i=1}^{p} \sum_{j=1}^{p} w_{ij}* \sum_{k=1}^{g} n_k (\overline{X}_{ik} - \overline{X}_i)(\overline{X}_{jk} - \overline{X}_j) \qquad \text{Equation 1.31}$$

where p is the number of variables in the model, g is the number of groups, n_k is the sample size in the kth group, $\overline{X}_{ik}$ is the mean of the ith variable for the kth group, $\overline{X}_i$ is the mean of the ith variable for all groups combined, and $w_{ij}*$ is an element of the inverse of the within-groups covariance matrix. The larger the differences between group means, the larger Rao's V.

One way to evaluate the contribution of a variable is to see how much it increases Rao's V when it is added to the model. The sampling distribution of V is approximately a chi-square with $p(g - 1)$ degrees of freedom. A test of the significance of the change in Rao's V when a variable is included can also be based on the chi-square distribution. It is possible for a variable to actually decrease Rao's V when it is added to a model.

1.32
Mahalanobis' Distance

Mahalanobis' distance, D^2, is a generalized measure of the distance between two groups. The distance between groups a and b is defined as

$$D_{ab}^2 = (n - g) \sum_{i=1}^{p} \sum_{j=1}^{p} w_{ij}* (\overline{X}_{ia} - \overline{X}_{ib})(\overline{X}_{ja} - \overline{X}_{jb}) \qquad \text{Equation 1.32}$$

where p is the number of variables in the model, $\overline{X}_{ia}$ is the mean for the ith variable in group a, and $w_{ij}*$ is an element from the inverse of the within-groups covariance matrix.

When Mahalanobis' distance is the criterion for variable selection, the Mahalanobis' distances between all pairs of groups are calculated first. The variable that has the largest D^2 for the two groups that are closest (have the smallest D^2 initially) is selected for inclusion.

1.33
Between-Groups F

A test of the null hypothesis that the two sets of population means are equal can be based on Mahalanobis' distance. The corresponding F statistic is

$$F = \frac{(n-1-p)n_1 n_2}{p(n-2)(n_1+n_2)} D^2_{ab} \qquad \text{Equation 1.33}$$

This F value can also be used for variable selection. At each step the variable chosen for inclusion is the one with the largest F value. Since the Mahalanobis' distance is weighted by the sample sizes when the between-groups F is used as the criterion for stepwise selection, the results from the two methods may differ.

1.34
Sum of Unexplained Variance

As mentioned previously, two-group discriminant analysis is analogous to multiple regression in which the dependent variable is either 0 or 1, depending on the group to which a case belongs. In fact, the Mahalanobis' distance and R^2 are proportional. Thus

$$R^2 = cD^2$$

Equation 1.34

For each pair of groups, a and b, the unexplained variation from the regression is $1 - R^2_{ab}$, where R^2_{ab} is the square of the multiple correlation coefficient when a variable coded as 0 or 1 (depending on whether the case is a member of a or b) is considered the dependent variable.

The sum of the unexplained variation for all pairs of groups can also be used as a criterion for variable selection. The variable chosen for inclusion is the one that minimizes the sum of the unexplained variation.

1.35
THREE-GROUP DISCRIMINANT ANALYSIS

The previous example used discriminant analysis to distinguish between members of two groups. This section presents a three-group discriminant example. The basics are the same as in two-group discriminant analysis, although there are several additional considerations.

One of the early applications of discriminant analysis in business was for credit-granting decisions. Many different models for extending credit based on a variety of predictor variables have been proposed. Churchill (1979) describes the case of the Consumer Finance Company, which must screen credit applicants. It has available for analysis 30 cases known to be poor, equivocal, and good credit risks. For each case, the annual income (in thousands of dollars), the number of credit cards, the number of children, and the age of the household head are known. The task is to use discriminant analysis to derive a classification scheme for new cases based on the available data.

1.36
The Number of Functions

With two groups, it is possible to derive one discriminant function that maximizes the ratio of between- to within-groups sums of squares. When there are three groups, two discriminant functions can be calculated. The first function, as in the two-group case, has the largest ratio of between-groups to within-groups sums of squares. The second function is uncorrelated with the first and has the next largest ratio. In general, if there are k groups, $k - 1$ discriminant functions can be computed. They are all uncorrelated with each other and maximize the ratio of between-groups to within-groups sums of squares, subject to the constraint of being uncorrelated.

Figure 1.36a contains the two sets of unstandardized discriminant function coefficients for the credit risk example. Based on these coefficients it is possible to compute two scores for each case, one for each function. Consider, for example, the first case in the file with an annual income of \$9,200, 2 credit cards, 3 children, and a 27-year-old head of household. For Function 1, the discriminant score is

$$D_{11} = -14.47 + 0.33(9.2) + 0.13(2) + 0.24(27) + 0.15(3) = -4.2$$

Equation 1.36

The discriminant score for Function 2 is obtained the same way, using the coefficients for the second function. Figure 1.36b shows the discriminant scores and other classification information.

Figure 1.36a   Unstandardized canonical discriminant function coefficients

```
DSCRIMINANT GROUPS=RISK(1,3)
 /VARIABLES=INCOME TO CHILDREN
 /STATISTICS=11.
```

```
Unstandardized Canonical Discriminant Function Coefficients

               FUNC  1        FUNC  2

INCOME         .3257077       -.2251991
CREDIT         .1344126       -.5564818D-02
AGEHEAD        .2444825        .1497008
CHILDREN       .1497964        .1778159
(constant)   -14.46811       -2.540298
```

Figure 1.36b   Classification output

```
DSCRIMINANT GROUPS=RISK(1,3)
 /VARIABLES=INCOME TO CHILDREN
 /STATISTICS=11 14.
```

Case Number	Mis Val	Sel	Actual Group	Highest Probability Group	P(D/G)	P(G/D)	2nd Highest Group	P(G/D)	Discriminant Scores...	
1			1	1	0.8229	0.9993	2	0.0007	-4.1524	-0.0479
2			1	1	0.2100	0.9999	2	0.0001	-4.7122	-1.3738
3			1	1	0.7864	0.9885	2	0.0115	-3.3119	0.5959
4			1	1	0.8673	0.9718	2	0.0282	-2.9966	-0.0155
5			1	1	0.7610	0.9646	2	0.0354	-2.9464	0.3933
6			1	1	0.8797	0.9865	2	0.0135	-3.2056	-0.4530
7			1	1	0.7589	0.9995	2	0.0005	-4.2685	-0.1243
8			1	1	0.5684	0.9812	2	0.0188	-3.1762	0.9402
9			1	1	0.8191	0.9980	2	0.0020	-3.7851	-0.6398
10			1	1	0.7160	0.9336	2	0.0664	-2.7267	0.0973
11			2	2	0.9923	0.9938	1	0.0060	-0.3287	-0.0043
12			2	2	0.7764	0.9922	1	0.0076	-0.3718	-0.5939
13			2	2	0.6003	0.9938	3	0.0059	0.5383	0.6958
14			2	2	0.2482	0.6334	1	0.3666	-1.7833	0.8513
15			2	2	0.5867	0.9856	3	0.0143	0.7262	-0.0908
16			2	2	0.5199	0.9770	3	0.0229	0.8454	-0.0539
17			2	2	0.5355	0.9788	3	0.0211	0.8312	0.1126
18			2	2	0.3812	0.7845	1	0.2155	-1.5451	0.6993
19			2	2	0.9734	0.9961	1	0.0036	-0.1879	0.3225
20			2	2	0.2789	0.7086	1	0.2914	-1.5878	-0.8148
21			3	3	0.8476	0.9977	2	0.0023	3.2486	0.0529
22			3	3	0.3037	1.0000	2	0.0000	4.2453	1.4329
23			3	3	0.4273	0.9996	2	0.0004	3.6041	-1.3365
24			3	3	0.0973	0.9997	2	0.0003	3.6535	-2.2021
25			3	3	0.5946	0.9861	2	0.0139	2.7974	-0.1220
26			3	3	0.2355	0.9988	2	0.0012	3.4655	1.6148
27		**	3	2	0.0585	0.7055	3	0.2945	1.6111	1.5539
28			3	3	0.2221	1.0000	2	0.0000	5.5428	0.0977
29			3	3	0.0510	1.0000	2	0.0000	4.2979	-2.4410
30			3	3	0.1170	1.0000	2	0.0000	5.6787	0.8533

1.37
Classification

When there is one discriminant function, classification of cases into groups is based on the values for the single function. When there are several groups, a case's values on all functions must be considered simultaneously.

Figure 1.37a contains group means for the two functions. Group 1 has negative means for both functions, Group 2 has a negative mean for Function 1 and a positive mean for Function 2, while Group 3 has a positive mean on Function 1 and a slightly negative mean on Function 2.

Figure 1.37a   Canonical discriminant function—group means

```
Canonical Discriminant Functions evaluated at Group Means (Group Centroids)

   Group     FUNC  1      FUNC  2

     1       -3.52816     -0.06276
     2       -0.28634      0.11238
     3        3.81449     -0.04962
```

Figure 1.37b shows the territorial map for the three groups on the two functions. The mean for each group is indicated by an asterisk (*). The numbered boundaries mark off the combination of function values that result in the classification of the cases into the three groups. All cases with values that fall into the region bordered by the 3's are classified into the third group, those that fall into the region bordered by 2's are assigned to the second group, and so on.

Figure 1.37b   Territorial map

```
DSCRIMINANT GROUPS=RISK(1,3)
 /VARIABLES=INCOME TO CHILDREN
 /STATISTICS=11 14 10.
```

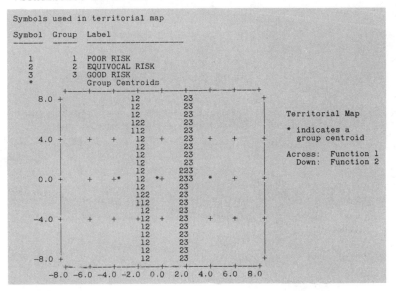

Figure 1.37c is a plot of the values of the two discriminant scores for each case. Cases are identified by their group number. When several cases fall into the same plotting location, only the symbol of the last case is printed.

Figure 1.37c   All-groups scatterplot

```
DSCRIMINANT GROUPS=RISK(1,3)
 /VARIABLES=INCOME TO CHILDREN
 /STATISTICS=11 14 10 15.
```

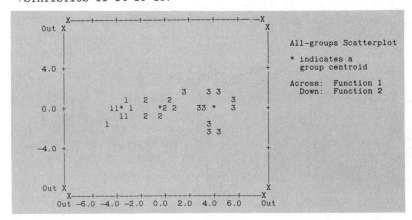

From Figures 1.36b and 1.37c you can see approximately how many cases are misclassified. For example, the case at the (1.6, 1.6) coordinates is denoted by a 3 but falls into the Group 2 region.

Figure 1.37d is the summary of the classification results. The diagonal elements are the number of cases classified correctly into the groups. For example, all poor and equivocal risks are classified correctly (10 out of 10 in each group). One of the good risks is misclassified as an equivocal risk. The overall percentage of cases classified correctly is the sum of the number of cases classified correctly in each group divided by the total number of cases. In this example, 29 out of 30 cases (96.7%) are classified correctly. These results may differ slightly from those obtained by counting plotted points in Figure 1.37c, since a single point in the plot may represent multiple cases.

Figure 1.37d   Classification table

```
DSCRIMINANT GROUPS=RISK(1,3)
 /VARIABLES=INCOME TO CHILDREN
 /STATISTICS=11 14 10 15 13.
```

```
Classification Results -

                        No. of     Predicted Group Membership
       Actual Group     Cases         1          2          3

Group      1             10           10          0          0
POOR RISK                          100.0%       0.0%       0.0%

Group      2             10            0         10          0
EQUIVOCAL RISK                       0.0%      100.0%       0.0%

Group      3             10            0          1          9
GOOD RISK                            0.0%       10.0%      90.0%

Percent of "grouped" cases correctly classified:   96.67%


Classification Processing Summary

       30 Cases were processed.
        0 Cases were excluded for missing or out-of-range group codes.
        0 Cases had at least one missing discriminating variable.
       30 Cases were used for printed output.
```

1.38
Additional Statistics

When more than one discriminant function is derived, several statistics other than those discussed in Section 1.17 are of interest. Consider Figure 1.38a. For each function, the eigenvalue is the ratio of between-groups to within-groups sums of squares. From Figure 1.38b (the analysis of variance tables for the two functions), the eigenvalue for Function 1 is 10.03 (270.8/27). For Function 2, it is 0.007 (0.19/27).

Figure 1.38a   Additional statistics

```
DSCRIMINANT GROUPS=RISK(1,3)
 /VARIABLES=INCOME TO CHILDREN.
```

```
                                  Canonical Discriminant Functions

                    Percent of  Cumulative   Canonical  : After
Function  Eigenvalue  Variance    Percent   Correlation : Function  Wilks' Lambda  Chi-squared  D.F.  Significance
                                                        :    0       0.0900296       61.394       8     0.0000
   1*     10.02971     99.93      99.93      0.9535910  :    1       0.9930012        .17910       3     0.9809
   2*      0.00705      0.07     100.00      0.0836587  :

* marks the   2 canonical discriminant functions remaining in the analysis.
```

Figure 1.38b   ONEWAY analysis of variance for the two functions

```
DSCRIMINANT GROUPS=RISK(1,3)
 /VARIABLES=INCOME TO CHILDREN
 /SAVE=SCORES=DISCORE.
ONEWAY DISCORE1 DISCORE2 BY RISK(1,3).
```

```
- - - - - - - - - - - - - - - O N E W A Y - - - - - - - - - - - - - - - - -

      Variable  DISCORE1   FIRST DISCRIMINANT SCORE
   By Variable  RISK

                              Analysis of Variance

                                Sum of        Mean          F      F
        Source          D.F.   Squares       Squares      Ratio  Prob.

Between Groups            2    270.8023      135.4011     135.4011 0.0

Within Groups            27     27.0000        1.0000

Total                    29    297.8023

- - - - - - - - - - - - - - - O N E W A Y - - - - - - - - - - - - - - - -

      Variable  DISCORE2   SECOND DISCRIMINANT SCORE
   By Variable  RISK

                              Analysis of Variance

                                Sum of        Mean          F      F
        Source          D.F.   Squares       Squares      Ratio  Prob.

Between Groups            2      .1903         .0951        .0951  .9095

Within Groups            27    27.0000        1.0000

Total                    29    27.1903
```

The canonical correlation for a function is the square root of the between-groups to total sums of squares. When squared, it is the proportion of total variability "explained" by differences between groups. For example, for Function 1 the canonical correlation is

$$\sqrt{\frac{270.8}{297.8}} = 0.953$$

Equation 1.38a

When two or more functions are derived, it may be of interest to compare their merits. One frequently encountered criterion is the percentage of the total between-groups variability attributable to each function. Remember from the two-group example that the canonical discriminant functions are derived so that the pooled within-groups variance is 1. (This is seen in Figure 1.38b by the value of 1 for the within-groups mean square.) Thus, each function differs only in the between-groups sum of squares.

The first function always has the largest between-groups variability. The remaining functions have successively less between-groups variability. From Figure 1.38a, Function 1 accounts for 99.93% of the total between-groups variability:

$$\frac{\text{Between Groups SS for Function 1}}{\text{Between Groups SS for Function 1} + \text{Between Groups SS for Function 2}} = 0.9993$$

Equation 1.38b

Function 2 accounts for the remaining 0.07% of the between-groups variability. These values are listed in the column labeled "Percent of Variance" in Figure 1.38a. The next column, Cumulative Percent, is simply the sum of the percentage of variance of that function and the preceding ones.

1.39
Testing the Significance of the Discriminant Functions

When there are no differences among the populations from which the samples are selected, the discriminant functions reflect only sampling variability. A test of the null hypothesis that, in the population, the means of all discriminant functions in all groups are really equal and 0 can be based on Wilks' lambda. Since several functions must be considered simultaneously, Wilks' lambda is not just the ratio of the between-groups to within-groups sums of squares but is the product of the univariate Wilks' lambda for each function. For example, the Wilks' lambda for both functions considered simultaneously is, from Figure 1.38b:

$$\Lambda = \left(\frac{27}{297.8}\right)\left(\frac{27}{27.19}\right) = 0.09$$

Equation 1.39

The significance level of the observed Wilks' lambda can be based on a chi-square transformation of the statistic. The value of lambda and its associated chi-square value, the degrees of freedom, and the significance level are shown in the second half of Figure 1.38a in the first row. Since the observed significance level is less than 0.00005, the null hypothesis that the means of both functions are equal in the three populations can be rejected.

When more than one function is derived, you can successively test the means of the functions by first testing all means simultaneously and then excluding one function at a time, testing the means of the remaining functions at each step. Using such successive tests, it is possible to find that a subset of discriminant functions accounts for all differences and that additional functions do not reflect true population differences, only random variation.

As shown in Figure 1.38a, DSCRIMINANT prints Wilks' lambda and the associated statistics as functions are removed successively. The column labeled "After Function" contains the number of the last function removed. The 0 indicates that no functions are removed, while a value of 2 indicates that the first two functions have been removed. For this example, the Wilks' lambda associated with Function 2 after Function 1 has been removed is 0.993. Since it is the last remaining function, the Wilks' lambda obtained is just the univariate value from Figure 1.38b. The significance level associated with the second function is 0.981, indicating that it does not contribute substantially to group differences. This can also be seen in Figure 1.37c, since only the first function determines the classification boundaries. All three groups have similar values for Function 2.

Figure 1.39 is a classification map that illustrates the situation in which both functions contribute to group separation. In other words, a case's values on both functions are important for classification. For example, a case with a value of -2 for the first discriminant function will be classified into Group 2 if the second function is negative and into Group 1 if the second function is positive.

Figure 1.39   Territorial map

```
TITLE INFANT SURVIVAL EXAMPLE--3-GROUP DISCRIMINANT.
COMPUTE CASE=$CASENUM.
RECODE CASE(1,2,3,4,5,6,18,22,23=2)(ELSE=1).
IF (CASE EQ 2) SURVIVAL=2.
RECODE SURVIVAL (2=2) (1=3) (0=1).
VALUE LABELS SURVIVAL 3'SURVIVE' 1'DIE' 2'DIE LATER'.
DSCRIMINANT GROUPS=SURVIVAL(1,3)
 /VARIABLES=TREATMNT TO RESP
 /STATISTICS=10.
```

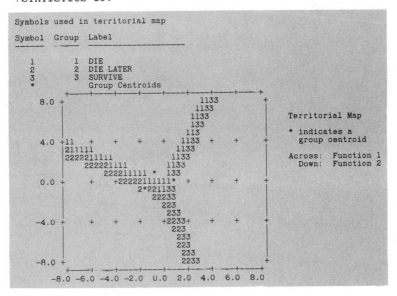

1.40
Classification with One Function

Instead of using all available functions to classify cases into groups, you can restrict the functions to the subset that has substantial between-groups variability. Eliminating weak functions should result in a more stable classification rule, since some of the sampling variability is removed.

When only one discriminant function is used to classify the credit risk cases, 96.67% of the cases are still classified correctly, as shown in Figure 1.40a.

Figure 1.40a   Classification table

```
DSCRIMINANT GROUPS=RISK(1,3)
 /VARIABLES=INCOME TO CHILDREN
 /FUNCTIONS= 1
 /STATISTICS=11 14 10 15 13.
```

Classification Results -

Actual Group	No. of Cases	Predicted Group Membership 1	2	3
Group 1 POOR RISK	10	10 100.0%	0 0.0%	0 0.0%
Group 2 EQUIVOCAL RISK	10	0 0.0%	10 100.0%	0 0.0%
Group 3 GOOD RISK	10	0 0.0%	1 10.0%	9 90.0%

Percent of "grouped" cases correctly classified: 96.67%

Figure 1.40b shows the all-groups histogram for the single discriminant function. Large negative values are associated with poor risks, large positive values with good risks, and small positive and negative values with equivocal risks.

Figure 1.40b   All-groups histogram

```
DSCRIMINANT GROUPS=RISK(1,3)
 /VARIABLES=INCOME TO CHILDREN
 /FUNCTIONS=1.0
 /STATISTICS=11 14 10 15 13.
```

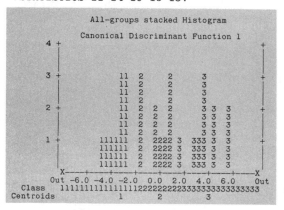

1.41
The Variables

To assess the contribution of each variable to the discriminant functions, you can compute standardized coefficients. From Figure 1.41a, income and age of the household head appear to be the variables with the largest standardized coefficients.

Figure 1.41a   Standardized canonical discriminant functions

```
DSCRIMINANT GROUPS=RISK(1,3)
 /VARIABLES=INCOME TO CHILDREN.
```

Standardized Canonical Discriminant Function Coefficients

	FUNC 1	FUNC 2
INCOME	0.89487	-0.61872
CREDIT	0.31363	-0.01298
AGEHEAD	0.84508	0.51746
CHILDREN	0.22936	0.27226

Another way to examine the contributions of the variables is to examine the correlation coefficients between the variables and the functions, as shown in Figure 1.41b. To help you interpret the functions, variables with large coefficients for a particular function are grouped together. These groupings are indicated with asterisks.

Figure 1.41b   Pooled within-groups correlation matrix

```
DSCRIMINANT GROUPS=RISK(1,3)
 /VARIABLES=INCOME TO CHILDREN
 /STATISTICS=11 14 10 15 13 4.
```

Structure Matrix:

Pooled-within-groups correlations between discriminating variables
                             and canonical discriminant functions
(Variables ordered by size of correlation within function)

	FUNC 1	FUNC 2
CREDIT	0.22728*	0.19774
INCOME	0.48482	-0.84832*
AGEHEAD	0.58577	0.72023*
CHILDREN	-0.00069	0.38568*

1.42
WHEN
ASSUMPTIONS ARE
VIOLATED

As previously indicated, the linear discriminant function minimizes the probability of misclassification if in each group the variables are from multivariate normal distributions and the covariance matrices for all groups are equal. A variety of tests for multivariate normality are available (see Andrews, 1973). A simple tactic is to examine first the distributions of each of the variables individually. If the variables are jointly distributed as a multivariate normal, it follows that each is individually distributed normally. Therefore, if any of the variables have markedly non-normal distributions, there is reason to suspect that the multivariate normality assumption is violated. However, if all variables are normally distributed, the joint distribution is not necessarily multivariate normal.

There are several ways to test equality of the group covariance matrices. DSCRIMINANT prints Box's M test, which is based on the determinants of the group covariance matrices. As shown in Figure 1.42, the significance probability is based on an F transformation. A small probablity might lead us to reject the null hypothesis that the covariance matrices are equal. However, when sample sizes in the groups are large, the significance probability may be small even if the group covariance matrices are not too dissimilar. The test is also sensitive to departures from multivariate normality. That is, it tends to call matrices unequal if the normality assumption is violated.

Figure 1.42   Test of equality of group covariance matrices

```
DSCRIMINANT GROUPS=SURVIVAL(1,2)
 /VARIABLES=TREATMNT TO RESP
 /MAXSTEPS=1
 /METHOD=WILKS
 /STATISTICS=7.
```

```
Test of equality of group covariance matrices using Box's M

   The ranks and natural logarithms of determinants printed are those
   of the group covariance matrices.

   Group Label                 Rank    Log Determinant

      1 DIE                      3        -1.722152
      2 SURVIVE                  3        -1.902866
   Pooled Within-Groups
   Covariance Matrix            3        -1.698660

   Box's M        Approximate F   Degrees of freedom   Significance
   4.8753           .75422        6,       14168.3        0.6058
```

If the covariance matrices are unequal but the joint distribution of the variables is multivariate normal, the optimum classification rule is the quadratic discriminant function. However, if the covariance matrices are not too dissimilar the linear discriminant function performs quite well, especially if the sample sizes are small (Wahl & Kronmal, 1977). Simulation studies suggest that with small sample sizes the quadratic rule can perform quite poorly. Since DSCRIMINANT uses the discriminant function values to classify cases, not the original variables, it is not possible to obtain the optimum quadratic rule. (When covariance matrices are assumed identical, classification based on the original variables and all canonical functions are equivalent.) However, results obtained using the functions and their covariance matrices might not be too different from those obtained using covariance matrices for the original variables (Tatsuoka, 1971).

In situations where the independent variables are all binary (yes-no, male-female) or a mixture of continuous and discrete variables, the linear discriminant function is not optimal. A variety of nonparametric procedures as well as special procedures for binary variables are available (see Hand, 1981; Goldstein & Dillon, 1978). In the case of dichotomous variables, most evidence suggests that the linear discriminant function often performs reasonably well (Gilbert, 1981; Moore, 1973).

1.43
RUNNING PROCEDURE DSCRIMINANT

DSCRIMINANT provides six methods for obtaining discriminant functions: forced entry and five stepwise procedures. You can use the discriminant functions to classify cases, and you can assess the accuracy of these classifications by examining classification results tables, plots of classified cases, and other statistical output provided by DSCRIMINANT.

Only two subcommands are required to obtain discriminant functions using the forced-entry method: the GROUPS subcommand, which specifies the grouping variable; and the VARIABLES subcommand, which specifies the predictor variables. These subcommands produce the eigenvalue and Wilks' lambda for each function, the standardized discriminant-function coefficients, the pooled within-groups correlations between the discriminant scores and the predictor variables, and the group centroids. To obtain unstandardized discriminant functions and coefficients, you must use the STATISTICS subcommand (see Section 1.56).

1.44
Specifying the Groups

Use the GROUPS subcommand to specify the grouping variable and its range of values. For example, the subcommand

```
/GROUPS=RISK(1,3)
```

indicates that RISK is the grouping variable, with integer values from 1 to 3. This command produces a three-group analysis. If there were no cases for one of the specified RISK values, DSCRIMINANT would perform a two-group analysis.

Cases with values outside the range specified for the grouping variable are not used to obtain the discriminant functions. However, such cases are classified into one of the existing groups if classification is requested.

You can specify only one GROUPS subcommand per DSCRIMINANT command.

1.45
Specifying the Variables

List all variables to be used as predictor variables on the VARIABLES subcommand. You can specify only numeric variables, and you can use only one VARIABLES subcommand per DSCRIMINANT command. For example, the command

```
DSCRIMINANT GROUPS=SURVIVAL(1,2)
 /VARIABLES=TREATMNT SEX APGAR AGE TIME WEIGHT PH RESP.
```

produces the output in Figures 1.2 and 1.17b.

1.46
Specifying the Analyses

The ANALYSIS subcommand is useful when you want several discriminant analyses, each with the same grouping variable but different predictor variables. Name all variables to be used in your analysis on the VARIABLES subcommand, and then use the ANALYSIS subcommand to specify subsets of these variables for particular analyses. In this way, you can specify several analyses on a single DSCRIMINANT command.

The variable list on ANALYSIS follows the usual SPSS/PC+ conventions for variable lists with one exception: the TO keyword refers to the order of variables on the VARIABLES subcommand, not their order on the active file. You can use the keyword ALL to refer to all variables listed on the VARIABLES subcommand. A maximum of ten ANALYSIS subcommands are allowed in any one execution of the DSCRIMINANT procedure.

The following command produces two discriminant analyses, both with RISK as the grouping variable:

```
DSCRIMINANT GROUPS=RISK(1,3)
 /VARIABLES=INCOME CREDIT AGEHEAD CHILDREN
 /ANALYSIS=INCOME CREDIT
 /ANALYSIS=INCOME TO CHILDREN.
```

The first analysis uses INCOME and CREDIT as the predictor variables. The second analysis uses INCOME, CREDIT, AGEHEAD, and CHILDREN as the predictor variables.

B

Statistics Guide

1.47
Specifying the Selection Method

Use the METHOD subcommand to specify the method for selecting variables for inclusion in the discriminant analysis. Specify METHOD after the ANALYSIS subcommand (or after the VARIABLES subcommand if ANALYSIS is not used). Each METHOD subcommand applies only to the previous ANALYSIS subcommand when multiple ANALYSIS subcommands are used.

DIRECT   *Forced entry.* All variables in the VARIABLES or ANALYSIS subcommand are entered simultaneously (if they satisfy tolerance criteria). This is the default. (See Sections 1.1 through 1.21.)

WILKS   *Stepwise analysis based on minimizing the overall Wilks' lambda.* (See Sections 1.24 through 1.29.)

RAO   *Stepwise analysis based on maximizing the increase in Rao's V.* (See Section 1.31.)

MAHAL   *Stepwise analysis based on maximizing Mahalanobis' distance between the two closest groups.* (See Section 1.32.)

MAXMINF   *Stepwise analysis based on maximizing the smallest F ratio for pairs of groups.* (See Section 1.33.)

MINRESID   *Stepwise analysis based on minimizing the sum of unexplained variation between groups.* (See Section 1.34.)

To obtain forced entry, do not specify a METHOD subcommand, or specify

```
DSCRIMINANT GROUPS=SURVIVAL(1,2)
 /VARIABLES=SEX APGAR AGE TIME WEIGHT PH TREATMNT RESP
 /METHOD=DIRECT.
```

The following command produces a stepwise analysis based on Wilks' lambda:

```
DSCRIMINANT GROUPS=RISK(1,3)
 /VARIABLES=INCOME CREDIT AGEHEAD CHILDREN
 /METHOD=WILKS.
```

1.48
Inclusion Levels

When you specify a stepwise method, you can use the ANALYSIS subcommand to control the order in which variables are considered for entry. By default, variables are examined for entry or removal on the basis of their partial *F* values. To control the order in which sets of variables are examined, specify an inclusion level in parentheses following the sets of variables on the ANALYSIS subcommand. The inclusion level can be any integer between 0 and 99, as in

```
DSCRIMINANT GROUPS=SURVIVAL(1,2)
 /VARIABLES=SEX APGAR AGE TIME WEIGHT PH TREATMNT RESP
 /ANALYSIS=SEX APGAR TIME PH(2) WEIGHT AGE RESP TREATMNT(1)
 /METHOD=WILKS.
```

The inclusion level controls the order in which variables are entered, the way in which they are entered, and whether or not they should be considered for removal, according to the rules outlined below. All variables must still pass the tolerance criterion to be entered.

- Variables with higher inclusion levels are considered for entry before variables with lower levels. Variables do not have to be ordered by their inclusion level on the subcommand itself.
- Variables with even inclusion levels are entered together.
- Variables with odd inclusion levels are entered one variable at a time according to the stepwise method specified on the METHOD subcommand.
- Only variables with an inclusion level of 1 may be considered for removal. To make a variable with a higher inclusion level eligible for removal, name it twice on the ANALYSIS subcommand, first specifying the desired inclusion level and then an inclusion level of 1.
- An inclusion level of 0 prevents a variable from being entered, although an entry criterion is computed and printed.
- The default inclusion level is 1.

Example of Backwards Elimination and Forward Selection. For example, to perform backward elimination of variables, all variables must first be entered. Those meeting criteria for removal can then be eliminated. The command

```
DSCRIMINANT GROUPS=SURVIVAL(1,2)
 /VARIABLES=SEX TP RESP
 /ANALYSIS SEX TO RESP(2)
          SEX TO RESP(1)
 /METHOD=WILKS.
```

enters all variables meeting the tolerance criteria and then removes those meeting removal criteria.

1.49
Specifying the Number of Steps

By default, the maximum number of steps in a stepwise analysis is twice the number of variables with inclusion level of 1 (the default), plus the number of variables with inclusion level greater than 1. Use the MAXSTEPS subcommand to decrease the maximum. Specify MAXSTEPS after the METHOD subcommand. The form of MAXSTEPS is MAXSTEPS=n where n is the maximum number of steps desired. MAXSTEPS applies only to the previous ANALYSIS subcommand.

1.50
Setting Statistical Criteria

Several subcommands are available to override the default statistical criteria for discriminant analysis. Specify these subcommands, in any order, after the METHOD subcommand. These subcommands apply only to the previous ANALYSIS subcommand.

TOLERANCE=n *Tolerance level.* The default tolerance level is .001. You can reset it to any decimal number between 0 and 1. This sets the minimum tolerance as well as the tolerance for individual variables. (See Section 1.24.)

FIN=n *F-to-enter.* The default *F*-to-enter is 1.0. You may reset it to any nonnegative number. (See Section 1.24.)

FOUT=n *F-to-remove.* The default *F*-to-remove is 1.0. You may reset it to any nonnegative number. (See Section 1.24.)

PIN=n *Probability of* F-to-enter. There is no default value, since *F*-to-enter is the default criterion used for selection. Use PIN to maintain a fixed significance level as the entry criterion. You can specify any number between 0 and 1. (See Section 1.24.)

POUT=n *Probability of* F-to-remove. There is no default value, since *F*-to-remove is the default criterion used for selection. Use POUT to maintain a fixed significance level as the removal criterion. You can specify any number between 0 and 1. (See Section 1.24.)

VIN=n *Rao's* V-to-enter. The default value is 0. (See Section 1.31.)

For example, the following command requests two discriminant analyses:

```
DSCRIMINANT GROUPS=RISK(1,3)
 /VARIABLES=INCOME CREDIT AGEHEAD CHILDREN
 /ANALYSIS=INCOME CREDIT
 /TOLERANCE=.01
 /ANALYSIS=INCOME TO CHILDREN
 /METHOD=RAO
 /VIN=.01.
```

The first requests a forced entry with the tolerance criterion reset to 0.01, and the second requests a stepwise analysis based on Rao's V, with the increase in Rao's V required to be at least 0.01 for entry.

1.51
Specifying the Number of Functions

By default, DSCRIMINANT calculates all discriminant functions available. To reduce the number of functions obtained, specify FUNCTIONS=nf, where nf is the number of functions desired. FUNCTIONS applies only to the previous ANALYSIS subcommand.

1.52
Selecting Cases

Use the SELECT subcommand to select a subset of cases for computing basic statistics and coefficients. You can then use these coefficients to classify either all the cases or only the unselected cases.

The specification for the SELECT subcommand is a variable name followed by a value in parentheses. Only cases with the specified value on the selection variable are used during the analysis phase. The value must be an integer, as in

```
DSCRIMINANT GROUPS=TYPE(1,5) /VARIABLES=A TO H
 /SELECT=LASTYEAR(81).
```

This command limits the analysis phase to cases containing the value 81 for variable LASTYEAR. The SELECT subcommand must precede the first ANALYSIS subcommand. It remains in effect for all analyses.

When you use the SELECT subcommand, DSCRIMINANT by default reports classification statistics separately for selected and unselected cases. To limit classification to unselected cases, use the options described in Section 1.55.

1.53
Specifying the Prior Probabilities

By default, DSCRIMINANT assumes the prior probabilities of group membership to be equal. You can specify other prior probabilities with the PRIORS subcommand. It follows the ANALYSIS subcommand and applies only to the previous ANALYSIS subcommand. You can specify any of the following:

EQUAL   *Equal prior probabilities.* This is the default specification.

SIZE   *Sample proportion of cases actually falling into each group.*

value list   *User-specified list of probabilities.* These must sum to 1, and there must be as many probabilities as there are groups.

For example, the command

```
DSCRIMINANT GROUPS=RISK(1,3)
 /VARIABLES=INCOME CREDIT AGEHEAD CHILDREN
 /PRIORS=.2 .4 .4.
```

specifies a prior probability of 0.2 for the first RISK group and 0.4 for the second and third groups.

1.54
Saving Discriminant Statistics

Much of the casewise information produced by Statistic 14 (Section 1.36) can be added to the active file. The SAVE subcommand specifies the type of information to be saved and the variable names assigned to each piece of information. Three different types of variables can be saved using the following keywords:

CLASS   *Save a variable containing the predicted group value.*

PROBS   *Save posterior probabilities of group membership for each case.* For example, if you have three groups, the first probability is the probability of the case being in Group 1 given its discriminant scores, the second probability is its probability of being in Group 2, and the third probability is its probability of being in Group 3. Since DSCRIMINANT produces more than one probability, a *rootname* used to create a set of variables of the form alpha1 to alpha*n* must be supplied. The rootname cannot exceed seven characters.

SCORES   *Save the discriminant scores.* The number of scores equals the number of functions derived. As with the PROBS parameter, the designated rootname is used to create a set of variables.

Consider the following example:

```
DSCRIMINANT GROUPS=RISK(1,3)
 /VARIABLES=INCOME CREDIT AGEHEAD CHILDREN
 /SAVE=CLASS=PRDCLAS SCORES=SCORE PROBS=PRB.
```

Since the number of groups is 3, DSCRIMINANT adds the 6 variables illustrated in Table 1.54 to the active file.

Table 1.54   Saved casewise results

Name	Description
PRDCLAS	Predicted Group
SCORE1	Discriminant score for Function 1
SCORE2	Discriminant score for Function 2
PRB1	Probability of being in Risk Group 1
PRB2	Probability of being in Risk Group 2
PRB3	Probability of being in Risk Group 3

Only the types of variables specified are saved. You can specify the keywords in any order, but the order in which the variables are added to the file is fixed. The group variable (CLASS) is always written first, followed by discriminant scores (SCORES), and probabilities (PROBS). Variable labels are provided automatically for the newly saved variables. Any value labels defined for the group variable are also saved for the predicted-group variable.

The SAVE subcommand applies only to the previous ANALYSIS subcommand. If there are multiple analyses and you want to save casewise materials from each, use multiple SAVE subcommands. Be sure to use different rootnames.

1.55
Specifying Options

You can request the following options by using the OPTIONS subcommand with the DSCRIMINANT command:

Missing Values. By default, cases missing on any of the variables named on the VARIABLES subcommand and cases out of range or missing on the GROUPS subcommand are not used during the analysis phase. Cases missing or out of range on the GROUPS variable are used during the classification phase.

Option 1   *Include missing values.* User-missing values are treated as valid values. Only the system-missing value is treated as missing.

Option 8 *Substitute means for missing values during classification.* Cases with missing values are not used during analysis. During classification, means are substituted for missing values and cases containing missing values are classified.

Display Options. Two options are available to reduce the amount of output produced during stepwise analysis.

Option 4 *Suppress printing of step-by-step output.*
Option 5 *Suppress printing of the summary table.*

These two options only affect printing, not the computation of intermediate results.

Rotation Options. The pattern and structure matrices printed during the analysis phase can be rotated to facilitate interpretation of results.

Option 6 *Rotate pattern matrix.*
Option 7 *Rotate structure matrix.*

Neither Option 6 nor Option 7 affects the classification of cases since the rotation is orthogonal.

Classification Options. Three options related to the classification phase are available via the associated OPTIONS subcommand.

Option 9 *Classify only unselected cases.* If you use the SELECT subcommand, by default DSCRIMINANT classifies all nonmissing cases. Two sets of classification results are produced, one for the selected cases and one for the nonselected cases. Option 9 suppresses the classification phase for cases selected via the SELECT subcommand.

Option 10 *Classify only unclassified cases.* Cases whose values on the grouping variable fall outside the range specified on the GROUPS subcommand are considered initially unclassified. During classification, these ungrouped cases are classified as a separate entry in the classification results table. Option 10 suppresses classification of cases that fall into the range specified on the GROUPS subcommand and classifies only cases falling outside the range.

Option 11 *Use separate-group covariance matrices of the discriminant functions for classification.* By default, DSCRIMINANT uses the pooled within-groups covariance matrix to classify cases. Option 11 uses the separate-group covariance matrices for classification. However, since classification is based on the discriminant functions and not the original variables, this option is not equivalent to quadratic discrimination (Tatsuoka, 1971).

1.56
Specifying Optional Statistics

You can request the following optional statistics by using the STATISTICS subcommand with the DSCRIMINANT command:

Statistic 1 *Means.* Requests total and group means for all variables named on the ANALYSIS subcommand. (See Section 1.3.)

Statistic 2 *Standard deviations.* Requests total and group standard deviations for all variables named on the ANALYSIS subcommand. (See Section 1.3.)

Statistic 3 *Pooled within-groups covariance matrix.*

Statistic 4 *Pooled within-groups correlation matrix.* (See Sections 1.5 and 1.41.)

Statistic 5 *Matrix of pairwise F ratios.* Requests the F ratio for each pair of groups. The F's are for significance tests for the Mahalanobis' distances between groups. This statistic is available only with stepwise methods. (See Section 1.25.)

Statistic 6 *Univariate F ratios.* Requests F for each variable. This is a one-way analysis of variance test for equality of group means for a single predictor variable. (See Section 1.3.)

Statistic 7   *Box's* M *test.* Tests the equality of group covariance matrices. (See Section 1.42.)

Statistic 8   *Group covariance matrices.*

Statistic 9   *Total covariance matrix.*

Statistic 11   *Unstandardized discriminant functions and coefficients.* (See Sections 1.6 and 1.36.)

Statistic 12   *Classification function coefficients.*

1.57
Classification Tables and Plots

To obtain the classification results table, specify Statistic 13 on the STATISTICS subcommand. For example, the following commands request the classification table shown in Figure 1.13:

```
DSCRIMINANT GROUPS=SURVIVAL(1,2)
 /VARIABLES=TREATMNT SEX APGAR AGE TIME WEIGHT PH RESP
 /STATISTICS=13.
```

Two types of classification plots are available, and a territorial map is available when there is more than one discriminant function (see Sections 1.37 and 1.39). If you have at least two functions, you can obtain separate-groups and all-groups scatterplots with the axes defined by the first two functions (see Section 1.37). If you have only one function, separate-groups and all-groups histograms are available (see Section 1.14).

To obtain any of these plots, use the STATISTICS subcommand:

Statistic 10   *Territorial map.* (See Sections 1.37 and 1.46.)

Statistic 13   *Classification results table.*

Statistic 15   *All-groups scatterplot or histogram.* (See Sections 1.14, 1.37, and 1.40.)

Statistic 16   *Separate-groups scatterplot or histogram.* (See Section 1.14.)

1.58
Discriminant Scores and Membership Probabilities

Use Statistic 14 to obtain casewise information that includes the observed group, the classified group, group membership probabilities, and discriminant scores (see Figures 1.12 and 1.36b).

Statistic 14   *Discriminant scores and classification information.* (See Sections 1.12 and 1.36.)

1.59
Annotated Example

The following commands produce the output in Figures 1.24, 1.25a, 1.25b, 1.25c, 1.25d, 1.26, 1.27, 1.28, and 1.29:

```
DATA LIST   /CASEID 1-2 SURVIVAL 4 TREATMNT 6 TIME 8-10(1)
    WEIGHT 12-15(3) APGAR 17-18 SEX 20 AGE 22-23 PH 33-35(2) RESP 37.
VARIABLE LABELS   SURVIVAL 'INFANT SURVIVAL'
   TREATMNT 'TREATMENT ADMINISTERED'
   TIME 'TIME TO SPONTANEOUS RESPIRATION'
   WEIGHT 'BIRTHWEIGHT IN KILOGRAMS'
   APGAR 'APGAR SCORE'
   SEX 'SEX OF RESPONDENT'
   AGE 'GESTATION AGE'
   PH 'PH LEVEL'
   RESP 'RESPIRATORY LEVEL'
VALUE LABELS SURVIVAL 1 'DIE' 2 'SURVIVE'/
   TREATMNT 1 'THAM' 0 'SODIUM BICARBONATE'/
   SEX 1 'MALE' 0 'FEMALE'/
   RESP 1 'YES' 0 'NO' 9 'NO ANSWER'.
RECODE SURVIVAL (0=1)(1=2).
MISSING VALUES  RESP(9).
BEGIN DATA.
lines of data
END DATA.
DSCRIMINANT GROUPS=SURVIVAL(1,2)
 /VARIABLES=TREATMNT TO RESP
 /METHOD=WILKS
 /STATISTICS=5
 /OPTIONS=6 7.
```

- The DATA LIST command gives the variable names and column locations for the variables in the analysis.
- The VARIABLE LABELS and VALUE LABELS commands provide descriptive labels to be used in the output.
- The RECODE command recodes the values of SURVIVAL.
- The MISSING VALUES command assigns the value 9 as a user-missing value for RESP.
- The DSCRIMINANT command requests the WILKS method for entering the variables into the analysis phase. It also requests a matrix of pairwise F ratios (Statistic 5) and a varimax rotation of both the function matrix and stucture matrix (Options 6 and 7).

Contents

Chapter 2   Identifying Dimensions of Communities: Factor Analysis

What are creativity, love, and altruism? Unlike variables such as weight, blood pressure, and temperature, they cannot be measured on a scale, sphygmomanometer, or thermometer, in units of pounds, millimeters of mercury, or degrees Fahrenheit. Instead they can be thought of as unifying constructs or labels that characterize responses to related groups of variables. For example, answers of "strongly agree" to items such as he (or she) sends me flowers, listens to my problems, reads my manuscripts, laughs at my jokes, and gazes deeply into my soul, may lead one to conclude that the love "factor" is present. Thus, love is not a single measurable entity but a construct which is derived from measurement of other, directly observable variables. Identification of such underlying dimensions or factors greatly simplifies the description and understanding of complex phenomena, such as social interaction. For example, postulating the existence of something called "love" explains the observed correlations between the responses to numerous and varied situations.

Factor analysis is a statistical technique used to identify a relatively small number of factors that can be used to represent relationships among sets of many interrelated variables. For example, variables such as scores on a battery of aptitude tests may be expressed as a linear combination of factors that represent verbal skills, mathematical aptitude, and perceptual speed. Variables such as consumer ratings of products in a survey can be expressed as a function of factors such as product quality and utility. Factor analysis helps identify these underlying, not directly observable, constructs.

A huge number of variables can be used to describe a community—degree of industrialization, commercial activity, population, mobility, average family income, extent of home ownership, birth rate, and so forth. However, descriptions of what is meant by the term "community" might be greatly simplified if it were possible to identify underlying dimensions, or factors, of communities. This was attempted by Jonassen and Peres (1960), who examined 82 community variables from 88 counties in Ohio. This chapter uses a subset of their variables (shown in Table 2.0) to illustrate the basics of factor analysis.

Table 2.0 Community variables

POPSTABL	population stability
NEWSCIRC	weekly per capita local newspaper circulation
FEMEMPLD	percentage of females 14 years or older in labor force
FARMERS	percentage of farmers and farm managers in labor force
RETAILNG	per capita dollar retail sales
COMMERCL	total per capita commercial activity in dollars
INDUSTZN	industrialization index
HEALTH	health index
CHLDNEGL	total per capita expenditures on county aid to dependent children
COMMEFFC	index of the extent to which a community fosters a high standard of living
DWELGNEW	percentage of dwelling units built recently
MIGRNPOP	index measuring the extent of in- and out-migration
UNEMPLOY	unemployment index
MENTALIL	extent of mental illness

2.1
THE FACTOR ANALYSIS MODEL

The basic assumption of factor analysis is that underlying dimensions, or factors, can be used to explain complex phenomena. Observed correlations between variables result from their sharing these factors. For example, correlations between test scores might be attributable to such shared factors as general intelligence, abstract reasoning skill, and reading comprehension. The correlations between the community variables might be due to factors like amount of urbanization, the socioeconomic level or welfare of the community, and the population stability. The goal of factor analysis is to identify the not-directly-observable factors based on a set of observable variables.

The mathematical model for factor analysis appears somewhat similar to a multiple regression equation. Each variable is expressed as a linear combination of factors which are not actually observed. For example, the industrialization index might be expressed as

$$\text{INDUSTZN} = a(\text{URBANISM}) + b(\text{WELFARE}) + c(\text{INFLUX}) + U_{\text{INDUSTZN}}$$ **Equation 2.1a**

This equation differs from the usual multiple regression equation in that URBANISM, WELFARE, and INFLUX are not single independent variables. Instead, they are labels for groups of variables that characterize these concepts. These groups of variables constitute the factors. Usually, the factors useful for characterizing a set of variables are not known in advance but are determined by factor analysis.

URBANISM, WELFARE, and INFLUX are called *common factors,* since all variables are expressed as functions of them. The *U* in Equation 2.1a is called a *unique factor,* since it represents that part of the industrialization index that cannot be explained by the common factors. It is unique to the industrialization index variable.

In general, the model for the *i*th standardized variable is written as

$$X_i = A_{i1}F_1 + A_{i2}F_2 + \ldots + A_{ik}F_k + U_i$$ **Equation 2.1b**

where the *F*'s are the common factors, the *U* is the unique factor, and the *A*'s are the constants used to combine the *k* factors. The unique factors are assumed to be uncorrelated with each other and with the common factors.

B

Statistics Guide

The factors are inferred from the observed variables and can be estimated as linear combinations of them. For example, the estimated urbanism factor is expressed as

$$\text{URBANISM} = C_1 \text{ POPSTABL} + C_2 \text{ NEWSCIRC} \quad\quad \text{Equation 2.1c}$$
$$+ \ldots + C_{14} \text{ MENTALIL}$$

While it is possible that all of the variables contribute to the urbanism factor, we hope that a only subset of variables characterizes urbanism, as indicated by their large coefficients. The general expression for the estimate of the jth factor F_j is

$$F_j = \sum_{i=1}^{p} W_{ji} X_i = W_{j1} X_1 + W_{j2} X_2 + \ldots + W_{jp} X_p \quad\quad \text{Equation 2.1d}$$

The W_i's are known as factor score coefficients, and p is the number of variables.

2.2
Ingredients of a Good Factor Analysis Solution

Before examining the mechanics of a factor analysis solution, let's consider the characteristics of a successful factor analysis. One goal is to represent relationships among sets of variables parsimoniously. That is, we would like to explain the observed correlations using as few factors as possible. If many factors are needed, little simplification or summarization occurs. We would also like the factors to be meaningful. A good factor solution is both simple and interpretable. When factors can be interpreted, new insights are possible. For example, if liquor preferences can be explained by such factors as sweetness and regional tastes (Stoetzel, 1960), marketing strategies can reflect this.

2.3
STEPS IN A FACTOR ANALYSIS

Factor analysis usually proceeds in four steps.

- First, the correlation matrix for all variables is computed, as in Figure 2.4a. Variables that do not appear to be related to other variables can be identified from the matrix and associated statistics. The appropriateness of the factor model can also be evaluated. At this step you should also decide what to do with cases that have missing values for some of the variables.

- In the second step, factor extraction—the number of factors necessary to represent the data and the method of calculating them—must be determined. At this step, you also ascertain how well the chosen model fits the data.

- The third step, rotation, focuses on transforming the factors to make them more interpretable.

- At the fourth step, scores for each factor can be computed for each case. These scores can then be used in a variety of other analyses.

2.4
Examining the Correlation Matrix

The correlation matrix for the 14 community variables is shown in Figure 2.4a. Since one of the goals of factor analysis is to obtain "factors" that help explain these correlations, the variables must be related to each other for the factor model to be appropriate. If the correlations between variables are small, it is unlikely that they share common factors. Figure 2.4a shows that almost half the coefficients are greater than 0.3 in absolute value. All variables, except the extent of mental illness, have large correlations with at least one of the other variables in the set.

Figure 2.4a   Correlation matrix and matrix input

```
DATA LIST MATRIX FREE
 / POPSTABL NEWSCIRC FEMEMPLD FARMERS RETAILNG COMMERCL INDUSTZN
   HEALTH CHLDNEGL COMMEFFC DWELGNEW MIGRNPOP UNEMPLOY MENTALIL.
N 88.
BEGIN DATA.
1.000
-.175 1.000
rest of matrix
END DATA.
FACTOR READ=COR TRIANGLE
 /VARIABLES=POPSTABL TO MENTALIL
 /PRINT=CORRELATION.
```

```
Correlation Matrix:

          POPSTABL  NEWSCIRC  FEMEMPLD  FARMERS  RETAILNG  COMMERCL  INDUSTZN

POPSTABL   1.00000
NEWSCIRC   -.17500   1.00000
FEMEMPLD   -.27600    .61600   1.00000
FARMERS     .36900   -.62500   -.63700   1.00000
RETAILNG   -.12700    .62400    .73600   -.51900   1.00000
COMMERCL   -.06900    .65200    .58900   -.30600    .72700   1.00000
INDUSTZN   -.10600    .71200    .74200   -.54500    .78500    .91100   1.00000
HEALTH     -.14900   -.03000    .24100   -.06800    .10000    .12300    .12900
CHLDNEGL   -.03900   -.17100   -.58900    .25700   -.55700   -.35700   -.42400
COMMEFFC   -.00500    .10000    .47100   -.21300    .45200    .28700    .35700
DWELGNEW   -.67000    .18800    .41300   -.57900    .16500    .03000    .20300
MIGRNPOP   -.47600   -.08600    .06400   -.19800    .00700   -.06800   -.02400
UNEMPLOY    .13700   -.37300   -.68900    .45000   -.65000   -.42400   -.52800
MENTALIL    .23700    .04600   -.23700    .12100   -.19000   -.05500   -.09500


           HEALTH   CHLDNEGL  COMMEFFC  DWELGNEW  MIGRNPOP  UNEMPLOY  MENTALIL

HEALTH     1.00000
CHLDNEGL   -.40700   1.00000
COMMEFFC    .73200   -.66000   1.00000
DWELGNEW    .29000   -.13800    .31100   1.00000
MIGRNPOP    .08300    .14800    .06700    .50500   1.00000
UNEMPLOY   -.34800    .73300   -.60100   -.26600    .18100   1.00000
MENTALIL   -.27900    .24700   -.32400   -.26600   -.30700    .21700   1.00000
```

Bartlett's test of sphericity can be used to test the hypothesis that the correlation matrix is an identity matrix. That is, all diagonal terms are 1 and all off-diagonal terms are 0. The test requires that the data be a sample from a multivariate normal population. From Figure 2.4b, the value of the test statistic for sphericity (based on a chi-square transformation of the determinant of the correlation matrix) is large and the associated significance level is small, so it appears unlikely that the population correlation matrix is an identity. If the hypothesis that the population correlation matrix is an identity cannot be rejected because the observed significance level is large, you should reconsider the use of the factor model.

Figure 2.4b   Test-statistic for sphericity

```
FACTOR READ=CORRELATION TRIANGLE
 /VARIABLES=POPSTABL TO MENTALIL
 /PRINT=CORRELATION  KMO  AIC.
```

```
Kaiser-Meyer-Olkin Measure of Sampling Adequacy =  .76968

Bartlett Test of Sphericity = 946.15313. Significance =     .00000
```

Another indicator of the strength of the relationship among variables is the partial correlation coefficient. If variables share common factors, the partial correlation coefficients between pairs of variables should be small when the linear effects of the other variables are eliminated. The partial correlations are then estimates of the correlations between the unique factors and should be close to zero when the factor analysis assumptions are met. (Recall that the unique factors are assumed to be uncorrelated with each other.)

The negative of the partial correlation coefficient is called the anti-image correlation. The matrix of anti-image correlations is shown in Figure 2.4c. If the proportion of large coefficients is high, you should reconsider the use of the factor model.

Figure 2.4c Anti-image correlation matrix

```
FACTOR READ=CORRELATION TRIANGLE
 /VARIABLES=POPSTABL TO MENTALIL
 /PRINT=CORRELATION KMO AIC.
```

```
Anti-Image Correlation Matrix:

           POPSTABL  NEWSCIRC  FEMEMPLD  FARMERS  RETAILNG  COMMERCL  INDUSTZN

POPSTABL   .58174
NEWSCIRC   .01578    .82801
FEMEMPLD   .10076    -.24223   .90896
FARMERS    .03198    .43797    -.00260   .73927
RETAILNG   .14098    .14206    .12037    .16426   .86110
COMMERCL   .20138    -.27622   .20714    -.49344  -.19535   .68094
INDUSTZN   -.23013   .08231    -.32790   .41040   -.04002   -.00499   .75501
HEALTH     .26114    -.02839   -.02332   .05845   .38421    -.16150   .08627
CHLDNEGL   .10875    -.24685   .27281    -.03446  .13062    .07043    -.07979
COMMEFFC   -.39878   .05772    .03017    -.16386  -.33700   .09427    -.06742
DWELGNEW   .55010    .04505    -.09493   .33479   .26678    .13831    -.13726
MIGRNPOP   .20693    .22883    -.06689   .11784   -.15886   -.07421   .06501
UNEMPLOY   -.17774   -.05946   .18631    -.12699  .19591    -.01262   -.02503
MENTALIL   -.08437   -.10058   .07770    .03053   .07842    -.02921   -.00056


           HEALTH    CHLDNEGL  COMMEFFC  DWELGNEW MIGRNPOP  UNEMPLOY  MENTALIL

HEALTH     .59124
CHLDNEGL   .02899    .87023
COMMEFFC   -.70853   .19554    .68836
DWELGNEW   .07480    -.04008   -.30434   .70473
MIGRNPOP   .07460    -.10809   -.14292   -.24074  .61759
UNEMPLOY   -.02904   -.33523   .19240    .02181   -.38208   .87230
MENTALIL   .06821    -.04163   .04728    -.02505  .20487    -.02708   .88390

Measures of sampling adequacy (MSA) are printed on the diagonal.
```

The Kaiser-Meyer-Olkin measure of sampling adequacy is an index for comparing the magnitudes of the observed correlation coefficients to the magnitudes of the partial correlation coefficients. It is computed as

$$\text{KMO} = \frac{\sum_{i \neq j} \sum r_{ij}^2}{\sum_{i \neq j} \sum r_{ij}^2 + \sum_{i \neq j} \sum a_{ij}^2}$$

Equation 2.4a

where r_{ij} is the simple correlation coefficient between variables i and j, and a_{ij} is the partial correlation coefficient between variables i and j. If the sum of the squared partial correlation coefficients between all pairs of variables is small when compared to the sum of the squared correlation coefficients, the KMO measure is close to 1. Small values for the KMO measure indicate that a factor analysis of the variables may not be a good idea, since correlations between pairs of variables cannot be explained by the other variables. Kaiser (1974) characterizes measures in the 0.90's as marvelous, in the 0.80's as meritorious, in the 0.70's as middling, in the 0.60's as mediocre, in the 0.50's as miserable, and below 0.5 as unacceptable. The value of the overall KMO statistic for this example is shown in Figure 2.4b. Since it is close to 0.8, we can comfortably proceed with the factor analysis.

A measure of sampling adequacy can be computed for each individual variable in a similar manner. Instead of including all pairs of variables in the summations, only coefficients involving that variable are included. For the ith variable, the measure of sampling adequacy is

$$\text{MSA}_i = \frac{\sum_{j \neq i} r_{ij}^2}{\sum_{j \neq i} r_{ij}^2 + \sum_{j \neq i} a_{ij}^2}$$

Equation 2.4b

These measures of sampling adequacy are printed on the diagonals of Figure 2.4c. Again, reasonably large values are needed for a good factor analysis. Thus, you might consider eliminating variables with small values for the measure of sampling adequacy.

The squared multiple correlation coefficient between a variable and all other variables is another indication of the strength of the linear association among the variables. These values are shown in the column labeled "COMMUNALITY" in Figure 2.9a. The extent of mental illness variable has a small multiple R^2, suggesting that it should be eliminated from the set of variables being analyzed. It will be kept in the analysis for illustrative purposes.

2.5
Factor Extraction

The goal of the factor extraction step is to determine the factors. In this example, we will obtain estimates of the initial factors from principal components analysis. Other methods for factor extraction are described in Section 2.10. In principal components analysis, linear combinations of the observed variables are formed. The first principal component is the combination that accounts for the largest amount of variance in the sample. The second principal component accounts for the next largest amount of variance and is uncorrelated with the first. Successive components explain progressively smaller portions of the total sample variance, and all are uncorrelated with each other.

It is possible to compute as many principal components as there are variables. If all principal components are used, each variable can be exactly represented by them, but nothing has been gained since there are as many factors (principal components) as variables. When all factors are included in the solution, all of the variance of each variable is accounted for, and there is no need for a unique factor in the model. The proportion of variance accounted for by the common factors, or the *communality* of a variable, is 1 for all the variables, as shown in Figure 2.5a. In general, principal components analysis is a separate technique from factor analysis. That is, it can be used whenever uncorrelated linear combinations of the observed variables are desired. All it does is transform a set of correlated variables to a set of uncorrelated variables (principal components).

To help us decide how many factors we need to represent the data, it is helpful to examine the percentage of total variance explained by each. The total variance is the sum of the variance of each variable. For simplicity, all variables and factors are expressed in standardized form, with a mean of 0 and a standard deviation of 1. Since there are 14 variables and each is standardized to have a variance of 1, the total variance is 14 in this example.

Figure 2.5a contains the initial statistics for each factor. The total variance explained by each factor is listed in the column labeled Eigenvalue. The next column contains the percentage of the total variance attributable to each factor. For example, the linear combination formed by Factor 2 has a variance of 2.35, which is 16.8% of the total variance of 14. The last column, the cumulative percentage, indicates the percentage of variance attributable to that factor and those that precede it in the table. Note that the factors are arranged in descending order of variance explained. Note also that although variable names and factors are displayed on the same line, there is no correspondence between the two parts of the table. The first two columns provide information about the individual variables, while the last four columns describe the factors. Note that there is no correspondence between the lines in the two halves of the table.

Figure 2.5a shows that almost 72% of the total variance is attributable to the first three factors. The remaining eleven factors together account for only 28.1% of the variance. Thus, a model with three factors may be adequate to represent the data.

Figure 2.5a Initial statistics

```
FACTOR READ=CORRELATION TRIANGLE
 /VARIABLES=POPSTABL TO MENTALIL.
```

```
Extraction  1  for Analysis  1. Principal-Components Analysis (PC)

Initial Statistics:

Variable    Communality  *  Factor  Eigenvalue  Pct of Var  Cum Pct
                         *
POPSTABL      1.00000    *    1      5.70658       40.8        40.8
NEWSCIRC      1.00000    *    2      2.35543       16.8        57.6
FEMEMPLD      1.00000    *    3      2.00926       14.4        71.9
FARMER3       1.00000    *    4       .80748        6.4        78.3
RETAILNG      1.00000    *    5       .75847        5.4        83.8
COMMERCL      1.00000    *    6       .53520        3.8        87.6
INDUSTZN      1.00000    *    7       .50886        3.6        91.2
HEALTH        1.00000    *    8       .27607        2.0        93.2
CHLDNEGL      1.00000    *    9       .24511        1.8        94.9
COMMEFFC      1.00000    *   10       .20505        1.5        96.4
DWELGNEW      1.00000    *   11       .19123        1.4        97.8
MIGRNPOP      1.00000    *   12       .16982        1.2        99.0
UNEMPLOY      1.00000    *   13       .10202         .7        99.7
MENTALIL      1.00000    *   14       .03946         .3       100.0
```

Several procedures have been proposed for determining the number of factors to use in a model. One criterion suggests that only factors that account for variances greater than 1 (the eigenvalue is greater than 1) should be included. Factors with a variance less than 1 are no better than a single variable, since each variable has a variance of 1. Although this is the default criterion in SPSS/PC+ FACTOR, it is not always a good solution (see Tucker, Koopman, & Linn, 1969).

Figure 2.5b is a plot of the total variance associated with each factor. Typically, the plot shows a distinct break between the steep slope of the large factors and the gradual trailing off of the rest of the factors. This gradual trailing off is called the *scree* (Cattell, 1966) because it resembles the rubble that forms at the foot of a mountain. Experimental evidence indicates that the scree begins at the *k*th factor, where *k* is the true number of factors. From the scree plot, it again appears that a three-factor model should be sufficient for the community example.

Figure 2.5b Scree plot

```
FACTOR READ=CORRELATION TRIANGLE
 /VARIABLES=POPSTABL TO MENTALIL
 /PLOT=EIGEN.
```

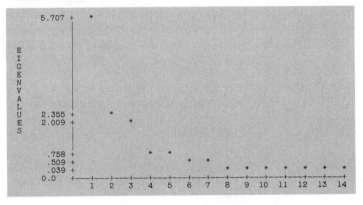

Figure 2.6 contains the coefficients that relate the variables to the three factors. The figure shows that the industrialization index can be expressed as

$$INDUSTZN = 0.844F_1 + 0.300F_2 + 0.238F_3$$

Equation 2.6a

Similarly, the health index is

$$HEALTH = 0.383F_1 - 0.327F_2 - 0.635F_3$$

Equation 2.6b

Figure 2.6   Factor matrix

```
FACTOR READ=CORRELATION TRIANGLE
 /VARIABLES=POPSTABL TO MENTALIL.
```

```
 Factor Matrix:

               FACTOR  1      FACTOR  2      FACTOR  3

 POPSTABL       -.30247        .68597        -.36451
 NEWSCIRC        .67238        .28096         .49779
 FEMEMPLD        .89461        .01131         .08063
 FARMERS        -.68659        .20002        -.40450
 RETAILNG        .85141        .24264         .09351
 COMMERCL        .72503        .39394         .19896
 INDUSTZN        .84436        .29956         .23775
 HEALTH          .38347       -.32718        -.63474
 CHLDNEGL       -.67430       -.12139         .52896
 COMMEFFC        .63205       -.15540        -.64221
 DWELGNEW        .45886       -.73940         .18706
 MIGRNPOP        .07894       -.74371         .24335
 UNEMPLOY       -.78714       -.09777         .30110
 MENTALIL       -.30025        .45463         .27134
```

Each row of Figure 2.6 contains the coefficients used to express a standardized variable in terms of the factors. These coefficients are called *factor loadings*, since they indicate how much weight is assigned to each factor. Factors with large coefficients (in absolute value) for a variable are closely related to the variable. For example, Factor 1 is the factor with the largest loading for the INDUSTZN variable. The matrix of factor loadings is called the *factor pattern* matrix.

When the estimated factors are uncorrelated with each other (orthogonal), the factor loadings are also the correlations between the factors and the variables. Thus, the correlation between the health index and Factor 1 is 0.383. Similarly, there is a slightly smaller correlation (−0.327) between the health index and Factor 2. The matrix of correlations between variables and factors is called the *factor structure* matrix. When the factors are orthogonal, the factor structure matrix and the factor pattern matrix are equivalent. As shown in Figure 2.6, such a matrix is labeled the factor matrix in SPSS/PC+ output.

There is yet another interpretation of the factor matrix in Figure 2.6. Whether the factors are orthogonal or not, the factor loadings are the standardized regression coefficients in the multiple regression equation with the original variable as the dependent variable and the factors as the independent variables. If the factors are uncorrelated, the values of the coefficients are not dependent on each other. They represent the unique contribution of each factor, and are the correlations between the factors and the variable.

To judge how well the three-factor model describes the original variables, we can compute the proportion of the variance of each variable explained by the three-factor model. Since the factors are uncorrelated, the total proportion of variance explained is just the sum of the variance proportions explained by each factor.

Consider, for example, the health index. Factor 1 accounts for 14.7% of the variance for this variable. This is obtained by squaring the correlation coefficient for Factor 1 and HEALTH (0.383). Similarly, Factor 3 explains 40.3% ($(-0.635)^2$) of the variance. The total percentage of variance in the health index accounted for by this three-factor model is therefore 65.7% (14.7 + 10.7 + 40.3). The proportion of variance explained by the common factors is called the *communality* of the variable.

The communalities for the variables are shown in Figure 2.7, together with the percentage of variance accounted for by each of the retained factors. This table is labeled as "Final Statistics," since it shows the communalities and factor statistics after the desired number of factors has been extracted. When factors are estimated using the method of principal components, the factor statistics are the same in the tables labeled as initial and final. However, the communalities are different since all of the variances of the variables are not explained when only a subset of factors is retained.

Figure 2.7 Communality of variables

```
FACTOR READ=CORRELATION TRIANGLE
/VARIABLES=POPSTABL TO MENTALIL.
```

```
Final Statistics:

Variable    Communality  *  Factor   Eigenvalue   Pct of Var   Cum Pct
                         *
POPSTABL      .69491     *    1       5.70658        40.8        40.8
NEWSCIRC      .77882     *    2       2.35543        16.8        57.6
FEMEMPLD      .80696     *    3       2.00926        14.4        71.9
FARMERS       .67503     *
RETAILNG      .79253     *
COMMERCL      .72044     *
INDUSTZN      .85921     *
HEALTH        .65699     *
CHLDNEGL      .74921     *
COMMEFFC      .83607     *
DWELGNEW      .79226     *
MIGRNPOP      .61855     *
UNEMPLOY      .71981     *
MENTALIL      .37047     *
```

Communalities can range from 0 to 1, with 0 indicating that the common factors explain none of the variance, and 1 indicating that all the variance is explained by the common factors. The variance that is not explained by the common factors is attributed to the unique factor and is called the *uniqueness* of the variable.

2.8
The Reproduced Correlation Matrix

One of the basic assumptions of factor analysis is that the observed correlation between variables is due to the sharing of common factors. Therefore, the estimated correlations between the factors and the variables can be used to estimate the correlations between the variables. In general, if factors are orthogonal, the estimated correlation coefficient for variables i and j is

$$r_{ij} = \sum_{f=1}^{k} r_{fi} r_{fj} = r_{1i} r_{1j} + r_{2i} r_{2j} + \ldots r_{ki} r_{kj}$$

Equation 2.8a

where k is the number of common factors, and r_{fi} is the correlation between the fth factor and the ith variable.

From Figure 2.6 and Equation 2.8a, the estimated correlation coefficient for HEALTH and COMMEFFC, based on the three-factor model, is

$$r_{8,10} = (0.38)(0.63) + (-0.33)(-0.16) + (-0.63)(-0.64) = 0.70$$

Equation 2.8b

Figure 2.4a shows that the observed correlation coefficient between HEALTH and COMMEFFC is 0.73, so the difference between the observed correlation coefficient and that estimated from the model is about −0.03. This difference is called a residual.

The estimated correlation coefficients and the residuals are shown in Figure 2.8. The residuals are listed above the diagonal and the estimated correlation coefficients are below the triangle. The values with asterisks (on the diagonal) are the communalities discussed in Section 2.7.

Figure 2.8 Estimated correlations and residuals

```
FACTOR READ=CORRELATION TRIANGLE
  /VARIABLES=POPSTABL TO MENTALIL
  /PRINT=REPR.
```

```
Reproduced Correlation Matrix:

                  POPSTABL    NEWSCIRC    FEMEMPLD    FARMERS     RETAILNG

  POPSTABL         .69491*     .01709      .01623     -.12332      -.00183
  NEWSCIRC        -.19209      .77882*    -.02883     -.01820      -.06320
  FEMEMPLD        -.29223      .64483      .80696*     .00758      -.03597
  FARMERS          .49232     -.60680     -.64458      .67503*      .05486
  RETAILNG        -.12517      .68720      .77197     -.57386       .79253*
  COMMERCL        -.02159      .69721      .66912     -.49948       .73149
  INDUSTZN        -.13656      .77024      .77793     -.61598       .81382
  HEALTH          -.10906     -.15005      .28818     -.07198       .18775
  CHLDNEGL        -.07212     -.22418     -.56196      .22473      -.55410
  COMMEFFC        -.06368      .06163      .51190     -.20527       .44037
  DWELGNEW        -.71418      .19390      .41722     -.53861       .22876
  MIGRNPOP        -.62274     -.03474      .08183     -.30139      -.09049
  UNEMPLOY         .06126     -.40684     -.68101      .39909      -.66575
  MENTALIL         .30378      .06093     -.24158      .18733      -.11995


                  COMMERCL    INDUSTZN    HEALTH      CHLDNEGL    COMMEFFC

  POPSTABL        -.04741      .03056     -.03994      .03312       .05868
  NEWSCIRC        -.04521     -.05824      .12005      .05318       .03837
  FEMEMPLD        -.08012     -.03593     -.04718     -.02704      -.04090
  FARMERS          .19348      .07098      .00398      .03227      -.00773
  RETAILNG        -.00449     -.02882     -.08775     -.00290       .01163
  COMMERCL         .72044*     .13350      .10014      .07447       .01773
  INDUSTZN         .77750      .85921*     .05413      .05596       .02256
  HEALTH           .02286      .07487      .65699*     .14761       .03114
  CHLDNEGL        -.43147     -.47996     -.55461      .74921*      .08703
  COMMEFFC         .26927      .33444      .70086     -.74703       .83607*
  DWELGNEW         .07863      .21042      .29914     -.12070       .28479
  MIGRNPOP        -.18732     -.09828      .11913      .16577       .00918
  UNEMPLOY        -.54931     -.62233     -.46098      .70191      -.67569
  MENTALIL         .01539     -.05282     -.43612      .29080      -.43468


                  DWELGNEW    MIGRNPOP    UNEMPLOY    MENTALIL

  POPSTABL         .04418      .14674      .07574     -.06678
  NEWSCIRC        -.00590     -.05126      .03384     -.01493
  FEMEMPLD        -.00422     -.01783     -.00799      .00458
  FARMERS         -.04039      .10339      .05091     -.06633
  RETAILNG        -.06376      .09749      .01575     -.07005
  COMMERCL        -.04863      .11932      .12531     -.07039
  INDUSTZN        -.00742      .07428      .09433     -.04218
  HEALTH          -.00914     -.03613      .11298      .15712
  CHLDNEGL        -.01730     -.01777      .03109     -.04380
  COMMEFFC         .02621      .05782      .07469      .11068
  DWELGNEW         .79226*    -.12664     -.03343      .15717
  MIGRNPOP         .63164      .61855*     .09715     -.01121
  UNEMPLOY        -.23257      .08385      .71981*    -.05659
  MENTALIL        -.42317     -.29579      .27359      .37047*


The lower left triangle contains the reproduced correlation matrix;  The
diagonal, communalities; and the upper right triangle, residuals between
the observed correlations and the reproduced correlations.

There are   42 (46.0%) residuals (above diagonal) that are > 0.05
```

Below the matrix is a message indicating how many residuals are greater than 0.05 in absolute value. In the community example, less than half (46%) are greater than 0.05 in absolute value. The magnitudes of the residuals indicate how well the fitted model reproduces the observed correlations. If the residuals are large, the model does not fit the data well and should probably be reconsidered.

2.9
Some Additional Considerations

If a method other than principal components analysis is used to extract the initial factors, there are differences in parts of the factor output. Consider, for example, Figure 2.9a, which contains the initial statistics obtained when the maximum-likelihood algorithm is used.

Regardless of the algorithm used, by default the number of factors to be retained is determined by the principal components solution because it is easily obtainable. Thus most of the output in Figure 2.9a is identical to that displayed in Figure 2.5a. The only exception is the column of communalities. In the principal components solution, all initial communalities are listed as 1's. In all other solutions, the initial estimate of the communality of a variable is the multiple R^2

from the regression equation that predicts that variable from all other variables. These initial communalities are used in the estimation algorithm.

Figure 2.9a   Maximum-likelihood extractions

```
FACTOR READ=CORRELATION TRIANGLE
 /VARIABLES=POPSTABL TO MENTALIL
 /EXTRACTION=ML.
```

```
Initial Statistics:

Variable    Communality  *  Factor   Eigenvalue   Pct of Var   Cum Pct
                         *
POPSTABL      .62385     *    1        5.70658       40.8        40.8
NEWSCIRC      .71096     *    2        2.35543       16.8        57.6
FEMEMPLD      .77447     *    3        2.00926       14.4        71.9
FARMERS       .74519     *    4         .89745        6.4        78.3
RETAILNG      .79259     *    5         .75847        5.4        83.8
COMMERCL      .90987     *    6         .53520        3.8        87.6
INDUSTZN      .92914     *    7         .50886        3.6        91.2
HEALTH        .66536     *    8         .27607        2.0        93.2
CHLDNEGL      .67987     *    9         .24511        1.8        94.9
COMMEFFC      .79852     *   10         .20505        1.5        96.4
DWELGNEW      .72576     *   11         .19123        1.4        97.8
MIGRNPOP      .50560     *   12         .16982        1.2        99.0
UNEMPLOY      .72549     *   13         .10202         .7        99.7
MENTALIL      .23825     *   14         .03946         .3       100.0
```

When a method other than principal components analysis is used to estimate the final factor matrix, the percentage of variance explained by each final factor is usually different. Figure 2.9b contains the final statistics from a maximum-likelihood solution. The final three factors extracted explain only 63% of the total variance, as compared to 72% for the first three principal components. The first factor accounts for 35.5% of the total variance, as compared to 40.8% for the first principal component.

Figure 2.9b   Maximum-likelihood final statistics

```
FACTOR READ=CORRELATION TRIANGLE
 /VARIABLES=POPSTABL TO MENTALIL
 /EXTRACTION=ML.
```

```
Final Statistics:

Variable    Communality  *  Factor   Eigenvalue   Pct of Var   Cum Pct
                         *
POPSTABL      .52806     *    1        4.96465       35.5        35.5
NEWSCIRC      .57439     *    2        2.17833       15.6        51.0
FEMEMPLD      .75057     *    3        1.67661       12.0        63.0
FARMERS       .56808     *
RETAILNG      .72089     *
COMMERCL      .87128     *
INDUSTZN      .96817     *
HEALTH        .33383     *
CHLDNEGL      .78341     *
COMMEFFC      .62762     *
DWELGNEW      .87445     *
MIGRNPOP      .35074     *
UNEMPLOY      .70833     *
MENTALIL      .15977     *
```

The proportion of the total variance explained by each factor can be calculated from the factor matrix. The proportion of the total variance explained by Factor 1 is calculated by summing the proportions of variance of each variable attributable to Factor 1. Figure 2.9c, the factor matrix for the maximum-likelihood solution, shows that Factor 1 accounts for $(-0.16)^2$ of the POPSTABL variance, 0.72^2 of the NEWSCIRC variance, 0.81^2 of the FEMEMPLD variance, and so on for the other variables. The total variance attributable to Factor 1 is therefore

Equation 2.9

$$
\begin{aligned}
\text{Total variance} \\
\text{for Factor 1} &= (-0.16)^2 + 0.72^2 + 0.81^2 + (-0.59)^2 + 0.83^2 + 0.89^2 \\
&\quad + 0.97^2 + 0.20^2 + (-0.52)^2 + 0.44^2 + 0.27^2 \\
&\quad + (-0.00)^2 + (-0.62)^2 + (-0.15)^2 = 4.96
\end{aligned}
$$

This is the eigenvalue displayed for Factor 1 in Figure 2.9b.

Figure 2.9c   Maximum-likelihood factor matrix

```
FACTOR READ=CORRELATION TRIANGLE
 /VARIABLES=POPSTABL TO MENTALIL
 /EXTRACTION=ML.
```

```
Factor Matrix:

              FACTOR  1      FACTOR  2      FACTOR  3

POPSTABL       -.16474        -.62235        -.33705
NEWSCIRC        .71934        -.04703         .23394
FEMEMPLD        .80703         .27934        -.14573
FARMERS        -.58607        -.43787        -.18130
RETAILNG        .83267         .00538        -.16588
COMMERCL        .88945        -.27142         .08063
INDUSTZN        .97436        -.10452         .08869
HEALTH          .19912         .35743        -.40795
CHLDNEGL       -.51856        -.17816         .69481
COMMEFFC        .44351         .33795        -.56277
DWELGNEW        .27494         .86373         .22983
MIGRNPOP       -.00353         .49141         .33052
UNEMPLOY       -.62354        -.25283         .50558
MENTALIL       -.14756        -.33056         .16948
```

2.10
Methods for Factor Extraction

Several different methods can be used to obtain estimates of the common factors. These methods differ in the criterion used to define "good fit." Principal axis factoring proceeds much as principal components analysis, except that the diagonals of the correlation matrix are replaced by estimates of the communalities. At the first step, squared multiple correlation coefficients can be used as initial estimates of the communalities. Based on these, the requisite number of factors is extracted. The communalities are reestimated from the factor loadings, and factors are again extracted with the new communality estimates replacing the old. This continues until negligible change occurs in the communality estimates.

The method of unweighted least squares produces, for a fixed number of factors, a factor pattern matrix that minimizes the sum of the squared differences between the observed and reproduced correlation matrices (ignoring the diagonals). The generalized least-squares method minimizes the same criterion; however, correlations are weighted inversely by the uniqueness of the variables. That is, correlations involving variables with high uniqueness are given less weight than correlations involving variables with low uniqueness.

The maximum-likelihood method produces parameter estimates that are the most likely to have produced the observed correlation matrix if the sample is from a multivariate normal distribution. Again, the correlations are weighted by the inverse of the uniqueness of the variables, and an iterative algorithm is employed.

The alpha method considers the variables in a particular analysis to be a sample from the universe of potential variables. It maximizes the alpha reliability of the factors. This differs from the previously described methods, which consider the cases to be a sample from some population and the variables to be fixed. With alpha factor extraction, the eigenvalues can no longer be obtained as the sum of the squared factor loadings and the communalities for each variable are not the sum of the squared loadings on the individual factors. See Harman (1967) and Kim and Mueller (1978) for discussions of the different factor estimation algorithms.

2.11
Goodness of Fit of the Factor Model

When factors are extracted using generalized least squares or maximum-likelihood estimation and it is assumed that the sample is from a multivariate normal population, it is possible to obtain goodness-of-fit tests for the adequacy of a k-factor model. For large sample sizes, the goodness-of-fit statistic tends to be distributed as a chi-squared variate. In most applications, the number of common factors is not known, and the number of factors is increased until a reasonably good fit is obtained—that is, until the observed significance level is no longer small. The statistics obtained in this fashion are not independent and the true significance level is not the same as the observed significance level at each step.

The value of the chi-squared goodness-of-fit statistic is directly proportional to the sample size. The degrees of freedom are a function of only the number of common factors and the number of variables. (For the chi-squared statistic to have positive degrees of freedom, the number of common factors cannot exceed the largest integer satisfying

$$m < 0.5\left(2p + 1 - \sqrt{8p + 1}\right) \qquad \text{Equation 2.11}$$

where m is the number of common factors to be extracted and p is the number of variables). For large sample sizes, the goodness-of-fit test may cause rather small discrepancies in fit to be deemed statistically significant, resulting in a larger number of factors being extracted than is really necessary.

Table 2.11 contains the goodness-of-fit statistics for maximum-likelihood extraction for different numbers of common factors. Using this criterion, six common factors are needed to adequately represent the community data.

Table 2.11 Goodness-of-fit statistics

Number of factors	Chi-square statistic	Iterations required	Significance
3	184.8846	13	0.0000
4	94.1803	8	0.0000
5	61.0836	11	0.0010
6	27.3431	15	0.1985

2.12
Summary of the Extraction Phase

In the factor extraction phase, the number of common factors needed to adequately describe the data is determined. This decision is based on eigenvalues and percentage of the total variance accounted for by different numbers of factors. A plot of the eigenvalues (the scree plot) is also helpful in determining the number of factors.

2.13
The Rotation Phase

Although the factor matrix obtained in the extraction phase indicates the relationship between the factors and the individual variables, it is usually difficult to identify meaningful factors based on this matrix. Often the variables and factors do not appear correlated in any interpretable pattern. Most factors are correlated with many variables. Since one of the goals of factor analysis is to identify factors that are substantively meaningful (in the sense that they summarize sets of closely related variables) the *rotation* phase of factor analysis attempts to transform the initial matrix into one that is easier to interpret.

Consider Figure 2.13a, which is a factor matrix for four hypothetical variables. From the factor loadings, it is difficult to interpret any of the factors, since the variables and factors are intertwined. That is, all factor loadings are quite high, and both factors explain all of the variables.

Figure 2.13a   Hypothetical factor matrix

```
FACTOR VARIABLES=V1 V2 V3 V4
 /READ=FACTOR(2)
 /PLOT=ROTATION(1,2).
```

```
Factor Matrix:

                FACTOR  1        FACTOR  2

V1              .50000           .50000
V2              .50000          -.40000
V3              .70000           .70000
V4             -.60000           .60000
```

Figure 2.13b   Rotated hypothetical factor matrix

```
Rotated Factor Matrix:

                FACTOR  1        FACTOR  2

V1              .70684          -.01938
V2              .05324          -.63809
V3              .98958          -.02713
V4              .02325           .84821
```

In the factor matrix in Figure 2.13b, variables V1 and V3 are highly related to Factor 1, while V2 and V4 load highly on Factor 2. By looking at what variables V2 and V4 have in common (such as a measurement of job satisfaction, or a characterization of an anxious personality), we may be able to identify Factor 2. Similar steps can be taken to identify Factor 1. The goal of rotation is to transform complicated matrices like that in Figure 2.13a into simpler ones like that in Figure 2.13b.

Consider Figure 2.13c, which is a plot of variables V1 to V4 using the factor loadings in Figure 2.13a as the coordinates, and Figure 2.13d, which is the corresponding plot for Figure 2.13b. Note that Figure 2.13c would look exactly like Figure 2.13d if the dotted lines were rotated to be the reference axes. When the axes are maintained at right angles, the rotation is called orthogonal. If the axes are not maintained at right angles, the rotation is called oblique. Oblique rotation is discussed in Section 2.16.

The purpose of rotation is to achieve a simple structure. This means that we would like each factor to have nonzero loadings for only some of the variables. This helps us interpret the factors. We would also like each variable to have nonzero loadings for only a few factors, preferably one. This permits the factors to be differentiated from each other. If several factors have high loadings on the same variables, it is difficult to ascertain how the factors differ.

Rotation does not affect the goodness of fit of a factor solution. That is, although the factor matrix changes, the communalities and the percentage of total variance explained do not change. The percentage of variance accounted for by each of the factors does, however, change. Rotation redistributes the explained variance for the individual factors. Different rotation methods may actually result in the identification of somewhat different factors.

A variety of algorithms are used for orthogonal rotation to a simple structure. The most commonly used method is the *varimax* method, which attempts to minimize the number of variables that have high loadings on a factor. This should enhance the interpretability of the factors.

Figure 2.13c   Prior to rotation

```
FACTOR VARIABLES=V1 V2 V3 V4
 /READ=FACTOR(2)
 /PLOT=ROTATION(1,2)
 /ROTATION=NOROTATE.
```

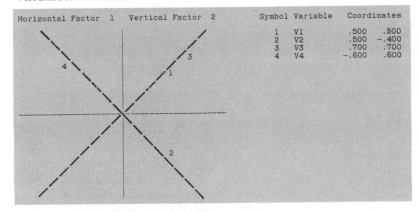

Figure 2.13d   Orthogonal rotation

```
FACTOR VARIABLES=V1 V2 V3 V4
 /READ=FACTOR(2)
 /ROTATION=VARIMAX
 /PLOT=ROTATION(1,2).
```

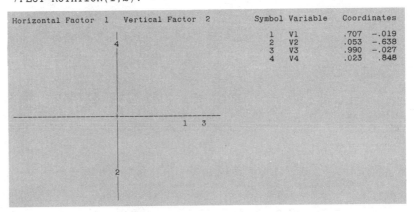

The *quartimax* method emphasizes simple interpretation of variables, since the solution minimizes the number of factors needed to explain a variable. A quartimax rotation often results in a general factor with high-to-moderate loadings on most variables. This is one of the main shortcomings of the quartimax method.

The *equamax* method is a combination of the varimax method, which simplifies the factors, and the quartimax method, which simplifies variables.

Consider Figure 2.13e, which shows the factor matrices for the community data before rotation and again after a varimax (and quartimax and equamax) orthogonal rotation procedure.

Figure 2.13e Factor matrices for community data

```
FACTOR READ=CORRELATION TRIANGLE
 /VARIABLES=POPSTABL TO MENTALIL
 /EXTRACT=PC
 /ROTATION=VARIMAX
 /ROTATION=QUARTIMAX
 /ROTATION=EQUAMAX.
```

Factor Matrix: (unrotated)

	FACTOR 1	FACTOR 2	FACTOR 3
POPSTABL	-.30247	.68597	-.36451
NEWSCIRC	.67238	.28096	.49779
FEMEMPLD	.89461	.01131	.08063
FARMERS	-.68659	.20002	-.40450
RETAILNG	.85141	.24264	.09351
COMMERCL	.72503	.39394	.19896
INDUSTZN	.84436	.29956	.23775
HEALTH	.38347	-.32718	-.63474
CHLDNEGL	-.67430	-.12139	.52896
COMMEFFC	.63205	-.15540	-.64221
DWELGNEW	.45886	-.73940	.18706
MIGRNPOP	.07894	-.74371	.24335
UNEMPLOY	-.78714	-.09777	.30110
MENTALIL	-.30025	.45463	.27134

Rotated Factor Matrix: (varimax)

	FACTOR 1	FACTOR 2	FACTOR 3
POPSTABL	-.13553	.00916	-.82247
NEWSCIRC	.86634	-.14256	.08920
FEMEMPLD	.78248	.37620	.23055
FARMERS	-.65736	-.04537	-.49077
RETAILNG	.83993	.29454	.01705
COMMERCL	.83432	.11068	-.11000
INDUSTZN	.91325	.15773	.01730
HEALTH	-.05806	.79424	.15101
CHLDNEGL	-.39791	-.75492	.14486
COMMEFFC	.21186	.88794	.05241
DWELGNEW	.17484	.22931	.84208
MIGRNPOP	-.12119	-.00660	.77706
UNEMPLOY	-.57378	-.62483	.01311
MENTALIL	.03133	-.47460	-.37979

Rotated Factor Matrix: (quartimax)

	FACTOR 1	FACTOR 2	FACTOR 3
POPSTABL	-.14884	.00769	-.82018
NEWSCIRC	.85549	-.20254	.07706
FEMEMPLD	.81105	.32272	.21214
FARMERS	-.66736	-.00515	-.47920
RETAILNG	.85885	.23432	-.00105
COMMERCL	.83802	.04963	-.12529
INDUSTZN	.92229	.09267	.00000
HEALTH	.00097	.79832	.14028
CHLDNEGL	-.44778	-.72272	.16242
COMMEFFC	.27508	.87127	.03590
DWELGNEW	.20527	.22763	.83565
MIGRNPOP	-.10781	.01249	.77896
UNEMPLOY	-.61627	-.58226	.03168
MENTALIL	-.00897	-.48069	-.37326

Rotated Factor Matrix: (equamax)

	FACTOR 1	FACTOR 2	FACTOR 3
POPSTABL	-.12961	.01218	-.82338
NEWSCIRC	.86917	-.12003	.09470
FEMEMPLD	.77037	.39514	.23949
FARMERS	-.65223	-.05898	-.49613
RETAILNG	.83157	.31678	.02580
COMMERCL	.83185	.13387	-.10273
INDUSTZN	.90854	.18199	.02554
HEALTH	-.08047	.79116	.15682
CHLDNEGL	-.37857	-.76645	.13585
COMMEFFC	.18756	.89284	.06103
DWELGNEW	.16236	.22710	.84518
MIGRNPOP	-.12675	-.01613	.77603
UNEMPLOY	-.55688	-.64006	.00379
MENTALIL	.04688	-.47050	-.38327

The unrotated factor matrix is difficult to interpret. Many variables have moderate-size correlations with several factors. After rotation, the number of large and small factor loadings increases. Variables are more highly correlated with single factors. Interpretation of the factors also appears possible. For example, the first factor shows string positive correlation with newspaper circulation, percentage of females in the labor force, sales, commercial activity, and the industrialization index. It also shows a strong negative correlation with the number of farmers. Thus Factor 1 might be interpreted as measuring something like "urbanism." The second factor is positively correlated with health and a high standard of living and negatively correlated with aid to dependent children, unemployment, and mental illness. This factor describes the affluence or welfare of a community. The last factor is associated with the instability or influx of a community. Thus, communities may be fairly well characterized by three factors—urbanism, welfare, and influx.

2.14
Factor Loading Plots

A convenient means of examining the success of an orthogonal rotation is to plot the variables using the factor loadings as coordinates. In Figure 2.14a, the variables are plotted using Factors 1 and 2 after varimax rotation of the two factors. The plotted numbers represent the number of the variable; e.g., 7 represents the seventh variable (INDUSTZN). The coordinates correspond to the factor loadings in Figure 2.13e for the varimax-rotated solution. The coordinates are also listed next to each plot. In Figure 2.14b, the variables are plotted using Factors 1 and 2 before rotation.

Figure 2.14a   Varimax-rotated solution

```
FACTOR READ=CORRELATION TRIANGLE
 /VARIABLES=POPSTABL TO MENTALIL
 /ROTATION=VARIMAX
 /PLOT=ROTATION(1,2).
```

Symbol	Variable	Coordinates	
1	POPSTABL	-.136	.009
2	NEWSCIRC	.866	-.143
3	FEMEMPLD	.782	.376
4	FARMERS	-.657	-.045
5	RETAILNG	.840	.295
6	COMMERCL	.834	.111
7	INDUSTZN	.913	.158
8	HEALTH	-.058	.794
9	CHLDNEGL	-.398	-.755
10	COMMEFFC	.212	.888
11	DWELGNEW	.175	.229
12	MIGRNPOP	-.121	-.007
13	UNEMPLOY	-.574	-.625
14	MENTALIL	.031	-.475

Figure 2.14b   Unrotated solution

```
FACTOR READ=CORRELATION TRIANGLE
 /VARIABLES=POPSTABL TO MENTALIL
 /ROTATION=NOROTATE
 /PLOT=ROTATION(1,2).
```

Symbol	Variable	Coordinates	
1	POPSTABL	-.302	.686
2	NEWSCIRC	.672	.281
3	FEMEMPLD	.895	.011
4	FARMERS	-.687	.200
5	RETAILNG	.851	.243
6	COMMERCL	.725	.394
7	INDUSTZN	.844	.300
8	HEALTH	.383	-.327
9	CHLDNEGL	-.674	-.121
10	COMMEFFC	.632	-.155
11	DWELGNEW	.459	-.739
12	MIGRNPOP	.079	-.744
13	UNEMPLOY	-.787	-.098
14	MENTALIL	-.300	.455

If a rotation has achieved a simple structure, clusters of variables should occur near the ends of the axes and at their intersection. Variables at the end of an axis are those that have high loadings on only that factor. Variables near the origin of the plot have small loadings on both factors. Variables that are not near the axes are explained by both factors. If a simple structure has been achieved, there should be few, if any, variables with large loadings on more than one factor.

2.15
Interpreting the Factors

To identify the factors, it is necessary to group the variables that have large loadings for the same factors. Plots of the loadings, as discussed in Section 2.14, are one way of determining the clusters of variables. Another convenient strategy is to sort the factor pattern matrix so that variables with high loadings on the same factor appear together, as shown in Figure 2.15a. Small factor loadings can be omitted from such a table. In Figure 2.15b, no loadings less than 0.5 in absolute value are displayed. Note that the mental illness variable, as expected, does not correlate highly with any of the factors.

Figure 2.15a Sorted loadings

```
FACTOR READ=CORRELATION TRIANGLE
 /VARIABLES=POPSTABL TO MENTALIL
 /FORMAT=SORT
 /ROTATION=VARIMAX.
```

Rotated Factor Matrix:

	FACTOR 1	FACTOR 2	FACTOR 3
INDUSTZN	.91325	.15773	.01730
NEWSCIRC	.86634	-.14256	.08920
RETAILNG	.83993	.29454	.01705
COMMERCL	.83432	.11068	-.11000
FEMEMPLD	.78248	.37620	.23055
FARMERS	-.65736	-.04537	-.49077
COMMEFFC	.21186	.88794	.05241
HEALTH	-.05806	.79424	.15101
CHLDNEGL	-.39791	-.75492	.14486
UNEMPLOY	-.57378	-.62483	.01311
MENTALIL	.03133	-.47460	-.37979
DWELGNEW	.17484	.22931	.84208
POPSTABL	-.13553	.00916	-.82247
MIGRNPOP	-.12119	-.00660	.77706

Figure 2.15b Sorted and blanked loadings

```
FACTOR READ=CORRELATION TRIANGLE
 /VARIABLES=POPSTABL TO MENTALIL
 /FORMAT=SORT BLANK(.5)
 /ROTATION=VARIMAX.
```

Rotated Factor Matrix:

	FACTOR 1	FACTOR 2	FACTOR 3
INDUSTZN	.91325		
NEWSCIRC	.86634		
RETAILNG	.83993		
COMMERCL	.83432		
FEMEMPLD	.78248		
FARMERS	-.65736		
COMMEFFC		.88794	
HEALTH		.79424	
CHLDNEGL		-.75492	
UNEMPLOY	-.57378	-.62483	
MENTALIL			
DWELGNEW			.84208
POPSTABL			-.82247
MIGRNPOP			.77706

2.16
Oblique Rotation

Orthogonal rotation results in factors that are uncorrelated. Although this is an appealing property, sometimes allowing for correlations among factors simplifies the factor pattern matrix. Consider Figure 2.16a, which is a plot of the factor loadings for six variables. Note that if the axes went through the points (the solid line), a simpler factor pattern matrix would result than with an orthogonal rotation (the dotted lines). Factor pattern matrices for both rotations are shown in Figure 2.16b.

Figure 2.16a   Plot of factor loadings

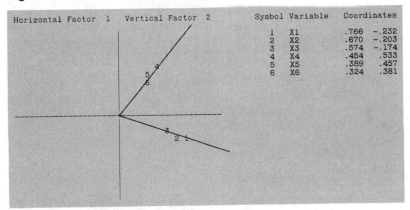

Symbol	Variable	Coordinates	
1	X1	.766	−.232
2	X2	.670	−.203
3	X3	.574	−.174
4	X4	.454	.533
5	X5	.389	.457
6	X6	.324	.381

Figure 2.16b   Rotated varimax and oblique factor loadings

```
Rotated Factor Matrix: (varimax)

                FACTOR  1      FACTOR  2

X1               .78313         .16345
X2               .68523         .14302
X3               .58734         .12259
X4               .14302         .68523
X5               .12259         .58734
X6               .10215         .48945


Pattern Matrix: (oblique)

                FACTOR  1      FACTOR  2

X1               .80000         .00000
X2               .70000        -.00000
X3               .60000        -.00000
X4               .00000         .70000
X5              -.00000         .60000
X6              -.00000         .50000
```

There are several reasons why oblique rotation has come into favor. It is unlikely that influences in nature are uncorrelated. And even if they are uncorrelated in the population, they need not be so in the sample. Thus, oblique rotations have often been found to yield substantively meaningful factors.

2.17
Factor Pattern and Structure Matrices

Oblique rotation preserves the communalities of the variables, as does orthogonal rotation. When oblique rotation is used, however, the factor loadings and factor variable correlations are no longer identical. The factor loadings are still partial regression coefficients, but since the factors are correlated, they are no longer equal to the simple factor variable correlations. (Remember that the regression coefficients depend on the interrelationships of the independent variables when these are correlated.) Therefore, separate factor loading and factor structure matrices are displayed as part of the output.

The method for oblique rotation available in SPSS/PC+ is called OBLIMIN. A parameter called δ (delta) controls the extent of obliqueness. When δ is zero, the factors are most oblique. For negative values of δ, the factors become less oblique as δ becomes more negative. Harman (1967) recommends that δ be either zero or negative.

The factor loadings for the communities data after an oblique rotation are shown in the factor pattern matrix in Figure 2.18a. The loadings are no longer constrained to a range from −1 to +1. The correlations between the factors and variables are shown in Figure 2.18b, the factor structure matrix.

Figure 2.18a   Factor pattern matrix

```
FACTOR READ=CORRELATION. TRIANGLE
  /VARIABLES=POPSTABL TO MENTALIL
  /FORMAT=SORT
  /ROTATION=OBLIMIN.
```

```
Pattern Matrix:

                FACTOR  1        FACTOR  2        FACTOR  3

    INDUSTZN      .91577          .02882          -.04731
    NEWSCIRC      .90594         -.06987           .26053
    COMMERCL      .84325          .15024          -.01504
    RETAILNG      .82253          .03760          -.19782
    FEMEMPLD      .74906         -.17274          -.27862
    FARMERS      -.65969          .46636          -.06041

    POPSTABL     -.12570          .82380          -.06787
    DWELGNEW      .13426         -.82258          -.17248
    MIGRNPOP     -.13720         -.78724           .03070

    COMMEFFC      .09940          .02770          -.88775
    HEALTH       -.16689         -.08909          -.81993
    CHLDNEGL     -.31128         -.22218           .73693
    UNEMPLOY     -.50651         -.08531           .57387
    MENTALIL      .10140          .34462           .47495
```

Figure 2.18b   Factor structure matrix

```
Structure Matrix:

                FACTOR  1        FACTOR  2        FACTOR  3

    INDUSTZN      .92553         -.04717          -.27457
    RETAILNG      .86963         -.05222          -.40031
    NEWSCIRC      .84545         -.10235           .02205
    COMMERCL      .83566          .08423          -.20712
    FEMEMPLD      .83252         -.26822          -.49178
    FARMERS      -.67979          .50798           .17096

    DWELGNEW      .24017         -.85671          -.32064
    POPSTABL     -.17101          .82390           .07829
    MIGRNPOP     -.08527         -.77258          -.04400

    COMMEFFC      .32149         -.10314          -.90901
    HEALTH        .04692         -.19032          -.79016
    CHLDNEGL     -.48053         -.09623           .78468
    UNEMPLOY     -.64496          .03280           .68993
    MENTALIL     -.04466          .40290           .49721
```

The correlation matrix for the factors is in Figure 2.18c. Note that there are small correlations between all three factors. In the case of an orthogonal rotation, the factor correlation matrix is an identity matrix: that is, there are 1's on the diagonal and 0's elsewhere.

Figure 2.18c   Factor correlation matrix

```
Factor Correlation Matrix:

                FACTOR  1        FACTOR  2        FACTOR  3

    FACTOR  1     1.00000
    FACTOR  2     -.07580         1.00000
    FACTOR  3     -.25253          .13890           1.00000
```

The oblique rotation resulted in the same grouping of variables as did the orthogonal rotation. The interpretation of the factors does not change based on it.

2.19
Factor Scores

Since one of the goals of factor analysis is to reduce a large number of variables to a smaller number of factors, it is often desirable to estimate factor scores for each case. The factor scores can be used in subsequent analyses to represent the values of the factors. Plots of factor scores for pairs of factors are useful for detecting unusual observations.

Recall from Section 2.1 that a factor can be estimated as a linear combination of the original variables. That is, for case k, the score for the jth factor is estimated as

$$\hat{F}_{jk} = \sum_{i=1}^{p} W_{ji} X_{ik}$$

Equation 2.19a

where X_{ik} is the standardized value of the ith variable for case k and W_{ji} is the factor score coefficient for the jth factor and the ith variable. Except for principal components analysis, exact factor scores cannot be obtained. Estimates are obtained instead.

There are several methods for estimating factor score coefficients. Each has different properties and results in different scores (see Tucker, 1971; Harman, 1967). The three methods available in SPSS/PC+ FACTOR (Anderson-Rubin, regression, and Bartlett) all result in scores with a mean of 0. The Anderson-Rubin method always produces uncorrelated scores with a standard deviation of 1, even when the original factors are estimated to be correlated. The regression factor scores (the default) have a variance equal to the squared multiple correlation between the estimated factor scores and the true factor values. (These are shown on the diagonal in Figure 2.19b.) Regression method factor scores can be correlated even when factors are assumed to be orthogonal. If principal components extraction is used, all three methods result in the same factor scores, which are no longer estimated but are exact.

Figure 2.19a contains the factor score coefficients used to calculate regression method factor scores for the community data. The correlation matrix for the estimated scores is shown in Figure 2.19b.

Figure 2.19a   Factor coefficient matrix

```
FACTOR READ=CORRELATION TRIANGLE
  /VARIABLES=POPSTABL TO MENTALIL
  /PRINT=FSCORES
  /EXTRACTION=ML
  /ROTATION=VARIMAX.
```

```
Factor Score Coefficient Matrix:
              FACTOR  1     FACTOR  2     FACTOR  3

POPSTABL      -.00150       .03191       -.15843
NEWSCIRC       .05487      -.06095        .03524
FEMEMPLD       .01729       .14014        .05328
FARMERS       -.01797       .00113       -.11462
RETAILNG       .03728       .09460       -.03577
COMMERCL       .20579      -.11667       -.10723
INDUSTZN       .77285      -.27024        .00882
HEALTH        -.02786       .09971       -.00161
CHLDNEGL       .08404      -.44657        .16521
COMMEFFC      -.05030       .23211       -.03623
DWELGNEW      -.05117       .07034        .68792
MIGRNPOP       .00029      -.03198        .09778
UNEMPLOY       .03856      -.26435        .05378
MENTALIL       .01264      -.04224       -.01691
```

Figure 2.19b Covariance matrix for estimated regression factor scores

```
FACTOR READ=CORRELATION TRIANGLE
 /VARIABLES=POPSTABL TO MENTALIL
 /PRINT=FSCORES
 /EXTRACTION=ML
 /ROTATION=VARIMAX.
```

```
Covariance Matrix for Estimated Regression Factor Scores:

                FACTOR  1      FACTOR  2      FACTOR  3

    FACTOR  1      .96763
    FACTOR  2      .03294        .87641
    FACTOR  3      .00042        .02544        .89452
```

To see how factor scores are calculated, consider Table 2.19 which contains standardized values for the original 14 variables for 5 counties, and factor score values for the three factors. For each factor, the factor scores are obtained by multiplying the standardized values by the corresponding factor score coefficients. Thus, for Adams county the value for Factor 1 is −1.328.

$$-.00150 \times -.36 + .05487 \times -.93 + .01729 \times -1.06 + \ldots$$
$$+.01264 \times -.76 = -1.328$$

Equation 2.19b

Table 2.19 Standardized values and factor scores

			County		
Variable	**Adams**	**Butler**	**Crawford**	**Cuyahoga**	**Hamilton**
POPSTABL	−0.36	−1.49	2.44	−0.13	−0.30
NEWSCIRC	−0.93	0.39	−0.26	2.04	1.17
FEMEMPLD	−1.06	0.41	0.24	1.30	1.03
FARMERS	2.20	−0.67	0.01	−0.93	−0.90
RETAILNG	−1.41	0.49	0.58	1.15	1.07
COMMERCL	−0.89	−0.30	−0.07	1.58	2.02
INDUSTZN	−1.14	−0.11	0.03	1.53	1.85
HEALTH	−0.25	−0.56	−1.32	−0.36	−1.17
CHLDNEGL	−1.26	0.79	−0.61	0.63	0.99
COMMEFFC	−0.20	0.78	−0.87	−0.78	−1.66
DWELGNEW	−0.52	0.52	−1.09	−0.01	−0.22
MIGRNPOP	−0.98	0.16	−0.60	0.63	1.13
UNEMPLOY	−0.75	−0.36	−0.44	1.56	0.76
MENTALIL	−0.76	−0.77	−0.46	−0.14	0.61
Factor			**Scores**		
Factor 1	−1.328	−0.089	0.083	1.862	2.233
Factor 2	0.897	0.027	0.197	−1.362	−1.79
Factor 3	−0.830	0.831	−1.290	0.342	0.226

2.20 RUNNING PROCEDURE FACTOR

A variety of extraction and rotation techniques are available in the SPSS/PC+ FACTOR procedure. The extraction methods available include principal components analysis (Section 2.5) and the maximum-likelihood factor method (Section 2.9). The factor rotation methods are varimax, equamax, quartimax, and oblimin.

You can also request scree plots and factor loading plots to help in selecting and interpreting factors. FACTOR will accept a correlation matrix or a factor loading matrix as input, as well as the original values of your variables for cases.

2.21 Global and Analysis Block Subcommands

There are two main types of FACTOR subcommands: global and analysis block. Global subcommands are specified once and are in effect for the entire FACTOR procedure. Analysis block subcommands apply only to the ANALYSIS subcommand that precedes them. Within an analysis block, there are extraction and rotation phase subcommands.

The global subcommands are VARIABLES, MISSING, and WIDTH. The VARIABLES subcommand identifies the subset of variables from the active file available for analysis by FACTOR. The MISSING subcommand provides several alternative missing-value treatments. WIDTH controls the width of the display.

An analysis block begins with an ANALYSIS subcommand, which names a subset of variables from the list specified on the VARIABLES subcommand. If you omit the ANALYSIS subcommand, all variables named on the VARIABLES subcommand are used.

Analysis block subcommands include EXTRACTION, ROTATION, CRITERIA, SAVE, etc. You also can tailor the statistics displayed for an analysis block by specifying the PRINT subcommand to request optional statistics, the FORMAT subcommand to reformat factor loading and structure matrices, and the PLOT subcommand to obtain scree plots and factor loading plots.

The extraction phase is initiated with the EXTRACTION subcommand. (A principal components analysis is performed if there is no EXTRACTION subcommand.) The CRITERIA subcommand controls the number of factors selected in subsequent extractions, and the DIAGONAL subcommand supplies initial diagonal values for principal axis factoring.

The rotation phase is initiated with the ROTATION subcommand, which specifies the rotation method to use. The default varimax rotation is obtained if you omit both EXTRACTION and ROTATION. No rotation occurs if EXTRACTION is specified without ROTATION. The CRITERIA subcommand controls subsequent rotation, as well as extraction, criteria.

Optional subcommands are available to write and read matrices for FACTOR (see Figure 2.4a for an example of matrix input).

2.22
Subcommand Order

The global subcommands VARIABLES and MISSING must be the first specifications. The remaining subcommands can appear in any logical order.

Within an analysis block, the placement of CRITERIA is important, as it affects all extractions and rotations that follow. Once specified, a CRITERIA subcommand is in effect for the remainder of the FACTOR procedure. However, you can specify more than one CRITERIA subcommand.

2.23
Specifying the Variables

The VARIABLES subcommand lists the variables to analyze. If you do not specify a subsequent EXTRACTION or ROTATION subcommand, the default principal components analysis with varimax rotation is produced. Thus, the command

```
FACTOR VARIABLES=POPSTABL NEWSCIRC FEMEMPLD FARMERS RETAILNG COMMERCL
    INDUSTZN HEALTH CHLDNEGL COMMEFFC DWELGNEW MIGRNPOP UNEMPLOY MENTALIL
```

or, if the variables exist on that order on the active file, the command

```
FACTOR VARIABLES=POPSTABL TO MENTALIL.
```

produces the output shown in Figures 2.5a, 2.6, and 2.7.

VARIABLES is the only required subcommand and must be placed before all other subcommands except MISSING and WIDTH. Only variables named on the VARIABLES subcommand can be referred to in subsequent subcommands. You can specify only one VARIABLES subcommand on a FACTOR command.

2.24
Missing Values

FACTOR results are based on the correlation matrix for the variables listed on the VARIABLES subcommand. Use the MISSING subcommand to specify the missing-value treatment for this matrix. If you omit the MISSING subcommand, or include it with no specifications, missing values are deleted listwise.

LISTWISE *Delete missing values listwise.* Only cases with valid values on all variables on the VARIABLES subcommand are used. This is the default.

PAIRWISE *Delete missing values pairwise.* Cases with complete data on each pair of variables correlated are used.

MEANSUB *Replace missing values with the variable mean.* This includes both user-missing and system-missing values.

INCLUDE *Include missing values.* Cases with user-missing values are treated as valid observations. System-missing values are excluded from analysis.

DEFAULT *Same as LISTWISE.*

For example, the command

```
FACTOR VARIABLES=IQ GPA TESTSCOR STRESS SAT PSYCHTST
 /MISSING=PAIRWISE.
```

requests a default analysis that uses pairwise missing-value treatment in calculating the correlation matrix.

You can specify only one MISSING subcommand per FACTOR command. The MISSING subcommand must be placed before all other subcommands except VARIABLES and WIDTH. MISSING is ignored with matrix input.

2.25
Specifying Output Width

The WIDTH subcommand controls the display width for factor output. For example, the subcommand

```
/WIDTH=80
```

requests output that is 80 characters wide. The value on WIDTH must be an integer. This value overrides the one specified on the SET command. You can specify only one WIDTH subcommand per FACTOR command. The WIDTH subcommand can be placed anywhere.

2.26
Specifying Analyses

The ANALYSIS subcommand allows you to perform analyses on subsets of variables named on the VARIABLES subcommand. For example, the command

```
FACTOR VARIABLES=POPSTABL TO MENTALIL
 /ANALYSIS=FEMEMPLD FARMERS INDUSTZN HEALTH CHILDNEGL DWELGNEW
 /ANALYSIS=POPSTABL NEWSCIRC FEMEMPLD COMMERCL UNEMPLOY MENTALIL.
```

requests two default principal components analyses. The first uses variables FEMEMPLD, FARMERS, INDUSTZN, HEALTH, CHLDNEGL, and DWELGNEW, and the second uses variables POPSTABL, NEWSCIRC, FEMEMPLD, COMMERCL, UNEMPLOY, and MENTALIL.

If you do not include the ANALYSIS subcommand, FACTOR uses all of the variables listed on the VARIABLES subcommand for the analysis.

The TO keyword in a variable list on the ANALYSIS subcommand refers to the order of variables on the VARIABLES subcommand, not to their order in the file. Otherwise, the usual SPSS/PC+ conventions for variable lists are followed. You can use the keyword ALL to refer to all of the variables listed on the VARIABLES subcommand.

If you follow the VARIABLES subcommand with another analysis block subcommand prior to the ANALYSIS subcommand, you implicitly initiate an analysis block. For example, the command

```
FACTOR VARIABLES=POPSTABL TO MENTALIL
 /PRINT=DEFAULTS CORRELATIONS
 /ANALYSIS=FEMEMPLD FARMERS INDUSTZN HEALTH CHILDNEGL DWELGNEW
 /ANALYSIS=POPSTABL NEWSCIRC FEMEMPLD COMMERCL UNEMPLOY MENTALIL.
```

requests three analyses. The first uses all variables and prints the correlation matrix along with the defaults, and the second and third use different subsets of the variable list and print only the defaults.

2.27
Specifying the Extraction Method

To specify the extraction method, use the EXTRACTION subcommand with one of the keywords shown below.

PC	*Principal components analysis.* This is the default.
PAF	*Principal axis factoring.*
ML	*Maximum likelihood.*
ALPHA	*Alpha factoring.*
IMAGE	*Image factoring.*
ULS	*Unweighted least squares.*
GLS	*Generalized least squares.*
PA1	*Same as PC.*
PA2	*Same as PAF.*
DEFAULT	*Same as PC.*

You can specify more than one EXTRACTION subcommand. For example, the command

```
FACTOR VARIABLES=IQ GPA TESTSCOR STRESS SAT PSYCHTST
 /EXTRACTION=ML
 /EXTRACTION=PC.
```

produces output based on two extraction methods—maximum likelihood and principal components. You can specify multiple EXTRACTION subcommands in each analysis block to produce output for different extraction methods for subsets of variables named on the VARIABLES subcommand.

If you use the EXTRACTION subcommand without a subsequent ROTATION subcommand, the factor pattern matrix is not rotated (see Section 2.30).

2.28
Specifying Diagonal Values

Use the DIAGONAL subcommand to specify initial diagonal values in conjunction with principal axis factoring (EXTRACTION=PAF). You can specify any one of the following:

value list	*Diagonal values.* User-supplied diagonal values are used only for principal axis factoring.
DEFAULT	*1's on the diagonal for principal components or initial communality estimates on the diagonal for factor methods.*

You must supply the same number of diagonal values as there are variables in the analysis. For example, the command

```
FACTOR VARIABLES=IQ GPA TESTSCOR SAT EDYEARS
 /DIAGONAL=.55 .45 .35 .40 .50
 /EXTRACTION=PAF.
```

assigns five diagonal values for the specified principal axis factoring. You can use the prefix *n* and an asterisk to indicate replicated values. For example, 5*0.80 is the same as specifying 0.80 five times.

2.29
Specifying Extraction and Rotation Criteria

Use CRITERIA to control criteria for extractions and rotations that follow the subcommand.

FACTORS(nf)	*Number of factors extracted.* The default is the number of eigenvalues greater than MINEIGEN (see below).
MINEIGEN(eg)	*Minimum eigenvalue used to control the number of factors.* The default value is 1.
ITERATE(ni)	*Number of iterations for the factor solution.* The default value is 25.

ECONVERGE(e1) *Convergence criterion for extraction. The default value is 0.001.*
RCONVERGE(e2) *Convergence criterion for rotation. The default value is 0.0001.*
KAISER   *Kaiser normalization in rotation. This is the default.*
NOKAISER   *No Kaiser normalization.*
DELTA(d)   *Value of delta for direct oblimin rotation. The default value is 0.*
DEFAULT   *Use default values for all criteria.*

Once specified, criteria stay in effect for the procedure until explicitly overridden. For example, the command

```
FACTOR VARIABLES=IQ GPA TESTSCOR STRESS SAT PSYCHTST
 /CRITERIA=FACTORS(2)
 /ANALYSIS=ALL
 /CRITERIA=DEFAULT.
```

produces two factor analyses for the same set of variables. The first analysis limits the number of factors extracted to 2, and the second extracts all factors whose eigenvalue is greater than 1.

2.30
Rotating Factors

Four rotation methods are available in FACTOR: varimax, equamax, quartimax, and oblimin (see Section 2.13). When both the EXTRACTION and ROTATION subcommands are omitted, the factors are rotated using the varimax method. However, if EXTRACTION is specified but ROTATION is not, the factors are not rotated. To specify a rotation method other than these defaults, use the ROTATION subcommand.

VARIMAX   *Varimax rotation. This is the default if both EXTRACTION and ROTATION are omitted.*
EQUAMAX   *Equamax rotation.*
QUARTIMAX   *Quartimax rotation.*
OBLIMIN   *Direct oblimin rotation.*
NOROTATE   *No rotation. This is the default if EXTRACTION is specified but ROTATION is not.*
DEFAULT   *Same as VARIMAX.*

OBLIMIN uses a default delta value of 0. Use the CRITERIA subcommand to change this default (see Section 2.29).

   To obtain a factor loading plot based on unrotated factors, use the PLOT subcommand (see Section 2.33) and specify NOROTATE in the ROTATION subcommand, as in

```
FACTOR VARIABLES=IQ GPA TESTSCOR STRESS SAT PSYCHTST
 /PLOT=EIGEN ROTATION(1,2)
 /ROTATION=NOROTATE.
```

You can specify more than one rotation for a given extraction by using multiple ROTATION subcommands. See Section 2.29 for information on controlling rotation criteria.

2.31
Optional Statistics

By default, the statistics listed below under INITIAL, EXTRACTION, and ROTATION are printed. Use the PRINT subcommand to request additional statistics. If you specify PRINT, only those statistics explicity named are displayed. You can use only one PRINT subcommand for each analysis block.

UNIVARIATE   *Numbers of valid observations, means, and standard deviations for the variables named on the ANALYSIS subcommand.*
INITIAL   *Initial communalities, eigenvalues, and percentage of variance explained. (See Sections 2.5 and 2.7.)*
CORRELATION   *Correlation matrix for the variables named on the ANALYSIS subcommand.*
SIG   *Significance levels of correlations. These are one-tailed probabilities.*
DET   *The determinant of the correlation matrix.*

INV	*The inverse of the correlation matrix.*
AIC	*The anti-image covariance and correlation matrices.*
KMO	*The Kaiser-Meyer-Olkin measure of sampling adequacy and Bartlett's test of sphericity. (See Section 2.4.)*
EXTRACTION	*Communalities, eigenvalues, and rotated factor loadings. (See Sections 2.5 through 2.10.)*
REPR	*Reproduced correlations and their residuals. (See Section 2.8.)*
ROTATION	*Rotated factor pattern and structure matrices, factor transformation matrix, and factor correlation matrix. (See Sections 2.13.)*
FSCORE	*The factor score coefficient matrix.* By default, this is based on a regression solution.
DEFAULT	*INITIAL, EXTRACTION, and ROTATION statistics.* If you use the EXTRACTION subcommand without a subsequent ROTATION subcommand, only the statistics specified by INITIAL and EXTRACTION are displayed by default.
ALL	*All available statistics.*

For example,

```
FACTOR VARIABLES=POPSTABL TO MENTALIL
 /PRINT=REPR.
```

produced the output in Figure 2.8.

2.32
Sorting the Factor Pattern Matrix

Use the FORMAT subcommand to reformat the display of the factor loading and structure matrices to help you interpret the factors (see Section 2.15). You can use only one FORMAT subcommand per analysis block. The following keywords may be specified on FORMAT:

SORT	*Order the factor loadings by magnitude.*
BLANK(n)	*Suppress coefficients lower in absolute value than* n.
DEFAULT	*Turn off blanking and sorting.*

For example, the command

```
FACTOR VARIABLES=POPSTABL TO MENTALIL
 /FORMAT=SORT BLANK(.5).
```

produced the output in Figure 2.15b.

2.33
Obtaining Plots

To obtain a scree plot (Section 2.5) or a factor loading plot (Section 2.14), use the PLOT subcommand with the following keywords:

EIGEN	*Scree plot.* Plots the eigenvalues in descending order.
ROTATION(n1 n2)	*Factor loading plot.* The specifications $n1$ and $n2$ refer to the factors used as the axes. Several pairs of factors in parentheses can be specified on one ROTATION specification. A plot is displayed for each pair of factor numbers enclosed in parentheses.

You can specify only one PLOT subcommand per analysis block. Plots are based on rotated factors. To get an unrotated factor plot, you must explicitly specify NOROTATE on the ROTATION subcommand (see Section 2.30).

The plots in Figures 2.5b and 2.14a can be augmented with two additional factor plots by specifying

```
FACTOR VARIABLES=POPSTABL TO MENTALIL
 /PLOT=EIGEN ROTATION(1 2)(1 3)(2 3).
```

2.34
Saving Factor Scores

Use the SAVE subcommand to compute and save factor scores on the active file. (Factor scores cannot be produced from matrix input.) The specifications on the SAVE subcommand include the method for calculating factor scores, how many factor scores to calculate, and a *rootname* to be used in naming the factor scores.

First, choose one of the following method keywords (see Section 2.19):

REG   *The regression method.* This is the default.
BART   *The Bartlett method.*
AR   *The Anderson-Rubin method.*
DEFAULT   *Same as REG.*

Next, specify within parentheses the number of desired factor scores and a rootname up to seven characters long to be used in naming the scores. The maximum number of scores equals the order of the factor solution. You can use keyword ALL to calculate factor scores for all extracted factors.

FACTOR uses the rootname to name the factor scores sequentially, as in root1, root2, root3, etc. If you are calculating factor scores for a many-factor solution, make sure that the rootname is short enough to accommodate the number of the highest-order factor score variable. When FACTOR saves the variables on the active file, it automatically supplies a variable label indicating the the method used to calculate it, its positional order, and the analysis number.

For example, the following FACTOR command saves factor scores for a study of abortion items:

```
FACTOR VARIABLES=ABDEFECT TO ABSINGLE
 /MISSING=MEANSUB
 /CRITERIA=FACTORS(2)
 /EXTRACTION=ULS
 /ROTATION=VARIMAX
 /SAVE=AR (ALL FSULS).
```

FACTOR calculates two factor scores named FSULS1 and FSULS2 using the Anderson-Rubin method and saves them on the active file.

You can use multiple SAVE subcommands for an extraction. For example,

```
FACTOR VARIABLES=ABDEFECT TO ABSINGLE
 /MISSING=MEANSUB
 /EXTRACTION=ULS
 /ROTATION=VARIMAX
 /SAVE=AR (ALL FSULS)
 /SAVE=BART (ALL BFAC).
```

saves two sets of factor scores. The first set is computed using the Anderson-Rubin method and the second is computed using the Bartlett method.

2.35
Reading and Writing Matrices

You can read either the correlation matrix or factor loadings into FACTOR by specifying *one* of the following keywords on the READ subcommand.

CORRELATION   *Read the correlation matrix.* This is the default.
FACTOR(nf)   *Read the factor matrix. nf* indicates the number of factors in the analysis.
DEFAULT   *Same as CORRELATION.*

You can enter a correlation matrix in lower-triangular form if it contains a diagonal of *1*'s by specifying the keyword TRIANGLE following the keyword CORRELATION on the READ subcommand, as in

```
/READ=CORRELATION TRIANGLE
```

When you read a correlation or factor loading matrix with FACTOR, you must first specify a DATA LIST MATRIX command that points to the file containing the matrix materials and names the variables that will be read. If you supply an N command, FACTOR is able to calculate significance levels for the extraction techniques that use chi-square as a test statistic for the adequacy of the model and Bartlett's test of sphericity, which is available with the KMO keyword on the PRINT subcommand.

When FACTOR reads correlation matrices written by other procedures such as CORRELATION, it skips the record or matrix of *n*'s and prints a message for each line of the matrix of *n*'s.

The following SPSS/PC+ commands read a correlation matrix from an external file:

```
DATA LIST MATRIX FILE='file name' / X1 TO X10.
FACTOR READ/VARIABLES=X1 TO X10.
```

Use the WRITE subcommand with one of the following keywords to write the correlation matrix or the factor loadings to a specified file:

CORRELATION   *Write the correlation matrix. This is the default.*

FACTOR   *Write the factor matrix.*

DEFAULT   *Same as CORRELATION.*

The matrix is written to the results file specified on the SET command (by default, SPSS.PRC).

2.36
Annotated Example

The following SPSS/PC+ commands produce the output in Figures 2.4a, 2.5a, 2.7, 2.8, 2.15a, and 2.19a:

```
DATA LIST MATRIX FREE
 / POPSTABL NEWSCIRC FEMEMPLD FARMERS RETAILNG COMMERCL INDUSTZN
   HEALTH CHLDNEGL COMMEFFC DWELGNEW MIGRNPOP UNEMPLOY MENTALIL.
N 88.
BEGIN DATA.
 1.000
 -.175 1.000
 -.276   .616 1.000
  .369 -.625 -.637 1.000
 -.127   .624   .736 -.519 1.000
 -.069   .652   .589 -.306   .727 1.000
 -.106   .712   .742 -.545   .785   .911 1.000
 -.149 -.030   .241 -.068   .100   .123   .129 1.000
 -.039 -.171 -.589   .257 -.557 -.357 -.424 -.407 1.000
 -.005   .100   .471 -.213   .452   .287   .357   .732 -.660 1.000
 -.670   .188   .413 -.579   .165   .030   .203   .290 -.138   .311 1.000
 -.476 -.086   .064 -.198   .007 -.068 -.024   .083   .148   .067   .505 1.000
  .137 -.373 -.689   .450 -.650 -.424 -.528 -.348   .733 -.601 -.266   .181 1.000
  .237   .046 -.237   .121 -.190 -.055 -.095 -.279   .247 -.324 -.266 -.307   .217
 1.000
END DATA.
FACTOR READ=COR TRIANGLE
 /VARIABLES=POPSTABL TO MENTALIL
 /PRINT=ALL
 /FORMAT=SORT
 /ROTATION=VARIMAX/
 /ROTATION=OBLIMIN.
FINISH.
```

- The DATA LIST command indicates the variable names used in the analysis and tells SPSS/PC+ that the data is input as a matrix.
- The N command tells SPSS/PC+ upon how many cases the matrix is based.
- The READ subcommand on the FACTOR command reads a correlation matrix in lower-triangular form (the keyword TRIANGLE).
- The VARIABLES subcommand indicates which variables can be included on subsequent subcommands.
- The PRINT subcommand specifies all possible factor results.
- The FORMAT subcommand requests that the factor loadings be ordered by magnitude.
- The first ROTATION subcommand produces an orthogonal varimax rotation. The second ROTATION subcommand requests an oblique oblimin rotation.

Contents

Chapter 3 Stacking Beers: Cluster Analysis

Despite the old adage that opposites attract, it appears instead that likes cluster together. Birds of a feather, yuppies, and many other animate and inanimate objects that share similar characteristics are found together. By studying such clusters, one can determine the characteristics the objects share, as well as those in which they differ. In statistics, the search for relatively homogeneous groups of objects is called *cluster analysis*.

In biology, cluster analysis is used to classify animals and plants. This is called numerical taxonomy. In medicine, cluster analysis is used to identify diseases and their stages. For example, by examining patients who are diagnosed as depressed, one finds that there are several distinct subgroups of patients with different types of depression. In marketing, cluster analysis is used to identify persons with similar buying habits. By examining their characteristics, one may be able to target future marketing strategies more efficiently. See Romesburg (1984) for more examples of the use of cluster analysis.

Although both cluster analysis and discriminant analysis classify objects or cases into categories, discriminant analysis requires you to know group membership for the cases used to derive the classification rule. For example, if you are interested in distinguishing among several disease groups, cases with known diagnoses must be available. Then, based on cases whose group membership is known, discriminant analysis derives a rule for allocating undiagnosed patients. In cluster analysis, group membership for all cases is unknown. In fact, even the number of groups is often unknown. The goal of cluster analysis is to identify homogeneous groups or clusters.

In this chapter the fundamentals of cluster analysis are illustrated using a subset of data presented in a Consumer Reports (1983) survey of beer. Each of 20 beers is characterized in terms of cost per 12 ounces, alcohol content, sodium content, and the number of calories per 12 ounce serving. From these variables is it possible to identify several distinct subgroups of beer?

3.1
BASIC STEPS

As in other statistical procedures, a number of decisions must be made before one embarks on the actual analysis. Which variables will serve as the basis for cluster formation? How will the distance between cases be measured? What criteria will be used for combining cases into clusters?

Selecting the variables to include in an analysis is always crucial. If important variables are excluded, poor or misleading findings may result. For example, in a regression analysis of salary, if variables such as education and experience are not included, the results may be questionable. In cluster analysis, the initial choice of variables determines the characteristics that can be used to identify subgroups. If one is interested in clustering schools within a city and does not include variables like the number of students or the number of teachers, size is automatically excluded as a criterion for establishing clusters. By excluding all measures of taste or quality from the beer data, only physical characteristics and price will determine which beers are deemed similar.

3.2
How Alike are the Cases?

The concepts of distance and similarity are basic to many statistical techniques. Distance is a measure of how far apart two objects are, and similarity measures closeness. Distance measures are small and similarity measures are large for cases that are similar. In cluster analysis, these concepts are especially important, since cases are grouped on the basis of their "nearness." There are many different definitions of distance and similarity. Selection of a distance measure should be based both on the properties of the measure and on the algorithm for cluster formation. See Section 3.11 for further discussion of distance measures.

To see how a simple distance measure is computed, consider Table 3.2a, which shows the values of calories and cost for two of the beers. There is a 13-calorie and 5-cent difference between the two beers. This information can be combined into a single index or distance measure in many different ways. A commonly used index is the *squared Euclidean distance,* which is the sum of the squared differences over all of the variables. In this example, the squared Euclidean distance is 13^2+5^2, or 194.

Table 3.2a   Values of calories and cost for two beers

	Calories	Cost
Budweiser	144	43
Lowenbrau	157	48

The squared Euclidean distance has the disadvantage that it depends on the units of measurement for the variables. For example, if the cost were given as pennies per ounce instead of per twelve ounces, the distance measure would change. Another disadvantage is that when variables are measured on different scales, as in this example, variables that are measured in larger numbers will contribute more to the distance than variables that are recorded in smaller numbers. For example, the 13-calorie difference contributes much more to the distance score than does the 5-cent difference in cost.

One means of circumventing this problem is to express all variables in standardized form. That is, all variables have a mean of 0 and a standard deviation of 1. This is not always the best strategy, however, since the variability of a particular measure can provide useful information (see Sneath & Sokal, 1973).

Table 3.2b shows the Z scores for calories and cost for Budweiser and Lowenbrau based on the means and standard deviations for all twenty beers. The squared Euclidean distance based on the standardized variables is $(0.38-0.81)^2+(-0.46-(-0.11))^2$, or 0.307. The differences in calories and cost are now weighted equally.

Table 3.2b   Z scores for the calories and cost variables

	Calories	Cost
Budweiser	0.38	-0.46
Lowenbrau	0.81	-0.11

3.3
Forming Clusters

Just as there are many methods for calculating distances between objects, there are many methods for combining objects into clusters. A commonly used method for forming clusters is hierarchical cluster analysis, using one of two methods: agglomerative, or divisive. In *agglomerative* hierarchical clustering, clusters are formed by grouping cases into bigger and bigger clusters until all cases are members of a single cluster. *Divisive* hierarchical clustering starts out with all cases grouped into a single cluster and splits clusters until there are as many clusters as there are cases. For a discussion of nonhierarchical clustering methods, see Everitt (1980).

3.4
Agglomerative Clustering

Before discussing the rules for forming clusters, consider what happens during the steps of agglomerative hierarchical cluster analysis. At the first step all cases are considered separate clusters: there are as many clusters as there are cases. At the second step, two of the cases are combined into a single cluster. At the third step, either a third case is added to the cluster already containing two cases, or two additional cases are merged into a new cluster. At every step, either individual cases are added to clusters or already existing clusters are combined. Once a cluster is formed, it cannot be split; it can only be combined with other clusters. Thus, hierarchical clustering methods do not allow cases to separate from clusters to which they have been allocated. For example, if two beers are deemed members of the same cluster at the first step, they will always be members of the same cluster, although they may be combined with additional cases at a later step.

3.5
Criteria for Combining Clusters

There are many criteria for deciding which cases or clusters should be combined at each step. All of these criteria are based on a matrix of either distances or similarities between pairs of cases. One of the simplest methods is *single linkage*, sometimes called "nearest neighbor." The first two cases combined are those that have the smallest distance (or largest similarity) between them. The distance between the new cluster and individual cases is then computed as the minimum distance between an individual case and a case in the cluster. The distances between cases that have not been joined do not change. At every step, the distance between two clusters is the distance between their two closest points.

Another commonly used method is called *complete linkage*, or the "furthest neighbor" technique. In this method, the distance between two clusters is calculated as the distance between their two furthest points. Other methods for combining clusters available in SPSS/PC+ are described in Section 3.11.

3.6
PERFORMING A CLUSTER ANALYSIS

Before considering other distance measures and methods of combining clusters, consider Figure 3.6a, which contains the matrix of squared Euclidean distance coefficients for all possible pairs of the 20 beers, based on standardized calories, sodium, alcohol, and cost. The standardized values were computed by procedure

DESCRIPTIVES. The listing of the original and standardized values for these variables is shown in Figure 3.6b.

The first entry in Figure 3.6a is the distance between Case 1 and Case 2, Budweiser and Schlitz. This can be calculated from the standardized values in Figure 3.6b as

$$D^2 = (0.38-0.61)^2 + (0.01-0.62)^2 + (0.34-0.61)^2$$
$$+ (-0.46-(-0.46))^2 = 0.49$$

Equation 3.6

Since the distance between pairs of cases is symmetric (that is, the distance between Case 3 and Case 4 is the same as the distance between Case 4 and Case 3), only the lower half of the distance matrix is displayed.

Figure 3.6a The squared Euclidean distance coefficient matrix

```
SET WIDTH=WIDE.
DATA LIST
  / ID 1-2 RATING 3 BEER 4-24 (A) ORIGIN 25 AVAIL 26
    PRICE 27-30 COST 31-34 CALORIES 35-37 SODIUM 38-39
    ALCOHOL 40-42 CLASS 43 LIGHT 44.
FORMATS PRICE COST (F4.2) ALCOHOL (F3.1).
MISSING VALUES CLASS(0).
BEGIN DATA.
lines of data
END DATA.
DESCRIPTIVES CALORIES SODIUM ALCOHOL COST
  /OPTIONS=3.
FORMATS ZCALORIE ZSODIUM ZALCOHOL ZCOST (F8.6).
CLUSTER ZCALORIE ZSODIUM ZALCOHOL ZCOST
  /PRINT=DISTANCE
  /METHOD=COMPLETE.
```

Squared Euclidean Dissimilarity Coefficient Matrix

Case	1	2	3	4	5	6	7	8
2	.4922							
3	.3749	.5297						
4	7.0040	8.2298	4.8424					
5	6.1889	7.0897	4.4835	.8700				
6	2.5848	1.6534	3.7263	17.0154	15.2734			
7	4.0720	1.8735	3.1573	12.1251	11.5371	3.1061		
8	3.3568	1.5561	3.6380	14.8000	12.0038	1.3526	2.0742	
9	3.0662	5.4473	4.9962	11.4721	9.5339	7.4577	13.3723	9.6850
10	3.9181	6.8702	5.8179	11.5391	10.0663	8.9551	15.7993	11.5019
11	.2474	.3160	.7568	8.4698	6.8353	1.8432	3.6498	1.9953
12	2.5940	4.1442	4.4322	12.1519	9.1534	5.4981	11.2604	6.4385
13	1.1281	2.8432	1.7663	5.9995	4.9519	6.0530	9.0610	6.8673
14	5.6782	5.3399	4.2859	4.2382	1.6427	11.5628	8.6397	7.0724
15	8.3245	10.1947	6.6075	.7483	.6064	19.5528	16.0117	16.9620
16	16.4081	19.7255	20.8463	33.3380	28.0650	17.6015	32.1339	20.5466
17	.5952	.6788	1.4051	10.0509	7.9746	1.6159	4.3782	1.8230
18	1.9394	.6307	2.1757	11.9216	9.5828	1.2688	1.7169	.3092
19	13.1887	17.6915	16.7104	23.2048	19.8574	19.0673	30.9530	22.3479
20	4.4010	7.4360	6.2635	10.8241	9.1372	10.4511	16.4825	12.7426

Case	9	10	11	12	13	14	15	16
10	.9349							
11	3.4745	4.5082						
12	.6999	1.5600	2.2375					
13	1.6931	1.3437	1.6100	1.6536				
14	10.2578	10.9762	5.1046	7.8646	5.4275			
15	10.2201	10.3631	9.6179	10.9556	5.9694	4.1024		
16	8.6771	6.9127	15.2083	7.1851	12.2231	24.6793	29.7992	
17	3.3828	4.2251	.1147	1.8315	1.7851	5.6395	10.9812	13.1806
18	7.3607	9.4595	1.0094	4.9491	5.0762	5.9553	13.7962	20.0105
19	4.6046	3.0565	13.4011	5.3477	7.9175	20.5149	19.3851	2.8209
20	.3069	.7793	5.1340	1.5271	1.9902	10.8954	9.0403	9.0418

Case	17	18	19
18	1.0802		
19	12.3170	20.1156	
20	5.1327	10.0114	3.6382

Figure 3.6b   Original and standardized values for the 20 beers from procedure LIST

```
DESCRIPTIVES CALORIES SODIUM ALCOHOL COST
  /OPTIONS=3.
FORMATS ZCALORIE ZSODIUM ZALCOHOL ZCOST (F5.2).
LIST VAR=ID BEER CALORIES SODIUM ALCOHOL
            COST ZCALORIE ZSODIUM ZALCOHOL ZCOST.
```

ID	BEER	CALORIES	SODIUM	ALCOHOL	COST	ZCALORIE	ZSODIUM	ZALCOHOL	ZCOST
1	BUDWEISER	144	15	4.7	.43	.38	.01	.34	-.46
2	SCHLITZ	151	19	4.9	.43	.61	.62	.61	-.46
3	LOWENBRAU	157	15	4.9	.48	.81	.01	.61	-.11
4	KRONENBOURG	170	7	5.2	.73	1.24	-1.21	1.00	1.62
5	HEINEKEN	152	11	5.0	.77	.65	-.60	.74	1.90
6	OLD MILWAUKEE	145	23	4.6	.28	.42	1.22	.21	-1.51
7	AUGSBERGER	175	24	5.5	.40	1.41	1.38	1.40	-.67
8	STROHS BOHEMIAN STYLE	149	27	4.7	.42	.55	1.83	.34	-.53
9	MILLER LITE	99	10	4.3	.43	-1.10	-.75	-.18	-.46
10	BUDWEISER LIGHT	113	8	3.7	.44	-.64	-1.06	-.97	-.39
11	COORS	140	18	4.6	.44	.25	.46	.21	-.39
12	COORS LIGHT	102	15	4.1	.46	-1.00	.01	-.45	-.25
13	MICHELOB LIGHT	135	11	4.2	.50	.09	-.60	-.32	.02
14	BECKS	150	19	4.7	.76	.58	.62	.34	1.83
15	KIRIN	149	6	5.0	.79	.55	-1.36	.74	2.04
16	PABST EXTRA LIGHT	68	15	2.3	.38	-2.13	.01	-2.82	-.81
17	HAMMS	136	19	4.4	.43	.12	.62	-.05	-.46
18	HEILEMANS OLD STYLE	144	24	4.9	.43	.38	1.38	.61	-.46
19	OLYMPIA GOLD LIGHT	72	6	2.9	.46	-2.00	-1.36	-2.03	-.25
20	SCHLITZ LIGHT	97	7	4.2	.47	-1.17	-1.21	-.32	-.18

```
Number of cases read =    20    Number of cases listed =    20
```

3.7
Icicle Plots

Once the distance matrix has been calculated, the actual formation of clusters can commence. Figure 3.7a summarizes a cluster analysis that uses the complete linkage method. This type of figure is sometimes called a vertical icicle plot because it resembles a row of icicles hanging from eaves.

Figure 3.7a   Vertical icicle plot for the 20 beers

```
CLUSTER ZCALORIE ZSODIUM ZALCOHOL ZCOST
  /ID=BEER
  /METHOD=COMPLETE/
  /PLOT=VICICLE.
```

The columns of Figure 3.7a correspond to the objects being clustered. They are identified both by a sequential number ranging from 1 to the number of cases and, when possible, by the labels of the objects. Thus, the first column corresponds to beer number 19, Olympia Gold Light, while the last column corresponds to the first beer in the file, Budweiser. In order to follow the sequence of steps in the cluster analysis, the figure is read from bottom to top.

As previously described, all cases are considered initially as individual clusters. Since there are twenty beers in this example, there are 20 clusters. At the first step the two "closest" cases are combined into a single cluster, resulting in 19 clusters. The bottom line of Figure 3.7a shows these 19 clusters. Each case is represented by a single X separated by blanks. The two cases that have been merged into a single cluster, Coors and Hamms, do not have blanks separating them. Instead they are represented by consecutive X's. The row labeled 18 in Figure 3.7a corresponds to the solution at the next step, when 18 clusters are present. At this step Miller Lite and Schlitz Light are merged into a single cluster. Thus, at this point there are 18 clusters, 16 consisting of individual beers and 2 consisting of pairs of beers. At each subsequent step an additional cluster is formed by joining either a case to an already existing multicase cluster, two separate cases into a single cluster, or two multicase clusters.

For example, the row labeled 5 in Figure 3.7a corresponds to a solution that has five clusters. Beers 19 and 16, the very light beers, form one cluster; beers 13, 12, 10, 20, and 9 form the next. These beers, Michelob Light, Coors Light, Budweiser Light, Schlitz Light, and Miller Light, are all light beers, but not as light as the two in the first cluster. The third cluster consists of Becks, Kirin, Heineken, and Kronenbourg. These are all imported beers. Although no variable in this example explicitly indicates whether beers are domestic or imported, the cost variable (see Figure 3.6b) causes the imported beers to cluster together since they are quite a bit more expensive than the domestic ones. A fourth cluster consists of Augsberger, Heilemans Old Style, Strohs Bohemian Style, and Old Milwaukee. Inspection of Figure 3.7b shows that all of these beers are distinguished by high sodium content. The last cluster consists of five beers, Hamms, Coors, Schlitz, Lowenbrau, and Budweiser. These beers share the distinction of being average. That is, they are neither particulary high nor particularly low on the variables measured. Note from Figure 3.7b that, based on the standard deviations, beers in the same cluster, when compared to all beers, are more homogeneous on the variables measured.

Figure 3.7b   Cluster characteristics (table from SPSS/PC+ TABLES)

```
CLUSTER ZCALORIE ZSODIUM ZALCOHOL ZCOST
  /ID=BEER
  /METHOD=COMPLETE(CLUSMEM)
  /SAVE=CLUSTER(5).
VALUE LABELS CLUSMEM5 1 'AVERAGE' 2 'EXPENSIVE' 3 'HIGH NA'
   4 'LIGHT' 5 'VERY LIGHT'.
TABLES OBSERVATION=COST CALORIES ALCOHOL SODIUM
  /FTOTAL=TOTAL
  /FORMAT=CWIDTH(10,9)
  /TABLE=CLUSMEM5+TOTAL BY CALORIES+COST+ALCOHOL+SODIUM
  /STATISTICS=MEAN STDDEV.
```

	CALORIES PER 12 FLUID OUNCES		COST PER 12 FLUID OUNCES		ALCOHOL BY VOLUME (IN %)		SODIUM PER 12 FLUID OUNCES IN MG	
	Mean	Standard Deviation	Mean	Standard Deviation	Mean	Standard Deviation	Mean	Standard Deviation
CLUSMEM5								
AVERAGE	146	8	.44	.02	4.7	.2	17	2
EXPENSIVE	155	10	.76	.03	5.0	.2	11	6
HIGH NA	153	15	.38	.07	4.9	.4	25	2
LIGHT	109	16	.46	.03	4.1	.2	10	3
VERY LIGHT	70	3	.42	.06	2.6	.4	11	6
TOTAL	132	30	.50	.14	4.4	.8	15	7

Cluster formation continues in Figure 3.7a until all cases are merged into a single cluster, as shown in the first row. Thus, all steps of the cluster analysis are displayed in Figure 3.7a. If we were clustering people instead of beers, the last row would be individual persons, higher up they would perhaps merge into families, these into neighborhoods, and so forth. Often there is not one single, meaningful cluster solution, but many, depending on what is of interest.

3.8 The Agglomeration Schedule

The results of the cluster analysis are summarized in the *agglomeration schedule* in Figure 3.8, which contains the number of cases or clusters being combined at each stage. The first line is Stage 1, the 19-cluster solution. Beers 11 and 17 are combined at this stage, as shown in the columns labeled "Clusters Combined." The squared Euclidean distance between these two beers is displayed in the column labeled "Coefficient." Since this is the first step, this coefficient is identical to the distance measure in Figure 3.6a for Cases 11 and 17. The last column indicates at which stage another case or cluster is combined with this one. For example, at the tenth stage, Case 1 is merged with Cases 11 and 17 into a single cluster. The column entitled "Stage Cluster 1st Appears" indicates at which stage a cluster is first formed. For example, the entry of 4 at Stage 5 indicates that Case 1 was first involved in a merge in the previous step (Stage 4). From the line for Stage 4, you can see that, at this point, Case 1 was involved in a merge with Case 3. From the last column of Stage 5 we see that the new cluster (Cases 1, 2, and 3) is next involved in a merge at Stage 10, where the cases combine with Cases 11 and 17.

Figure 3.8   Agglomeration schedule using complete linkage

```
CLUSTER ZCALORIE ZSODIUM ZALCOHOL ZCOST
 /ID=BEER
 /PRINT=SCHEDULE
 /METHOD=COMPLETE.
```

Agglomeration Schedule using Complete Linkage

Stage	Clusters Combined Cluster 1	Cluster 2	Coefficient	Stage Cluster 1st Appears Cluster 1	Cluster 2	Next Stage
1	11	17	.114695	0	0	10
2	9	20	.306903	0	0	8
3	8	18	.309227	0	0	9
4	1	3	.374859	0	0	5
5	1	2	.529696	4	0	10
6	5	15	.606378	0	0	7
7	4	5	.870016	0	6	15
8	9	10	.934909	2	0	11
9	6	8	1.352617	0	3	14
10	1	11	1.405148	5	1	16
11	9	12	1.559987	8	0	12
12	9	13	1.990205	11	0	17
13	16	19	2.820896	0	0	19
14	6	7	3.106108	9	0	16
15	4	14	4.238164	7	0	17
16	1	6	4.378198	10	14	18
17	4	9	12.151937	15	12	18
18	1	4	19.552841	16	17	19
19	1	16	33.338028	18	13	0

The information in Figure 3.8 that is not available in the icicle plot is the value of the distance between the two most dissimilar points of the clusters being combined at each stage. By examining these values, you can get an idea of how unlike the clusters being combined are. Small coefficients indicate that fairly homogeneous clusters are being merged. Large coefficients indicate that clusters containing quite dissimilar members are being combined. The actual value depends on the clustering method and the distance measure used.

These coefficients can also be used for guidance in deciding how many clusters are needed to represent the data. One usually wishes to stop agglomeration as soon as the increase between two adjacent steps becomes large. For example, in Figure 3.8 there is a fairly large increase in the value of the distance measure from a four-cluster to a three-cluster solution (Stages 16 and 17).

3.9
The Dendrogram

Another way of visually representing the steps in a hierarchical clustering solution is with a display called a *dendrogram*. The dendrogram shows the clusters being combined and the values of the coefficients at each step. The dendrogram produced by the SPSS/PC+ CLUSTER procedure does not plot actual distances but rescales them to numbers between 0 and 25. Thus, the ratio of the distances between steps is preserved. The scale displayed at the top of the figure does not correspond to actual distance values.

To understand how a dendrogram is constructed, consider a simple four-beer example. Figure 3.9a contains the icicle plot for the clustering of Kirin, Becks, Old Milwaukee, and Budweiser. From the icicle plot, you can see that at the first step Budweiser and Old Milwaukee are combined, at the second step Becks and Kirin are merged, and all four beers are merged into a single cluster at the last step.

Figure 3.9a Vertical icicle plot for the four-beer example

```
CLUSTER ZCALORIE ZSODIUM ZALCOHOL ZCOST
 /ID=BEER
 /METHOD=COMPLETE
 /PLOT=VICICLE.
```

```
Vertical Icicle Plot using Complete Linkage

  (Down) Number of Clusters   (Across) Case Label and number

        K   B   O       B
        I   E   L       U
        R   C   D       D
        I   K   M       W
        N   S   I       E
                L       I
                W       S
                A       E
                U       R
                K
                E
                E



        4   3   2   1
 1 +XXXXXXXXXX
 2 +XXXX   XXXX
 3 +X   X   XXXX
```

The distances at which the beers are combined are shown in the agglomeration schedule in Figure 3.9b. From this schedule, we see that the distance between Budweiser and Old Milwaukee is 2.017 when they are combined. Similarly when Becks and Kirin are combined, their distance is 6.323. Since the method of complete linkage is used, the distance coefficient displayed for the last stage is the largest distance between a member of the Budweiser-Milwaukee cluster and a member of the Becks-Kirin cluster. This distance is 16.789.

Figure 3.9b   Agglomeration schedule for the four-beer example

```
CLUSTER ZCALORIE ZSODIUM ZALCOHOL ZCOST
 /ID=BEER
 /PRINT=SCHEDULE
 /METHOD=COMPLETE.
```

```
Agglomeration Schedule using Complete Linkage

            Clusters    Combined                  Stage Cluster 1st Appears   Next
    Stage  Cluster 1  Cluster 2   Coefficient     Cluster 1    Cluster 2     Stage
      1        1          2        2.017018           0            0           3
      2        3          4        6.323439           0            0           3
      3        1          3       16.789215           1            2           0
```

The information in Figure 3.9b is displayed in the dendrogram in Figure 3.9c, which is read from left to right. Vertical lines denote joined clusters. The position of the line on the scale indicates the distance at which clusters were joined. Since the distances are rescaled to fall in the range of 1 to 25, the largest distance, 16.8, corresponds to the value of 25. The smallest distance, 2.017, corresponds to the value 1. Thus, the second distance (6.32) corresponds to a value of about 8. Note that the ratio of the rescaled distances is, after the first, the same as the ratios of the original distances.

The first two clusters that are joined are Budweiser and Old Milwaukee. They are connected by a line that is 1 unit from the origin since this is the rescaled distance between these points. When Becks and Kirin are joined, the line that connects them is 8 units from the origin. Similarly, when these two clusters are merged into a single cluster, the line that connects them is 25 units from the origin. Thus, the dendrogram indicates not only which clusters are joined but also the distance at which they are joined.

Figure 3.9c   Dendrogram for the four-beer example

```
CLUSTER ZCALORIE ZSODIUM ZALCOHOL ZCOST
 /ID=BEER
 /METHOD=COMPLETE
 /PLOT=DENDROGRAM.
```

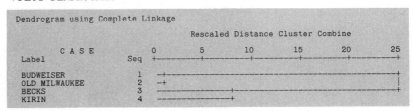

```
Dendrogram using Complete Linkage

                               Rescaled Distance Cluster Combine

            C A S E        0         5        10        15        20        25
    Label            Seq   +---------+---------+---------+---------+---------+

    BUDWEISER         1     -+---------------------------------------------+
    OLD MILWAUKEE     2     -+                                             |
    BECKS             3     -------------+-------------------------------- +
    KIRIN             4     -------------+
```

Figure 3.9d contains the dendrogram for the complete 20-beer example. Since many of the distances at the beginning stages are similar in magnitude, one cannot tell the sequence in which some of the early clusters are formed. However, at the last three stages the distances at which clusters are being combined are fairly large. Looking at the dendrogram, it appears that the five-cluster solution (very light beers, light beers, imported beers, high-sodium beers, and "average" beers) may be appropriate since it is easily interpretable and occurs before the distances at which clusters are combined become too large.

Figure 3.9d   Dendrogram using complete linkage for the 20 beers

```
CLUSTER ZCALORIE ZSODIUM ZALCOHOL ZCOST
 /ID=BEER
 /METHOD=COMPLETE
 /PLOT=DENDROGRAM.
```

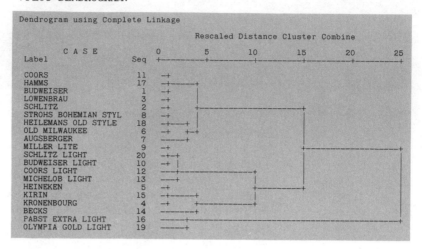

3.10
Some Additional Displays and Modifications

The agglomeration schedule, the icicle plot, and the dendrogram illustrate the results produced by a hierarchical clustering solution. Several variations of these plots may also be useful. For example, when there are many cases, the initial steps of the cluster analysis may not be of particular interest. You might want to display solutions for only certain numbers of clusters. Or you might want to see the results at every *k*th step. Figure 3.10a contains the icicle plot of results at every fifth step.

Figure 3.10a   Icicle plot with results at every fifth step

```
CLUSTER ZCALORIE ZSODIUM ZALCOHOL ZCOST
 /ID=BEER
 /METHOD=COMPLETE
 /PLOT=VICICLE(1,19,5).
```

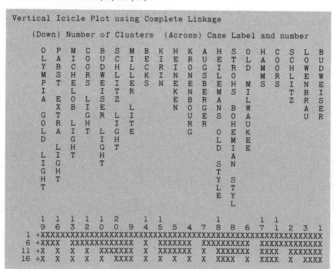

When there are many cases, all of them may not fit across the top of a single page. In this situation it may be useful to turn the icicle plot on its side. This is called a horizontal icicle plot. Figure 3.10b contains the horizontal icicle plot corresponding to Figure 3.7a.

Figure 3.10b   Horizontal icicle plot

```
CLUSTER ZCALORIE ZSODIUM ZALCOHOL ZCOST
 /ID=BEER
 /METHOD=COMPLETE
 /PLOT=HICICLE.
```

```
Horizontal Icicle Plot Using Complete Linkage

                            Number of Clusters

                            1111111111
          C A S E           1234567890123456789
    Label             Seq   +++++++++++++++++++

  OLYMPIA GOLD LIGHT   19   XXXXXXXXXXXXXXXXXXX
                            XXXXXX
                            XXXXXX
  PABST EXTRA LIGHT    16   XXXXXXXXXXXXXXXXXXX
                            X
                            X
  MICHELOB LIGHT       13   XXXXXXXXXXXXXXXXXXX
                            XXXXXXXX
                            XXXXXXXX
  COORS LIGHT          12   XXXXXXXXXXXXXXXXXXX
                            XXXXXXXXX
                            XXXXXXXXX
  BUDWEISER LIGHT      10   XXXXXXXXXXXXXXXXXXX
                            XXXXXXXXXXX
                            XXXXXXXXXXX
  SCHLITZ LIGHT        20   XXXXXXXXXXXXXXXXXXX
                            XXXXXXXXXXXXXXXX
                            XXXXXXXXXXXXXXXX
  MILLER LITE           9   XXXXXXXXXXXXXXXXXXX
                            XXX
                            XXX
  BECKS                14   XXXXXXXXXXXXXXXXXXX
                            XXXXX
                            XXXXX
  KIRIN                15   XXXXXXXXXXXXXXXXXXX
                            XXXXXXXXXXXXX
                            XXXXXXXXXXXXX
  HEINEKEN              5   XXXXXXXXXXXXXXXXXXX
                            XXXXXXXXXXXX
                            XXXXXXXXXXXX
  KRONENBOURG           4   XXXXXXXXXXXXXXXXXXX
                            XX
                            XX
  AUGSBERGER            7   XXXXXXXXXXXXXXXXXXX
                            XXXXXX
                            XXXXXX
  HEILEMANS OLD STYLE  18   XXXXXXXXXXXXXXXXXXX
                            XXXXXXXXXXXXXXXX
                            XXXXXXXXXXXXXXXX
  STROHS BOHEMIAN STYL  8   XXXXXXXXXXXXXXXXXXX
                            XXXXXXXXXXX
                            XXXXXXXXXXX
  OLD MILWAUKEE         6   XXXXXXXXXXXXXXXXXXX
                            XXXX
                            XXXX
  HAMMS                17   XXXXXXXXXXXXXXXXXXX
                            XXXXXXXXXXXXXXXX
                            XXXXXXXXXXXXXXXX
  COORS                11   XXXXXXXXXXXXXXXXXXX
                            XXXXXXXXXX
                            XXXXXXXXXX
  SCHLITZ               2   XXXXXXXXXXXXXXXXXXX
                            XXXXXXXXXXXXXX
                            XXXXXXXXXXXXXX
  LOWENBRAU             3   XXXXXXXXXXXXXXXXXXX
                            XXXXXXXXXXXXXX
                            XXXXXXXXXXXXXX
  BUDWEISER             1   XXXXXXXXXXXXXXXXXXX
```

Although the composition of clusters at any stage can be discerned from the icicle plots, it is often helpful to display the information in tabular form. Figure 3.10c contains the cluster memberships for the cases at different stages of the solution. From Figure 3.10c, you can easily tell which clusters cases belong to in the two- to five-cluster solutions.

Figure 3.10c Cluster membership at different stages

```
CLUSTER ZCALORIE ZSODIUM ZALCOHOL ZCOST
  /ID=BEER
  /PRINT=CLUSTER(2,5)
  /METHOD=COMPLETE.
```

```
Cluster Membership of Cases using Complete Linkage

                                        Number of Clusters

    Label                    Case     5    4    3    2

    BUDWEISER                  1       1    1    1    1
    SCHLITZ                    2       1    1    1    1
    LOWENBRAU                  3       1    1    1    1
    KRONENBOURG                4       2    2    2    1
    HEINEKEN                   5       2    2    2    1
    OLD MILWAUKEE              6       3    1    1    1
    AUGSBERGER                 7       3    1    1    1
    STROHS BOHEMIAN STYL       8       3    1    1    1
    MILLER LITE                9       4    3    2    1
    BUDWEISER LIGHT           10       4    3    2    1
    COORS                     11       1    1    1    1
    COORS LIGHT               12       4    3    2    1
    MICHELOB LIGHT            13       4    3    2    1
    BECKS                     14       2    2    2    1
    KIRIN                     15       2    2    2    1
    PABST EXTRA LIGHT         16       5    4    3    2
    HAMMS                     17       1    1    1    1
    HEILEMANS OLD STYLE       18       3    1    1    1
    OLYMPIA GOLD LIGHT        19       5    4    3    2
    SCHLITZ LIGHT             20       4    3    2    1
```

3.11
More on Calculating Distances and Similarities

There are many methods for estimating the distance or similarity between two cases. But even before these measures are computed, you must decide whether the variables need to be rescaled. When the variables have different scales, such as cents and calories, and they are not standardized, any distance measure will reflect primarily the contributions of variables measured in the large units. For example, the beer data variables were standardized prior to cluster analysis to have a mean of 0 and a standard deviation of 1. Besides standardization to Z-scores, variables can be standardized by dividing by just the standard deviation, the range, the mean, or the maximum. See Romesburg (1984) or Anderberg (1973) for further discussion.

Based on the transformed data it is possible to calculate many different types of distance and similarity measures. Different distance and similarity measures weight data characteristics differently. The choice among the measures should be based on which differences or similarities in the data are important for a particular application. For example, if one is clustering animal bones, what may matter is not the actual differences in bone size but relationships among the dimensions, since we know that even animals of the same species differ in size. Bones with the same relationship between length and diameter should be judged as similar, regardless of their absolute magnitudes. See Romesburg (1984) for further discussion.

The most commonly used distance measure, the squared Euclidean distance, has been discussed previously. Sometimes its square root, the Euclidean distance, is also used. A distance measure that is based on the absolute values of differences is the *city-block* or *Manhattan* distance. For two cases it is just the sum of the absolute differences of the values for all variables. Since the differences are not squared, large differences are not weighted as heavily as in the squared Euclidean distances. The *Chebychev* distance defines the distance between two cases as the maximum absolute difference in the values over all variables. Thus, it ignores much of the available information.

3.12
Methods for Combining Clusters

Many methods can be used to decide which cases or clusters should be combined at each step. In general, clustering methods fall into three groups: linkage methods, error sums of squares or variance methods, and centroid methods. All are based on either a matrix of distances or a matrix of similarities between pairs of cases. The methods differ in how they estimate distances between clusters at successive steps. Since the merging of clusters at each step depends on the distance measure, different distance measures can result in different cluster solutions for the same clustering method. See Milligan (1980) for comparisons of the performance of some of the different clustering methods.

One of the simplest methods for joining clusters is *single linkage,* sometimes called "nearest neighbor." The first two cases combined are those with the smallest distance, or greatest similarity, between them. The distance between the new cluster and individual cases is then computed as the minimum distance between an individual case and a case in the cluster. The distances between cases that have not been joined do not change. At every step the distance between two clusters is taken to be the distance between their two closest points.

Another commonly used method is called *complete linkage,* or the "furthest neighbor" technique. In this method the distance between two clusters is calculated as the distance between their two furthest points.

The *average linkage between groups method,* often called UPGMA (unweighted pair-group method using arithmetic averages), defines the distance between two clusters as the average of the distances between all pairs of cases in which one member of the pair is from each of the clusters. For example, if Cases 1 and 2 form cluster A and Cases 3, 4, and 5 form cluster B, the distance between clusters A and B is taken to be the average of the distances between the following pairs of cases: (1,3) (1,4) (1,5) (2,3) (2,4) (2,5). This differs from the linkage methods in that it uses information about all pairs of distances, not just the nearest or the furthest. For this reason it is usually preferred to the single and complete linkage methods for cluster analysis.

The UPGMA method considers only distances between pairs of cases in different clusters. A variant of it, *the average linkage within groups,* combines clusters so that the average distance between all cases in the resulting cluster is as small as possible. Thus, the distance between two clusters is taken to be the average of the distances between all possible pairs of cases in the resulting cluster.

Another frequently used method for cluster formation is *Ward's method.* For each cluster the means for all variables are calculated. Then for each case the squared Euclidean distance to the cluster means is calculated. These distances are summed for all of the cases. At each step, the two clusters that merge are those that result in the smallest increase in the overall sum of the squared within-cluster distances.

The *centroid method* calculates the distance between two clusters as the distance between their means for all of the variables. One disadvantage of the centroid method is that the distance at which clusters are combined can actually decrease from one step to the next. Since clusters merged at later stages are more dissimilar than those merged at early stages, this is an undesirable property.

In the centroid method, the centroid of a merged cluster is a weighted combination of the centroids of the two individual clusters, where the weights are proportional to the sizes of the clusters. In the *median method,* the two clusters being combined are weighted equally in the computation of the centroid, regardless of the number of cases in each. This allows small groups to have equal effect on the characterization of larger clusters into which they are merged. Squared Euclidean distances should be used with both centroid and median methods.

Some of the above methods, such as single and complete linkage and the average distances between and within clusters, can be used with similarity or distance measures. Other methods require particular types of distance measures. In particular, the median, centroid, and Ward's methods should use squared Euclidean distances. When similarity measures are used, the criteria for combining is reversed. That is, clusters with large similarity-based measures are merged.

3.13
Clustering Variables

In the previous example, the units used for cluster analysis were individual cases (the different brands of beer). Cluster analysis can also be used to find homogeneous groups of variables. For example, consider the 14 community variables described in Chapter 2. We could use cluster analysis to group the 88 counties included in the study and then examine the resulting clusters to establish the characteristics they share. Another approach is to cluster the 14 variables used to describe the communities. In this case, the unit used for analysis is the variable. The distance or similarity measures are computed for all pairs of variables.

Figure 3.13 contains the results of clustering the community variables using the absolute value of the correlation coefficient as a measure of similarity. The absolute value of the coefficient is used since it is a measure of the strength of the relationship. The sign indicates only the direction. If you want clusters for positively correlated variables only, the sign of the coefficient should be maintained.

Figure 3.13   Cluster analysis of the community variables

```
* CLUSTERING THE COMMUNITY VARIABLES USING THE ABSOLUTE VALUE OF
  THE CORRELATION COEFFICIENT AS A MEASURE OF SIMILARITY.
SET DISK=ON.
DATA LIST MATRIX FREE
  / POPSTABL NEWSCIRC FEMEMPLD FARMERS RETAILNG COMMERCL INDUSTZN HEALTH
  CHLDNEGL COMMEFFC DWELGNEW MIGRNPOP UNEMPLOY MENTALIL.
N 88.
BEGIN DATA.
1.000
 .175 1.000
 .276  .616 1.000
 .369  .625  .637 1.000
 .127  .624  .736  .519 1.000
 .069  .652  .589  .306  .727 1.000
 .106  .712  .742  .545  .785  .911 1.000
 .149  .030  .241  .068  .100  .123  .129 1.000
 .039  .171  .589  .257  .557  .357  .424  .407 1.000
 .005  .100  .471  .213  .452  .287  .357  .732  .660 1.000
 .670  .188  .413  .579  .165  .030  .203  .290  .138  .311 1.000
 .476  .086  .064  .198  .007  .068  .024  .083  .148  .067  .505 1.000
 .137  .373  .689  .450  .650  .424  .528  .348  .733  .601  .266  .181 1.000
 .237  .046  .237  .121  .190  .055  .095  .279  .247  .324  .266  .307  .217
1.000
END DATA.
CLUSTER POPSTABL TO MENTALIL
 /READ=TRIANGLE SIMILAR.
FINISH.
```

The clustering procedure is the same whether variables or cases are clustered. It starts out with as many clusters as there are variables. At each successive step, variables or clusters of variables are merged, as shown in the icicle plot in Figure 3.13.

Consider the four-cluster solution. The HEALTH, COMMEFFC, CHLD-NEGL, and UNEMPLOY variables form one cluster, the FARMERS, INDUSTZN, COMMERCL, RETAILNG, FEMEMPLD, and NEWSCIRC variables form the second cluster, MENTALIL is a cluster by itself, and the fourth cluster is MIGRNPOP, DWELGNEW, and POPSTABL.

For readers of Chapter 2, this solution should appear familiar. The groupings of the variables are exactly those established by the factor analysis. The first cluster is the WELFARE factor, the second the URBANISM, and the fourth INFLUX. In both cases the extent of mental illness does not appear to be related to the remainder of the variables.

This is not a chance occurrence. Although factor analysis has an underlying theoretical model and cluster analysis is much more ad hoc, both identify related groups of variables. However, factor analysis allows variables to be either positively or negatively related to a factor. Cluster analysis can be restricted to search only for positive associations between variables. Thus, if the absolute values of the correlation coefficients are not taken, variables that correlate negatively with a factor do not appear in the same cluster with variables that correlate positively. For example, the FARMERS variable would not appear with the other urbanism variables. Factor analysis and cluster analysis need not always arrive at the same variable groupings, but it is comforting when they do.

3.14
RUNNING PROCEDURE CLUSTER

Use the CLUSTER procedure to obtain hierarchical clusters for cases when the number of cases is not too large. Variables can also be clustered if the data are in the appropriate format (for example, if you have a correlation matrix or some other measure of distance). CLUSTER provides several measures of dissimilarity and allows you to specify missing-value treatment. A matrix of similarity or dissimilarity coefficients can be entered and used to cluster cases or variables.

3.15
Specifying the Variables

The first specification on CLUSTER is a list of variables to use in computing similarities or distances between cases, as in

```
CLUSTER ZCALORIE ZSODIUM ZALCOHOL ZCOST.
```

The variable list is the only required specification and must precede any optional subcommands. When a matrix is read, the variable list identifies the variables represented in the similarity or distance matrix. These variables are then clustered.

3.16
Selecting the Clustering Method

The METHOD subcommand specifies the clustering method. If you do not specify a method, CLUSTER uses the average-linkage between-groups method (see Section 3.12). You can use more than one method on a single matrix.

BAVERAGE *Average linkage between groups (UPGMA). This is the default.*

WAVERAGE *Average linkage within groups.*

SINGLE *Single linkage or nearest neighbor.*

COMPLETE *Complete linkage or furthest neighbor.*

CENTROID *Centroid clustering (UPGMC). Squared Euclidean distances should be used with this method.*

MEDIAN *Median clustering (WPGMC). Squared Euclidean distances should be used with this method.*

WARD *Ward's method. Squared Euclidean distances should be used with this method.*

DEFAULT *Same as BAVERAGE.*

For example, the command

```
CLUSTER ZCALORIE ZSODIUM ZALCOHOL ZCOST
  /METHOD=SINGLE COMPLETE.
```

requests clustering with both the single and complete methods.

3.17
Specifying the Distance Measure

Use the MEASURE subcommand to specify the distance measure to use for clustering cases (see Section 3.2 and 3.11). If you omit MEASURE, CLUSTER uses squared Euclidean distances. You can specify only one distance measure.

MEASURE has the following keywords:

SEUCLID *Squared Euclidean distances.* This is the default. This measure should be used with the centroid, median, and Ward's methods of clustering. The distance between two cases is the sum of the squared differences in values for each variable:

$$\text{Distance}(X, Y) = \sum_i (X_i - Y_i)^2$$

EUCLID *Euclidean distances.* The distance between two cases is the square root of the sum of the squared differences in values for each variable:

$$\text{Distance}(X, Y) = \sqrt{\sum_i (X_i - Y_i)^2}$$

COSINE *Cosine of vectors of variables.* This is a pattern similarity measure:

$$\text{Similarity}(X, Y) = \frac{\sum_i (X_i Y_i)}{\sqrt{\sum_i (X_i^2) \sum_i (Y_i^2)}}$$

BLOCK *City-block or Manhattan distances.* The distance between two cases is the sum of the absolute differences in values for each variable:

$$\text{Distance}(X, Y) = \sum_i |X_i - Y_i|$$

CHEBYCHEV *Chebychev distance metric.* The distance between two cases is the maximum absolute difference in values for any variable:

$$\text{Distance}(X, Y) = MAX_i |X_i - Y_i|$$

POWER(p,r) *Distances in an absolute power metric.* The distance between two cases is the *r*th root of the sum of the absolute differences to the *p*th power in values on each variable.

$$\text{Distance}(X, Y) = \left(\sum_i (X_i - Y_i)^p \right)^{1/r}$$

Appropriate selection of integer parameters *p* and *r* yields Euclidean, squared Euclidean, Minkowski, city-block, minimum, maximum, and many other distance metrics.

DEFAULT *Same as SEUCLID.*

3.18
Specifying Output

CLUSTER automatically displays the clustering method, the similarity or distance measure used for clustering, and the number of cases. The following additional output is controlled by the PRINT subcommand:

SCHEDULE *Agglomeration schedule.* Display the order in which and distances at which clusters combine to form new clusters as well as the last cluster level at which a case (or variable) joined the cluster (see Figures 3.8 and 3.9b). The agglomeration schedule is displayed by default if you do not specify PRINT or if you specify PRINT without any keywords. If you specify any other keywords on PRINT, you must request SCHEDULE explicitly.

CLUSTER(min,max) *Cluster membership. Min* and *max* specify the minimum and maximum numbers of clusters in the cluster solutions. For each case, CLUSTER displays an identifying label and values indicating which cluster the case belongs to in a given cluster solution (see Figure 3.10c). For example, PRINT=CLUSTER(3,5) displays the clusters to which each case belongs when three, four, and five clusters are produced. Cases are identified by case number plus the value of any string variable specified on the ID subcommand (see Section 3.20).

DISTANCE   *Matrix of distances or similarities between items.* The type of matrix produced (similarities or dissimilarities) depends upon the measure selected. With a large number of clustered cases, DISTANCE uses considerable computer processing time.

DEFAULT   *Same as SCHEDULE.*

NONE   *None of the above.* Use PRINT=NONE when you want to suppress all display output, such as when you are using SAVE.

3.19
Requesting Plots

CLUSTER produces the verticle icicle plot by default. Use the PLOT subcommand to obtain a horizontal icicle plot or a dendrogram. When you specify PLOT, only the requested plots are produced.

VICICLE[(min,max,inc)]   *Verticle icicle plot. Min* and *max* specify the minimum and maximum numbers of cluster solutions to plot, and *inc* specifies the increment to use between cluster levels. Min, max, and inc must be integers. By default, the increment is 1 and all cluster solutions are plotted. For example, PLOT = VICICLE (2,10,2) plots cluster solutions with two, four, six, eight, and ten clusters. VICICLE is the default. (See Figures 3.7a, 3.9a, and 3.10a.)

HICICLE[(min,max,inc)]   *Horizontal icicle plot.* Has the same specifications as VICICLE. (See Figure 3.10b.)

DENDROGRAM   *Dendrogram.* The dendrogram is scaled by joining the distances of the clusters. (See Figures 3.9c and 3.9d.)

NONE   *No plots.*

If there is insufficient memory to plot a dendrogram or icicle plot, CLUSTER performs the cluster analysis, skips the plot, and displays an error message. To obtain a plot when this occurs specify an increment for VICICLE or HICICLE.

3.20
Identifying Cases

By default, CLUSTER identifies cases by case number. Name a string variable on the ID subcommand to identify cases with string values. For example, the subcommand

    / ID=BEER

produces the beer-name labels in Figures 3.7a, 3.9a, 3.9c, 3.9d, 3.10a, 3.10b, and 3.10c.

3.21
Missing Values

CLUSTER uses listwise deletion as the default missing-value treatment. A case with missing values for any clustering variable is excluded from the analysis. Use the MISSING subcommand to treat user-defined missing values as valid.

LISTWISE   *Delete cases with missing values listwise.* This is the default.

INCLUDE   *Include user-missing values.*

DEFAULT   *Same as LISTWISE.*

Cases with system-missing values for clustering variables are never included in the analysis.

3.22
Matrix Materials

The CLUSTER procedure can read and write similarity and distance matrices. Use the READ subcommand to read a matrix (such as a correlation matrix created by CORRELATION). This allows you to cluster variables or cases using a distance measure not available in CLUSTER. Three keywords indicate the type of matrix to read:

SIMILAR   *Matrix of similarity values.* By default, CLUSTER assumes that a dissimilarity or distance matrix is read.

TRIANGLE   *Matrix in lower-triangular form.* By default, CLUSTER assumes that a square matrix is read.

LOWER   *Matrix in lower-subdiagonal form.* The matrix is in lower-triangular form but without the diagonal elements.

It may be necessary to use more than one of the above keywords to correctly indicate the type of matrix being read. For example, since CLUSTER assumes a square matrix is read, if you have a similarity matrix which is in lower-triangular form, you would have to specify

```
/READ=TRIANGLE SIMILAR
```

as shown in Figure 3.13. Only one similarity or distance matrix can be read in a single procedure.

The WRITE subcommand saves a computed similarity or distance matrix in a file named on the PROCEDURE OUTPUT command. The optional DISTANCE keyword indicates that the saved matrix is a distance matrix.

DISTANCE   *Write a distance matrix.* This is the default.

3.23
Saving Cluster Memberships

You can use the SAVE subcommand to save cluster memberships at specified cluster levels as new variables on the active file. You must specify a rootname on the METHOD subcommand for each cluster method for which you wish to save cluster membership, as in

```
CLUSTER A B C
   /METHOD=BAVERAGE(CLUSMEM)
   /SAVE=CLUSTERS(3,5).
```

This command saves each case's cluster memberships for the three-, four-, and five-cluster solutions. The names for the new variables are CLUSMEM5, CLUSMEM4, and CLUSMEM3, and they will appear on the active file in that order. CLUSTER prints the names of variables it adds to the active file.

3.24
Annotated Example

The following commands produce the output in Figures 3.6a, 3.7a, 3.8, 3.9d, 3.10b, and 3.10c.

```
SET WIDTH=WIDE.
DATA LIST
   / ID 1-2 RATING 3 BEER 4-24 (A) ORIGIN 25 AVAIL 26
     PRICE 27-30 COST 31-34 CALORIES 35-37 SODIUM 38-39
     ALCOHOL 40-42 CLASS 43 LIGHT 44.
FORMATS PRICE COST (F4.2) ALCOHOL (F3.1).
MISSING VALUES CLASS(0).
BEGIN DATA.
lines of data
END DATA.
DESCRIPTIVES CALORIES SODIUM ALCOHOL COST
   /OPTIONS=3.
FORMATS ZCALORIE ZSODIUM ZALCOHOL ZCOST (F8.6).
CLUSTER ZCALORIE ZSODIUM ZALCOHOL ZCOST
   /ID=BEER
   /PRINT=CLUSTER(2,5) DISTANCE SCHEDULE
   /METHOD=COMPLETE
   /PLOT=HICICLE VICICLE DENDOGRAM.
FINISH.
```

• The SET command tells SPSS/PC+ to change the width to 132 characters.

• The DATA LIST gives the variable names and column locations for the variables in the analysis.

- The FORMATS command assigns display and write formats to the variables PRICE, COST, and ALCOHOL.
- The MISSING VALUES command assigns the value 0 user-missing status for the variable CLASS.
- The DESCRIPTIVES command adds the Z scores for CALORIES, SODIUM, ALCOHOL, and COST to the active file so they can be used by procedure CLUSTER.
- The FORMATS command assigns print and write formats for the new variables ZCALORIE, ZSODIUM, ZALCOHOL, and ZCOST.
- The CLUSTER command requests a cluster analysis of the standardized values for calories, sodium content, alcohol content, and cost.
- The ID subcommand requests that the values for the string variable BEER be used to identify cases.
- The PRINT command gives the values 2 and 5 as the minimum and maximum numbers of clusters in the cluster membership display. It also requests that a matrix of distances between items and an agglomeration schedule be displayed.
- The METHOD subcommand asks for complete linkage.
- The PLOT subcommand requests a horizontal icicle plot and a dendrogram in addition to the verticle icicle plot.

Contents

Chapter 4   Another Round: Cluster Analysis for Large Files

Chapter 3 discusses the basics of cluster analysis and describes a commonly used method for cluster formation—agglomerative hierarchical clustering. This is but one of many methods available for cluster formation. For a particular problem, selection of a method to use depends not only on the characteristics of the various methods but also on the data set to be analyzed. For example, when the number of cases is large, algorithms that require many computations or storage of all cases in a computer's "memory" may pose difficulties in terms of either time required to perform the computations or available memory.

This chapter describes the QUICK CLUSTER procedure, which can be used to cluster large numbers of cases efficiently without requiring substantial computer resources. Unlike the CLUSTER procedure, which results in a series of solutions corresponding to different numbers of clusters, the QUICK CLUSTER procedure produces only one solution for the number of clusters requested. The number of clusters must be specified by the user.

4.1
THE METHOD

The algorithm used for determining cluster membership in the QUICK CLUSTER procedure is based on nearest centroid sorting (Anderberg, 1973). That is, a case is assigned to the cluster for which the distance between the case and the center of the cluster (centroid) is smallest. The actual mechanics of the procedure depend on the information available. If the cluster centers are known, they can be specified, and case assignment is based on them. Otherwise, cluster centers are estimated from the data.

4.2
Classification When Cluster Centers Are Known

Consider the beer data described in Chapter 3. Using the CLUSTER procedure, we identified five interpretable clusters. If there are additional beers that we want to classify into one of these five clusters, we can use the QUICK CLUSTER procedure as a quick and efficient means of doing so. Each of the new beers is assigned to the cluster to whose center it is closest. For each cluster, the center is just the mean of the four variables for cases in the cluster. These values, standardized, are shown in Figure 4.2a. (The unstandardized values are shown in Chapter 3.)

Figure 4.2a Standardized values for the 5 clusters from TABLES

```
TABLES OBSERVATION=ZCOST ZCALORIE ZSODIUM ZALCOHOL
   /FTOTAL=TOTAL
   /FORMAT=CWIDTH(10,9)
   /TABLE=CLUSMEM5+TOTAL BY ZCALORIE+ZCOST+ZALCOHOL+ZSODIUM
   /STATISTICS=MEAN STDDEV.
```

	ZCALORIE		ZCOST		ZALCOHOL		ZSODIUM	
	Mean	Standard Deviation	Mean	Standard Deviation	Mean	Standard Deviation	Mean	Standard Deviation
CLUSMEM5								
AVERAGE	.44	.28	−.38	.15	.34	.28	.34	.31
EXPENSIVE	.76	.33	1.85	.17	.70	.27	−.64	.90
HIGH NA	.69	.48	−.79	.48	.64	.53	1.45	.26
LIGHT	−.77	.52	−.25	.19	−.45	.31	−.72	.47
VERY LIGHT	−2.06	.09	−.53	.39	−2.42	.56	−.68	.97
TOTAL	−.00	1.00	.00	1.00	−.00	1.00	.00	1.00

The centers of the five original clusters are called "Classification Cluster Centers," since they will be used to assign cases to clusters. These values are shown in Figure 4.2b from procedure QUICK CLUSTER.

Figure 4.2b Classification cluster centers

```
COMPUTE ZCALORIE=(CALORIES-132.4)/30.26.
COMPUTE ZCOST=(COST-49.65)/14.38.
COMPUTE ZALCOHOL=(ALCOHOL-4.44)/.76.
COMPUTE ZSODIUM=(SODIUM-14.95)/6.58.
PROCESS IF (SELECT EQ 0).
QUICK CLUSTER ZCALORIE ZCOST ZALCOHOL ZSODIUM
   /CRITERIA=CLUSTERS(5) NOUPDATE
   /INITIAL=(.436   -.379    .342     .342
              .755  1.85     .704    -.639
              .689  -.793    .638    1.45
             -.767  -.254   -.447    -.722
             -2.06  -.532   -2.42    -.676).
```

```
Classification Cluster Centers.

   Cluster    ZCALORIE      ZCOST       ZALCOHOL     ZSODIUM

      1          .4360      -.3790         .3420        .3420
      2          .7550     1.8500         .7040       -.6390
      3          .6890      -.7930         .6380       1.4500
      4         -.7670      -.2540        -.4470       -.7220
      5        -2.0600      -.5320       -2.4200       -.6760
```

The cases in the new data set are standardized using the means and standard deviations of the original data set. These values are shown in Figure 4.2c. For each case the Euclidean distance (Chapter 3) to each of the cluster centers is calculated. For example, the first new beer to be classified is Miller High Life. Its standardized value for calories is 0.55, for cost is −0.53, for alcohol is 0.34, and for sodium is 0.31. Its Euclidean distance to Cluster 1 is

$$\sqrt{(0.55-0.44)^2 + (-0.53-(-0.38))^2 + (0.34-0.34)^2 + (0.31-0.34)^2}$$ **Equation 4.2a**

$$= 0.19$$

Distances to the other cluster centers are computed in the same way. The distance to Cluster 2 is 2.6, to Cluster 3 is 1.21, to Cluster 4 is 1.87, and to Cluster 5 is 3.92. Since the distance is smallest to Cluster 1, Miller High Life is assigned to it.

Figure 4.2c Original and standardized values for the 15 beers

```
COMPUTE ZCALORIE=(CALORIES-132.4)/30.26.
COMPUTE ZCOST=(COST-49.65)/14.38.
COMPUTE ZALCOHOL=(ALCOHOL-4.44)/.76.
COMPUTE ZSODIUM=(SODIUM-14.95)/6.58.
FORMATS ZCALORIE ZCOST ZALCOHOL ZSODIUM (F5.2).
PROCESS IF (SELECT EQ 0).
LIST VAR=BEER CALORIES SODIUM ALCOHOL COST
         ZCALORIE ZSODIUM ZALCOHOL ZCOST.
```

BEER	CALORIES	SODIUM	ALCOHOL	COST	ZCALORIE	ZSODIUM	ZALCOHOL	ZCOST
MILLER HIGH LIFE	149	17	4.7	.42	.55	.31	.34	-3.42
MICHELOB	162	10	5.0	.50	.98	-.75	.74	-3.42
LABATTS	147	17	5.0	.53	.48	.31	.74	-3.42
MOLSON	154	17	5.1	.56	.71	.31	.87	-3.41
HENRY WEINHARD	149	7	4.7	.61	.55	-1.21	.34	-3.41
ANCHOR STEAM	154	17	4.7	1.20	.71	.31	.34	-3.37
SCHMIDTS	147	7	4.7	.30	.48	-1.21	.34	-3.43
PABST BLUE RIBBON	152	8	4.9	.38	.65	-1.06	.61	-3.43
OLYMPIA	153	27	4.6	.44	.68	1.83	.21	-3.42
DOS EQUIS	145	14	4.5	.70	.42	-.14	.08	-3.40
SCOTCH BUY (SAFEWAY)	145	18	4.5	.27	.42	.46	.08	-3.43
BLATZ	144	13	4.6	.30	.38	-.30	.21	-3.43
ROLLING ROCK	144	8	4.7	.36	.38	-1.06	.34	-3.43
TUBORG	155	13	5.0	.43	.75	-.30	.74	-3.42
ST PAULI GIRL	144	21	4.7	.77	.38	.92	.34	-3.40

Number of cases read = 15   Number of cases listed = 15

Figure 4.2d contains the cluster numbers to which the new beers are assigned, as well as the Euclidean distance from the case to the center of the cluster to which it is assigned. As shown in Figure 4.2e, ten beers are assigned to Cluster 1, four to Cluster 2, and one to Cluster 3. No beers are assigned to the last two clusters.

Figure 4.2d Case listing of cluster membership

```
QUICK CLUSTER ZCALORIE ZCOST ZALCOHOL ZSODIUM
 /CRITERIA=CLUSTERS(5) NOUPDATE
 /INITIAL=(.436  -.379   .342    .342
            .755  1.85    .704   -.639
            .689  -.793   .638   1.45
           -.767  -.254  -.447   -.722
           -2.06  -.532  -2.42   -.676)
 /PRINT=ID(BEER) CLUSTER.
```

Case listing of Cluster membership.		
BEER	Cluster	Distance
MILLER HIGH LIFE	1	.192
MICHELOB	1	1.345
LABATTS	1	.730
MOLSON	1	1.014
HENRY WEINHARD	2	1.274
ANCHOR STEAM	2	3.208
SCHMIDTS	1	1.839
PABST BLUE RIBBON	1	1.502
OLYMPIA	3	.699
DOS EQUIS	2	.969
SCOTCH BUY (SAFEWAY)	1	1.231
BLATZ	1	1.184
ROLLING ROCK	1	1.511
TUBORG	1	.817
ST PAULI GIRL	2	1.643

Figure 4.2e Number of cases in each cluster

```
Number of Cases in each Cluster.

   Cluster       unweighted cases      weighted cases

        1               10.0                  10.0
        2                4.0                   4.0
        3                1.0                   1.0
        4                0.0                   0.0
        5                0.0                   0.0

Missing                  0
Total                   15.0                  15.0
```

Once the beers have been assigned to clusters, it is possible to calculate the actual centers of the resulting clusters, which are just the average values of the variables for cases in the cluster. These values, labeled "Final Cluster Centers," are shown in Figure 4.2f. Since no cases were assigned to the last two clusters, system-missing values are printed. From this table, we can see that the clusters do not differ much in average calories, since all three have similar standardized values. Cluster 2 has the beers with the highest cost, while Cluster 3 contains the high sodium beers.

Figure 4.2f Final cluster centers

```
Final Cluster Centers.

   Cluster     ZCALORIE      ZCOST         ZALCOHOL      ZSODIUM

        1         .5783       -.6363          .5000        -.3267
        2         .5155       2.2497          .2763        -.0304
        3         .6808       -.3929          .2105        1.8313
        4          .            .              .             .
        5          .            .              .             .
```

Once clusters have been formed, it is useful to assess how "well-separated" they are by calculating the distances between their centers. Hopefully, the clusters will have centers that are far apart, with cases within a cluster hovering fairly closely to the cluster's center.

Euclidean distances between pairs of final cluster centers are displayed in Figure 4.2g. For example, the distance between Clusters 1 and 2 is

$$\sqrt{(0.58-0.52)^2 + (-0.64-2.25)^2 + (0.50-0.28)^2 + (0.33-(-0.03))^2} \quad \textbf{Equation 4.2b}$$
$$= 2.91$$

Similarly, the distance between Clusters 1 and 3 is 2.19, while the distance between Clusters 2 and 3 is 3.24.

Figure 4.2g Euclidean distances between clusters

```
QUICK CLUSTER ZCALORIE ZCOST ZALCOHOL ZSODIUM
 /CRITERIA=CLUSTERS(5) NOUPDATE
 /INITIAL=(.436   -.379     .342      .342
           .755   1.85      .704     -.639
           .689   -.793     .638     1.45
          -.767   -.254    -.447     -.722
          -2.06   -.532   -2.42      -.676)
 /PRINT=DISTANCE.
```

```
Distances between Final Cluster centers.

  Cluster           1              2           3           4           5

       1           0.0
       2           2.9104         0.0
       3           2.1933         3.2374      0.0
       4            .              .           .          0.0
       5            .              .           .           .          0.0
```

The table of final cluster centers (Figure 4.2f) contains the average values of the variables for each cluster but provides no idea of the variability. One way of assessing the between-cluster to within-cluster variability is to compute a one-way analysis of variance for each of the variables and examine the ratio of the between-cluster to within-cluster mean squares.

Figure 4.2h contains the mean squares for examining differences between the clusters. The between-clusters mean square is labeled "Cluster MS," and the within-cluster mean square is labeled "Error MS." Their ratio is in the column labeled "F." Large ratios and small observed significance levels are associated with variables that differ between the clusters. However, the *F*-tests should only be used for descriptive purposes since the clusters have been chosen to maximize the differences among cases in different clusters. The observed significance levels are not corrected for this and thus cannot be interpreted as tests of the hypothesis that the cluster means are equal.

Figure 4.2h Cluster mean squares

```
QUICK CLUSTER ZCALORIE ZCOST ZALCOHOL ZSODIUM
 /CRITERIA=CLUSTERS(5) NOUPDATE
 /INITIAL=( .436  -.379   .342    .342
            .755  1.85    .704   -.639
            .689  -.793   .638   1.45
           -.767  -.254  -.447   -.722
          -2.06   -.532  -2.42   -.676)
 /PRINT=ANOVA.
```

Analysis of Variance.

Variable	Cluster MS	DF	Error MS	DF	F	Prob
ZCALORIE	.0124	2	.0334	12.0	.3712	.698
ZCOST	12.0558	2	1.2003	12.0	10.0438	.003
ZALCOHOL	.0952	2	.0586	12.0	1.6256	.237
ZSODIUM	2.1316	2	.5242	12.0	4.0665	.045

As expected from Figure 4.2f, the CALORIES variable does not differ between the clusters. The *F*-value is small, and the associated significance level is large. Beers in the three clusters also have fairly similar alcohol content. However, they do seem to be different in sodium and cost.

4.3
Classification When Cluster Centers Are Unknown

In the previous example, the cluster centers for classifying cases were already known. The initial cluster solution and the center values were obtained from the CLUSTER solution. In many situations the center values for the clusters are not known in advance. Instead, they too must be estimated from the data. Several different methods for estimating cluster centers are available. Most of them involve examining the data several times.

Good cluster centers separate the cases well. One strategy is to choose cases that have large distances between them and use their values as initial estimates of the cluster centers. The number of cases selected is the number of clusters specified.

The algorithm for this strategy proceeds as follows. The first *k* cases in the data file, where *k* is the number of clusters requested, are selected as temporary centers. As subsequent cases are processed, a case replaces a center if its smallest distance to a center is greater than the distance between the two closest centers. The center that is closer to the case is replaced. A case also replaces a center if the smallest distance from the case to a center is larger than the smallest distance between that center and all other centers. Again, it replaces the center closest to it.

To illustrate the basics of the QUICK CLUSTER procedure when centers are estimated from the data, let's consider the beers again, this time using QUICK CLUSTER to cluster all 35 beers into 5 clusters.

4.4
Selecting Initial Cluster Centers

The first step of cluster formation, as previously described, is selection of the first guesses at cluster centers. Although we need not specify anything else about the clusters, we must indicate the number of clusters to be formed. Figure 4.4a contains the values of five centers selected by the program. They are labeled "Initial Cluster Centers." Each center corresponds to a beer. The first center is Schlitz Light, the second, Kronenbourg, the third, Pabst Extra Light, the next, Anchor Steam, and the last, Heileman's Old Style. These are, in terms of the variables under consideration, well-separated beers. Schlitz Light is a low calorie beer; Kronenbourg is a low sodium beer; Pabst Extra Light is a very light beer; Anchor Steam is a very expensive beer; and Heileman's Old Style is a rather average beer, though somewhat higher in sodium than most.

Figure 4.4a   Initial cluster centers for all 35 beers

```
DESCRIPTIVES CALORIES (ZCAL) SODIUM (ZSOD) ALCOHOL (ZALC) COST(ZCST)
 /OPTIONS=3.
QUICK CLUSTER ZCAL ZSOD ZALC ZCST
 /CRITERIA=CLUST(5).
```

Initial Cluster Centers.

Cluster	ZCAL	ZSOD	ZALC	ZCST
1	-1.7496	-1.2461	-.6255	-.1907
2	1.2365	-1.2461	1.0330	1.1973
3	-2.9358	.0558	-3.7765	-.6711
4	.5820	.3813	.2038	3.7064
5	.1730	1.5204	.5354	-.4042

After the initial cluster centers have been selected, all cases are grouped into the cluster with the closest center. Once all cases have been assigned to clusters, average values for the variables are computed from the cases that have been assigned to each cluster and the cases that were the initial cluster centers. These values, shown in Figure 4.4b are the "Classification Cluster Centers" since they will be used to classify the cases at the next step.

Figure 4.4b   Classification cluster centers

Classification Cluster Centers.

Cluster	ZCAL	ZSOD	ZALC	ZCST
1	-1.5138	-.9695	-.6928	-.2315
2	.8498	-1.0563	.7817	.8577
3	-2.9085	-.1534	-3.6521	-.6237
4	.5820	.3813	.2038	3.7064
5	.3333	.8370	.4196	-.3716

Examination of the classification cluster centers shows that the "average profile" of the clusters has not changed much from that suggested by the initial centers. The first cluster remains the light beers; the second, low sodium beers; and so forth. The fourth cluster contains only Anchor Steam, a beer far removed from the others because of its very steep price, almost four standard deviations above the rest.

4.5
A Second Round of
Classification

Although at this step all cases have been allocated to clusters based on the initial center values, clustering results can be improved by classifying the cases again using the classification cluster centers. Again, the same rule is used for the formation of clusters. Each case is assigned to the cluster for which its distance to the classification center is smallest. Beer names, cluster numbers, and distances to the cluster centers are shown in Figure 4.5a for the first 10 beers. The count of the number of cases in each cluster is shown in Figure 4.5b.

Figure 4.5a   Case listing of cluster membership

```
QUICK CLUSTER ZCAL ZSOD ZALC ZCST
 /CRITERIA=CLUST(5)
 /PRINT=ID(BEER) CLUSTER.
```

```
Case listing of Cluster membership.

BEER                      Cluster      Distance

  MILLER HIGH LIFE            5          .513
  BUDWEISER                   5          .827
  SCHLITZ                     5          .217
  LOWENBRAU                   5          .904
  MICHELOB                    2          .942
  LABATTS                     5          .735
  MOLSON                      5          .953
  HENRY WEINHARD              2          .827
  KRONENBOURG                 2          .603
  HEINEKEN                    2          .805
  .
  .
  .
```

Figure 4.5b   Number of cases in each cluster

```
Number of Cases in each Cluster.

Cluster      unweighted cases      weighted cases

    1              5.0                  5.0
    2              9.0                  9.0
    3              2.0                  2.0
    4              1.0                  1.0
    5             18.0                 18.0

Missing            0
Total             35.0                 35.0
```

Once the cases have been classified a second time, average values of the variables are again computed. These are termed final cluster centers and are shown in Figure 4.5c. The resulting five clusters are quite similar to those obtained with the CLUSTER procedure (Chapter 3) using a subset of the beers. Cluster 1 is the light beers, Cluster 3 is the very light beers, and Cluster 5 is the average beers. Anchor Steam, which was not included in the previous analysis, constitutes a separate cluster.

Figure 4.5c   Final cluster centers

```
Final Cluster Centers.

Cluster      ZCAL        ZSOD        ZALC        ZCST

    1       -1.2505     -.7253      -.7913      -.2440
    2         .5093     -.9748       .4617       .3491
    3       -2.8540     -.6765     -3.2790      -.4576
    4         .5820      .3813       .2038      3.7064
    5         .3775      .7429       .3420      -.2618
```

Euclidean distances between the final cluster centers are shown in Figure 4.5d. Based on this, one can assess how different the final clusters are. The largest distance is between the very light beers and Anchor Steam; the smallest distance is between the average beers and the light beers. From Figure 4.5e, it appears that for all of the variables, variability within a cluster is less than the variability between the clusters.

Figure 4.5d   Euclidean distances between clusters

```
QUICK CLUSTER ZCAL ZSOD ZALC ZCST
 /CRITERIA=CLUST(5)
 /PRINT=DISTANCE.
```

Distances between Final Cluster centers.					
Cluster	1	2	3	4	5
1	0.0				
2	2.2541	0.0			
3	2.9678	5.1034	0.0		
4	4.6020	3.6307	6.5110	0.0	
5	2.4679	1.8318	5.0603	3.9923	0.0

Figure 4.5e   Cluster mean squares

```
QUICK CLUSTER ZCAL ZSOD ZALC ZCST
 /CRITERIA=CLUST(5)
 /PRINT=ANOVA.
```

Analysis of Variance.						
Variable	Cluster MS	DF	Error MS	DF	F	Prob
ZCAL	7.3370	4	.1551	30.0	47.3136	.000
ZSOD	5.5445	4	.3941	30.0	14.0701	.000
ZALC	7.1748	4	.1767	30.0	40.6070	.000
ZCST	4.1961	4	.5738	30.0	7.3123	.000

4.6
RUNNING PROCEDURE QUICK CLUSTER

The QUICK CLUSTER procedure allocates cases to clusters when the number of clusters to be formed is known. It is particularly useful when the number of cases is large, since it requires substantially less computer memory and computation time than does the CLUSTER procedure. The algorithm classifies cases into clusters based on distances to the cluster centers. Cluster centers can either be specified by the user or estimated from the data.

Available output includes estimates of initial, updated, and final cluster centers, distances between all pairs of final cluster centers, cluster membership and distance to the cluster center for all cases, and analysis of variance tables for variables used in the clustering. For each case, cluster membership and distance can be saved as new variables on the active file.

4.7
Specifying the Variables

The only required specification for QUICK CLUSTER is the list of variables to be used for forming the clusters. The command

```
QUICK CLUSTER ZCALORIE ZCOST ZALCOHOL ZSODIUM.
```

produces a default clustering of cases into two groups based on the values of the four variables. The variable list must precede any optional subcommands.

4.8
Specifying the Number of Clusters

The CRITERIA subcommand is used to specify various options for the clustering algorithm. The following keywords are available:

CLUSTERS(k)   *Number of clusters to be formed.* The default is two clusters.

NOUPDATE   *Initial cluster centers are used for classification.* The centers are not updated to the observed means of the initial clusters. This keyword is required if cluster centers specified with the INITIAL subcommand are to be used for classification.

For example, the command

```
QUICK CLUSTER ZCALORIE ZCOST ZALCOHOL ZSODIUM
 /CRITERIA=CLUST(5).
```

asks for 5 clusters.

4.9
Specifying the Cluster Centers

The INITIAL subcommand specifies either the selection method for initial cluster centers or the actual values for the centers. These centers are then updated to actual cluster means for classification purposes. If the NOUPDATE keyword is used on the CRITERIA subcommand (see Section 4.8) the initial cluster centers are used for classification.

Available keywords are:

SELECT *Select well-spaced cases from the data file as initial centers.* This requires an extra pass of the data. This is the default.

FIRST *The first* k *cases in the data file are used as initial cluster centers, where* k *is the number of clusters.* This does not require an extra pass of the data but may result in a poor solution.

(value list) *Values for the initial cluster centers.* The values must be enclosed in parentheses. List all the values for each cluster together. For example, if there are two clusters, the values of all variables for Cluster 1 are followed by the values of all variables for Cluster 2.

For example, the command

```
QUICK CLUSTER ZCALORIE ZCOST ZALCOHOL ZSODIUM
 /CRITERIA=CLUSTERS(5) NOUPDATE
 /INITIAL=(.436   -.379    .342     .342
            .755   1.85     .704    -.639
            .689   -.793    .638    1.45
           -.767   -.254   -.447    -.722
          -2.06    -.532  -2.42     -.676).
```

requests 5 clusters. The values for the initial cluster centers are given, and the NOUPDATE keyword on the CRITERIA subcommand specifies that these initial cluster centers be used for classification.

4.10
Displaying Optional Output

By default, QUICK CLUSTER prints the initial cluster centers, the centers used for classification, and, when clustering is complete, average values for the variables in each cluster as well as the number of cases in each cluster. The PRINT subcommand with the following keywords is used to obtain additional output:

CLUSTER *Displays for each case an identifying number or label, the number of the cluster to which it is assigned, and its Euclidean distance to the center of the cluster.* (See Figures 4.2d and 4.5a.)

ID(varname) *Identifies cases on output by the values of the variable specified.* By default, cases are identified by their sequential number in the active file. (See Figures 4.2d and 4.5a.)

DISTANCE *Displays Euclidean distances between all pairs of final cluster centers.* (See Figures 4.2g and 4.5d.)

ANOVA *Displays an analysis of variance table for each variable used for classification.* (See Figures 4.2h and 4.5e.)

For example, the command

```
QUICK CLUSTER ZCALORIE ZCOST ZALCOHOL ZSODIUM
 /CRITERIA=CLUSTERS(5) NOUPDATE
 /INITIAL=(.436   -.379    .342     .342
            .755   1.85     .704    -.639
            .689   -.793    .638    1.45
           -.767   -.254   -.447    -.722
          -2.06    -.532  -2.42     -.676)
 /PRINT=DISTANCE ANOVA.
```

requests that the Euclidean distances between pairs of final clusters and an analysis of variance table be included in the display.

4.11
Missing Values

By default, QUICK CLUSTER eliminates from the analysis cases with system- or user-missing values for any variable on the variable list. Use the MISSING subcommand with one of the following four keywords to change the missing-value treatment:

LISTWISE *Delete cases with missing values on any variable.* This is the default.

PAIRWISE *Assign cases to clusters based on distances computed from all variables with non-missing values.*

INCLUDE *Treat user-defined missing values as non-missing.*

DEFAULT *Same as LISTWISE.*

For example, the command

```
QUICK CLUSTER ZCALORIE ZCOST ZALCOHOL ZSODIUM
   /MISSING=INCLUDE.
```

requests that user-missing values be included as non-missing.

4.12
Saving Cluster Membership and Distance

The SAVE subcommand saves cluster membership and distance as new variables on the active file. To use these results for use in subsequent sessions, you must save the active file using the SAVE or EXPORT commands.

Available keywords for SAVE are

CLUSTER(varname) *The cluster number of each case is stored in the variable name specified.* The numbers range from 1 to k, where k is the number of clusters.

DISTANCE(varname) *For each case the distance to the cluster center is stored in the variable name specified.*

For example, the subcommand

```
/SAVE=CLUSTER(MEMBER).
```

requests that the cluster number of each case be stored in the variable MEMBER.

4.13
Writing the Final Cluster Centers

The WRITE subcommand writes the final cluster centers onto the results file specified on the SET command (the default is SPSS.PRC). By editing this file, you can use these cluster centers on an INITIAL subcommand in a subsequent session. The WRITE subcommand has no specifications.

4.14
Annotated Example

The following SPSS/PC+ commands created the output in Figures 4.2b, 4.2d, 4.2e, 4.2f, 4.2g, and 4.2h.

```
DATA LIST FREE /SELECT RATING BEER (A21) ORIGIN AVAIL
       PRICE COST CALORIES SODIUM ALCOHOL CLASS LIGHT.
COMPUTE ZCALORIE=(CALORIES-132.4)/30.26.
COMPUTE ZCOST=(COST-49.65)/14.38.
COMPUTE ZALCOHOL=(ALCOHOL-4.44)/.76.
COMPUTE ZSODIUM=(SODIUM-14.95)/6.58.
BEGIN DATA.
data lines
END DATA.
PROCESS IF (SELECT EQ 0).
QUICK CLUSTER ZCALORIE ZCOST ZALCOHOL ZSODIUM
   /CRITERIA=CLUSTERS(5) NOUPDATE
   /INITIAL=(.436   -.379    .342     .342
             .755   1.85     .704    -.639
             .689   -.793    .638    1.45
            -.767   -.254   -.447    -.722
           -2.06    -.532   -2.42    -.676)
   /PRINT=ID(BEER) CLUSTER DISTANCE ANOVA.
FINISH.
```

- The DATA LIST command defines the variables names and tells SPSS/PC+ that the data are in freefield format.
- The four COMPUTE commands create the standardized variables needed for input to the QUICK CLUSTER command. COMPUTE statements, rather than procedure DESCRIPTIVES, are used so that the standardized values are based on the means and standard deviations of the original 20 beers analyzed in Chapter 3.
- PROCESS IF command temporarily selects only those beers that were not analyzed in Chapter 3 The variable SELECT is coded 0 for the new beers and 1 for the beers previously analyzed.
- The QUICK CLUSTER command names the four standardized variables as the variables to be used for forming clusters. The CRITERIA subcommand tells SPSS/PC+ to form 5 clusters. Since the values of the initial cluster centers are given on the INITIAL subcommand, the keyword NOUPDATE is included on the CRITERIA sucommand. The PRINT subcommand asks for all available output, with the values of string variable BEER used to label cases.

Contents

Chapter 5   Balancing on Beams: Multivariate Analysis of Variance

"Tilted" houses featured in amusement parks capitalize on the challenge of navigating one's way in the presence of misleading visual cues. It's difficult to maintain balance when walls are no longer parallel and rooms assume strange shapes. We are all dependent on visual information to guide movement, but the extent of this dependence has been found to vary considerably.

Based on a series of experiments, Witkin (1954) classified individuals into two categories: those who can ignore misleading visual cues, termed field independent, and those who cannot, termed field dependent. Field dependence has been linked to a variety of psychological characteristics such as self-image and intelligence. Psychologists theorize that it derives from childhood socialization patterns—field-dependent children learn to depend on highly structured environments while field independent children learn to cope with ambiguous situations.

In this chapter, the relationship between field dependence, sex, and various motor abilities is examined, using data reported by Barnard (1973). Students (63 female and 71 male) from the College of Southern Idaho were administered a test of field independence, the rod and frame test. On the basis of this test, subjects were classified as field dependent, field independent, or intermediate. Four tests of motor ability were also conducted: two tests of balance, a test of gross motor skills, and a test of fine motor skills.

For the balance test, subjects were required to maintain balance while standing on one foot on a rail. Two trials for each of two conditions, eyes open and eyes closed, were administered and the average number of seconds a subject maintained balance under each condition was recorded. Gross motor coordination was assessed with the side-stepping test. For this test, three parallel lines are drawn four feet apart on the floor and a subject stands on the middle line. At the start signal the subject must sidestep to the left until the left foot crosses the left line. He or she then sidesteps to the right until the right line is crossed. A subject's score is the average number of lines crossed in three ten second trials. The Purdue Pegboard Test was used to quantify fine motor skills. Subjects are required to place small pegs into pegholes using only the left hand, only the right hand, and then both hands simultaneously. The number of pegs placed in two 30-second trials for each condition was recorded and the average over six trials calculated.

The experiment described above is fairly typical of many investigations. There are several "classification" or independent variables, sex and field independence in this case, and a dependent variable. The goal of the experiment is to examine the relationship between the classification variables and the dependent variable. For example, is motor ability related to field dependence? Does the relationship differ for men and women? Analysis of variance techniques are usually used to answer these questions.

In this experiment, however, the dependent variable is not a single measure but four different scores obtained for each student. Although ANOVA tests can be computed separately for each of the dependent variables, this approach ignores the interrelation among the dependent variables. As explained in the previous chapters, substantial information may be lost when correlations between variables are ignored. For example, several bivariate regression analyses cannot substitute for a multiple regression model which considers the independent variables jointly. Only when the independent variables are uncorrelated with each other are the bivariate and multivariate regression results equivalent. Similarly, analyzing multiple two dimensional tables cannot substitute for an analysis that considers the variables simultaneously.

5.1 MULTIVARIATE ANALYSIS OF VARIANCE

The extension of univariate analysis of variance to the case of multiple dependent variables is termed *multivariate analysis of variance,* abbreviated as MANOVA. Univariate analysis of variance is just a special case of MANOVA, the case with a single dependent variable. The hypotheses tested with MANOVA are similar to those tested with ANOVA. The difference is that sets (sometimes called a vector) of means replace the individual means specified in ANOVA. In a one-way design, for example, the hypothesis tested is that the populations from which the groups are selected have the same means for all dependent variables. Thus, the hypothesis might be that the population means for the four motor-ability variables are the same for the three field dependence categories.

5.2 Assumptions

For the case of a single dependent variable, two assumptions are necessary for the proper application of the ANOVA test: the groups must be random samples from normal populations with the same variance. Similar assumptions are necessary for MANOVA. Since we are dealing with several dependent variables, however, we must make assumptions about their joint distribution, that is, the distribution of the variables considered together. The extension of the ANOVA assumptions to MANOVA requires that the dependent variables have a multivariate normal distribution with the same variance-covariance matrix in each group. A variance-covariance matrix, as its name indicates, is a square arrangement of elements, with the variances of the variables on the diagonal, and the covariances of pairs of variables off the diagonal. A variance-covariance matrix can be transformed into a correlation matrix by dividing each covariance by the standard deviations of the two variables. Later sections of the chapter will present tests for these assumptions.

5.3 One-Sample Hotelling's T^2

Before considering more complex generalizations of ANOVA techniques, let's consider the simple one-sample t test and its extension to the case of multiple dependent variables. As you will recall, the one-sample t test is used to test the hypothesis that the sample originates from a population with a known mean. For example, you might want to test the hypothesis that schizophrenics do not differ in mean IQ from the general population, which is assumed to have a mean IQ of 100. If additional variables such as reading comprehension, mathematical aptitude, and motor dexterity are also to be considered, a test that allows comparison of several observed means to a set of constants is required.

A test developed by Hotelling, called Hotelling's T^2, is often used for this purpose. It is the simplest example of MANOVA. To illustrate this test and introduce some of the SPSS/PC+ MANOVA output, we will use the field-dependence and motor-ability data to test the hypothesis that the observed sample comes from a population with specified values for the means of the four tests. That is, we will assume that normative data are available for the four tests and we will test the hypothesis that our sample is from a population having the normative means.

For illustrative purposes, the standard values are taken to be 13 seconds for balancing with eyes open, 3 seconds for balancing with eyes closed, 18 lines for the side-stepping test, and 10 pegs for the pegboard test. Since SPSS/PC+ MANOVA automatically tests the hypothesis that a set of means is equal to 0, the normative values must be subtracted from the observed scores and the hypothesis that the differences are 0 is tested.

Figure 5.3 contains the message displayed by SPSS/PC+ MANOVA when the cases are processed. It indicates the number of cases to be used in the analysis as well as the number of cases to be excluded. In this example, 134 cases will be included in the analysis. SPSS/PC+ also indicates whether any cases contain missing values for the variables being analyzed or have independent-variable (factor) values outside of the designated range. Such cases are excluded from the analysis.

Since the hypothesis being tested involves only a test of a single sample, all observations are members of one "cell," in ANOVA terminology. If two independent samples, for example males and females, were compared, two "cells" would exist. The last line of Figure 5.3 indicates how many different MANOVA models have been specified.

Figure 5.3 Case information

```
COMPUTE BALOMEAN=((TEST1+TEST2)/2)-13.
COMPUTE BALCMEAN=((TEST3+TEST4)/2)-3.
COMPUTE SSTMEAN=((TEST5+TEST6)/2)-18.
COMPUTE PP=((TEST7+TEST8)/2)-10.
MANOVA BALOMEAN BALCMEAN SSTMEAN PP
 /DESIGN.
```

```
 134 cases accepted.
   0 cases rejected because of out-of-range factor values.
   0 cases rejected because of missing data.
   1 non-empty cells.

   1 design will be processed.
```

5.4
Descriptive Statistics

One of the first steps in any statistical analysis, regardless of how simple or complex it may be, is examination of the individual variables. This preliminary screening provides information about a variable's distribution and permits identification of unusual or outlying values.

Of course, when multivariate analyses are undertaken, it is not sufficient just to look at the characteristics of the variables individually. Information about their joint distribution must also be obtained. Similarly, identification of outliers must be based on the joint distribution of variables. For example, a height of six feet is not very unusual, and neither is a weight of 100 pounds nor being a man. A six-foot-tall male who weighs 100 pounds, however, is fairly atypical and needs to be identified, not for any humanitarian reasons, but to ascertain that the values have been correctly recorded, and if so to gauge the effect of such a lean physique on subsequent analyses.

Figure 5.4 contains means, standard deviations, and confidence intervals for each of the four motor-ability variables after the normative values have been subtracted. The sample exceeds the norm for balancing with eyes closed and peg insertion and is poorer than the norm for balancing with eyes open and side-stepping. The only confidence interval that includes 0 is for the balancing-with-eyes-closed variable.

Figure 5.4 Cell means and standard deviations

```
SET WIDTH=WIDE.
MANOVA BALOMEAN BALCMEAN SSTMEAN PP
  /PRINT=CELLINFO(MEANS)
  /DESIGN.
```

```
Cell Means and Standard Deviations
Variable .. BALOMEAN
                                   Mean   Std. Dev.      N    95 percent Conf. Interval

For entire sample                 -1.540   5.860        134   -2.541      -.539

 _ _ _ _ _ _ _ _ _ _
Variable .. BALCMEAN
                                   Mean   Std. Dev.      N    95 percent Conf. Interval

For entire sample                   .143   1.405        134    -.097       .383

 _ _ _ _ _ _ _ _ _ _
Variable .. SSTMEAN
                                   Mean   Std. Dev.      N    95 percent Conf. Interval

For entire sample                 -2.597   2.681        134   -3.055      -2.139

 _ _ _ _ _ _ _ _ _ _
Variable .. PP
                                   Mean   Std. Dev.      N    95 percent Conf. Interval

For entire sample                  4.973   1.495        134    4.717       5.228
```

The 95% confidence intervals that are displayed are individual confidence intervals. This means that no adjustment has been made for the fact that the confidence intervals for several variables have been computed. We have 95% confidence that each of the individual intervals contains the unknown parameter value. We do not have 95% confidence that *all* intervals considered jointly contain the unknown parameters. The distinction here is closely related to the problem of multiple comparisons in ANOVA.

When many tests are done, the chance that some observed differences appear to be statistically significant when there are no true differences in the populations increases with the number of comparisons made. To protect against calling too many differences "real" when in fact they are not, the criterion for how large a difference must be before it is considered "significant" is made more stringent. That is, larger differences are required, depending on the number of comparisons made. The larger the number of comparisons, the greater the observed difference must be. Similarly, if a confidence region that simultaneously contains values of observed population parameters with a specified overall confidence level is to be constructed, the confidence interval for each variable must be wider than that needed if only one variable is considered.

5.5
Further Displays for Checking Assumptions

Although the summary statistics presented in Figure 5.4 provide some information about the distributions of the dependent variables, more detailed information is often desirable. Figure 5.5 is a stem-and-leaf plot of the peg-board variable after the normative values have been subtracted. Stem-and-leaf plots provide a convenient way to examine the distribution of a variable.

In Figure 5.5, the numbers to the left of the dotted line are called the *stem*, while those to the right are the *leaves*. Each case is represented by a leaf. For example, the first line of the plot is for a case with a value of 1.2 and a case with a value of 1.3. The stem, 1, is the same for both cases while the values of the leaves (2 and 3) differ. When there are several cases with the same values, the leaf value is repeated. For example, there are two cases with a value of 2.7 and four cases with a value of 2.8. In this example, each stem value occurs twice, once for cases with leaves 0 through 4, and once for cases with leaves 5 through 9. This is not always the case, since the stem values depends on the actual data. In this example, the decimal point for each case occurs between the value of the stem and the leaf. This also is not always the case. SPSS/PC+ MANOVA scales the variables so that the stem-and-leaf plot is based on the number of significant digits. Since the purpose of the plot is to display the distribution of the variable, the actual scale is not important.

Figure 5.5   Stem-and-leaf plot—pegboard test

```
MANOVA BALOMEAN BALCMEAN SSTMEAN PP
 /PLOT=STEMLEAF
 /DESIGN.
```

```
Stem-and-leaf display for variable .. PP
   1 . 23
   1 . 8
   2 . 033
   2 . 778888
   3 . 02333
   3 . 555555577777778888
   4 . 002222222223
   4 . 5555555557777778888
   5 . 00000222222333
   5 . 55555555777788888
   6 . 0000222223333
   6 . 5577777778
   7 . 00000223
   7 . 5778
   8 . 2
   8 .
   9 . 3
```

One assumption needed for hypothesis testing in MANOVA is the assumption that the dependent variables have a multivariate normal distribution. If variables have a multivariate normal distribution, each one taken individually must be normally distributed. (However, variables that are normally distributed individually will not necessarily have a multivariate normal distribution when considered together.) The stem-and-leaf plots for each variable allows us to assess the reasonableness of the normality assumption, since if any distribution appears to be markedly nonnormal, the assumption of multivariate normality is likely to be violated.

5.6
Normal Plots

Although the stem-and-leaf plot gives a rough idea of the normality of the distribution of a variable, other plots that are especially designed for assessing normality can also be obtained. For example, we can assess normality using a normal probability plot, which is obtained by ranking the observed values of a variable from smallest to largest and then pairing each value with an expected normal value for a sample of that size from a standard normal distribution.

Figure 5.6a is a normal probability plot of the peg-board variable. The symbols represent the number of cases that fall in the same position on the plot. If the observed scores are from a normal distribution, the plot in should be approximately a straight line. Since the distribution of the peg-board scores appeared fairly normal in the stem-and-leaf plot (Figure 5.5), the normal probability plot should be fairly linear, and it is.

Figure 5.6a   Normal probability plot—pegboard test

```
MANOVA BALOMEAN BALCMEAN SSTMEAN PP
 /PLOT=NORMAL
 /DESIGN.
```

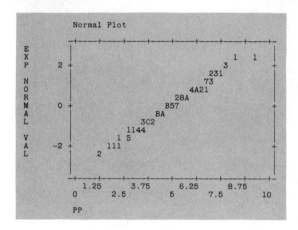

To further assess the linearity of the normal probability plot, we can calculate the difference between the observed point and the expected point under the assumption of normality and plot this difference for each case. If the observed sample is from a normal distribution, these differences should be fairly close to 0 and be randomly distributed.

Figure 5.6b is a plot of the differences for the normal probability plot shown in Figure 5.6a. This plot is called a detrended normal plot since the trend in Figure 5.6a, the straight line, has been removed. Note that the values fall roughly in a horizontal band about 0, though there appears to be some pattern. Also notice the two outliers, one in the lower-right corner and the other in the upper-left corner. These correspond to the smallest and largest observations in the sample and indicate that the observed distribution doesn't have quite as much spread in the tails as expected. For the smallest value, the deviation from the expected line is positive, indicating that the smallest value is not quite as small as would be expected. For the largest value, the value is not as large as would be expected. Since most of the points cluster nicely around 0, this small deviation is probably not of too much concern. Nonetheless, it is usually a good idea to check outlying points to ascertain that they have been correctly recorded and entered. If the distribution of a variable appears markedly nonnormal, transformation of the data should be considered.

Figure 5.6b Detrended normal plot—pegboard test

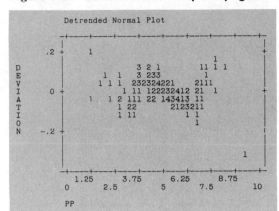

```
        Detrended Normal Plot
      -+---+---+---+---+---+---+---+---+-
     .2 +     1                              1                    +
 D                          3  2  1           11  1  1
 E                     1  1   3  233            1
 V                  1  1  1  232324221       2111
 I      0 +            1  11  122232412   21   1                  +
 A               1     1  2  111   22  143413  11
 T                     1  22          2123211
 I                     1  11              1  1
 O                                         1
 N    -.2 +                                                       |
                                                       1
      -+---+---+---+---+---+---+---+---+-
          1.25      3.75      6.25      8.75
       0        2.5        5        7.5        10
      PP
```

5.7
Another Plot

To get a little more practice in interpreting the previously described plots, consider Figure 5.7a, which is the plot for the balancing-with-eyes-closed variable. From this stem-and-leaf plot, you can see that the distribution of the data is skewed to the right. That is, there are several large values that are quite removed from the rest.

Figure 5.7a Stem-and-leaf plot—balance variable

```
Stem-and-leaf display for variable .. BALCMEAN

 -2 .
 -2 . 00
 -1 . 866555
 -1 . 4444333333222110000
 -0 . 988888888866666666555555
 -0 . 444433333322111110000000
  0 . 111222233444444
  0 . 55555556788899999
  1 . 00000112222344
  1 . 555889
  2 . 244
  2 .
  3 . 2
  3 .
  4 .
  4 . 88
  5 .
  5 .
  6 . 2
  6 . 5
```

Figure 5.7b is the corresponding normal probability plot. Note that the plot is no longer linear but is curved, especially for larger values of the variable. This downward curve indicates that the observed values are larger than predicted by the corresponding expected normal values. This is also seen in the stem-and-leaf plot. The detrended normal plot for this variable is shown in Figure 5.7c, which shows that there is a definite pattern to the deviations. The values no longer cluster in a horizontal band about 0. A transformation might be considered.

Figure 5.7b   Normal probability plot—balance variable

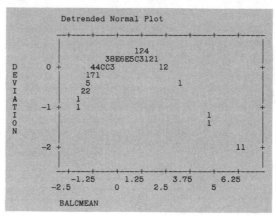

```
              Normal Plot
          --+----+----+----+----+----+----+----+--
  E                                               |
  X                                               |
  P                                  11           |
  N    2 +          1        2                   +
  O                           2112               |
  R                      55                      |
  M                     4D                       |
  A                    5E1                       |
  L    0 +           8E1                         +
  V                 2F3                          |
  A               25A                            |
  L              1A                              |
                6                                |
  V   -2 +     21                               +
  A          2                                   |
  L                                              |
          --+----+----+----+----+----+----+----+--
         -1.25      1.25     3.75      6.25
       -2.5      0       2.5       5
              BALCMEAN
```

Figure 5.7c   Detrended normal plot—balance variable

```
           Detrended Normal Plot
         --+----+----+----+----+----+----+----+--
  D                   124                        |
  E                38E6E5C3121                   |
  V    0 +      44CC3          12               +
  I            171                               |
  A            5                                 |
  T            22                                |
  I          1                                   |
  O   -1 +   1                                   +
  N                              1               |
                                 1               |
                                                 |
      -2 +                          11          +
                                                 |
         --+----+----+----+----+----+----+----+--
        -1.25      1.25     3.75      6.25
      -2.5      0       2.5       5
             BALCMEAN
```

**5.8
Bartlett's Test of Sphericity**

Since there is no reason to use the multivariate analysis of variance procedure if the dependent variables are not correlated, it is useful to examine the correlation matrix of the dependent variables. If the variables are independent, the observed correlation matrix is expected to have small off-diagonal elements. Bartlett's test of sphericity can be used to test the hypothesis that the population correlation matrix is an identity matrix, that is, all diagonal terms are 1 and all off-diagonal terms are 0.

The test is based on the determinant of the within-cells correlation matrix. A determinant that is close in value to 0 indicates that one or more of the variables can almost be expressed as a linear function of the other dependent variables. Thus the hypothesis that the variables are independent is rejected if the determinant is small. Figure 5.8a contains output from Bartlett's test of sphericity. The determinant is displayed first, followed by a transformation of the determinant (which has a chi-square distribution). Since the observed significance level is small (less than 0.0005), the hypothesis that the population correlation matrix is an identity matrix is rejected.

Figure 5.8a Bartlett's test of sphericity

```
MANOVA BALOMEAN BALCMEAN SSTMEAN PP
  /PRINT=ERROR(COR)
  /DESIGN.
```

```
Statistics for WITHIN CELLS correlations

Determinant =                       .82942
Bartlett test of sphericity =    24.46993 with 6 D. F.
Significance =                      .000
```

A graphical test of the hypothesis that the correlation matrix is an identity matrix is described by Everitt (1978). The observed correlation coefficients are transformed using Fisher's Z-transform, and then a half-normal plot of the transformed coefficients is obtained. A half-normal plot is very similar to the normal plot described above. The only difference is that both positive and negative values are treated identically. If the population correlation matrix is an identity matrix, the plot should be fairly linear and the line should pass through the origin.

Figure 5.8b is the plot of the transformed correlation coefficients for the correlation matrix in Figure 5.4. The plot shows deviations from linearity, suggesting that the dependent variables are not independent, a result also indicated by Bartlett's test.

Figure 5.8b A half-normal plot of the correlation coefficients

```
MANOVA BALOMEAN BALCMEAN SSTMEAN PP
  /PLOT=ZCORR
  /DESIGN.
```

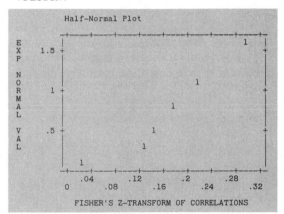

5.9
Testing Hypotheses

Once the distributions of the variables have been examined, we are ready to test the hypothesis that there is no difference between the population means and the hypothesized values. To test the various hypotheses of interest, SPSS/PC+ MANOVA computes a design matrix whose columns correspond to the various effects in the model (see Section 5.16). Figure 5.9a shows the table displayed by SPSS/PC+ MANOVA containing the names of the effects to be tested and their corresponding columns in the design matrix. In the one-sample MANOVA design, there is only one effect, labeled the CONSTANT.

Figure 5.9a   The effects matrix

```
MANOVA BALOMEAN BALCMEAN SSTMEAN PP
 /DESIGN.
```

```
Correspondence between Effects and Columns of BETWEEN-Subjects DESIGN 1
   Starting  Ending
    Column   Column    Effect Name
      1        1       CONSTANT
```

To understand how the statistic for testing the hypothesis that all differences are 0 is constructed, recall the one-sample t test. The statistic for testing the hypothesis that the population mean is some known constant, which we will call μ_0, is

$$t = \frac{\overline{X} - \mu_0}{S/\sqrt{N}}$$

Equation 5.9a

where $\overline{X}$ is the sample mean and S is the standard deviation. The numerator of the t value is a measure of how much the sample mean differs from the hypothesized value, while the denominator is a measure of how variable the sample mean is.

When you simultaneously test the hypothesis that several population means do not differ from a specified set of constants, a statistic that considers all variables together is required. Hotelling's T^2 statistic is usually used for this purpose. It is computed as

$$T^2 = N(\overline{X} - \mu_0)' S^{-1}(\overline{X} - \mu_0)$$

Equation 5.9b

where S^{-1} is the inverse of the variance-covariance matrix of the dependent variables and $\overline{X} - \mu_0$ is the vector of differences between the sample means and the hypothesized constants. The two matrices upon which Hotelling's T^2 is based can be displayed by SPSS/PC+ MANOVA. The matrix that contains the differences between the observed sample means and the hypothesized values is shown in Figure 5.9b.

Figure 5.9b   The hypothesis sum of squares and cross-products matrix

```
MANOVA BALOMEAN BALCMEAN SSTMEAN PP
 /PRINT=SIGNIF(HYPOTH)
 /DESIGN.
```

```
EFFECT .. CONSTANT
Adjusted Hypothesis Sum-of-Squares and Cross-Products

              BALOMEAN    BALCMEAN    SSTMEAN        PP

BALOMEAN       317.764
BALCMEAN       -29.490       2.737
SSTMEAN        535.894     -49.733    903.761
PP           -1026.104      95.226  -1730.478    3313.434
```

The diagonal elements are just the squares of the sample means minus the hypothesized values, multiplied by the sample size. For example, from Figure 5.4, the difference between the eyes-open balance score and the hypothesized value is −1.54. Squaring this difference and multiplying it by the sample size of 134, we get 317.76, the entry for BALOMEAN in Figure 5.9b. The off-diagonal elements are the product of the differences for the two variables, multiplied by the sample size. For example, the cross-products entry for the BALOMEAN and BALCMEAN is, from Figure 5.4, $-1.54 \times 0.14 \times 134 = -29.49$. For a fixed sample size, as the magnitude of the differences between the sample means and hypothesized values increases, so do the entries of this sums-of-squares and cross-products matrix.

The matrix whose entries indicate how much variability there is in the dependent variables is called the within-cells sums-of-squares and cross-products matrix. It is designated as S in the previous formula and is shown in Figure 5.9c. The diagonal entries are $(N-1)$ times the variance of the dependent variables. For example, the entry for the pegboard variable is, from Figure 5.4, $1.49^2 \times (133) = 297.12$. The off-diagonal entries are the sums of the cross-products for the two variables. For example, for variables X and Y the cross-product is

$$\text{CPSS}_{xy} = \sum_{i=1}^{N} (X_i - \overline{X})(Y_i - \overline{Y})$$

Equation 5.9c

To compute Hotelling's T^2, the inverse of this within-cells sums-of-squares matrix is required, as well as the hypothesis sums-of-squares matrix in Figure 5.9b. The significance level associated with T^2 can be obtained from the F distribution. Figure 5.9d contains the value of Hotelling's T^2 divided by $(N-1)$, its transformation to a variable that has an F distribution, and the degrees of freedom associated with the F statistic. Since there are four dependent variables in this example, the hypothesis degrees of freedom are 4, while the remaining degrees of freedom, 130, are associated with the error sums of squares. Since the observed significance level is small (less than 0.0005), the null hypothesis that the population means do not differ from the hypothesized constants is rejected.

Figure 5.9c Within-cells sums-of-squares and cross-products matrix

```
MANOVA BALOMEAN BALCMEAN SSTMEAN PP
  /PRINT=ERROR(SSCP)
  /DESIGN.
```

```
WITHIN CELLS Sum-of-Squares and Cross-Products

            BALOMEAN    BALCMEAN    SSTMEAN         PP

BALOMEAN    4567.274
BALCMEAN     311.080     262.501
SSTMEAN      459.656      94.833    956.239
PP            26.795      40.782     70.422    297.122
```

Figure 5.9d Hotelling's statistic

```
MANOVA BALOMEAN BALCMEAN SSTMEAN PP
  /DESIGN.
```

```
Multivariate Tests of Significance (S = 1, M = 1 , N = 64 )

Test Name        Value  Approx. F Hypoth. DF   Error DF  Sig. of F

Hotellings    13.20587  429.19091      4.00     130.00       0.0
```

5.10
Univariate Tests

When the hypothesis of no difference is rejected, it is often informative to examine the univariate test results to get some idea of where the differences may be. Figure 5.10a contains the univariate results for the four dependent variables. The hypothesis and error sums of squares are the diagonal terms in Figures 5.9b and 5.9c. The mean squares are obtained by dividing the sums of squares by their degrees of freedom, 1 for the hypothesis sums of squares and 133 for the error sums of squares. The ratio of the two mean squares is displayed in the column labeled F. These F values are nothing more than the squares of one-sample t values. Thus, from Figure 5.4, the mean difference for the BALOMEAN variable is -1.54 and the standard deviation is 5.86. The corresponding t value is

$$t = \frac{-1.54}{5.86/\sqrt{134}} = -3.04$$

Equation 5.10

Squaring this produces the value 9.25, which is the entry in Figure 5.10a. From Figure 5.10a, we can see that the balancing-with-eyes-closed variable is the only one whose t value is not significant. This is to be expected, since it has a 95% confidence interval that includes 0. The significance levels for the univariate statistics are not adjusted for the fact that several comparisons are being made and thus should be used with a certain amount of caution. For a discussion of the problem of multiple comparisons, see Miller, 1981, or Burns, 1984.

Figure 5.10   Univariate *F* tests

```
MANOVA BALOMEAN BALCMEAN SSTMEAN PP
 /PRINT=SIGNIF(UNIV)
 /DESIGN.
```

```
Univariate F-tests with (1,133) D. F.

Variable   Hypoth. SS   Error SS  Hypoth. MS   Error MS          F  Sig. of F

BALOMEAN    317.76355  4567.27368  317.76355   34.34040    9.25334      .003
BALCMEAN      2.73673   262.50070    2.73673    1.97369    1.38661      .241
SSTMEAN     903.76111   956.23869  903.76111    7.18976  125.70107      0.0
PP         3313.43322   297.12189 3313.43322    2.23400 1483.18463      0.0
```

5.11
The Two-Sample Multivariate T-Test

In the previous sections, we were concerned with testing the hypothesis that the sample was drawn from a population with a particular set of means. There was only one sample involved, though there were several dependent variables. In this section, we will consider the multivariate generalization of the two-sample t test. The hypothesis that men and women do not differ on the four motor-ability variables will be tested.

Figure 5.11a contains descriptive statistics for each variable according to sex. The female subjects are coded as *1*'s, and the males are coded as *2*'s. Males appear to maintain balance with eyes open longer than females and cross more lines in the stepping test.

Figure 5.11a   Cell means and standard deviations

```
SET WIDTH=WIDE.
MANOVA BALOMEAN BALCMEAN SSTMEAN PP BY SEX(1,2)
 /PRINT=CELLINFO(MEANS)
 /DESIGN.
```

```
Cell Means and Standard Deviations
Variable .. BALOMEAN
     FACTOR          CODE          Mean   Std. Dev.      N   95 percent Conf. Interval

SEX                  1            9.748     5.707       63       8.311      11.186
SEX                  2           12.979     5.605       71      11.652      14.306
For entire sample                11.460     5.860      134      10.459      12.461
- - - - - - - - -
Variable .. BALCMEAN
     FACTOR          CODE          Mean   Std. Dev.      N   95 percent Conf. Interval

SEX                  1            3.191     1.518       63       2.809       3.574
SEX                  2            3.100     1.306       71       2.791       3.409
For entire sample                3.143     1.405      134       2.903       3.383
- - - - - - - - -
Variable .. SSTMEAN
     FACTOR          CODE          Mean   Std. Dev.      N   95 percent Conf. Interval

SEX                  1           14.095     2.255       63      13.527      14.663
SEX                  2           16.563     2.501       71      15.972      17.155
For entire sample                15.403     2.681      134      14.945      15.861
- - - - - - - - -
Variable .. PP
     FACTOR          CODE          Mean   Std. Dev.      N   95 percent Conf. Interval

SEX                  1           15.466     1.453       63      15.100      15.831
SEX                  2           14.535     1.401       71      14.204      14.867
For entire sample                14.973     1.495      134      14.717      15.228
```

Another way to visualize the distribution of scores in each of the groups is with box-and-whisker plots, as shown in Figure 5.11b for the two balance variables. The upper and lower boundaries of the boxes are the upper and lower quartiles. The box length is the interquartile distance and the box contains the middle 50% of values in a group. The asterisk (*) inside the box identifies the group median. The larger the box, the greater the spread of the observations. The lines emanating from each box (the whiskers) extend to the smallest and largest observations in a group that are less than one interquartile range from the end of the box. These are marked with an *X*. Any points outside of this range but less than one-and-a-half interquartile ranges from the end of the box are marked with *O*'s for outlying. Points more than 1.5 interquartile distances away are marked with *E*'s for extreme. If there are multiple points at a single position, the number of points is also displayed.

Figure 5.11b Box-and-whisker plots

```
MANOVA BALOMEAN BALCMEAN SSTMEAN PP BY SEX(1,2)
  /PLOT=BOXPLOTS
  /DESIGN.
```

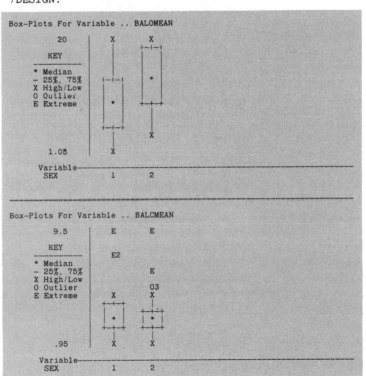

**5.12
Tests of Homogeneity of Variance**

In the one-sample Hotelling's T² test, there was no need to worry about the homogeneity of the variance-covariance matrices since there was only one matrix. In the two-sample test, there are two matrices (one for each group) and tests for their equality are necessary.

The variance-covariance matrices are shown in Figure 5.12a. They are computed for each group using the means of the variables within that group. Thus, each matrix indicates how much variability there is in a group. Combining these individual matrices into a common variance-covariance matrix results in the pooled matrix displayed in Figure 5.12b.

Figure 5.12a   Variance-covariance matrices for BALOMEAN and BALCMEAN

```
SET WIDTH=WIDE.
MANOVA BALOMEAN BALCMEAN SSTMEAN PP BY SEX(1,2)
 /PRINT=CELLINFO(COV)
 /DESIGN.
```

```
Cell Number .. 1
Variance-Covariance matrix

            BALOMEAN    BALCMEAN    SSTMEAN          PP

BALOMEAN    32.57185
BALCMEAN     3.39103     2.30400
SSTMEAN       .42704      .55622    5.08397
PP           1.43677      .36703    1.30888     2.11036

 - - - - - - - - -

Cell Number .. 2
Variance-Covariance matrix

            BALOMEAN    BALCMEAN    SSTMEAN          PP

BALOMEAN    31.42090
BALCMEAN     1.58111     1.70536
SSTMEAN      2.38612      .96952    6.25267
PP            .54349      .21702     .94178     1.96263
```

Figure 5.12b   Pooled matrix

```
Pooled within-cells Variance-Covariance matrix

            BALOMEAN    BALCMEAN    SSTMEAN          PP

BALOMEAN    31.96150
BALCMEAN     2.43122     1.98654
SSTMEAN      1.46594      .77540    5.70374
PP            .96306      .28748    1.11421     2.03202
```

Figure 5.12c contains two homogeneity-of-variance tests (Cochrans C and the Bartlett-Box F) for each variable individually. The significance levels indicate that there is no reason to reject the hypotheses that the variances in the two groups are equal. Although these univariate tests are a convenient starting point for examining the equality of the covariance matrices, they are not sufficient. A test that simultaneously considers both the variances and covariances is required.

Box's M test, which is based on the determinants of the variance-covariance matrices in each cell as well as of the pooled variance-covariance matrix, provides a multivariate test for the homogeneity of the matrices. However, Box's M test is very sensitive to departures from normality. The significance level can be based on either an F or a χ^2 statistic, and both approximations are given in the output, as shown in Figure 5.12d. Given the result of Box's M test, there appears to be no reason to suspect the homogeneity-of-dispersion-matrices assumption.

Figure 5.12c   Univariate homogeneity of variance tests

```
MANOVA BALOMEAN BALCMEAN SSTMEAN PP BY SEX(1,2)
 /PRINT=HOMOGENEITY(COCHRAN BARTLETT)
 /DESIGN.
```

```
Univariate Homogeneity of Variance Tests

Variable .. BALOMEAN

     Cochrans C(66,2) =                          .50899, P =  .884 (approx.)
     Bartlett-Box F(1,51762) =                   .02113, P =  .884

Variable .. BALCMEAN

     Cochrans C(66,2) =                          .57466, P =  .224 (approx.)
     Bartlett-Box F(1,51762) =                  1.48033, P =  .224

Variable .. SSTMEAN

     Cochrans C(66,2) =                          .55155, P =  .403 (approx.)
     Bartlett-Box F(1,51762) =                   .69438, P =  .405

Variable .. PP

     Cochrans C(66,2) =                          .51813, P =  .769 (approx.)
     Bartlett-Box F(1,51762) =                   .08603, P =  .769
```

Figure 5.12d   Homogeneity of dispersion matrices

```
MANOVA BALOMEAN BALCMEAN SSTMEAN PP BY SEX(1,2)
 /PRINT=HOMOGENEITY(COCHRAN BARTLETT BOXM)
 /DESIGN.
```

```
Cell Number .. 1
Determinant of Variance-Covariance matrix =        538.89601
LOG(Determinant) =                                   6.28952


- - - - - - -


Cell Number .. 2
Determinant of Variance-Covariance matrix =        522.34684
LOG(Determinant) =                                   6.25833


- - - - - - - - -


Determinant of pooled Variance-Covariance matrix    557.40536
LOG(Determinant) =                                   6.32329


- - - - - - - - -


Multivariate test for Homogeneity of Dispersion matrices


Boxs M =                           6.64101
F WITH (10,80608) DF =              .64228,  P =    .779 (Approx.)
Chi-Square with 10 DF =            6.42361,  P =    .779 (Approx.)
```

5.13
Hotelling's T² for Two Independent Samples

The actual statistic for testing the equality of several means with two independent samples is also based on Hotelling's T^2. The formula is

$$T^2 = \frac{N_1 N_2}{N_1 + N_2} (\bar{X}_1 - \bar{X}_2)' S^{-1} (\bar{X}_1 - \bar{X}_2)$$

Equation 5.13a

where $\bar{X}_1$ is the vector of means for the first group (females), $\bar{X}_2$ is the vector for the second group (males), and S^{-1} is the inverse of the pooled within-groups covariance matrix. The statistic is somewhat similar to the one described for the one-sample test in Section 5.9.

Again, two matrices are used in the computation of the statistic. The pooled within-groups covariance matrix has been described previously and is displayed in Figure 5.12b. The second matrix is the adjusted hypothesis sums-of-squares and cross-products matrix. It is displayed under the heading EFFECT .. SEX and in Figure 5.13a. The entries in this matrix are the weighted squared differences of the group means from the combined mean. For example, the entry for the balancing-with-eyes-open variable is

$$SS = 63(9.75-11.46)^2 + 71(12.98-11.46)^2 = 348.36$$

Equation 5.13b

where, from Figure 5.11a, 9.75 is the mean value for the 63 females, 12.98 is the value for the 71 males, and 11.46 is the mean for the entire sample. The first off-diagonal term for balancing with eyes open (BALOMEAN) and eyes closed (BALCMEAN) is similarly

$$SS = (9.75-11.46)(3.19-3.14)63 + (12.98-11.46)(3.10-3.14)71$$
$$= -9.84$$

Equation 5.13c

The diagonal terms should be recognizable to anyone familiar with analysis of variance methodology. They are the sums of squares due to groups for each variable.

Figure 5.13a   Adjusted hypothesis sums of squares and cross-products matrix

```
SET WIDTH=WIDE.
MANOVA BALOMEAN BALCMEAN SSTMEAN PP BY SEX(1,2)
 /PRINT=SIGNIF(HYPOTH)
 /DESIGN.
```

```
EFFECT .. SEX
Adjusted Hypothesis Sum-of-Squares and Cross-Products

              BALOMEAN      BALCMEAN      SSTMEAN             PP

BALOMEAN      348.35572
BALCMEAN       -9.84205       .27807
SSTMEAN       266.15115     -7.51953     203.34512
PP           -100.32892      2.83458     -76.65342       28.89544
```

Figure 5.13b contains the value of Hotelling's T^2 statistic divided by $N-2$ for the test of the hypothesis that men and women do not differ on the motor-ability test scores. The significance level is based on the F distribution with 4 and 129 degrees of freedom. The observed significance level is small (less than 0.0005), so the null hypothesis that men and women perform equally well on the motor-ability tests is rejected.

Figure 5.13b   Hotelling's T^2 statistic

```
MANOVA BALOMEAN BALCMEAN SSTMEAN PP BY SEX(1,2)
 /PRINT=SIGNIF(HYPOTH MULTIV)
 /DESIGN.
```

```
Multivariate Tests of Significance (S = 1, M = 1 , N = 63 1/2)

Test Name           Value  Approx. F Hypoth. DF    Error DF   Sig. of F

Hotellings         .66953  21.59224       4.00      129.00        .000
```

5.14
Univariate Tests

To get some idea of where the differences between men's and women's scores occur, the univariate tests for the individual variables may be examined. These are the same as the F values from one-way analyses of variance. In the case of two groups, the F values are just the squares of the two-sample t values.

Figure 5.14   Univariate F tests

```
MANOVA BALOMEAN BALCMEAN SSTMEAN PP BY SEX(1,2)
 /PRINT=SIGNIF(HYPOTH MULTIV UNIV)
 /DESIGN.
```

```
EFFECT .. SEX (CONT.)
Univariate F-tests with (1,132) D. F.

Variable   Hypoth. SS   Error SS Hypoth. MS    Error MS          F  Sig. of F

BALOMEAN    348.35572 4218.91817  348.35572    31.96150   10.89923       .001
BALCMEAN       .27807  262.22270     .27807     1.98654     .13998       .709
SSTMEAN     203.34512  752.89249  203.34512     5.70373   35.65125       .000
PP           28.89544  268.22570   28.89544     2.03201   14.22011       .000
```

From Figure 5.14, we can see that there are significant univariate tests for all variables except balancing with eyes closed. Again, the significance levels are not adjusted for the fact that four tests, rather than one, are being performed.

5.15
Discriminant Analysis

In Chapter 1, we considered the problem of finding the best linear combination of variables for distinguishing among several groups. Coefficients for the variables are chosen so that the ratio of between-groups sums of squares to total sums of squares is as large as possible. Although the equality of means hypotheses tested in MANOVA may initially appear quite unrelated to the discriminant problem, the two procedures are closely related. In fact, MANOVA can be viewed as a problem of first finding linear combinations of the dependent variables that best separate the groups and then testing whether these new variables are significantly different for the groups. For this reason, the usual discriminant analysis statistics can be obtained as part of the SPSS/PC+ MANOVA output.

Figure 5.15a contains the eigenvalues and canonical correlation for the canonical discriminant function that separates males and females. Remember that the eigenvalue is the ratio of the between-groups sum of squares to the within-groups sum of squares, while the square of the canonical correlation is the ratio of the between-groups sums of squares to the total sum of squares. Thus, about 40% of the variablility in the discriminant scores is attributable to between-group differences ($0.633^2 = 0.401$).

Figure 5.15a   Eigenvalue and canonical correlation

```
SET WIDTH=WIDE.
MANOVA BALOMEAN BALCMEAN SSTMEAN PP BY SEX(1,2)
 /PRINT=SIGNIF(HYPOTH MULTIV UNIV EIGEN)
 /DESIGN.
```

Eigenvalues and Canonical Correlations				
Root No.	Eigenvalue	Pct.	Cum. Pct.	Canon Cor.
1	.66953	100.00000	100.00000	.63327

As discussed in Chapter 1, when there are two groups Wilks' lambda can be interpreted as a measure of the proportion of total variability not explained by group differences. As shown in Figure 5.15b, almost 60% of the observed variability is not explained by the group differences. The hypothesis that in the population there are no difference between the group means can be tested using Wilks' lambda. Lambda is transformed to a variable that has an F distribution. For the two-group situation, the F value for Wilks' lambda is identical to that given for Hotelling's T^2 (Figure 5.13b).

Figure 5.15b   Wilks' lambda

```
MANOVA BALOMEAN BALCMEAN SSTMEAN PP BY SEX(1,2)
 /DESIGN.
```

Multivariate Tests of Significance (S = 1, M = 1 , N = 63 1/2)					
Test Name	Value	Approx. F	Hypoth. DF	Error DF	Sig. of F
Wilks	.59897	21.59224	4.00	129.00	.000

Both raw and standardized discriminant function coefficients can be displayed by SPSS/PC+ MANOVA. The raw coefficents are the multipliers of the dependent variables in their original units, while the standardized coefficients are the multipliers of the dependent variables when the latter have been standardized to a mean of 0 and a standard deviation of 1. Both sets of coefficients are displayed in Figure 5.15c.

Figure 5.15c   Raw and standardized discriminant function coefficients

```
SET WIDTH=WIDE.
MANOVA BALOMEAN BALCMEAN SSTMEAN PP BY SEX(1,2)
 /DISCRIM=RAW STAN
 /DESIGN.
```

```
EFFECT .. SEX (CONT.)
Raw discriminant function coefficients
         Function No.

Variable           1

BALOMEAN      -.07465
BALCMEAN       .19245
SSTMEAN       -.36901
PP             .49189

- - - - - - - - -

Standardized discriminant function coefficients
         Function No.

Variable           1

BALOMEAN      -.42205
BALCMEAN       .27125
SSTMEAN       -.88128
PP             .70118
```

The side-stepping and pegboard scores have the largest standardized coefficients and, as you will recall from Figure 5.9a, they also have the largest univariate F's, suggesting that they are important for separating the two groups. Of course, when variables are correlated, the discriminant function coefficients must be interpreted with care, since highly correlated variables "share" the discriminant weights.

The correlation coefficients for the discriminant scores and each dependent variable are somewhat less likely to be strongly influenced by the correlations between the variables. These coefficients, sometimes called *structure coefficients*, are displayed in Figure 5.15d. Once again, the side-stepping test and the pegboard test are most highly correlated with the discriminant function, while the correlation coefficient between balancing with eyes closed and the discriminant function is near 0. Again, balancing with eyes closed had a nonsignificant univariate F.

Figure 5.15d   Correlations between dependent variables and canonical variables

```
SET WIDTH=WIDE.
MANOVA BALOMEAN BALCMEAN SSTMEAN PP BY SEX(1,2)
 /DISCRIM=RAW STAN CORR
 /DESIGN.
```

```
Correlations between DEPENDENT and canonical variables
               Canonical Variable

Variable              1

BALOMEAN         -.35118
BALCMEAN          .03980
SSTMEAN          -.63514
PP                .40113
```

An additional statistic displayed as part of the discriminant output in MANOVA is an estimate of the effect for the canonical variable. Consider Figure 5.15e (from procedure DSCRIMINANT), which gives the average canonical function scores for the two groups. We can estimate the effect of a canonical variable by measuring its average distance from 0 across all groups. In this example the average distance is $(0.862 + 0.765)/2 = 0.814$, as shown in Figure 5.15f. Canonical variables with small effects do not contribute much to separation between groups.

Figure 5.15e   Average canonical function scores from DSCRIMINANT

```
DSCRIMINANT GROUPS=SEX(1,2)
 /VARIABLES=BALOMEAN SSTMEAN BALCMEAN PP
 /METHOD=DIRECT
 /DESIGN.
```

```
Canonical Discriminant Functions evaluated at Group Means (Group Centroids)

  Group      FUNC  1
     1      -.86214
     2       .76500
```

Figure 5.15f   Estimates of effects for canonical variables

```
SET WIDTH=WIDE.
MANOVA BALOMEAN BALCMEAN SSTMEAN PP BY SEX(1,2)
 /DISCRIM=RAW STAN CORR ESTIM
 /DESIGN.
```

```
Estimates of effects for canonical variables
              Canonical Variable

Parameter            1

    2            .81357
```

5.16
Parameter Estimates

As for most other statistical techniques, there is for MANOVA a mathematical model that expresses the relationship between the dependent variable and the independent variables. Recall, for example, that in a univariate analysis of variance model with four groups, the mean for each group can be expressed as

$$Y_{.1} = \mu + \alpha_1 \qquad\qquad\quad + E_{.1}$$

$$Y_{.2} = \mu \quad\; + \alpha_2 \qquad\qquad + E_{.2}$$

$$Y_{.3} = \mu \qquad\quad + \alpha_3 \qquad + E_{.3}$$

$$Y_{.4} = \mu \qquad\qquad\quad + \alpha_4 + E_{.4}$$

Equation 5.16a

In matrix form this can be written as

$$
\begin{bmatrix} Y_{.1} \\ Y_{.2} \\ Y_{.3} \\ Y_{.4} \end{bmatrix}
=
\begin{bmatrix}
1 & 1 & 0 & 0 & 0 \\
1 & 0 & 1 & 0 & 0 \\
1 & 0 & 0 & 1 & 0 \\
1 & 0 & 0 & 0 & 1
\end{bmatrix}
\begin{bmatrix} \mu \\ \alpha_1 \\ \alpha_2 \\ \alpha_3 \\ \alpha_4 \end{bmatrix}
+
\begin{bmatrix} E_{.1} \\ E_{.2} \\ E_{.3} \\ E_{.4} \end{bmatrix}
$$

Equation 5.16b

or

$$Y = A\Theta^* + E$$

Equation 5.16c

Since the Θ matrix has more columns than rows, it does not have a unique inverse. We are unable to estimate five parameters (μ and α_1 to α_4) on the basis of four sample means. Instead we can estimate four linear combinations, termed contrasts, of the parameters (see Finn, 1974).

Several types of contrasts are available in SPSS/PC+ MANOVA, resulting in different types of parameter estimates. Deviation contrasts, the default, estimate each parameter as its difference from the overall average for that parameter. This results in parameter estimates of the form $\mu_j - \mu$. Deviation contrasts do not require any particular ordering of the factor levels.

Simple contrasts are useful when one of the factor levels is a comparison or control group. All parameter estimates are then expressed as a deviation from the value of the control group. When factor levels have an underlying metric, orthogonal polynomial contrasts may be used to determine whether group means are related to the values of the factor level. For example, if three doses of an agent are administered (10 units, 20 units, and 30 units), you can test whether response is related to dose in a linear or quadratic fashion.

Figure 5.16 contains parameter estimates corresponding to the default deviation contrasts. For each dependent variable, the entry under CONSTANT is just the unweighted average of the means in the two groups. For example, from Figure 5.11a, we see that the mean for balancing with eyes open is 9.748 for females and 12.979 for males. The estimate for the average time balanced with eyes open, the constant term in Figure 5.16, is 11.364, the average of 12.979 and 9.748.

Figure 5.16 Parameter estimates

```
Estimates for BALOMEAN
CONSTANT

  Parameter      Coeff.    Std. Err.    t-Value    Sig. t   Lower -95% CL- Upper
       1     11.3636425      .48926    23.22635      0.0     10.39584    12.33144
SEX

  Parameter      Coeff.    Std. Err.    t-Value    Sig. t   Lower -95% CL- Upper
       2     -1.6152302      .48926    -3.30140     .001     -2.58303     -.64743
- - - - - - - - -

Estimates for BALCMEAN
CONSTANT

  Parameter      Coeff.    Std. Err.    t-Value    Sig. t   Lower -95% CL- Upper
       1      3.14563447     .12198    25.78916      0.0      2.90436     3.38691
SEX

  Parameter      Coeff.    Std. Err.    t-Value    Sig. t   Lower -95% CL- Upper
       2       .045634894    .12198      .37413     .709      -.19564      .28691
- - - - - - - - -

Estimates for SSTMEAN
CONSTANT

  Parameter      Coeff.    Std. Err.    t-Value    Sig. t   Lower -95% CL- Upper
       1     15.3293074      .20668    74.16860      0.0     14.92047    15.73814
SEX

  Parameter      Coeff.    Std. Err.    t-Value    Sig. t   Lower -95% CL- Upper
       2     -1.2340701      .20668    -5.97087     .000     -1.64291     -.82523
- - - - - - - - -

Estimates for PP
CONSTANT

  Parameter      Coeff.    Std. Err.    t-Value    Sig. t   Lower -95% CL- Upper
       1     15.0004080      .12336   121.59533      0.0     14.75638    15.24443
SEX

  Parameter      Coeff.    Std. Err.    t-Value    Sig. t   Lower -95% CL- Upper
       2       .465197766    .12336     3.77096     .000       .22117      .70922
```

There are two estimates for the sex parameter, one for females and one for males. The output includes only values for the first parameter (females), since the value for the second parameter is just the negative of the value for the first. The sex effect for females is estimated as the difference between the mean score of females and the overall unweighted mean. For balancing with eyes open it is 9.75 − 11.36 = −1.61, the value displayed in Figure 5.16. Confidence intervals and t tests for the null hypothesis that a parameter value is 0 can also be calculated. Again, these are calculated on a parameter-by-parameter basis and do not offer an overall protection level against Type 1 errors. Note that the t values displayed for each parameter are equal to the square root of the F values displayed for the univariate F tests in Figure 5.14.

5.17
A Multivariate Factorial Design

So far we have considered two very simple multivariate designs, generalizations of the one- and two-sample t tests to the case of multiple dependent variables. We are now ready to examine a more complex design. Recall that in the experiment conducted by Barnard, the hypothesis of interest concerned the relationship among field dependence, sex, and motor abilities. Since subjects are classified into one of three field-dependence categories—low, intermediate, and high—we have a two-way factorial design with three levels of field dependence and two categories of sex.

Figure 5.17a contains the location of the effects in the design matrix. The number of columns required by each effect equals its degrees of freedom. Thus, there is one column for sex, two for field-dependence, and two for the sex-by-field-dependence interaction.

Figure 5.17a   Correspondence table

```
MANOVA BALCMEAN BY SEX(1,2) FIELD(1,3) WITH BALOMEAN
 /DESIGN.
```

```
Correspondence between Effects and Columns of BETWEEN-Subjects DESIGN 1

Starting  Ending
 Column   Column    Effect Name
   1        1       CONSTANT
   2        2       SEX
   3        4       FIELD
   5        6       SEX BY FIELD
```

When orthogonal contrasts are requested for a factor, that is, when the sum of the products of corresponding coefficients for any two contrasts is zero, the numbers in the columns of the design matrix are the coefficients of the contrasts, except for scaling. When nonorthogonal contrasts, such as "deviation" or "simple," are requested for a factor, the columns of the matrix are not the contrast coefficients but arc the "basis" for the contrast requested (see Bock, 1975; Finn, 1974). The actual parameter estimates always correspond to the contrast requested.

Descriptive statistics are available for each cell in the design. Some additional plots may also be useful. Plotting the mean of a variable for all the cells in the design, as shown in Figure 5.17b, gives an idea of the spread of the means. The top row of numbers indicates how many cell means there are in each interval. You can see from the plot that there are two cells with means close to 14 seconds, three cells with means less than 10 seconds, and 1 cell with a mean in between.

Figure 5.17b   Distribution of cell means for BALOMEAN

```
SET WIDTH=WIDE.
MANOVA BALCMEAN BY SEX(1,2) FIELD(1,3) WITH BALOMEAN
 /PLOT=CELLPLOTS
 /DESIGN.
```

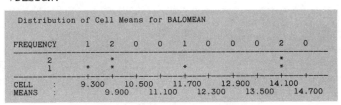

Although both univariate and multivariate analyses of variance require equal variances in the cells, there are many situations in which cell means and standard deviations, or cell means and variances, are proportional. Figure 5.17c shows plots of cell means versus cell variances and cell standard deviations. There appears to be no relationship between the means and the measures of variability. If patterns were evident, transformations of the dependent variables might be used to stabilize the variances.

Figure 5.17c   Plots of cell means, cell variances, and cell standard deviations

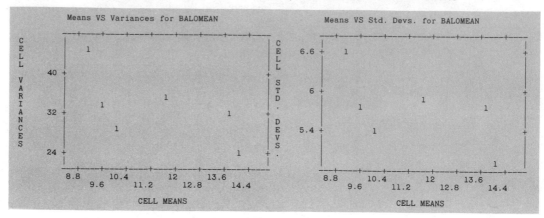

5.18
**Principal Components
Analysis**

Bartlett's test of sphericity provides information about the correlations among the dependent variables by testing the hypothesis that the correlation matrix is an identity matrix. Another way to examine dependencies among the dependent variables is to perform a principal components analysis of their within-cells correlation or covariance matrix (see Chapter 2 for a discussion of principal components analysis). If principal components analysis reveals that one of the variables can be expressed as a linear combination of the others, the error sums-of-squares and cross-products matrix will be singular and a unique inverse cannot be obtained.

Figure 5.18a contains the within-cells correlation matrix for the two-way factorial design. The eigenvalues and percent of variance explained by each are shown in Figure 5.18b. The first two principal components account for about two-thirds of the total variance, and the remaining two components account for the rest. None of the eigenvalues is close enough to 0 to cause concern about the error matrix being singular.

Figure 5.18a   Within-cells correlation matrix

```
SET WIDTH=WIDE.
MANOVA BALOMEAN BALCMEAN SSTMEAN PP BY SEX(1,2) FIELD(1,3)
 /PRINT=ERROR(COR)
 /DESIGN.
```

WITHIN CELLS Correlations with Std. Devs. on Diagonal			
	BALOMEAN	BALCMEAN	SSTMEAN	PP
BALOMEAN	5.67488			
BALCMEAN	.30019	1.41485		
SSTMEAN	.11506	.24341	2.39327	
PP	.11100	.14334	.34698	1.43842

Figure 5.18b   Eigenvalues and percent of variance

```
SET WIDTH=WIDE.
MANOVA BALOMEAN BALCMEAN SSTMEAN PP BY SEX(1,2) FIELD(1,3)
 /PCOMPS=CORR
 /DESIGN.
```

Eigenvalues of WITHIN CELLS correlation matrix			
	Eigenvalue	Pct of Var	Cum Pct
1	1.63610	40.90258	40.90258
2	1.02780	25.69499	66.59757
3	.72258	18.06447	84.66204
4	.61352	15.33796	100.00000

Figure 5.18c contains the loadings, which in this case are equivalent to correlations, between the principal components and dependent variables. The components can be rotated, as shown in Figure 5.18d, to increase interpretability. Each variable loads highly on only one of the components, suggesting that none is redundant or highly correlated with the others. When there are many dependent variables, a principal components analysis may indicate how the variables are related to each other. This information is useful for establishing the number of unique dimensions being measured by the dependent variables.

Figure 5.18c   Correlations between principal components and dependent variable

```
SET WIDTH=WIDE.
MANOVA BALOMEAN BALCMEAN SSTMEAN PP BY SEX(1,2) FIELD(1,3)
  /PCOMPS=CORR ROTATE(VARIMAX)
  /DESIGN.
```

```
Normalized principal components
          Components
Variables         1          2          3          4

BALOMEAN    -.55200    -.63056    -.48683     .24635
BALCMEAN    -.66950    -.41517     .49417    -.36770
SSTMEAN     -.69880     .41598     .27636     .51212
PP          -.62837     .53366    -.40619    -.39416
```

Figure 5.18d   Rotated correlations between components and dependent variable

```
VARIMAX rotated correlations between components and DEPENDENT variable
          Can. Var.
DEP. VAR.         1          2          3          4

BALOMEAN     .98696     .04774     .14699     .04503
BALCMEAN     .15005     .05958     .98016     .11501
SSTMEAN      .04632     .17390     .11608     .97680
PP           .04835     .98230     .05905     .17104
```

5.19
Tests of Multivariate Differences

Once the preliminary steps of examining the distribution of the variables for outliers, nonnormality, and inequality of variances have been taken and no significant violations have been found, hypothesis testing can begin. In the one- and two-sample test, Hotelling's T^2, a multivariate generalization of the univariate t value, is used. For more complicated designs, an extension of the familiar analysis of variance F test to the multivariate case is needed.

The univariate F tests in ANOVA are the ratios of the hypothesis mean squares to the error mean squares. When there is more than one dependent variable, there is no longer a single number that represents the hypothesis and error sums of squares. Instead, as shown in Section 5.9, there are matrices for the hypothesis and error sums of squares and cross-products. These matrices must be combined into some type of test statistic.

Most univariate test statistics are based on the determinant of HE^{-1}, where H is the hypothesis sums-of-squares and cross-products matrix and E^{-1} is the inverse of the error sums-of-squares and cross-products matrix. The determinant is a measure of the generalized variance, or dispersion, of a matrix. This determinant can be calculated as the product of the eigenvalues of a matrix, since each eigenvalue represents a portion of the generalized variance. In fact, the process of extracting eigenvalues can be viewed as a principal components analysis on the HE^{-1} matrix.

There are a variety of test statistics for evaluating multivariate differences based on the eigenvalues of HE^{-1}. Four of the most commonly used tests are displayed by SPSS/PC+ MANOVA:

- Pillai's Trace

$$V = \sum_{i=1}^{s} \frac{1}{1 + \lambda_i}$$

Equation 5.19a

- Wilks' Lambda

$$W = \prod_{i=1}^{s} \frac{1}{1 + \lambda_i}$$

Equation 5.19b

- Hotelling's Trace

$$T = \sum_{i=1}^{s} \lambda_i$$

Equation 5.19c

- Roy's Largest Root

$$R = \frac{\lambda_{MAX}}{1 + \lambda_{MAX}}$$

Equation 5.19d

where λ_{max} is the largest eigenvalue, λ_i is the ith eigenvalue, and s is the number of nonzero eigenvalues of HE^{-1}.

Although the exact distributions of the four criteria differ, they can be transformed into statistics that have approximately an F distribution. Tables of the exact distributions of the statistics are also available.

When there is a single dependent variable, all four criteria are equivalent to the ordinary ANOVA F statistic. When there is a single sample or two independent samples with multiple dependent variables, they are all equivalent to Hotelling's T^2. In both situations, the transformed statistics are distributed exactly as F's.

Two concerns dictate the choice of the multivariate criterion—power and robustness. That is, the test statistic should detect differences when they exist and not be much affected by departures from the assumptions. For most practical situations, when differences among groups are spread along several dimensions, the ordering of the test criteria in terms of decreasing power is Pillai's, Wilks', Hotelling's, and Roy's. Pillai's trace is also the most robust criterion. That is, the significance level based on it is reasonably correct even when the assumptions are violated. This is important since a test that results in distorted significance levels in the presence of mild violations of homogeneity of covariance matrices or multivariate normality is of limited use (Olson, 1976).

5.20
Testing the Effects

Since our design is a two-by-three factorial (two sexes and three categories of field dependence), there are three effects to be tested: the sex and field-dependence main effects and the sex-by-field-dependence interaction. As in univariate analysis of variance, the terms are tested in reverse order. That is, higher-order effects are tested before lower-order ones, since it is difficult to interpret lower-order effects in the presence of higher order interactions. For example, if there is a sex-by-field-dependence interaction, testing for sex and field-dependence main effects is not particularly useful and can be misleading.

SPSS/PC+ MANOVA displays separate output for each effect. Figure 5.20a shows the label displayed on each page to identify the effect being tested. The hypothesis sums-of-squares and cross-products matrix can be displayed for each effect. The same error matrix (the pooled within-cells sums-of-squares and cross-products matrix) is used to test all effects and is displayed only once before the effect-by-effect output. Figure 5.20b contains the error matrix for the factorial design. Figure 5.20c is the hypothesis sums-of-squares and cross-product matrix. These two matrices are the ones involved in the computation of the test statistic displayed in Figure 5.20d.

Figure 5.20a   Label for effect being tested

```
EFFECT .. SEX BY FIELD
```

Figure 5.20b   Error sums-of-squares and cross-products matrix

```
SET WIDTH=WIDE.
MANOVA BALOMEAN BALCMEAN SSTMEAN PP BY SEX(1,2) FIELD(1,3)
 /PRINT=ERROR(SSCP)
 /DESIGN.
```

```
WITHIN CELLS Sum-of-Squares and Cross-Products

               BALOMEAN    BALCMEAN     SSTMEAN          PP

BALOMEAN     4122.15198
BALCMEAN      308.51396   256.22940
SSTMEAN       200.02101   105.49892   733.14820
PP            115.98110    37.33887   152.89478   264.83723
```

Figure 5.20c   Hypothesis sums-of-squares and cross-products matrix

```
SET WIDTH=WIDE.
MANOVA BALOMEAN BALCMEAN SSTMEAN PP BY SEX(1,2) FIELD(1,3)
 /PRINT=SIGNIF(HYPOTH)
 /DESIGN.
```

```
Adjusted Hypothesis Sum-of-Squares and Cross-Products

               BALOMEAN    BALCMEAN     SSTMEAN          PP

BALOMEAN       18.10216
BALCMEAN        8.23621     3.77316
SSTMEAN         2.49484      .55197    13.52285
PP             -.00369       .21322    -4.85733     1.78987
```

Figure 5.20d   Multivariate tests of significance

```
MANOVA BALOMEAN BALCMEAN SSTMEAN PP BY SEX(1,2) FIELD(1,3)
 /PRINT=SIGNIF(HYPOTH MULTIV)
 /DESIGN.
```

```
Multivariate Tests of Significance (S = 2, M = 1/2, N = 61 1/2)

Test Name         Value  Approx. F Hypoth. DF   Error DF  Sig. of F

Pillais          .05245    .84827      8.00      252.00       .561
Hotellings       .05410    .83848      8.00      248.00       .570
Wilks            .94813    .84339      8.00      250.00       .565
Roys             .03668
```

The first line of Figure 5.20d contains the values of the parameters (S, M, N) used to find significance levels in tables of the exact distributions of the statistics. For the first three tests, the value of the test statistic is given, followed by its transformation to a statistic that has approximately an F distribution. The next two columns contain the numerator (hypothesis) and denominator (error) degrees of freedom for the F statistic. The observed significance level (the probability of observing a difference at least as large as the one found in the sample when there is no difference in the populations) is given in the last column. All of the observed significance levels are large, causing us not to reject the hypothesis that the sex-by-field-dependence interaction is 0. There is no straight-forward transformation for Roy's largest root criterion to a statistic with a known distribution, so only the value of the largest root is displayed.

Since the multivariate results are not statistically significant, there is no reason to examine the univariate results shown in Figure 5.20e. When the multivariate results are significant, however, the univariate statistics may help determine which variables contribute to the overall differences. The univariate F tests for the SEX by FIELD interaction are the same as the F's for SEX by FIELD in a two-way ANOVA. Figure 5.20f contains a two-way analysis of variance for the balancing-with-eyes-open (BALOMEAN) variable. The within-cells sum of squares is identical to the diagonal entry for BALOMEAN in Figure 5.20b. Similarly, the SEX by FIELD sum of squares is identical to the diagonal entry for BALOMEAN in Figure 5.20c. The F value for the interaction term, 0.281, is the same as in the first line of Figure 5.20e.

Figure 5.20e   Univariate F tests

```
MANOVA BALOMEAN BALCMEAN SSTMEAN PP BY SEX(1,2) FIELD(1,3)
 /PRINT=SIGNIF(HYPOTH MULTIV UNIV)
 /DESIGN.
```

```
EFFECT .. SEX BY CAT (CONT.)
Univariate F-tests with (2,128) D. F.

Variable    Hypoth. SS   Error SS Hypoth. MS   Error MS         F  Sig. of F

BALOMEAN     18.10216  4122.15198    9.05108   32.20431    .28105      .755
BALCMEAN      3.77316   256.22940    1.88658    2.00179    .94244      .392
SSTMEAN      13.52285   733.14820    6.76143    5.72772   1.18047      .310
PP            1.78987   264.83723     .89493    2.06904    .43254      .650
```

Figure 5.20f   Two-way analysis of variance

```
MANOVA BALOMEAN BY SEX(1,2) FIELD(1,3)
 /DESIGN.
```

```
Tests of Significance for BALOMEAN using UNIQUE sums of squares
Source of Variation          SS     DF        MS         F  Sig of F

WITHIN CELLS             4122.15    128     32.20
CONSTANT                16042.05      1  16042.05    498.13      .000
SEX                       389.33      1    389.33     12.09      .001
CAT                        55.19      2     27.59       .86      .427
SEX BY CAT                 18.10      2      9.05       .28      .755
```

5.21
Discriminant Analysis

As discussed in Section 5.15 for the two-group situation, the MANOVA problem can also be viewed as one of finding the linear combinations of the dependent variables that best separate the categories of the independent variables. For main effects, the analogy with discriminant analysis is clear: What combinations of the variables distinguish men from women and what combinations distinguish the three categories of field dependence? When interaction terms are considered, we must distinguish among the six (two sex and three field-dependence) categories jointly. This is done by finding the linear combination of variables that maximizes the ratio of the hypothesis to error sums-of-squares. Since the interaction effect is not significant, there is no particular reason to examine the discriminant analysis results. However, we will consider them for illustrative purposes.

Figure 5.21a contains the standardized discriminant function coefficients for the interaction term. The number of functions that can be derived is equal to the degrees of freedom for that term if it is less than the number of dependent variables. The two variables that have the largest standardized coefficients are the side-stepping test and the Purdue Pegboard Test. All warnings concerning the interpretation of coefficients when variables are correlated apply in this situation as well. However, the magnitude of the coefficients may give us some idea of the variables contributing most to group differences.

Figure 5.21a Standardized discriminant function coefficients

```
SET WIDTH=WIDE.
MANOVA BALOMEAN BALCMEAN SSTMEAN PP BY SEX(1,2) FIELD(1,3)
 /DISCRIM=STAN ALPHA(1)
 /DESIGN.
```

```
EFFECT .. SEX BY FIELD (CONT.)
Standardized discriminant function coefficients
        Function No.

Variable         1            2

BALOMEAN       .02621      -.27281
BALCMEAN      -.19519      -.90129
SSTMEAN        .98773       .02421
PP            -.73005       .15206
```

As discussed in Chapter 1, a measure of the strength of the association between the discriminant functions and the grouping variables is the canonical correlation coefficient. Its square is the proportion of variability in the discriminant function scores "explained" by the independent variables. All multivariate significance tests, which were expressed as functions of the eigenvalues in Section 5.19, can also be expressed as functions of the canonical correlations.

Figure 5.21b contains several sets of statistics for the discriminant functions. The entry under eigenvalues is the dispersion associated with each function. The next column is the percentage of the total dispersion associated with each function. (It is obtained by dividing each eigenvalue by the sum of all eigenvalues and multiplying by 100.) The last column contains the canonical correlation coefficients. The results in Figure 5.21b are consistent with the results of the multivariate significance tests. Both the eigenvalues and canonical correlation coefficients are small, indicating that there is no interaction effect.

Figure 5.21b Eigenvalues and canonical correlations

```
SET WIDTH=WIDE.
MANOVA BALOMEAN BALCMEAN SSTMEAN PP BY SEX(1,2) FIELD(1,3)
 /PRINT=SIGNIF(EIGEN)
 /DESIGN.
```

```
EFFECT .. SEX BY FIELD (CONT.)
Eigenvalues and Canonical Correlations

Root No.     Eigenvalue        Pct.       Cum. Pct.     Canon Cor.

    1          .03808        70.39068     70.39068        .19152
    2          .01602        29.60932    100.00000        .12556
```

When more than one discriminant function can be derived, you should examine how many functions contribute to group differences. The same tests for successive eigenvalues described in Chapter 1 can be obtained from SPSS/PC+ MANOVA. The first line in Figure 5.21c is a test of the hypothesis that all eigenvalues are equal to 0. The value for Wilks' lambda in the first line of Figure 5.21c is equal to the test of multivariate differences in Figure 5.20d. Successive lines in Figure 5.21c correspond to tests of the hypothesis that all remaining functions are equal in the groups. These tests allow you to assess the number of dimensions on which the groups differ.

Figure 5.21c Dimension reduction analysis

```
MANOVA BALOMEAN BALCMEAN SSTMEAN PP BY SEX(1,2) FIELD(1,3)
 /PRINT=SIGNIF(EIGEN DIMENR)
 /DESIGN.
```

```
EFFECT .. SEX BY FIELD (CONT.)
- - - - - - - - - -
Dimension Reduction Analysis

Roots       Wilks L.      F Hypoth. DF    Error DF   Sig. of F

1 TO 2       .94813       .84339    8.00    250.00      .565
2 TO 2       .98424       .67273    3.00    126.00      .570
```

5.22
Testing for Differences Among Field Dependence and Sex Categories

Since the field-dependence-by-sex interaction term is not significant, the main effects can be tested. Figure 5.22a contains the multivariate tests of significance for the field-dependence variable. All four criteria indicate that there is not sufficient evidence to reject the null hypothesis that the means of the motor-ability variables do not differ for the three categories of field dependence.

Figure 5.22a Multivariate tests of significance for FIELD

```
MANOVA BALOMEAN BALCMEAN SSTMEAN PP BY SEX(1,2) FIELD(1,3)
  /PRINT=SIGNIF(EIGEN DIMENR MULTIV)
  /DESIGN.
```

```
EFFECT .. FIELD
- - - - - - - - -
Multivariate Tests of Significance (S = 2, M = 1/2, N = 61 1/2)

Test Name        Value    Approx. F  Hypoth. DF   Error DF   Sig. of F

Pillais          .04152    .66780       8.00       252.00      .720
Hotellings       .04244    .65789       8.00       248.00      .728
Wilks            .95889    .66285       8.00       250.00      .724
Roys             .02533
```

The multivariate tests of significance for the sex variable are shown in Figure 5.22b. All four criteria indicate that there are significant differences between men and women on the motor-ability variables. Compare Figure 5.22b with Figure 5.13b, which contains Hotelling's statistic for the two-group situation. Note that although the two statistics are close in value—0.669 when SEX is considered alone and 0.609 when SEX is included in a model containing field dependence and the sex-by-field-dependence interaction—they are not identical. The reason is that in the second model the sex effect is "adjusted" for the other effects in the model (see Section 5.24).

Figure 5.22b Multivariate tests of significance for SEX

```
EFFECT .. SEX
- - - - - - - - -
Multivariate Tests of Significance (S = 1, M = 1 , N = 61 1/2)

Test Name        Value    Approx. F  Hypoth. DF   Error DF   Sig. of F

Pillais          .37871   19.04870      4.00       125.00      .000
Hotellings       .60956   19.04870      4.00       125.00      .000
Wilks            .62129   19.04870      4.00       125.00      .000
Roys             .37871
```

5.23
Stepdown F Tests

If the dependent variables are ordered in some fashion, it is possible to test for group differences of variables adjusting for effects of other variables. This is termed a *stepdown* procedure. Consider Figure 5.23a, which contains the stepdown tests for the motor-ability variables. The first line is just a univariate *F* test for the balancing-with-eyes-open variable. The value is the same as that displayed in Figure 5.23b, which contains the univariate *F* tests. The next line in Figure 5.23a is the univariate *F* test for balancing with eyes closed when balancing with eyes open is taken to be a covariate. That is, differences in balancing with eyes open are eliminated from the comparison of balancing with eyes closed. Figure 5.23c is the ANOVA table for the BALCMEAN variable when BALO-MEAN is treated as the covariate. Note that the *F* value of 1.76 for SEX in Figure 5.23c is identical to that for BALCMEAN in Figure 5.23a.

Figure 5.23a Stepdown tests

```
MANOVA BALOMEAN BALCMEAN SSTMEAN PP BY SEX(1,2) FIELD(1,3)
  /PRINT=SIGNIF(EIGEN DIMENR MULTIV STEPDOWN)
  /DESIGN.
```

```
EFFECT .. SEX (CONT.)
- - - - - - - - - -
Roy-Bargman Stepdown F - tests

Variable   Hypoth. MS   Error MS  StepDown F  Hypoth. DF   Error DF   Sig. of F

BALOMEAN    389.32559   32.20431   12.08924           1        128       .001
BALCMEAN      3.24111    1.83574    1.76556           1        127       .186
SSTMEAN     149.80319    5.46262   27.42333           1        126       .000
PP           44.19749    1.84899   23.90357           1        125       .000
```

Figure 5.23b Univariate F tests

```
MANOVA BALOMEAN BALCMEAN SSTMEAN PP BY SEX(1,2) FIELD(1,3)
  /PRINT=SIGNIF(EIGEN DIMENR MULTIV STEPDOWN UNIV)
  /DESIGN.
```

```
EFFECT .. SEX (CONT.)
- - - - - - - - - -
Univariate F-tests with (1,128) D. F.

Variable   Hypoth. SS   Error SS  Hypoth. MS   Error MS         F   Sig. of F

BALOMEAN    389.32559  4122.15198  389.32559   32.20431  12.08924      .001
BALCMEAN       .16537   256.22940      .16537    2.00179    .08261      .774
SSTMEAN     172.11227   733.14820   172.11227    5.72772  30.04900      .000
PP           23.56111   264.83723    23.56111    2.06904  11.38746      .001
```

Figure 5.23c ANOVA table for BALCMEAN with BALOMEAN as the covariate

```
MANOVA BALOMEAN BALCMEAN SSTMEAN PP BY SEX(1,2) FIELD(1,3)
  /ANALYSIS=BALCMEAN WITH BALOMEAN
  /DESIGN.
```

Tests of Significance for BALCMEAN using UNIQUE sums of squares

Source of Variation	SS	DF	MS	F	Sig of F
WITHIN CELLS	233.14	127	1.84		
REGRESSION	23.09	1	23.09	12.58	.001
CONSTANT	135.46	1	135.46	73.79	.000
SEX	3.24	1	3.24	1.77	.186
CAT	2.40	2	1.20	.65	.522
SEX BY CAT	2.63	2	1.32	.72	.490

The third line of Figure 5.23a, the test for the side-stepping variable, is adjusted for both the balancing-with-eyes-open variable and the balancing-with-eyes-closed variable. Similarly, the last line, the Purdue Pegboard Test score, has balancing with eyes open, balancing with eyes closed, and the side-stepping test as covariates. Thus each variable in Figure 5.23a is adjusted for variables that precede it in the table.

The order in which variables are displayed on the stepdown tests in MANOVA output depends only on the order in which the variables are specified for the procedure. If this order is not meaningful, the stepdown tests that result will not be readily interpretable or meaningful.

5.24
Different Types of Sums of Squares

When there is more than one factor and unequal numbers of cases in each cell in univariate analysis of variance, the total sums of squares cannot be partitioned into additive components for each effect. That is, the sums of squares for all effects do not add up to the total sums of squares. Differences between factor means are "contaminated" by the effects of the other factors.

There are many different algorithms for calculating the sums of squares for unbalanced data. Different types of sums of squares correspond to tests of different hypotheses. Two frequently used methods for calculating the sums of squares are the regression method, in which an effect is adjusted for all other effects in the model, and the sequential method, in which an effect is adjusted only for effects that precede it in the model.

In multivariate analysis of variance, unequal sample sizes in the cells lead to similar problems. Again, different procedures for calculating the requisite statistics are available. SPSS/PC+ MANOVA offers two options—the regression solution (requested by keyword UNIQUE) and the sequential solution (requested by keyword SEQUENTIAL). All output displayed in this chapter is obtained from the regression solution, the default (see Milliken & Johnson, 1984).

For any connected design, the hypotheses associated with the sequential sums of squares are weighted functions of the population cell means, with weights depending on the cell frequencies (see Searle, 1971). For designs in which every cell is filled, it can be shown that the hypotheses corresponding to the regression model sums of squares are the hypotheses about the unweighted cell means. With empty cells, the hypotheses will depend on the pattern of missingness. In such cases, you can display the solution matrix, which contains the coefficients of the linear combinations of the cell means being tested.

5.25
Problems with Empty Cells

When there are no observations in one or more cells in a design, the analysis is greatly complicated. This is true for both univariate and multivariate designs. Empty cells results in the inability to estimate uniquely all of the necessary parameters. Hypotheses that involve parameters corresponding to the empty cells usually cannot be tested. Thus, the output from an analysis involving empty cells should be treated with caution (see Freund, 1980; Milliken & Johnson 1984).

5.26
Examining Residuals

Residuals—the differences between observed values and those predicted from a model—provide information about the adequacy of fit of the model and the assumptions. Previous chapters have discussed residual analysis for regression and log-linear models. The same techniques are appropriate for analysis of variance models as well.

In the two-factor model with interactions, the equation is

$$\widehat{Y}_{ij} = \widehat{\mu} + \widehat{\alpha}_i + \widehat{\beta}_j + \widehat{\delta}_{ij}$$

Equation 5.26a

where $\widehat{Y}_{ij}$ is the predicted value for the cases in the ith category of the first variable and the jth category of the second. As before, $\widehat{\mu}$ is the grand mean, $\widehat{\alpha}_i$ the effect of the ith category of the first variable, $\widehat{\beta}_j$ is the effect of the jth category of the second variable, and $\widehat{\delta}_{ij}$ is their interaction.

Consider Figure 5.26a, which contains deviation parameter estimates for the balancing-with-eyes-open variable. From this table, the predicted value for females in the low field-dependence category is

$$\widehat{Y}_{11} = 11.42 - 1.78 - 0.97 + 0.51 = 9.18$$

Equation 5.26b

Similarly, the predicted value for males in the high field-dependence category is

$$\widehat{Y}_{23} = 11.42 + 1.78 + 0.53 + 0.09 = 13.82$$

Equation 5.26c

Note that only independent parameter estimates are displayed and the other estimates must be derived from these. (For the main effects these can be requested with the keyword NEGSUM.) For example, the parameter estimate displayed for the sex variable is for the first category, females. The estimate for males is the negative of the estimate for females, since the two values must sum to 0. The value for the third category of field dependence is 0.53, the negative of the sum of the values for the first two categories. The two parameter estimates displayed for the interaction effects are for females with low field dependence and females with medium field dependence. The remaining estimates can be easily calculated. For example, the value for males in the low field-dependence category is −0.51, the negative of that for females. Similarly, the value for females in the high field-dependence category is −0.087, the negative of the sum of the values for females in low and medium field-dependence categories.

Figure 5.26a Parameter estimates

```
MANOVA BALOMEAN BALCMEAN SSTMEAN PP BY SEX(1,2) FIELD(1,3)
 /PRINT=PARAMETERS(ESTIM)
 /ANALYSIS=BALOMEAN
 /DESIGN.
```

```
Estimates for BALOMEAN
CONSTANT

 Parameter      Coeff.   Std. Err.    t-Value    Sig. t  Lower -95% CL- Upper

        1    11.4196871    .51166    22.31890      0.0    10.40728    12.43209
SEX

 Parameter      Coeff.   Std. Err.    t-Value    Sig. t  Lower -95% CL- Upper

        2    -1.7790199    .51166    -3.47696      .001   -2.79143     -.76661
CAT

 Parameter      Coeff.   Std. Err.    t-Value    Sig. t  Lower -95% CL- Upper

        3    -.97446433    .74485    -1.30827      .193   -2.44828      .49935
        4    .445727366    .70743     .63006       .530    -.95405     1.84551

SEX BY CAT

 Parameter      Coeff.   Std. Err.    t-Value    Sig. t  Lower -95% CL- Upper

        5    .514565980    .74485     .69083       .491    -.95925     1.98838
        6    -.42730430    .70743    -.60402       .547   -1.82709      .97248
```

Figure 5.26b contains an excerpt of some cases in the study and their observed and predicted values for the balancing-with-eyes-open variable. The fourth column is the residual, the difference between the observed and predicted values. The residuals can be standardized by dividing each one by the error standard deviation (Column 5).

Figure 5.26b Observed and predicted values

```
SET WIDTH=WIDE.
MANOVA BALOMEAN BALCMEAN SSTMEAN PP BY SEX(1,2) FIELD(1,3)
 /RESIDUALS=CASEWISE PLOT
 /ANALYSIS=BALOMEAN
 /DESIGN.
```

```
Observed and Predicted Values for Each Case
Dependent Variable.. BALOMEAN

Case No.    Observed  Predicted Raw Resid. Std Resid.

      1     4.00000   10.08214   -6.08214   -1.07176
      2     8.85000    9.18077    -.33077    -.05829
      3    10.00000    9.65909     .34091     .06007
      4     3.55000   10.08214   -6.53214   -1.15106
      5     2.80000    9.65909   -6.85909   -1.20867
      6    14.50000    9.65909    4.84091     .85304
      .         .          .          .          .

    127     5.00000   13.81470   -8.81470   -1.55328
    128    20.00000   11.70968    8.29032    1.46088
    129    20.00000   13.81470    6.18530    1.08994
    130    19.00000   11.70968    7.29032    1.28466
    131    16.14999   14.07174    2.07826     .36622
    132    20.00000   14.07174    5.92826    1.04465
      .         .          .          .          .
```

As in regression analysis, a variety of plots are useful for checking the assumptions. Figure 5.26c is a plot of the observed and predicted values for the BALOMEAN variable. The cases fall into six rows for the predicted values, since all cases in the same cell have the same predicted value. Residuals are plotted against the predicted values in Figure 5.26d and against the case numbers in Figure 5.26e. The plot against the case numbers is useful if the data are gathered and entered into the file sequentially. Any patterns in this plot lead to suspicions that the data are not independent of each other. Of course, if the data have been sorted before being entered, a pattern is to be expected.

Figure 5.26c Plot of observed and predicted values

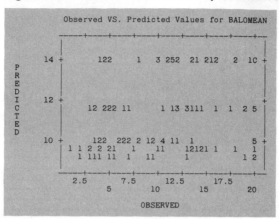

Figure 5.26d Plot of predicted and residual values

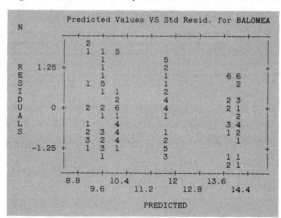

Figure 5.26e Plot of case numbers and residuals

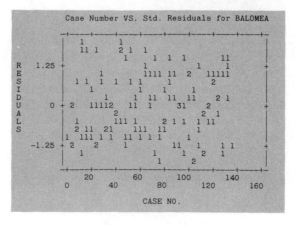

If the assumption of multivariate normality is met, the distribution of the residuals for each variable should be approximately normal. Figure 5.26f is a normal plot of the residuals for the balancing-with-eyes-open variable, while Figure 5.26g is the detrended normal plot of the same variable. Both of these plots suggest that there may be reason to suspect that the distribution of the residuals is not normal.

Figure 5.26f   Normal plot of residuals

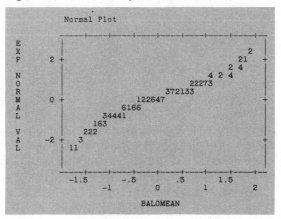

Figure 5.26g   Detrended normal plot

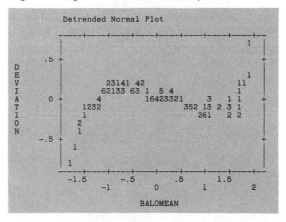

5.27
Predicted Means

Figure 5.27a shows a table that contains observed and predicted means for all cells in the design, as well as residuals, for the balancing-with-eyes-open variable. The first column of the table, labeled "Obs. Mean," is the observed mean for that cell. The next value, labeled "Adj. Mean" is the mean predicted from the model adjusted for the covariates. The column labeled "Est. Mean" contains the predicted means without correcting for covariates. When covariates are present, the differences between the adjusted and estimated means provide an indication of the effectiveness of the covariate adjustment (see Finn, 1974). For a complete factorial design without covariates the observed, adjusted and estimated means will always be equal. The difference between them, the residual, will also be equal to 0.

If the design is not a full-factorial model, the observed means and those predicted using the parameter estimates will differ. Consider Figure 5.27b, which contains a table of means for the main-effects-only model. The observed cell means are no longer equal to those predicted by the model. The difference between the observed and estimated mean is shown in the column labeled "Raw Resid." The residual divided by the error standard deviation is shown in the column labeled "Std. Resid." From this table it is possible to identify cells for which the model does not fit well.

Figure 5.27a Table of predicted means

```
MANOVA BALOMEAN BALCMEAN SSTMEAN PP BY SEX (1,2) FIELD (1,3)
 /PMEANS=TABLES(SEX BY FIELD)
 /DESIGN.
```

```
Adjusted and Estimated Means
Variable .. BALOMEAN
  CELL       Obs. Mean    Adj. Mean    Est. Mean  Raw Resid. Std. Resid.

    1           9.181        9.181        9.181        0.0        0.0
    2           9.659        9.659        9.659        0.0        0.0
    3          10.082       10.082       10.082        0.0        0.0
    4          11.710       11.710       11.710        0.0        0.0
    5          14.072       14.072       14.072        0.0        0.0
    6          13.815       13.815       13.815        0.0        0.0
```

It is also possible to obtain various combinations of the adjusted means. For example, Figure 5.27b contains the combined adjusted means for the SEX and FIELD variables for the main effects design. The means are labeled as unweighted, since the sample sizes in the cells are not used when means are combined over the categories of a variable.

Figure 5.27b Table of predicted means

```
MANOVA BALOMEAN BALCMEAN SSTMEAN PP BY SEX (1,2) FIELD (1,3)
 /PMEANS=TABLES(SEX,FIELD)
 /DESIGN SEX FIELD.
```

```
Adjusted and Estimated Means
Variable .. BALOMEAN
  CELL       Obs. Mean    Adj. Mean    Est. Mean  Raw Resid. Std. Resid.

    1           9.181        8.410        8.410       .771       .136
    2           9.659       10.062       10.062      -.403      -.071
    3          10.082       10.123       10.123      -.041      -.007
    4          11.710       12.033       12.033      -.323      -.057
    5          14.072       13.686       13.686       .386       .068
    6          13.815       13.747       13.747       .068       .012

Combined Adjusted Means for SEX
Variable .. BALOMEAN
       SEX
        1       UNWGT.      9.53176
        2       UNWGT.     13.15531

Combined Adjusted Means for FIELD
Variable .. BALOMEAN
       FIELD
        1       UNWGT.     10.22132
        2       UNWGT.     11.87418
        3       UNWGT.     11.93510
```

5.28
Some Final Comments

In this chapter, only the most basic aspects of multivariate analysis of variance have been covered. The MANOVA procedure is capable of testing more elaborate models of several types. Chapter 6 considers a special class of designs called repeated measures designs. In such designs, the same variable or variables are measured on several occassions. For further discussion about multivariate analysis of variance, consult Morrison (1967) and Tatsuoka (1971).

5.29
RUNNING PROCEDURE MANOVA

MANOVA is a generalized analysis of variance and covariance program that performs both univariate and multivariate procedures. You can analyze such designs as block, split-plot, nested, and repeated measures designs. (Repeated measures designs and the MANOVA commands needed to analyze them are discussed in Chapter 6.) MANOVA can also be used to obtain multivariate regression coefficients, principal components, discriminant function coefficients, canonical correlations, and other statistics.

A program with so many facilities naturally has a large number of subcommands available. This section concentrates on the most commonly used subcommands and briefly describes the rest. The repeated measures subcommands WSFACTORS, WSDESIGN, and RENAME are discussed in Chapter 6. For further information and examples, see Command Reference: MANOVA.

5.30
Specifying Factors and the Structure of the Data

To run MANOVA, you must indicate which variables are dependent variables, which (if any) are factors, and which (if any) are covariates. You also need to specify the design to be used.

The simplest MANOVA specification is a list of variables. If no other subcommands or keywords are used, all variables listed are treated as dependent variables and a one-sample Hotelling's T^2 is calculated. Thus, the output in Figure 5.9d was produced by specifying

```
MANOVA BALOMEAN BALCMEAN SSTMEAN PP.
```

5.31
The Dependent Variable List

The first variables specified are the dependent variables in the analysis. By default, MANOVA treats a list of dependent variables as jointly dependent and therefore uses a multivariate design. This default can be changed by using the ANALYSIS subcommand (see Section 5.34).

5.32
The Factor List

If factors are to be used in the analysis, they are specified following the dependent variable list and the keyword BY. Each factor is followed by two integer values enclosed in parentheses and separated by a comma, specifying the lowest and highest values for the factor. For example,

```
MANOVA BALOMEAN BALCMEAN SSTMEAN PP BY SEX(1,2) FIELD(1,3).
```

indicates that there are two factors: SEX with possible values 1 and 2, and FIELD with possible values 1, 2, and 3. Cases with values outside the range specified are excluded from the analysis. Since MANOVA requires factor levels to be integer, you need to recode any noninteger factor values. Factors with empty categories must also be recoded, since MANOVA expects the levels of a factor to be adjacent.

If several factors have the same value range, you can specify a list of factors followed by a single value range, in parentheses, as in the command

```
MANOVA SALES BY TVAD RADIOAD MAGAD NEWSPAD(2,5).
```

Certain analyses, such as regression, canonical correlation, and the one-sample Hotelling's T^2, do not require a factor specification. For these analyses, the factor list and the keyword BY should be omitted.

5.33
The Covariate List

The covariate list specifies any covariates to be used in the analysis. It follows the factor list and is separated from it by the keyword WITH, as in

```
MANOVA BALOMEAN BALCMEAN SSTMEAN PP BY SEX(1,2) FIELD(1,3) WITH IQ.
```

5.34
Specifying the Model

Use the ANALYSIS subcommand to specify a model based on a subset of variables in the variable list. You can also use ANALYSIS to change the model specified in the variable list by changing dependent variables to covariates or covariates to dependent variables. When ANALYSIS is specified, it completely overrides the dependent variable list and covariate list in the MANOVA specification, but it does not affect the factors. Only variables in the original MANOVA variable list (or covariate list) can be specified on the ANALYSIS subcommand, as in

```
MANOVA BALOMEAN BALCMEAN SSTMEAN PP BY SEX(1,2) FIELD(1,3) WITH IQ
 /ANALYSIS=BALOMEAN BALCMEAN PP WITH SSTMEAN.
```

This command changes SSTMEAN from a dependent variable to a covariate. The command

```
MANOVA BALOMEAN BALCMEAN SSTMEAN BY SEX(1,2) FIELD(1,3) WITH IQ PP
 /ANALYSIS=BALOMEAN BALCMEAN SSTMEAN PP WITH IQ.
```

changes PP from a covariate to a dependent variable. The factors SEX and FIELD are still used in the analysis (unless eliminated with a DESIGN subcommand; see Section 5.35).

Dependent variables or covariates can be eliminated from the analysis, as in

```
MANOVA SALES OPINION BY TVAD RADIOAD NEWSPAD(2,5) WITH PCTBUSNS
 /ANALYSIS=OPINION.
```

which deletes the variables SALES and PCTBUSNS from the analysis.

Although only one ANALYSIS subcommand can be specified per DESIGN subcommand, a single ANALYSIS subcommand can be used to obtain multiple analyses, as long as the lists of dependent variables do not overlap. For example, the command

```
MANOVA BALOMEAN BALCMEAN SSTMEAN PP BY SEX(1,2) FIELD (1,3)
        WITH EDUC IQ
 /ANALYSIS=(BALOMEAN BALCMEAN /SSTMEAN /PP WITH IQ).
```

specifies three analyses. The first has BALOMEAN and BALCMEAN as dependent variables and no covariates, the second has SSTMEAN as the dependent variable and no covariates, and the third has PP as the dependent variable and IQ as a covariate. (Note that none of the variable lists overlap.) Although three separate ANALYSIS and DESIGN subcommands could be used to get the same results, this would increase processing time.

To request three separate analyses with EDUC as the covariate for all of them, specify

```
MANOVA BALOMEAN BALCMEAN SSTMEAN PP BY SEX (1,2) FIELD(1,3)
        WITH EDUC IQ
 /ANALYSIS=(BALOMEAN BALCMEAN /SSTMEAN /PP WITH IQ) WITH EDUC
 /DESIGN.
```

This is equivalent to

```
MANOVA BALOMEAN BALCMEAN SSTMEAN PP BY SEX(1,2) FIELD(1,3)
        WITH EDUC IQ
 /ANALYSIS=BALOMEAN BALCMEAN WITH EDUC
 /DESIGN
 /ANALYSIS=SSTMEAN WITH EDUC
 /DESIGN
 /ANALYSIS=PP WITH IQ EDUC
 /DESIGN.
```

When specifying multiple analyses in this fashion, you may sometimes find the keywords CONDITIONAL and UNCONDITIONAL useful. CONDITIONAL indicates that subsequent variable lists should include as covariates all previous dependent variables on that ANALYSIS subcommand. UNCONDITIONAL (the default) indicates that each list should be used as is, independent of the others. For example, the command

```
MANOVA SALES LEADS OPINIONS CONTRACT BY TVAD RADIOAD MAGAD NEWSPAD(2,5)
       WITH PCTHOMES PCTBUSNS
  /ANALYSIS(CONDITIONAL)=(LEADS OPINIONS CONTRACT/SALES) WITH PCTBUSNS
  /DESIGN.
```

is equivalent to

```
MANOVA SALES LEADS OPINIONS CONTRACT BY TVAD RADIOAD MAGAD NEWSPAD(2,5)
       WITH PCTHOMES PCTBUSNS
  /ANALYSIS=LEADS OPINIONS CONTRACT WITH PCTBUSNS
  /DESIGN
  /ANALYSIS=SALES WITH LEADS OPINIONS CONTRACT PCTBUSNS
  /DESIGN.
```

5.35
Specifying the Design

Use the DESIGN subcommand to specify the structure of the model. DESIGN must be the *last* subcommand for any given model, and it can be used more than once to specify different models. The default model (obtained when DESIGN is used without further specification) is the full-factorial model.

Because of its importance the DESIGN subcommand is discussed at this point in the chapter. Remember that the other subcommands discussed later on must *precede* the DESIGN subcommand(s) to which they apply.

5.36
Specifying Effects

When a full-factorial model is not desired, the DESIGN subcommand can be used to specify the effects in the model. The format is simply

```
/DESIGN=list of effects
```

with the effects separated by blanks or commas. For example, a model with only main effects is specified by the command

```
MANOVA BALOMEAN BALCMEAN SSTMEAN PP BY SEX(1,2) FIELD(1,3)
  /DESIGN=SEX FIELD.
```

Interaction terms are indicated with the keyword BY, so that the command

```
MANOVA SALES BY TVAD RADIOAD MAGAD NEWSPAD(2,5)
  /DESIGN=TVAD RADIOAD MAGAD NEWSPAD TVAD BY RADIOAD TVAD BY RADIOAD
          BY NEWSPAD.
```

specifies a model with all main effects, the two-way interaction between TVAD and RADIOAD, and the three-way interaction between TVAD, RADIOAD, and NEWSPAD.

If single-degree-of-freedom effects are to be included, a PARTITION subcommand may be used before specifying these effects in the DESIGN subcommand, as in

```
MANOVA RELIEF BY DRUG(1,4)
  /CONTRAST(DRUG)=SPECIAL(1 1 1 1, 1 -1 0 0, 4 4 -8 0, 4 4 1 -9)
  /PARTITION(DRUG)
  /DESIGN=DRUG(1) DRUG(2) DRUG(3).
```

The above command is equivalent to

```
MANOVA RELIEF BY DRUG(1,4)
  /CONTRAST(DRUG)=SPECIAL(1 1 1 1, 1 -1 0 0, 4 4 -8 0, 4 4 1 -9)
  /DESIGN=DRUG(1) DRUG(2) DRUG(3).
```

For further information about the PARTITION subcommand, see Section 5.46. For the CONTRAST subcommand, see Section 5.47.

The keyword POOL is used with DESIGN to incorporate continuous variables into a single effect. The variables to be incorporated must not have been specified in the previous ANALYSIS subcommand as dependent variables or covariates. When you use POOL on DESIGN, dependent variables must be defined with an ANALYSIS subcommand. For example, the command

```
MANOVA SALES TEST1 TEST2 TEST3 BY TVAD RADIOAD MAGAD NEWSPAD(2,5)
     WITH PCTBUSNS
 /ANALYSIS=SALES WITH PCTBUSNS
 /DESIGN=POOL(TEST1 TEST2 TEST3).
```

incorporates TEST1, TEST2, and TEST3 into a single effect with three degress of freedom. See Command Reference: MANOVA for further information about POOL.

To specify interactions between factors and continuous variables, simply list these interaction effects on the DESIGN subcommand using keyword BY. You cannot specify interactions between two continuous variables (including covariates), and you cannot use variables that are included in the model by an ANALYSIS subcommand.

Effects can be pooled together into a single effect by using a plus sign. For example,

```
 /DESIGN=TVAD + TVAD BY RADIOAD
```

combines the effects of TVAD and TVAD BY RADIOAD into a single effect. (The BY keyword is evaluated before the plus sign.)

To obtain estimates that consist of the sum of the constant term and the parameter values, use the MUPLUS keyword. The constant term μ is then combined with the parameter following the MUPLUS keyword. For example, if the subcommand

```
 /DESIGN=MUPLUS SEX
```

is specified, the mean of each dependent variable is added to the SEX parameters for that variable. This produces conditional means or "marginals" for each dependent variable. Since these means are adjusted for any covariates in the model, they are also the usual adjusted means when covariates are present. When the adjusted means cannot be estimated, MUPLUS produces estimates of the constant plus the requested effect. These are no longer the predicted means.

The MUPLUS approach is the only way you can obtain the standard errors of the conditional means. (However, conditional and adjusted means can be obtained by using the OMEANS and PMEANS subcommands; see Section 5.48). You can obtain unweighted conditional means for a main effect by specifying the full factorial model and specifying MUPLUS before the effect whose means are to be found. (For an interaction effect, the DESIGN should not include any lower-order effects contained in it.) For example, the subcommand

```
 /DESIGN=MUPLUS SEX FIELD SEX BY FIELD
```

obtains the unweighted marginal means for SEX in a two-factor design. Only one MUPLUS keyword may be used per DESIGN subcommand.

Although MANOVA automatically includes the constant term (the correction for the mean), it will not be included if you specify NOCONSTANT on a METHOD subcommand. You can override NOCONSTANT by specifying CONSTANT on the DESIGN subcommand. A variable named CONSTANT is not recognized on DESIGN.

5.37
Specifying Nested Designs

The WITHIN keyword, or W, indicates that the term to its left is nested in the term to its right. For example, the subcommand

```
/DESIGN=TREATMNT WITHIN TESTCAT
```

indicates that TREATMNT is nested within TESTCAT, while the subcommand

```
/DESIGN=TREATMNT WITHIN TESTCAT BY EDUC BY MOTIVTN
```

indicates that TREATMNT is nested within the interaction TESTCAT by EDUC by MOTIVTN.

5.38
Specifying Error Terms

Error terms for individual effects are specified on the DESIGN subcommand with the following keywords:

WITHIN	*Within-cells error terms.* Alias W.
RESIDUAL	*Residual error terms.* Alias R.
WITHIN+RESIDUAL	*Combined within-cells and residual error terms.* Alias WR or RW.

To test a term against one of these error terms, specify the term to be tested, followed by the VS keyword and the error-term keyword. For example, to test the SEX BY FIELD term against the residual error term, specify

```
/DESIGN=SEX BY FIELD VS RESIDUAL
```

You can also create up to ten user-defined error terms by declaring any term in the model as an error term. To create such a term, specify the term followed by an equals sign and an integer from 1 to 10 on the DESIGN subcommand, as in

```
/DESIGN=SEX BY FIELD=1 FIELD VS 1 SEX VS 1
```

This command designates the SEX by FIELD term as error term 1, which is then used to test the sex and field main effects. To use a special error term in a test of significance, specify

```
term=n  VS  error-term keyword
```

or

```
term  VS  term=n
```

Any term present in the design but not specified on DESIGN is lumped into the residual error term. The default error term for all tests is WITHIN.

5.39
Specifying the Error Term

To specify the default error term for each between-subjects effect in subsequent designs, use the ERROR subcommand with the following keywords:

WITHIN	*Within-cells error term.* Alias W.
RESIDUAL	*Residual error term.* Alias R.
WITHIN+RESIDUAL	*Pooled within-class and residual error terms.* Alias WR or RW.
n	*Model term.*

You can designate a model term (*n*) as the default error term only if you explicitly define error term numbers on the DESIGN subcommand. If the specified error term number is not defined for a particular design, MANOVA does not carry out the significance tests involving that error term, although the parameter estimates and hypothesis sums of squares will be computed. For example, if the command

```
MANOVA BALOMEAN BALCMEAN SSTMEAN PP BY SEX(1,2) FIELD(1,3)
  /ERROR=1
  /DESIGN=SEX FIELD SEX BY FIELD=1
  /DESIGN=SEX FIELD.
```

is specified, no significance tests for SEX or FIELD are displayed for the second design, which contains no term defined as error term 1.

5.40
Specifying Within-Subjects Factors

The WSFACTORS subcommand is used for repeated measures analysis (see Chapter 6). It provides the names and number of levels for within-subjects factors when you use the multivariate data setup. For example, to supply a within-subjects factor name for DRUG1 to DRUG4, specify

```
MANOVA DRUG1 TO DRUG4
  /WSFACTORS=TRIAL(4).
```

Each name follows the naming conventions of SPSS/PC+, and each name must be unique. That is, a within-subjects factor name cannot be the same as that of any dependent variable, between-subjects factor, or covariate in the MANOVA job. The within-subjects factors exist only during the MANOVA analysis.

WSFACTORS must be the first subcommand after the MANOVA specification, and it can be specified only once per MANOVA command. You can specify up to 20 within-subjects and grouping factors altogether. Presence of a WSFACTORS subcommand invokes special repeated-measures processing. See Chapter 6 for a complete discussion of the WSFACTORS subcommand.

5.41
Specifying a Within-Subjects Model

The WSDESIGN subcommand specifies a within-subjects model and a within-subjects transformation matrix based on the ordering of the continuous variables and the levels of the within-subjects factors. See Chapter 6 for a complete discussion of the WSDESIGN subcommand.

5.42
Analyzing Doubly Multivariate Designs

You can use SPSS/PC+ MANOVA to analyze doubly multivariate repeated measures designs, in which subjects are measured on two or more responses on two or more occasions. When the data are entered using the multivariate setup, you can use the MEASURE subcommand to name the multivariate pooled results, as in

```
MANOVA TEMP1 TO TEMP6, WEIGHT1 TO WEIGHT6 BY GROUP(1,4)
  /WSFACTOR=AMPM(2), DAYS(3)
  /MEASURE=TEMP WEIGHT
  /WSDESIGN=AMPM DAYS, AMPM BY DAYS.
```

See Chapter 6 for a discussion of the MEASURE subcommand.

5.43
Specifying Linear Transformations

To specify linear transformations of the dependent variables and covariates, use the TRANSFORM subcommand. The first specification on TRANSFORM is the list of variables to be transformed in parentheses. Multiple variable lists can be used if they are separated by slashes and each list contains the same number of variables. MANOVA then applies the indicated transformation to each list. By default, MANOVA transforms all dependent variables and covariates. If a list is specified, however, only variables included in the list are transformed.

Any number of TRANSFORM subcommands may be specified in a MANOVA command. A TRANSFORM subcommand remains in effect until MANOVA encounters another one. Transformations are *not* cumulative; each transformation applies to the original variables.

Transformed variables should be renamed to avoid possible confusion with the original variables. If you use TRANSFORM but do not supply a RENAME subcommand, MANOVA names the transformed variables T1, T2, and so on. You must use the new names for the continuous variables in all subsequent subcommands except OMEANS.

Seven types of transformations are available. These are

DEVIATIONS(refcat)	*Compare a dependent variable to the means of the dependent variables in the list.* By default, MANOVA omits the comparison of the last variable to the list of variables. You can omit a variable other than the last by specifying the number of the omitted variable in parentheses.
DIFFERENCE	*Compare a dependent variable with the mean of the previous dependent variables in the list.* Also known as reverse Helmert.
HELMERT	*Compare a dependent variable to the means of the subsequent dependent variables in the list.*
SIMPLE(refcat)	*Compare each dependent variable with the last.* You can specify a variable other than the last as the reference variable by giving the number of the variable in parentheses.
REPEATED	*Compare contiguous variable pairs, thereby producing difference scores.*
POLYNOMIAL(metric)	*Fit orthogonal polynomials to the variables in the transformation list.* The default metric is equal spacing, but you can specify your own metric.
SPECIAL(matrix)	*Fit your own transformation matrix reflecting combinations of interest.* The matrix must be square, with the number of rows and columns equal to the number of variables being transformed.

For example, the subcommand

```
/TRANSFORM(SALES LEADS OPINIONS CONTRACT)=POLYNOMIAL
```

fits orthogonal polynomials to variables SALES, LEADS, OPINIONS, and CONTRACT, with equal spacing assumed.

The type of transformation can be preceded by the keywords CONTRAST, BASIS, or ORTHONORM. CONTRAST and BASIS are alternatives; ORTHONORM may be used with either CONTRAST or BASIS, or alone, which implies CONTRAST.

CONTRAST	*Generate the transformation matrix directly from the contrast matrix of the given type.* This is the default.
BASIS	*Generate the transformation matrix from the one-way basis corresponding to the specified CONSTRAST.*
ORTHONORM	*Orthonormalize the transformation matrix by rows before use.* MANOVA does not, by default, orthonormalize rows.

CONTRAST or BASIS can be used with any of the available methods for defining contrasts on the CONTRAST subcommand (see Section 5.47). On the TRANS-

FORM subcommand, keywords CONTRAST and BASIS are used to generate the transformed variables for later analysis, rather than simply to specify the contrasts on which significance testing and parameter estimation will be based.

For further information on the TRANSFORM subcommand, see Command Reference: MANOVA.

5.44
Renaming Transformed Variables

Use the RENAME subcommand to rename dependent variables and covariates after they have been transformed using TRANSFORM or WSFACTORS. The format is

```
/RENAME=newname1 newname2 ... newnamek
```

The number of new names must be equal to the number of dependent variables and covariates. For further information about RENAME, see Command Reference: MANOVA.

5.45
Specifying the Method

The METHOD subcommand is used to control some of the computational aspects of MANOVA. The following keywords are available:

MODELTYPE   *The model for parameter estimation.*
ESTIMATION   *The method for estimating parameters.*
SSTYPE   *The method of partitioning sums of squares.*

Each keyword has associated options as listed below. These options are specified in parentheses after the keyword.

The options available on **MODELTYPE** are

MEANS   *Use the cell-means model for parameter estimation.*
OBSERVATIONS   *Use the observations model for parameter estimation.*

If continuous variables are specified on the DESIGN subcommand, MANOVA automatically uses the observations model. Otherwise, MEANS is the default. Since the observations model is computationally less efficient than the means model and the same estimates are obtained, the observations model should be used only when it is appropriate.

Up to four keywords, one from each of the following pairs, may be specified on **ESTIMATION**. The first keyword in each pair is the default.

QR/CHOLESKY   QR estimates parameters using the Householder transformations to effect an orthogonal decomposition of the design matrix. A less expensive (and sometimes less accurate) procedure is the Cholesky method, selected by specifying the alternative CHOLESKY keyword.

NOBALANCED/BALANCED   NOBALANCED assumes that the design is unbalanced. If your design is balanced and orthogonal, request balanced processing by specifying the alternative BALANCED keyword. BALANCED should be specified only when no cell is empty, the cell-means model applies, all cell sizes are equal, and the contrast type for each factor is orthogonal.

NOLASTRES/LASTRES   NOLASTRES calculates sums of squares for all effects. The alternative LASTRES keyword computes the last effect in the design by subtracting the between-groups sums of squares and cross-products from the total sums of squares and cross-products. When applicable, LASTRES can significantly decrease processing costs. Parameter estimates will not be available for the effect whose sum of squares was computed by subtraction. If LASTRES is specified, you may not use the POOL specification on

DESIGN to include continuous variables in the last effect (see Section 5.36). Do not use LASTRES unless you have specified SEQUENTIAL for the SSTYPE parameter (see below). It should not be used with UNIQUE (the default) since component sums of squares do not add up to the total sum of squares in a UNIQUE decomposition.

CONSTANT/NOCONSTANT   CONSTANT requests that the model contain a constant term. The alternative keyword NOCONSTANT suppresses the constant term. NOCONSTANT can be overridden on a subsequent DESIGN subcommand (see Section 5.36).

The following options may be specified on **SSTYPE:**

UNIQUE   *Requests sums of squares corresponding to unweighted combinations of means* (the regression approach). These sums of squares are not orthogonal unless the design is balanced. SSTYPE(UNIQUE) is the default.

SEQUENTIAL   *Requests an orthogonal decomposition of the sums of squares.* A term is corrected for all terms to its left in a given DESIGN specification, and confounded with all terms to its right.

For example, the subcommand

```
/METHOD=ESTIMATION(CHOLESKY,LASTRES) SSTYPE(SEQUENTIAL)
```

requests the less-expensive CHOLESKY estimation method, with the sums of squares for the last effect calculated by subtraction. SEQUENTIAL decomposition is requested, as is required for LASTRES. We assume that parameter estimates are not needed for the last effect and that the POOL keyword will not appear in the last effect on a DESIGN statement for this METHOD subcommand.

5.46
Subdividing the Degrees of Freedom

The degrees of freedom associated with a factor can be subdivided by using a PARTITION subcommand. Specify the factor name in parentheses, an equals sign, and a list of integers in parentheses indicating the degrees of freedom for each partition. For example, if EDUCATN has six values (five degrees of freedom), it can be partitioned into single degrees of freedom by specifying

```
/PARTITION(EDUCATN)=(1,1,1,1,1)
```

or, more briefly, by specifying

```
/PARTITION(EDUCATN)=(5*1)
```

Since the default degrees-of-freedom partition consists of the single degrees-of-freedom partition, these subcommands are equivalent to

```
/PARTITION(EDUCATN)
```

The subcommand

```
/PARTITION(EDUCATN)=(2,2,1)
```

partitions EDUCATN into three subdivisions, the first two with 2 degrees of freedom and the third with 1 degree of freedom. This subcommand can also be specified as

```
/PARTITION(EDUCATN)=(2,2)
```

since MANOVA automatically generates a final partition with the remaining degree(s) of freedom (1 in this case). If you were to then specify ED(1) on the DESIGN subcommand, it would refer to the first partition, which in this case has 2 degrees of freedom.

5.47
Specifying the Contrasts

The contrasts desired for a factor are specified by the CONTRAST subcommand. Specify the factor name in parentheses, followed by an equals sign and a contrast keyword. The constrast keyword can be any of the following:

DEVIATION *The deviations from the grand mean.* This is the default.

DIFFERENCE *Difference or reverse Helmert contrast.* Compare levels of a factor with the mean of the previous levels of the factor.

SIMPLE *Simple contrasts.* Compare each level of a factor to the last level.

HELMERT *Helmert contrasts.* Compare levels of a factor with the mean of the subsequent levels of the factor.

POLYNOMIAL *Orthogonal polynomial contrasts.*

REPEATED *Adjacent levels of a factor.*

SPECIAL *A user-defined contrast.* See the example in Section 5.36.

If you want to see the parameter estimates of the specified contrast use PRINT=PARAM(ESTIM).

5.48
Specifying Printed Output

The PRINT and NOPRINT subcommands control the output produced by MANOVA. PRINT requests specified output, while NOPRINT suppresses it. On both PRINT and NOPRINT, you specify keywords followed by the keyword options in parentheses. For example, the command

```
MANOVA SALES BY TVAD RADIOAD MAGAD NEWSPAD(2,5)
 /PRINT=CELLINFO(MEANS).
```

requests the display of cell means of SALES for all combinations of values of TVAD, RADIOAD, MAGAD, and NEWSPAD.

The specifications available on PRINT and NOPRINT are listed below, followed by the options available for each.

CELLINFO *Cells information.*

HOMOGENEITY *Homogeneity of variance tests.*

DESIGN *Design information.*

ERROR *Error matrices.*

SIGNIF *Significance tests.*

PARAMETERS *Estimated parameters.*

TRANSFORM *Transformation matrix.*

The options for **CELLINFO** are

MEANS *Cell means, standard deviations, and counts.*

SSCP *Cell sums-of-squares and cross-products matrices.*

COV *Cell variance-covariance matrices.*

COR *Cell correlation matrices.*

The options for **HOMOGENEITY** are

BARTLETT *Bartlett-Box F test.*

COCHRAN *Cochran's C.*

BOXM *Box's M (multivariate case only).*

The options for **DESIGN** are

ONEWAY	*The one-way basis for each factor.*
OVERALL	*The overall reduced-model basis (design matrix).*
DECOMP	*The QR/CHOLESKY decomposition of the design.*
BIAS	*Contamination coefficients displaying the bias present in the design.*
SOLUTION	*Coefficients of the linear combination of the cell means being tested.*

The options available for **ERROR** are

SSCP	*Error sums-of-squares and cross-product matrix.*
COV	*Error variance-covariance matrix.*
COR	*Error correlation matrix and standard deviations.*
STDDEV	*Error standard deviations (univariate case).*

If ERROR(COR) is specified in the multivariate case, MANOVA automatically displays the determinant and Bartlett's test of sphericity.

The options for **SIGNIF** are

MULTIV	*Multivariate F tests for group differences (default display).*
EIGEN	*Eigenvalues of $S_h S_e^{-1}$.*
DIMENR	*A dimension-reduction analysis.*
UNIV	*Univariate F tests (default display).*
HYPOTH	*The hypothesis SSCP matrix.*
STEPDOWN	*Roy-Bargmann step-down F tests.*
AVERF	*An averaged F test. Use with repeated measures (default display for repeated measures).*
BRIEF	*A shortened multivariate output. BRIEF overrides any of the preceding SIGNIF keywords.*
AVONLY	*Averaged results only. Use with repeated measures (overrides other SIGNIF keywords).*
SINGLEDF	*Single-degree-of-freedom listings of effects.*

When BRIEF is used, the output consists of a table similar in appearance to a univariate ANOVA table, but with the generalized F and Wilks' lambda replacing the univariate F.

The options available for **PARAMETERS** are

ESTIM	*The estimates themselves, along with their standard errors, t tests, and confidence intervals.*
ORTHO	*The orthogonal estimates of parameters used to produce the sums of squares.*
COR	*Correlations between the parameters.*
NEGSUM	*For main effects, the negative sum of the other parameters (representing the parameter for the omitted category).*

Parameters are not displayed by default.

TRANSFORM produces the transformation matrix, which shows how MANOVA transforms variables when a multivariate repeated measures design and a WSFACTORS subcommand are used (see Chapter 6). There are no subspecifications for PRINT=TRANSFORM.

5.49
Specifying Principal Components Analysis

The PCOMPS subcommand produces a principal components analysis of the error sums-of-squares and cross-products matrices in a multivariate design. The options for the PCOMPS subcommand are

COR	*Principal components analysis of the error correlation matrix.*
COV	*Principal components analysis of the error variance-covariance matrix.*
ROTATE(rottype)	*Rotation of the principal component loadings. For rottype, substitute VARIMAX, EQUAMAX, QUARTIMAX, or NOROTATE.*
NCOMP(n)	*The number of principal components to be rotated. Specify n, or let n default to all components extracted.*
MINEIGEN(eigcut)	*The eigenvalue cutoff value for principal components extraction.*

5.50
Specifying Canonical Analyses

The DISCRIM subcommand requests a canonical analysis of dependent and independent variables in multivariate analyses. If the independent variables are continuous, MANOVA produces a canonical correlation analysis; if they are categorical, MANOVA produces a canonical discriminant analysis. Available options are

RAW	*Raw discriminant function coefficients.*
STAN	*Standardized discriminant function coefficients.*
ESTIM	*Effect estimates in discriminant function space.*
COR	*Correlations between the dependent and canonical variables defined by the discriminant functions.*
ROTATE(rottyp)	*Rotation of the matrix of correlations between dependent and canonical variates. For rottype, specify VARIMAX, EQUAMAX, or QUARTIMAX.*
ALPHA(alpha)	*The significance level for the canonical variate. The default is 0.15.*

MANOVA does not perform rotation unless there are at least two significant canonical variates.

5.51
Producing Tables of Combined Observed Means

OMEANS produces tables of combined observed means. The specifications on OMEANS may consist of the keywords VARIABLES, TABLES, or both. With no specifications, the OMEANS subcommand produces a table of observed means for all of the continuous variables. The keyword VARIABLES allows you to enter, in parentheses, names of the dependent variables and covariates for which means are desired. When you explicitly specify variables on the OMEANS subcommand, you must also enter a TABLES specification as described below, as in

```
MANOVA BALOMEAN BALCMEAN SSTMEAN PP BY SEX(1,2) FIELD(1,3)
 /OMEANS VARIABLES(BALOMEAN) TABLES(SEX BY FIELD).
```

If the variable list is omitted, MANOVA displays combined means for all variables. MANOVA also displays both weighted and unweighted means. Tables of observed means are displayed if the keyword TABLES is used, with a list of *factors* by which the tables should be displayed. The subcommand

```
 /OMEANS TABLES(SEX,FIELD,SEX BY FIELD)
```

results in three tables, one collapsed over SEX, one collapsed over FIELD, and one showing the observed means themselves.

When a transformation has been requested with TRANSFORM or with WSFACTORS (described in repeated-measures MANOVA), OMEANS produces means of the original, untransformed, variables. Always use the original variable names in the VARIABLES specification on OMEANS.

5.52
Computing Predicted and Adjusted Means

PMEANS computes predicted and adjusted (for covariates) means, which are displayed for each error term in each design. VARIABLES and TABLES are two specifications that can be used; the format is the same as that for OMEANS. For designs with covariates and multiple error terms, use the ERROR(error) specification to indicate which error term's regression coefficients to use in calculating the predicted means. The format for specifying an error term with ERROR is the same as for the ERROR subcommand (see Section 5.39). If no error term is given when one is needed, MANOVA will not calculate predicted means. Predicted means are also suppressed if the last term is being calculated by subtraction (METHOD=ESTIM(LASTRES)) or if the design contains the MUPLUS keyword (see Section 5.36).

If the WSFACTORS subcommand is used to specify a repeated measures design (see Chapter 6), the means of the orthonormalized variables are displayed when PMEANS is used. If the TRANSFORM or WSFACTORS subcommands are used for a design, PMEANS displays the means of the transformed variables. Therefore the VARIABLES specification on PMEANS, unlike that on OMEANS, uses the names of the *transformed* variables in analyses which use the WSFACTORS or TRANSFORM subcommand. These are either the names you specify on the RENAME subcommand, or the names supplied by SPSS/PC+ if there is no RENAME subcommand (T1, T2, etc.). The keyword PLOT on the PMEANS subcommand produces a group-order plot of the estimated, adjusted, and observed means for each dependent variable, and a group-order plot of the mean residuals for each dependent variable. When there is more than one factor in the analysis, the rightmost factor changes most quickly.

5.53
Producing Residual Listings and Plots

The RESIDUALS subcommand produces listings or plots of predicted values and residuals. Casewise listings of residuals are produced by the keyword CASE-WISE. This output includes, for each case, the observed and predicted value of each dependent variable, the residual, and the standardized residual. Like PMEANS, RESIDUALS requires an ERROR specification for designs with covariates and multiple error terms, as in

```
MANOVA SALES BY TVAD RADIOAD(2,5) WITH PCTBUSNS
 /RESIDUALS=CASEWISE ERROR(WITHIN)
 /DESIGN TVAD VS 1,RADIOAD VS 1, TVAD BY RADIOAD = 1 VS WITHIN.
```

No output results if the error term is not specified when needed. Predicted observations are suppressed if the last term is calculated by subtraction (METHOD=ESTIM(LASTRES)) or if the DESIGN subcommand contains the MUPLUS keyword. If the designated error term does not exist for a given design, no predicted values or residuals are calculated.

The keyword PLOT on the RESIDUALS subcommand prints the following plots: observed values vs. standardized residuals, predicted values vs. standardized residuals, case number vs. standardized residuals, a normal probability plot, and a detrended normal probability plot for the standardized residuals.

5.54
Producing Plots

Plots are requested with the PLOT subcommand. The following keywords are available:

CELLPLOTS *Plot cell statistics,* including a plot of cell means vs. cell variances, a plot of cell means vs. cell standard deviations, and a histogram of cell means, for each of the continuous variables (dependent variables and covariates) defined in the MANOVA specification.

BOXPLOTS *Plot a boxplot* for each continuous variable.

NORMAL *Plot a normal plot and a detrended normal plot* for each continuous variable.

STEMLEAF *Plot a stem-and-leaf display* for each continuous variable.

ZCORR *Plot a half-normal plot* of the within-cells correlations between the dependent variables in a multivariate analysis.

If there is not enough memory to produce a plot, MANOVA displays a warning and does not produce the plot.

5.55
Reading and Writing Matrix Materials

MANOVA can write out a set of matrix materials, which it can then use for subsequent jobs. The WRITE subcommand is used to write these materials and the READ subcommand to read them. The WRITE subcommand has the format

/WRITE

This sends results to the "results file," which by default is named SPSS.PRC.

The READ subcommand reads the materials written by using WRITE and has the format

/READ

READ is used in conjunction with the DATA LIST MATRIX statement. See Command Reference: DATA LIST Matrix Materials for details.

5.56
Missing Value Treatment

By default, missing values for any of the variables named in the MANOVA specification are excluded from the analysis. To include user-missing values in the analysis, enter the subcommand MISSING=INCLUDE. The alternative specification, MISSING=LISTWISE, is the default. The missing subcommand can be used only once.

The missing values for factors must be within the ranges specified on the MANOVA variables specification in order to be included in the analysis.

5.57
Annotated Example   The following SPSS/PC+ commands produced the output in Figures 5.15b, 5.15c, 5.15d, 5.15f, and 5.16.

```
DATA LIST FREE/X1 TO X22.
IF    (X1 LT 200) SEX=1.
IF    (X1 GE 200) SEX=2.
COMPUTE BALOMEAN=(X10+X11)/2.
COMPUTE  BALCMEAN=(X12+X13)/2.
COMPUTE SSTMEAN=(X14+X15+X16)/3.
COMPUTE PP=(X17+X18+X19+X20+X21+X22)/6.
BEGIN DATA.
lines of data
END DATA.
MANOVA BALOMEAN BALCMEAN SSTMEAN PP BY SEX(1,2)
 /DISCRIM=RAW STAN CORR ESTIM
 /PRINT=SIGNIF(DIMENR) PARAMETERS(ESTIM)
 /DESIGN.
FINISH.
```

• The DATA LIST command reads in the variables in freefield format.

• The IF commands set up the variable SEX.

• The COMPUTE statements compute the dependent variables as averages of the original variables.

• The MANOVA command begins by specifying BALOMEAN, BALCMEAN, SST-MEAN and PP as the dependent variables and SEX as a factor. The DISCRIM subcommand requests a canonical analysis of the dependent and independent variables. The PRINT subcommand requests parameter estimates and a dimension-reduction analysis.

Contents

Chapter 6   Storing Memories: Repeated Measures Analysis of Variance

Anyone who experiences difficulties sorting through piles of output, stacks of bills, or assorted journals must be awed by the brain's ability to organize, update, and maintain the memories of a lifetime. It seems incredible that someone can instantly recall the name of his first-grade teacher. On the other hand, that same person might spend an entire morning searching for a misplaced shoe.

Memory has two components—storage and retrieval. Many different theories explaining its magical operation have been proposed (for example, see Eysenck, 1977). In this chapter, an experiment concerned with latency—the length of time required to search a list of items in memory—is examined.

Bacon (1980) conducted an experiment in which subjects were instructed to memorize a number. They were then given a "probe" digit and told to indicate whether it was included in the memorized number. One hypothesis of interest is the relationship between the number of digits in the memorized number and the latency. Is more time required to search through a longer number than a shorter one? Twenty-four subjects were tested on 60 memorized numbers, 20 each of two, three, and four digits in random order. The average latencies, in milliseconds, were calculated for each subject on the two-, three-, and four-digit numbers. Thus, three scores are recorded for each subject, one for each of the number lengths. The probe digit was included in the memorized number in a random position.

6.1
REPEATED
MEASURES

When the same variable is measured on several occasions for each subject, it is a *repeated measures* design. The simplest repeated measures design is one in which two measurements are obtained for each subject—such as pre- and post-test scores. These type of data are usually analyzed with a paired *t* test.

The advantages of repeated measurements are obvious. Besides requiring fewer experimental units (in this study, human subjects), they provide a control on their differences. That is, variability due to differences between subjects can be eliminated from the experimental error. Less attention has been focused on some of the difficulties that may be encountered with repeated measurements. Broadly, these problems can be classified as the carry-over effect, the latent effect, and the order or learning effect.

The carry-over effect occurs when a new treatment is administered before the effect of a previous treatment has worn off. For example, Drug B is given while Drug A still has an effect. The carry-over effect can usually be controlled by increasing the time between treatments. In addition, special designs that allow one to assess directly the carry-over effects are available (Cochran & Cox, 1957).

The latent effect—when one treatment may activate the dormant effect of the previous treatment, or interact with the previous treatment—is not so easily countered. This effect is especially problematic in drug trials and should be considered before using a repeated measures experimental design. Usually, if a latency effect is suspected, a repeated measures design should not be used.

The learning effect occurs when the response may improve merely by repetition of a task, independent of any treatment. For example, subjects' scores on a test may improve each time they take the test. Thus, treatments that are administered later may appear to improve performance, even though they have no effect. In such situations it is important to pay particular attention to the sequencing of treatments. Learning effects can be assessed by including a control group that performs the same tasks repeatedly without receiving any treatment.

6.2
Describing the Data

In a repeated measures experiment, as well as any other, the first step is to obtain descriptive statistics. These provide some idea of the distributions of the variables as well as their average values and dispersions. Figure 6.2a contains cell means and standard deviations, as well as individual confidence intervals, for the variables P2DIGIT, P3DIGIT, and P4DIGIT. The shortest average latency time (520 milliseconds) was observed for the two-digit numbers (P2DIGIT). The longest (581 milliseconds) was observed for the four-digit numbers. A plot of the mean latency times against the number of digits is shown in Figure 6.2b. Note that there appears to be a linear relationship between the latency time and the number of digits in the memorized number.

Figure 6.2a   Means and standard deviations

```
SET WIDTH=WIDE.
MANOVA P2DIGIT P3DIGIT P4DIGIT
  /PRINT=CELLINFO (MEANS)
  /DESIGN.
```

```
Cell Means and Standard Deviations
Variable .. P2DIGIT
                            Mean    Std. Dev.      N    95 percent Conf. Interval
For entire sample          520.583   131.366      24     465.112     576.054
 - - - - - - - - - -
Variable .. P3DIGIT
                            Mean    Std. Dev.      N    95 percent Conf. Interval
For entire sample          560.000   118.776      24     509.845     610.155
 - - - - - - - - - -
Variable .. P4DIGIT
                            Mean    Std. Dev.      N    95 percent Conf. Interval
For entire sample          581.250   117.325      24     531.708     630.792
 - - - - - - - - - -
```

Figure 6.2b   Plot of means from procedure PLOT

```
COMPUTE CONS=1.
AGGREGATE OUTFILE=*
 /BREAK=CONS
 /MPDIG2 MPDIG3 MPDIG4=MEAN(P2DIGIT P3DIGIT P4DIGIT).
COMPUTE C2=2.
COMPUTE C3=3.
COMPUTE C4=4.
PLOT SYMBOLS='***'/VSIZE=15/HSIZE=30
 /FORMAT=OVERLAY
 /TITLE 'MEAN LATENCY TIMES'
 /HORIZONTAL 'NUMBER OF DIGITS'/VERTICAL 'MEAN LATENCY'
 /PLOT=MPDIG2 WITH C2;MPDIG3 WITH C3;MPDIG4 WITH C4.
```

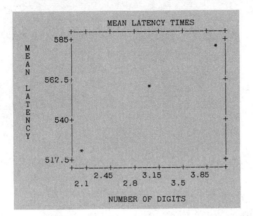

The stem-and-leaf plot of latencies for the P4DIGIT is shown in Figure 6.2c. The corresponding normal probability plot is shown in Figure 6.2d. From this, it appears that the values are somewhat more "bunched" than one would expect if they were normally distributed. The bunching of the data might occur because of limitations in the accuracy of the measurements. Similar plots can be obtained for the other two variables.

Figure 6.2c   Stem-and-leaf plot for P4DIGIT

```
MANOVA P2DIGIT P3DIGIT P4DIGIT
 /PLOT=STEMLEAF
 /DESIGN.
```

```
Stem-and-leaf display for variable .. P4DIGIT

    3 . 9
    4 . 347
    5 . 01111225558
    6 . 2889
    7 . 0125
    8 . 6
```

Figure 6.2d   Normal probability plot for P4DIGIT

```
MANOVA P2DIGIT P3DIGIT P4DIGIT
  /PLOT=NORMAL
  /DESIGN.
```

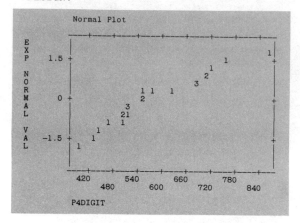

6.3
Analyzing Differences

Since multiple observations are made on the same experimental unit in a repeated measures design, special procedures that incorporate dependencies within an experimental unit must be used. For example, in the paired *t* test design, instead of analyzing each score separately, we analyze the difference between the two scores. When there are more than two scores for a subject, the analysis becomes somewhat more complicated. For example, if each subject receives three treatments, there are three pairwise differences: the difference between the first two treatments, the difference between the second two treatments, and the difference between the first and third treatments.

Performing three paired *t* tests of the differences may seem to be the simplest analysis, but it is not, for several reasons, the best strategy. First, the three *t* tests are not statistically independent, since they involve the same means in overlapping combinations. Some overall protection against calling too many differences significant is needed, especially as the number of treatments increases. Second, since there are three separate *t* tests, a single test of the hypothesis that there is no difference between the treatments is not available.

There are several approaches for circumventing such problems in the analysis of data from repeated measures experiments. These approaches are described in the remainder of this chapter.

6.4
Transforming the Variables

To test the null hypothesis that the mean latencies are the same for the three digit lengths, the original three variables must be "transformed." That is, instead of analyzing the original three variables, we analyze linear combinations of their differences. (In the paired t-test, the transformation is the difference between the values for each subject or pair.) For certain methods of analysis, these linear combinations, sometimes called *contrasts,* must be chosen so that they are statistically independent (orthogonal) and so that the sum of the squared coefficients is 1 (normalized). Such contrasts are termed *orthonormalized.* The number of statistically independent contrasts that can be formed for a factor is one less than the number of levels of the factor. In addition, a contrast corresponding to the overall mean (the constant term in the model) is always formed. For this example, this contrast is

CONTRAST 1 = P2DIGIT + P3DIGIT + P4DIGIT $\qquad$ **Equation 6.4a**

There are many types of transformations available. One is the difference contrast, which compares each level of a factor to the average of the levels that precede it. (Another transformation, orthogonal polynomials, is discussed in Section 6.12.)

The first difference contrast for the DIGIT factor is

CONTRAST 2 = P3DIGIT − P2DIGIT $\qquad$ **Equation 6.4b**

The second difference contrast is

CONTRAST 3 = 2 × P4DIGIT − P3DIGIT − P2DIGIT $\qquad$ **Equation 6.4c**

The contrasts can be normalized by dividing each contrast by the square root of the sum of the coefficients squared. The contrast for the overall mean is divided by

$$\sqrt{3}$$ $\qquad$ **Equation 6.4d**

and the second difference contrast is divided by

$$\sqrt{2^2 + 1^2 + 1^2} = \sqrt{6}$$ $\qquad$ **Equation 6.4e**

Figure 6.4 shows the orthonormalized transformation matrix from MANOVA for creating new variables from P2DIGIT, P3DIGIT, and P4DIGIT with the difference transformation. A column contains the coefficients for a particular contrast. Each row corresponds to one of the original variables. Thus, the first linear combination is

CONSTANT = 0.57735(P2DIGIT + P3DIGIT + P4DIGIT) $\qquad$ **Equation 6.4f**

This new variable is, for each case, the sum of the values of the three original variables, multiplied by 0.57735. Again, the coefficients are chosen so that the sum of their squared values is 1. The next two variables are the normalized difference contrasts for the DIGIT effect.

Figure 6.4 Orthonormalized transformation matrix for difference contrasts

```
SET WIDTH=WIDE.
MANOVA P2DIGIT P3DIGIT P4DIGIT
  /WSFACTORS=DIGIT(3)
  /CONTRAST(DIGIT)=DIFFERENCE
  /RENAME=CONS DIF12 DIF12V3
  /WSDESIGN
  /PRINT=TRANSFORM
  /DESIGN.
```

```
Orthonormalized Transformation Matrix (Transposed)

             CONS       DIF12      DIF12V3

P2DIGIT     .57735     -.70711     -.40825
P3DIGIT     .57735      .70711     -.40825
P4DIGIT     .57735     0.0          .81650
```

What do these new variables represent? The first variable, the sum of the original variables, is the average response over all treatments. It measures latency times over all digit lengths. The hypothesis that the average response, the constant, is equal to 0 is based on this variable. The second two contrasts together represent the treatment (DIGIT) effect. These two contrasts are used to test hypotheses about differences in latencies for the three digit lengths.

6.5
Testing for Differences

In Chapter 5, analysis of variance models with more than one dependent variable are described. The same techniques can be used for repeated measures data. For example, we can use the single-sample tests to test whether particular sets of the transformed variables in the Bacon experiment have means of 0. If the number of digits does not affect latency times, the mean values of the two contrasts for the DIGIT effect are expected to be 0. Different hypotheses are tested using different transformed variables.

6.6
Testing the Constant Effect

When a repeated measures design is specified in SPSS/PC+ MANOVA, several hypotheses are automatically tested. The first hypothesis is that the overall mean latency time is 0. It is based on the first transformed variable, which corresponds to the CONSTANT effect.

To help identify results, MANOVA prints the names of the transformed variables used to test a hypothesis. In this example, we assigned new names to the transformed variables within the MANOVA procedure (see Figure 6.4). These new names will appear on the output. The first transformed variable is renamed to CONS, the second to DIF12, and the third to DIF12V3. If new names are not assigned to the transformed variables, MANOVA assigns the names T1, T2, and so on, to the transformed variables.

Figure 6.6 shows the explanation displayed when the CONSTANT effect is tested. The column labeled "Variates" indicates which transformed variables are involved in the test of a particular effect. Since the test for the constant is based only on variable CONS, its name appears in that column. When there are no covariates in the analysis, the column labeled "Covariates" is empty, as shown. The note below the table is a reminder that analyses are based on the transformed variables, and that the particular analysis is for the CONSTANT effect.

Figure 6.6   Renamed variables used in the analysis

```
MANOVA P2DIGIT P3DIGIT P4DIGIT
  /WSFACTORS=DIGIT(3)
  /CONTRAST(DIGIT)=DIFFERENCE
  /RENAME=CONS DIF12 DIF12V3
  /WSDESIGN
  /PRINT=TRANSFORM
  /DESIGN.
```

```
Order of Variables for Analysis

  Variates      Covariates

   CONS

  1 Dependent Variable
  0 Covariates

- - - - - - - - - -
Note..  TRANSFORMED variables are in the variates column.
        These TRANSFORMED variables correspond to the
        Between-subject effects.
```

6.7
The Analysis of Variance Table

Since the test for the constant is based on a single variable, the results are displayed in the usual univariate analysis of variance table (Figure 6.7a). The large F value and the small observed significance level indicate that the hypothesis that the constant is 0 is rejected. This finding is of limited importance here, since we do not expect the time required to search a number to be 0. Tests about the constant might be of interest if the original variables are difference scores—change from baseline for example—since the test of the constant would then correspond to the test that there has been no overall change from baseline.

Figure 6.7a   Analysis of variance table

```
MANOVA P2DIGIT P3DIGIT P4DIGIT
 /WSFACTORS=DIGIT(3)
 /CONTRAST(DIGIT)=DIFFERENCE
 /RENAME=CONS DIF12 DIF12V3
 /WSDESIGN
 /PRINT=PARAMETERS(ESTIM)
 /DESIGN.
```

Tests of Significance for CONS using UNIQUE sums of squares Source of Variation	SS	DF	MS	F	Sig of F
WITHIN CELLS	995411.11	23	43278.74		
CONSTANT	22093520.22	1	22093520	510.49	.000

After the ANOVA table, SPSS/PC+ MANOVA prints parameter estimates and tests of the hypotheses that the individual transformed variables have means of 0. These are shown in Figure 6.7b. For the CONSTANT effect, the parameter estimate is nothing more than

$$0.57735 \times (520.58 + 560.00 + 581.25)$$

Equation 6.7

where the numbers within the parentheses are just the means of the original three variables shown in Figure 6.2a. The 0.57735 is the value used to normalize the contrast from Figure 6.4. The test of the hypothesis that the true value of the first parameter is 0 is equivalent to the test of the hypothesis that the constant is 0. Therefore, the t value printed for the test is the square root of the F value from the ANOVA table (the square root of 510.49 = 22.59). (When the t statistic is squared it is equal to an F statistic with one degree of freedom for the numerator and the same degrees of freedom for the denominator as the t statistic.)

Figure 6.7b   Parameter estimates

Estimates for CONS CONSTANT						
Parameter	Coeff.	Std. Err.	t-Value	Sig. t	Lower -95% CL-	Upper
1	959.459922	42.46506	22.59410	0.0	871.61426	1047.30558

**6.8
Testing the Digit Effect**

The hypothesis of interest in this study is whether latency time depends on the number of digits in the memorized number. As shown in Figure 6.8a, this test is based on the two transformed variables, labeled DIF12 and DIF12V3. Figure 6.8b contains the multivariate tests of the hypothesis that the means of these two variables are 0. In this situation, all multivariate criteria are equivalent and lead to rejection of the hypothesis that the number of digits does not affect latency time.

Figure 6.8a   Transformed variables used

```
MANOVA P2DIGIT P3DIGIT P4DIGIT
 /WSFACTORS=DIGIT(3)
 /CONTRAST(DIGIT)=DIFFERENCE
 /RENAME=CONS DIF12 DIF12V3
 /WSDESIGN
 /PRINT=TRANSFORM
 /DESIGN.
```

```
Order of Variables for Analysis

  Variates        Covariates

  DIF12
  DIF12V3

  2 Dependent Variables
  0 Covariates

 _ _ _ _ _ _ _ _ _
Note.. TRANSFORMED variables are in the variates column.
       These TRANSFORMED variables correspond to the
       'DIGIT' WITHIN-SUBJECT effect.
```

Figure 6.8b Multivariate hypothesis tests

```
EFFECT .. DIGIT
Multivariate Tests of Significance (S = 1, M = 0, N = 10 )

Test Name          Value    Approx. F Hypoth. DF    Error DF  Sig. of F

Pillais           .60452    16.81439      2.00       22.00      .000
Hotellings       1.52858    16.81439      2.00       22.00      .000
Wilks             .39548    16.81439      2.00       22.00      .000
Roys              .60452
```

Univariate F tests for the individual transformed variables are shown in Figure 6.8c. The first row corresponds to a test of the hypothesis that there is no difference in average latency times for numbers consisting of two digits and those consisting of three. (This is equivalent to a one-sample t test that the mean of the second transformed variable DIF12 is 0.) The second row of Figure 6.8c provides a test of the hypothesis that there is no difference between the average response to numbers with two and three digits and numbers with four digits. The average value of this contrast is also significantly different from 0, since the observed significance level is less than 0.0005. (See Section 6.12 for an example of a different contrast type.)

Figure 6.8c Univariate hypothesis tests

```
MANOVA P2DIGIT P3DIGIT P4DIGIT
 /WSFACTORS=DIGIT(3)
 /CONTRAST(DIGIT)=DIFFERENCE
 /RENAME=CONS DIF12 DIF12V3
 /WSDESIGN
 /PRINT=SIGNIF(UNIV)
 /DESIGN.
```

```
Univariate F-tests with (1,23) D. F.

Variable   Hypoth. SS    Error SS Hypoth. MS    Error MS          F  Sig. of F

DIF12     18644.0833  19800.9167 18644.0833  860.90942   21.65627      .000
DIF12V3   26841.3611  22774.3056 26841.3611  990.18720   27.10736      .000
```

To estimate the magnitudes of differences among the digit lengths, we can examine the values of each contrast. These are shown in Figure 6.8d. The column labeled Coeff is the average value for the normalized contrast. As shown in Section 6.4, the second contrast is 0.707 times the difference between two- and three-digit numbers, which is $0.707 \times (520.58 - 560.00) = 27.87$, the value shown in Figure 6.8d. To obtain an estimate of the absolute difference between mean response to two and three digits, the parameter estimate must be divided by 0.707. This value is 39.42. Again, the t value for the hypothesis that the contrast is 0 is equivalent to the square root of the F value from the univariate analysis of variance table.

Figure 6.8d Estimates for contrasts

```
Estimates for DIF12
DIGIT

Parameter      Coeff.  Std. Err.    t-Value    Sig. t  Lower -95% CL- Upper

       1   27.8717923   5.98926    4.65363      .000    15.48207    40.26152
- - - - - - - - - -
Estimates for DIF12V3
DIGIT

Parameter      Coeff.  Std. Err.    t-Value    Sig. t  Lower -95% CL- Upper

       1   33.4423391   6.42322    5.20647      .000    20.15489    46.72979
```

Similarly, the parameter estimate for the third contrast, the normalized difference between the average of two and three digits and four digits, is 33.44. The actual value of the difference is 40.96 (33.44 divided by 0.8165). The t value, the ratio of the parameter estimate to its standard error, is 5.206, which when squared equals the F value in Figure 6.8c. The t-values are the same for normalized and nonnormalized contrasts.

The parameter estimates and univariate F tests help identify which individual contrasts contribute to overall differences. However, the observed significance levels for the individual parameters are not adjusted for the fact that several comparisons are being made (see Miller, 1981; Burns, 1984). Thus, the significance levels should serve only as guides for identifying potentially important differences.

6.9
Averaged Univariate Results

The individual univariate tests can be "pooled" to obtain the averaged F test shown in Figure 6.9. The entries in Figure 6.9 are obtained from Figure 6.8c by summing the hypothesis and error sums of squares and the associated degrees of freedom. In this example, the averaged F test also leads us to reject the hypothesis that average latency times do not differ for numbers of different lengths. This is the same F statistic obtained by specifying a repeated measures design as a "mixed-model" univariate analysis of variance (Winer, 1971).

Figure 6.9   Averaged univariate hypothesis tests

```
MANOVA P2DIGIT P3DIGIT P4DIGIT
 /WSFACTORS=DIGIT(3)
 /CONTRAST(DIGIT)=DIFFERENCE
 /RENAME=CONS DIF12 DIF12V3
 /WSDESIGN
 /PRINT=SIGNIF(AVERF)
 /DESIGN.
```

AVERAGED Tests of Significance for MEAS.1 using UNIQUE sums of squares					
Source of Variation	SS	DF	MS	F	Sig of F
WITHIN CELLS	42575.22	46	925.55		
DIGIT	45485.44	2	22742.72	24.57	.000

6.10
Choosing Multivariate or Univariate Results

In the previous section, we saw that hypothesis tests for the DIGIT effect could be based on multivariate criteria such as Wilks' lambda, or on the averaged univariate F tests. When both approaches lead to similar results, choosing between them is not of much importance. However, there are situations in which the multivariate and univariate approaches lead to different results and the question of which is appropriate arises.

The multivariate approach considers the measurements on a subject to be a sample from a multivariate normal distribution, and makes no assumption about the characteristics of the variance-covariance matrix. The univariate (sometimes called *mixed-model*) approach requires certain assumptions about the variance-covariance matrix. If these conditions are met, especially for small sample sizes, the univariate approach is more powerful than the multivariate approach. That is, it is more likely to detect differences when they exist.

Modifications of the univariate results when the assumptions are violated have also been proposed. These corrected results are approximate and are based on the adjustment of the degrees of freedom of the F ratio (Greenhouse-Geisser, 1959; Huynh & Feldt, 1976). The significance levels for the corrected tests will always be larger than for the uncorrected. Thus, if the uncorrected test is not significant, there is no need to calculate corrected values.

6.11
Assumptions Needed for the Univariate Approach

Since subjects in the current example are not subdivided by any grouping characteristics, the only assumption required for using the univariate results is that the variances of all the transformed variables for an effect be equal and that their covariances be 0. (Assumptions required for more complicated designs are described in Section 6.22.)

Mauchly's test of sphericity is available in MANOVA for testing the hypothesis that the covariance matrix of the transformed variables has a constant variance on the diagonal and zeroes off the diagonal (Morrison (1976)). For small sample sizes this test is not very powerful. For large sample sizes the test may be significant even when the impact of the departure on the analysis of variance results may be small.

Figure 6.11 contains Mauchly's test of sphericity and the observed significance level based on a chi-square approximation. The observed significance level is 0.149, so the hypothesis of sphericity is not rejected. If the observed significance level is small and the sphericity assumption appears to be violated, an adjustment to the numerator and denominator degrees of freedom can be made. Two estimates of this adjustment, called epsilon, are available in MANOVA. These are also shown in Figure 6.11. Both the numerator and denominator degrees of freedom must be multiplied by epsilon, and the significance of the F-ratio evaluated with the new degrees of freedom. The Huynh-Feldt epsilon is an attempt to correct the Greenhouser-Geisser epsilon which tends to be overly conservative, especially for small sample sizes. The lowest value possible for epsilon is also printed. The Huynh-Feldt epsilon sometimes exceeds the value of one. When this occurs MANOVA prints a value of one.

Figure 6.11   Within-cells correlation

```
MANOVA P2DIGIT P3DIGIT P4DIGIT
   /WSFACTORS=DIGIT(3)
   /CONTRAST(DIGIT)=DIFFERENCE
   /RENAME=CONS DIF12 DIF12V3
   /DESIGN.
```

```
Tests involving 'DIGIT' Within-Subject Effect.


Mauchly sphericity test, W =         .84103
Chi-square approx. =                3.80873 with 2 D. F.
Significance =                       .149

Greenhouse-Geisser Epsilon =         .86284
Huynh-Feldt Epsilon =                .92638
Lower-bound Epsilon =                .50000
```

6.12
Selecting Other Contrasts

Based on the orthonormalized transformation matrix shown in Figure 6.4 and the corresponding parameter estimates in Figure 6.8d, hypotheses about particular combinations of the means were tested. Remember, the second contrast compared differences between the two- and three-digit numbers, while the third contrast compared the average of the two- and three-digit numbers to the four-digit numbers. A variety of other hypotheses can be tested by selecting different orthogonal contrasts.

For example, to test the hypothesis that latency time increases linearly with the number of digits in the memorized number, orthogonal polynomial contrasts can be used. (In fact, polynomial contrasts should have been the first choice for data of this type. Difference contrasts were used for illustrative purposes.) When polynomial contrasts are used, the first contrast for the DIGIT effect represents the linear component, and the second contrast represents the quadratic component. Figure 6.12 contains parameter estimates corresponding to the polynomial contrasts. You can see that there is a significant linear trend, but the quadratic trend is not significant. This is also shown in the plot in Figure 6.2b, since the means fall more or less on a straight line, which does not appear to curve upward or downward.

Figure 6.12   Parameter estimates for polynomial contrasts

```
MANOVA P2DIGIT P3DIGIT P4DIGIT
 /WSFACTORS=DIGIT(3)
 /CONTRAST(DIGIT)=POLYNOMIAL
 /RENAME=CONS LIN QUAD
 /WSDESIGN
 /PRINT=PARAMETERS(ESTIM)
 /DESIGN.
```

```
Estimates for LIN
DIGIT

 Parameter      Coeff.    Std. Err.    t-Value     Sig. t   Lower -95% CL- Upper

        1    42.8683486    7.28780     5.88221      .000    27.79239    57.94430

- - - - - - - - - -
Estimates for QUAD
DIGIT

 Parameter      Coeff.    Std. Err.    t-Value     Sig. t   Lower -95% CL- Upper

        1    -7.3995003    4.91598    -1.50519      .146   -17.56898     2.76998
```

The requirement that contrasts be orthonormalized is necessary for the averaged F tests. It is not required for the multivariate approach. The SPSS/PC+ MANOVA procedure, however, requires all contrasts for the within-subjects factors to be orthonormal. If nonorthogonal contrasts, such as simple or deviation are requested, they are orthonormalized prior to the actual analysis. The transformation matrix should always be printed so that the parameter estimates and univariate F ratios can be properly interpreted.

6.13
Adding Another Factor

The experimental design discussed so far is a very simple one. Responses to all levels of one factor (number of digits) were measured for all subjects. However, repeated measures designs can be considerably more complicated. Any factorial design can be applied to a single subject. For example, we can administer several different types of medication at varying dosages and times of day. Such a design has three factors (medication, dosage, and time) applied to each subject.

All of the usual analysis of variance hypotheses for factorial designs can be tested when each subject is treated as a complete replicate of the design. However, since observations from the same subject are not independent, the usual ANOVA method is inappropriate. Instead, we need to extend the previously described approach to analyzing repeated measures experiments.

To illustrate the analysis of a two-factor repeated measures design, consider the Bacon data again. The experiment was actually more involved than first described. The single "probe" digit was not always present in the memorized number. Instead, each subject was tested under two conditions—probe digit present and probe digit absent. Presence and absence of the probe digit was randomized. The two conditions were included to test the hypothesis that it takes longer to search through numbers when the probe digit is not present than when it is present. If memory searches are performed sequentially, one would expect that when the probe digit is encountered, searching stops. When the probe digit is not present in a number, searching must continue through all digits of the memorized number.

Thus, each subject has in fact six observations: latency times for the three number lengths when the probe is present, and times for the numbers when the probe is absent. This design has two factors—number of digits, and the probe presence/absence condition. The DIGIT factor has three levels (two, three, and four digits) and the CONDITION factor has two levels (probe present and probe absent).

6.14
Testing a Two-Factor Model

The analysis of this modified experiment proceeds similarly to the analysis described for the single-factor design. However, instead of testing only the DIGIT effect, tests for the DIGIT effect, the CONDITION effect, and the DIGIT by CONDITION interaction are required. Figure 6.14 is the orthonormalized transformation matrix for the two-factor design.

Figure 6.14 Orthonormalized transformation matrix for the two-factor design

```
SET WIDTH=WIDE.
MANOVA P2DIGIT P3DIGIT P4DIGIT NP2DIGIT NP3DIGIT NP4DIGIT
  /WSFACTORS=COND(2) DIGIT(3)
  /CONTRAST(DIGIT)=DIFFERENCE
  /RENAME=CONS TCONDIF TDIGIT1 TDIGIT2 TINT1 TINT2
  /WSDESIGN
  /PRINT=TRANSFORM PARAM(ESTIM) SIGNIF(AVERF)
  /DESIGN.
```

```
Orthonormalized Transformation Matrix (Transposed)

               CONS     TCONDIF    TDIGIT1    TDIGIT2    TINT1     TINT2

P2DIGIT       .40825     .40825    -.50000    -.28868   -.50000   -.28868
P3DIGIT       .40825     .40825     .50000    -.28868    .50000   -.28868
P4DIGIT       .40825     .40825     0.0        .57735    0.0       .57735
NP2DIGIT      .40825    -.40825    -.50000    -.28868    .50000    .28868
NP3DIGIT      .40825    -.40825     .50000    -.28868   -.50000    .28868
NP4DIGIT      .40825    -.40825     0.0        .57735    0.0      -.57735
```

6.15
The Transformed Variables

The coefficients of the transformation matrix indicate that the first contrast is an average of all six variables. The second contrast is the average response under the "present" condition compared to the average response under the "absent" condition. The third contrast is the difference between two and three digits averaged over the two conditions. The fourth contrast is the average of two and three digits compared to four digits, averaged over both conditions. As before, these two contrasts jointly provide a test of the DIGIT effect. The last two contrasts are used for the test of interaction. If there is no interaction effect, the difference between the two- and three-digit numbers should be the same for the two probe conditions. The contrast labeled TINT1 is the difference between two and three digits for Condition 1, minus two and three digits for Condition 2. Similarly, if there is no interaction between probe presence and the number of digits, the average of two and three digits compared to four should not differ for the two probe conditions. The contrast labeled TINT2 is used to test this hypothesis.

6.16
Testing Hypotheses

Hypothesis testing for this design proceeds similarly to the single factor design. Each effect is tested individually. Both multivariate and univariate results can be obtained for tests of each effect. (When a factor has only two levels, there is one contrast for the effect and the multivariate and univariate results are identical.) Since the test of the constant is not of interest, we will proceed to the test of the CONDITION effect.

6.17
The CONDITION Effect

The table in Figure 6.17a explains that variable TCONDIF is being used in the analysis of the CONDITION effect. The analysis of variance table in Figure 6.17b indicates that the CONDITION effect is significant. The F value of 52 has an observed significance level of less than 0.0005. The parameter estimate for the difference between the two conditions is -75 as shown in Figure 6.17c. The estimate of the actual difference between mean response under the two conditions is obtained by dividing -75 by 0.408, since the contrast is actually

$$\text{contrast} = 0.408 \times (\text{mean present} - \text{mean absent}) \qquad \textbf{Equation 6.17}$$

Since the contrast value is negative, the latency times for the absent condition are larger than the latency times for the present condition. This supports the notion that memory searching may be sequential, terminating when an item is found rather than continuing until all items are examined.

Figure 6.17a   Test of the CONDITION effect

```
Order of Variables for Analysis

  Variates      Covariates

  TCONDIF

  1 Dependent Variable
  0 Covariates

- - - - - - - - -
Note..  TRANSFORMED variables are in the variates column.
        These TRANSFORMED variables correspond to the
        'COND' WITHIN-SUBJECT effect.
```

Figure 6.17b   Analysis of variance table for the CONDITION effect

```
Tests of Significance for TCONDIF using UNIQUE sums of squares
Source of Variation          SS       DF        MS          F  Sig of F

WITHIN CELLS            58810.08      23    2556.96
COND                   134322.25       1  134322.25      52.53      .000
```

Figure 6.17c   Parameter estimates for the CONDITION effect

```
Estimates for TCONDIF
COND

 Parameter      Coeff.   Std. Err.    t-Value    Sig. t  Lower -95% CL- Upper

        1   -74.811499   10.32182   -7.24790      .000   -96.16381   -53.45918
```

6.18
The Number of Digits

The next effect to be tested is the number of digits in the memorized number. As shown in Figure 6.18a, the test is based on the two contrasts labeled TDIGIT1 and TDIGIT2. To use the univariate approach, the assumption of sphericity is necessary.

Figure 6.18a   Test of the DIGIT effect

```
Order of Variables for Analysis

  Variates      Covariates

    TDIGIT1
    TDIGIT2

    2 Dependent Variables
    0 Covariates

 _ _ _ _ _ _ _ _ _
Note..  TRANSFORMED variables are in the variates column.
        These TRANSFORMED variables correspond to the
        'DIGIT' WITHIN-SUBJECT effect.
```

Based on the multivariate criteria in Figure 6.18b, the hypothesis that there is no DIGIT effect should be rejected. From Figure 6.18c, we see that both of the contrasts are also individually different from 0. This can also be seen from Figure 6.18d, which contains the parameter estimates for the contrasts. Note that the tests that the parameter values are 0 are identical to the corresponding univariate F tests. The averaged tests of significance for the DIGIT effect, as shown in Figure 6.18e, lead to the same conclusion as the multivariate results in Figure 6.18b.

Figure 6.18b   Multivariate tests of significance

```
EFFECT .. DIGIT
Multivariate Tests of Significance (S = 1, M = 0, N = 10 )

Test Name        Value  Approx. F Hypoth. DF   Error DF  Sig. of F

Pillais         .64216  19.73989      2.00      22.00       .000
Hotellings     1.79454  19.73989      2.00      22.00       .000
Wilks           .35784  19.73989      2.00      22.00       .000
Roys            .64216
```

Figure 6.18c   Univariate tests of significance

```
Univariate F-tests with (1,23) D. F.

Variable  Hypoth. SS   Error SS Hypoth. MS     Error MS          F  Sig. of F

TDIGIT1  41002.6667 34710.8333 41002.6667 1509.16667   27.16908       .000
TDIGIT2  53682.7222 30821.4444 53682.7222 1340.06280   40.05986       .000
```

Figure 6.18d   Parameter estimates for the DIGIT contrasts

```
Estimates for TDIGIT1
DIGIT

Parameter     Coeff.   Std. Err.     t-Value   Sig. t  Lower -95% CL- Upper

       1   41.3333333    7.92981     5.21240     .000   24.92926    57.73740

_ _ _ _ _ _ _ _ _
Estimates for TDIGIT2
DIGIT

Parameter     Coeff.   Std. Err.     t-Value   Sig. t  Lower -95% CL- Upper

       1   47.2946096    7.47235     6.32929     .000   31.83688    62.75233
```

Figure 6.18e   Averaged tests of significance

```
AVERAGED Tests of Significance for MEAS.1 using UNIQUE sums of squares
Source of Variation          SS       DF        MS          F   Sig of F

WITHIN CELLS            65532.28      46     1424.61
DIGIT                   94685.39       2    47342.69      33.23     .000
```

6.19
The Interaction
The interaction between the number of digits in the memorized number and the presence or absence of the probe digit is based on the last two contrasts, labeled TINT1 and TINT2, as indicated in Figure 6.19a. Based on the multivariate criteria shown in Figure 6.19b and the averaged univariate results in Figure 6.19c, the hypothesis that there is no interaction is not rejected.

Figure 6.19a   Test of the interaction effect

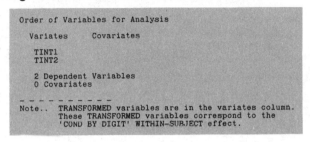

```
Order of Variables for Analysis

   Variates     Covariates

     TINT1
     TINT2

     2 Dependent Variables
     0 Covariates
- - - - - - - - - -
Note.. TRANSFORMED variables are in the variates column.
       These TRANSFORMED variables correspond to the
       'COND BY DIGIT' WITHIN-SUBJECT effect.
```

Figure 6.19b   Multivariate tests of significance

```
EFFECT .. COND BY DIGIT
Multivariate Tests of Significance (S = 1, M = 0, N = 10 )

Test Name        Value   Approx. F Hypoth. DF   Error DF  Sig. of F

Pillais         .00890    .09873      2.00       22.00      .906
Hotellings      .00898    .09873      2.00       22.00      .906
Wilks           .99110    .09873      2.00       22.00      .906
Roys            .00890
```

Figure 6.19c   Averaged tests of significance

```
AVERAGED Tests of Significance for MEAS.1 using UNIQUE sums of squares
Source of Variation          SS       DF        MS          F   Sig of F

WITHIN CELLS            20751.50      46      451.12
COND BY DIGIT              88.17       2       44.08        .10     .907
```

6.20
Putting it Together
Consider Figure 6.20a, which contains a plot of the average latencies for each of the three number lengths and conditions. Means and standard deviations are shown in Figure 6.20b. Note that the average latency times for the absent condition are always higher than those for the present condition. The test for the statistical significance of this observation is based on the CONDITION factor. Figure 6.20a shows that as the number of digits in a number increases, so does the average latency time. The test of the hypothesis that latency time is the same regardless of the number of digits is based on the DIGIT factor. Again, the hypothesis that there is no DIGIT effect is rejected. The relationship between

latency time and the number of digits appears to be fairly similar for the two probe conditions. This is tested by the CONDITION by DIGIT interaction, which was not found to be statistically significant. If there is a signficant interaction, the relationship between latency time and the number of digits would differ for the two probe conditions.

Figure 6.20a   Plot of average latencies from procedure PLOT

```
COMPUTE CONS=1.
AGGREGATE OUTFILE=*/BREAK=CONS/MPDIG2 MPDIG3 MPDIG4
 MNPDIG2 MNPDIG3 MNPDIG4=MEAN(P2DIGIT P3DIGIT P4DIGIT
 NP2DIGIT NP3DIGIT NP4DIGIT).
COMPUTE C2=2.
COMPUTE C3=3.
COMPUTE C4=4.
PLOT SYMBOLS='PPPAAA'
 /VSIZE=45
 /HSIZE=45
 /TITLE 'LATENCY TIMES (P=PROBE PRESENT A=PROBE ABSENT)'
 /FORMAT=OVERLAY
 /HORIZONTAL 'NUMBER OF DIGITS' /VERTICAL 'MEAN LATENCY TIME'
 /PLOT=MPDIG2 WITH C2;MPDIG3 WITH C3;MPDIG4 WITH C4;
       MNPDIG2 WITH C2;MNPDIG3 WITH C3;MNPDIG4 WITH C4.
```

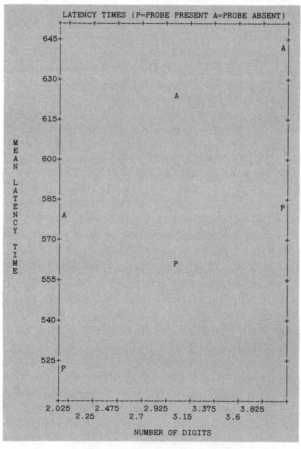

Figure 6.20b   Means and standard deviations from TABLES

```
COMPUTE DUMMY1=1.
COMPUTE DUMMY2=1.
VARIABLE LABEL DUMMY1 'PRESENT'/DUMMY2 'ABSENT'
  /P2DIGIT '2 DIGIT'/P3DIGIT '3 DIGIT' /P4DIGIT '4 DIGIT'
  /NP2DIGIT '2 DIGIT'/NP3DIGIT '3 DIGIT' /NP4DIGIT '4 DIGIT'.
VALUE LABEL DUMMY1 DUMMY2 1 ''.
TABLES OBSERV=P2DIGIT TO NP4DIGIT
  /TABLE DUMMY1 BY P2DIGIT+P3DIGIT+P4DIGIT
  /STATISTICS MEAN STDDEV
  /TABLE DUMMY2 BY NP2DIGIT+NP3DIGIT+NP4DIGIT
  /STATISTICS MEAN STDDEV.
```

	2 DIGIT		3 DIGIT		4 DIGIT	
	Mean	Standard Deviation	Mean	Standard Deviation	Mean	Standard Deviation
PRESENT	520.58	131.37	560.00	118.78	581.25	117.32

	2 DIGIT		3 DIGIT		4 DIGIT	
	Mean	Standard Deviation	Mean	Standard Deviation	Mean	Standard Deviation
ABSENT	579.75	132.17	623.00	135.14	642.33	144.81

6.21
Within-Subjects and Between-Subjects Factors

Both number of digits and probe status are called "within-subjects" factors since all combinations occur within each of the subjects. It is also possible to have "between-subjects" factors in repeated measures designs. Between-subjects factors subdivide the sample into discrete subgroups. Each subject has only one value for a between-subjects factor. For example, if cases in the previously described study are subdivided into males and females, sex is a between-subjects factor. Similarly, if cases are classified as those who received "memory enhancers" and those who did not, the memory enhancement factor is a between-subjects factor. If the same subject is tested with and without memory enhancers, memory enhancement would be a within-subjects factor. Thus, the same factor can be either a within-subjects or between-subjects factor, depending on the experimental design. Some factors, such as sex and race, can only be between-subjects factors since the same subject can be of only one sex or race.

6.22
Additional Univariate Assumptions

In a within-subjects design, a sufficient condition for the univariate model approach to be valid is that, for each effect, the variance-covariance matrix of the transformed variables used to test the effect has covariances of 0 and equal variances. Including between-subjects factors in a design necessitates an additional assumption. The variance-covariance matrices for the transformed variables for a particular effect must be equal for all levels of the between-subjects factors. These two assumptions are often called the "symmetry conditions." If they are not tenable, the F ratios from the averaged univariate results may not be correct.

6.23
Back to Memory

In addition to the two within-subjects factors, Bacon's experiment also included a between-subjects factor—the hand subjects used to press the instrument that signaled the presence or absence of the probe digit. All subjects were right-handed, but half were required to signal with the right hand and half with the left. (If a subject had been tested under both conditions, right hand and left hand, hand would be a within-subjects factor.) The hypothesis of interest was whether latency would increase for subjects using the left hand.

The hypothesis that the variance-covariance matrices are equal across all levels of the between-subjects factor can be examined using the multivariate generalization of Box's *M* test. It is based on the determinants of the variance-covariance matrices for all between-subjects cells in the design. Figure 6.23a contains the multivariate test for equality of the variance-covariance matrices for the two levels of the HAND factor (which hand the subject used). Note that in SPSS/PC+ MANOVA, this test is based on all the original variables for the within-subjects effects.

Figure 6.23a   Box's *M*

```
MANOVA P2DIGIT P3DIGIT P4DIGIT NP2DIGIT NP3DIGIT NP4DIGIT BY HAND(1,2)
 /WSFACTORS=COND(2) DIGIT(3)
 /CONTRAST(DIGIT)=DIFFERENCE
 /RENAME=CONS TCONDIF TDIGIT1 TDIGIT2 TINT1 TINT2
 /WSDESIGN
 /PRINT=HOMOGENEITY(BOXM) PARAM(ESTIM)
 /DESIGN.
```

```
Multivariate test for Homogeneity of Dispersion matrices


Boxs M =                            25.92434
F WITH (21,1780) DF =                 .86321, P =    .641 (Approx.)
Chi-Square with 21 DF =             18.43322, P =    .621 (Approx.)
```

Adding a between-subjects factor to the experiment introduces more terms into the analysis of variance model. Besides the DIGIT, CONDITION, and CONDITION by DIGIT effects, the model includes the main effect HAND and the interaction terms HAND by DIGIT, HAND by CONDITION, and HAND by DIGIT by CONDITION.

The analysis proceeds as before. Variables corresponding to the within-subjects factors are again transformed using the transformation matrix shown in Figure 6.23b. The between-subjects factors are not transformed.

Figure 6.23b   Transformation matrix

```
SET WIDTH=WIDE.
MANOVA P2DIGIT P3DIGIT P4DIGIT NP2DIGIT NP3DIGIT NP4DIGIT BY HAND(1,2)
 /WSFACTORS=COND(2) DIGIT(3)
 /CONTRAST(DIGIT)=DIFFERENCE
 /RENAME=CONS TCONDIF TDIGIT1 TDIGIT2 TINT1 TINT2
 /WSDESIGN
 /PRINT=HOMOGENEITY(BOXM) TRANSFORM
 /DESIGN.
```

Orthonormalized Transformation Matrix (Transposed)

	CONS	TCONDIF	TDIGIT1	TDIGIT2	TINT1	TINT2
P2DIGIT	.40825	.40825	−.50000	−.28868	−.50000	−.28868
P3DIGIT	.40825	.40825	.50000	−.28868	.50000	−.28868
P4DIGIT	.40825	.40825	0.0	.57735	0.0	.57735
NP2DIGIT	.40825	−.40825	−.50000	−.28868	.50000	.28868
NP3DIGIT	.40825	−.40825	.50000	−.28868	−.50000	.28868
NP4DIGIT	.40825	−.40825	0.0	.57735	0.0	−.57735

The within-subjects factors and their interactions are tested as when there were no between-subject factors in the design. Tests of the between-subjects factors and the interactions of the between- and within-subjects factors treat the transformed within-subjects variables as dependent variables. For example, the test of the HAND effect is identical to a two-sample *t* test, with the transformed variable corresponding to the constant as the dependent variable. The test of the CONDITION by HAND interaction treats the transformed variable corresponding to the CONDITION effect as the dependent variable. Similarly, the DIGIT by HAND interaction considers the two transformed variables for the DIGIT effect as dependent variables. The test of the three-way interaction HAND by DIGIT by CONDITION treats the two variables corresponding to the interaction of DIGIT by CONDITION as the dependent variables. HAND is always the grouping variable.

The SPSS/PC+ output for a design with both within- and between-subjects factors looks much like before. The variables used for each analysis are first identified, as shown for the CONSTANT effect in Figure 6.23c.

Figure 6.23c   Test of the HAND effect

```
Order of Variables for Analysis

   Variates      Covariates

   CONS

   1 Dependent Variable
   0 Covariates

- - - - - - - - -
Note..  TRANSFORMED variables are in the variates column.
        These TRANSFORMED variables correspond to the
        Between-subject effects.
```

All tests based on the same transformed variables are presented together. Since the test of the HAND effect is based on the same variable as the test for the CONSTANT effect, the tests are displayed together, as shown in Figure 6.23d. The table is the usual analysis of variance table since there is only one dependent variable in the analyses. From the ANOVA table, it appears that the CONSTANT is significantly different from 0, an uninteresting finding we have made before. The HAND effect, however, is not statistically significant since its observed significance level is very close to 1. This means that there is not sufficient evidence to reject the null hypothesis that there is no difference in average latency times for subjects who used their right hand and subjects who used their left.

Figure 6.23d   Tests of significance using unique sums of squares

```
Tests of Significance for CONS using UNIQUE sums of squares
Source of Variation           SS       DF        MS           F  Sig of F

WITHIN CELLS            2196663.86     22   99848.36
CONSTANT               49193858.03      1   49193858      492.69      .000
HAND                        300.44      1     300.44         .00      .957
```

For the transformed variable used to test the HAND effect, the overall mean is 1,432. The mean for the right-hand subjects is 1435 and for the left-hand subjects is 1,428. The parameter estimates in Figure 6.23e are based on these means. The parameter estimate for CONSTANT is the unweighted grand mean, while the parameter estimate for HAND is the deviation of the right-hand group from the overall mean. (For between-subjects variables such as HAND, deviation parameter estimates are the default.)

Figure 6.23e   Parameter estimates for the HAND contrasts

```
Estimates for CONS
CONSTANT

   Parameter      Coeff.   Std. Err.    t-Value     Sig. t  Lower -95% CL- Upper

          1   1431.69273   64.50076   22.19652        0.0   1297.92634 1565.45913
HAND

   Parameter      Coeff.   Std. Err.    t-Value     Sig. t  Lower -95% CL- Upper

          2    3.53815185   64.50076     .05485       .957  -130.22824  137.30454
```

Figure 6.23f is the ANOVA table based on the transformed variable for the CONDITION effect. Again there is a significant effect for CONDITION, but the HAND by CONDITION effect is not significant.

Figure 6.23f Analysis of variance for the interaction

```
Tests of Significance for TCONDIF using UNIQUE sums of squares
Source of Variation           SS      DF      MS          F   Sig of F

WITHIN CELLS             57889.97     22   2631.36
COND                    134322.25      1  134322.25     51.05    .000
HAND BY COND                920.11      1     920.11      .35    .560
```

Since the DIGIT effect has two degrees of freedom, its test is based on two transformed variables, and both univariate and multivariate results are printed for hypotheses involving DIGIT. The multivariate results for the HAND by DIGIT interaction are shown in Figure 6.23g. It appears that there is no interaction between number of digits and the hand used to signal the response. The multivariate results for the DIGIT effect are shown in Figure 6.23h. Again, they are highly significant. Figure 6.23i shows the averaged univariate results for terms involving the DIGIT effect.

Figure 6.23g Multivariate tests of significance for the HAND by DIGIT interaction

```
EFFECT .. HAND BY DIGIT
Multivariate Tests of Significance (S = 1, M = 0, N = 9 1/2)

Test Name       Value   Approx. F  Hypoth. DF   Error DF  Sig. of F

Pillais         .08477    .97258      2.00        21.00     .394
Hotellings      .09263    .97258      2.00        21.00     .394
Wilks           .91523    .97258      2.00        21.00     .394
Roys            .08477
```

Figure 6.23h Multivariate tests of significance for DIGIT effect

```
EFFECT .. DIGIT
Multivariate Tests of Significance (S = 1, M = 0, N = 9 1/2)

Test Name       Value   Approx. F  Hypoth. DF   Error DF  Sig. of F

Pillais         .64219  18.84488      2.00        21.00     .000
Hotellings     1.79475  18.84488      2.00        21.00     .000
Wilks           .35781  18.84488      2.00        21.00     .000
Roys            .64219
```

Figure 6.23i Averaged tests of significance

```
MANOVA P2DIGIT P3DIGIT P4DIGIT NP2DIGIT NP3DIGIT NP4DIGIT BY HAND(1,2)
  /WSFACTORS=COND(2) DIGIT(3)
  /CONTRAST(DIGIT)=DIFFERENCE
  /RENAME=CONS TCONDIF TDIGIT1 TDIGIT2 TINT1 TINT2
  /WSDESIGN
  /PRINT=HOMOGENEITY(BOXM) TRANSFORM ERROR(COR) SIGNIF(AVERF)
  /DESIGN.
```

```
AVERAGED Tests of Significance for MEAS.1 using UNIQUE sums of squares
Source of Variation           SS      DF      MS          F   Sig of F

WITHIN CELLS             64376.89     44   1463.11
DIGIT                    94685.39      2  47342.69     32.36    .000
HAND BY DIGIT             1155.39      2    577.69      .39    .676
```

Figure 6.23j shows the multivariate results for the HAND by CONDITION by DIGIT effect. Again these are not significant. The univariate tests, shown in Figure 6.23k, agree with the multivariate results.

Figure 6.23j   Multivariate tests of significance for the three-way interaction

```
EFFECT .. HAND BY COND BY DIGIT
Multivariate Tests of Significance (S = 1, M = 0, N = 9 1/2)

Test Name          Value    Approx. F Hypoth. DF   Error DF  Sig. of F

Pillais           .07632     .86760      2.00       21.00      .434
Hotellings        .08263     .86760      2.00       21.00      .434
Wilks             .92368     .86760      2.00       21.00      .434
Roys              .07632
```

Figure 6.23k   Averaged tests of significance for the three-way interaction

```
AVERAGED Tests of Significance for MEAS.1 using UNIQUE sums of squares
Source of Variation          SS       DF        MS        F    Sig of F

WITHIN CELLS             20138.11     44      457.68
COND BY DIGIT               88.17      2       44.08      .10     .908
HAND BY COND BY DIGI       613.39      2      306.69      .67     .517
T
```

6.24
Summarizing the Results

The hand used by the subject to signal the response does not seem to affect overall latency times. It also does not appear to interact with the number of digits in the memorized number, nor the presence or absence of the probe digit. This is an interesting finding, since it was conceivable that using a nonpreferred hand would increase the time required to signal. Or, subjects using their right hands might have had shorter latency times because of the way different activities are governed by the hemispheres of the brain. Memory is thought to be a function of the left hemisphere, which also governs the activity of the right hand. Thus, using the right hand would not necessitate a "switch" of hemispheres and might result in shorter latency times.

6.25
Analysis of Covariance with a Constant Covariate

The speed with which a subject signals that the probe digit is or is not present in the memorized number may depend on various characteristics of the subject. For example, some subjects may generally respond more quickly to stimuli than others. The reaction time or "speed" of a subject may influence performance in the memory experiments. To control for differences in responsiveness, we might administer a reaction-time test to each subject. This time can then be used as a covariate in the analysis. If subjects responding with the right hand are generally slower than subjects responding with their left, we may be able to account for the fact that no differences between the two groups were found.

To adjust for differences in covariates, the regression between the dependent variable and the covariate is calculated. For each subject, the response that would have been obtained if they had the same average "speed" is then calculated. Further analyses are based on these corrected values.

In a repeated measures design, the general idea is the same. The between-subjects effects are adjusted for the covariates. There is no need to adjust the within-subjects effects for covariates whose values do not change during the course of an experiment, since within-subjects factor differences are obtained from the same subject. That is, a subject's "quickness" or "slowness" is the same for all within-subjects factors.

To see how this is done, consider a hypothetical extension of Bacon's experiment. Let's assume that prior to the memory tests, each subject was given a series of trials in which he or she pressed a bar as soon as a light appeared. The interval between the time the light appeared and the time the subject pressed the bar will be termed the reaction time. For each subject, the average reaction time over a series of trials is calculated. This reaction time will be considered a covariate in the analysis.

As in the previous examples, all analyses are based on the transformed within-subjects variables. Figure 6.25a shows the orthonormalized transformation matrix. It is similar to the one used before, except that there are now six additional rows and columns that are used to transform the covariates. Although there is only one covariate in this example, the MANOVA procedure requires you to specify a covariate for each within-subjects variable, which is done by repeating the same covariate. The transformation applied to the covariates is the same as the transformation for the within-subjects factors.

Figure 6.25a Transformation matrix with covariates

```
COMPUTE C1=REACT.
COMPUTE C2=REACT.
COMPUTE C3=REACT.
COMPUTE C4=REACT.
COMPUTE C5=REACT.
COMPUTE C6=REACT.
SET WIDTH=WIDE.
MANOVA P2DIGIT P3DIGIT P4DIGIT NP2DIGIT NP3DIGIT NP4DIGIT BY HAND(1,2)
       WITH C1 C2 C3 C4 C5 C6
 /WSFACTORS=COND(2) DIGIT(3)
 /CONTRAST(DIGIT)=DIFFERENCE
 /RENAME=CONS TCONDIF TDIGIT1 TDIGIT2 TINT1 TINT2
         TC1 TC2 TC3 TC4 TC5 TC6
 /WSDESIGN
 /PRINT=TRANSFORM
 /DESIGN.
```

```
Orthonormalized Transformation Matrix (Transposed)

              CONS    TCONDIF   TDIGIT1   TDIGIT2    TINT1     TINT2      TC1       TC2       TC3       TC4       TC5

P2DIGIT      .40825    .40825   -.50000   -.28868   -.50000   -.28868    0.0       0.0       0.0       0.0       0.0
P3DIGIT      .40825    .40825    .50000   -.28868    .50000   -.28868    0.0       0.0       0.0       0.0       0.0
P4DIGIT      .40825    .40825   0.0        .57735   0.0        .57735    0.0       0.0       0.0       0.0       0.0
NP2DIGIT     .40825   -.40825   -.50000   -.28868    .50000    .28868    0.0       0.0       0.0       0.0       0.0
NP3DIGIT     .40825   -.40825    .50000   -.28868   -.50000    .28868    0.0       0.0       0.0       0.0       0.0
NP4DIGIT     .40825   -.40825   0.0        .57735   0.0       -.57735    0.0       0.0       0.0       0.0       0.0
C1           0.0      0.0       0.0       0.0       0.0       0.0        .40825    .40825   -.50000   -.28868   -.50000
C2           0.0      0.0       0.0       0.0       0.0       0.0        .40825    .40825    .50000   -.28868    .50000
C3           0.0      0.0       0.0       0.0       0.0       0.0        .40825    .40825   0.0        .57735   0.0
C4           0.0      0.0       0.0       0.0       0.0       0.0        .40825   -.40825   -.50000   -.28868    .50000
C5           0.0      0.0       0.0       0.0       0.0       0.0        .40825   -.40825    .50000   -.28868   -.50000
C6           0.0      0.0       0.0       0.0       0.0       0.0        .40825   -.40825   0.0        .57735   0.0

              TC6

P2DIGIT      0.0
P3DIGIT      0.0
P4DIGIT      0.0
NP2DIGIT     0.0
NP3DIGIT     0.0
NP4DIGIT     0.0
C1          -.28868
C2          -.28868
C3           .57735
C4           .28868
C5           .28868
C6          -.57735
```

Figure 6.25b is a description of the variables used in the analysis of the constant and the between-subjects variable. The dependent variable is CONSTANT, the covariate TC1. All of the other variables, including the five transformed replicates of the same covariate labeled TC2 to TC6, are not used for this analysis.

Figure 6.25b Test of the constant effect

```
Order of Variables for Analysis

  Variates      Covariates

   CONS           TC1

  1 Dependent Variable
  1 Covariate

- - - - - - - - - -
Note..  TRANSFORMED variables are in the variates column.
        These TRANSFORMED variables correspond to the
        Between-subject effects.
```

The analysis of variance table for the HAND and CONSTANT effects is shown in Figure 6.25c. Note how the table has changed from Figure 6.23d, the corresponding table without the reaction-time covariate. In Figure 6.25c, the within-cells error term is subdivided into two components—error sums of squares and sums of squares due to the regression. In an analysis of covariance model, we are able to explain some of the variability within a cell of the design by the fact that cases have different values for the covariates. The regression sum of squares is the variability attributable to the covariate. If one were to calculate a regression between the transformed constant term and the transformed covariate, the regression sums of squares would be identical to those in Figure 6.25c. The test for the HAND effect is thus no longer based on the CONSTANT, but on the CONSTANT adjusted for the covariate. Thus, differences between the groups in overall reaction time are eliminated. The HAND effect is still not significant, however. The sums of squares attributable to the CONSTANT have also changed. This is because the hypothesis tested is no longer that the overall mean is 0, but that the intercept in the regression equation for the constant and the reaction time is 0.

Figure 6.25c Analysis of covariance

```
Tests of Significance for CONS using UNIQUE sums of squares
Source of Variation          SS      DF        MS           F   Sig of F

WITHIN CELLS            656243.80    21   31249.70
REGRESSION             1540420.06     1  1540420.1       49.29    .000
CONSTANT                   126.81     1     126.81        .00    .950
HAND                      3745.90     1    3745.90        .12    .733
```

Figure 6.25d shows that the regression coefficient for the transformed reaction time is 97.5746. The test of the hypothesis that the coefficient is 0 is identical to the test of the regression effect in the ANOVA table.

Figure 6.25d Regression coefficient for reaction time

```
Regression analysis for WITHIN CELLS error term
Dependent variable .. CONS

COVARIATE           B         Beta      Std. Err.    t-Value    Sig. of t    Lower -95%    CL- Upper

TC1       97.5746661658    .8374092999   13.89762     7.02096      .000       68.67298     126.47635
```

When constant covariates are specified, messages such as that shown in Figure 6.25e are displayed. All the message says is that since all the covariates are identical, they are linearly dependent. You can simply ignore this message.

Figure 6.25e Linear dependency warning message

```
*    W A R N I N G    * For WITHIN CELLS error matrix, these covariates
*                     * appear LINEARLY DEPENDENT on preceding
*                     * variables ...
                          TC2
                       1 D.F. will be returned to this error term.
```

6.26
Doubly Multivariate
Repeated Measures
Designs

There is only one dependent variable in Bacon's experiment, latency time, which was measured for all subjects. In some situations, more than one dependent variable may be measured for each factor combination. For example, to test the effect of different medications on blood pressure, both systolic and diastolic blood pressures may be recorded for each treatment. This is sometimes called a doubly multivariate repeated measures design, since each subject has multiple variables measured at multiple times.

Analysis of doubly multivariate repeated measures data is similar to the analyses above. Each dependent variable is transformed using the same orthonormalized transformation. All subsequent analyses are based on these transformed variables. The tests for each effect are based on the appropriate variables for all dependent variables. For example, in the memory experiment, if two dependent variables had been measured for the three number lengths, the test of the DIGIT effect would be based on four transformed variables, two for the first dependent variable and two for the second. Similarly, the test for CONSTANT would have been based on two variables corresponding to averages for each dependent variable.

6.27
RUNNING MANOVA FOR REPEATED MEASURES DESIGNS

The operation of the MANOVA procedure is more fully documented in Chapter 5. Most of the subcommands described there can be used with repeated measures designs as well. This chapter covers only the subcommands needed to specify repeated measures designs.

6.28
Specifying the Variables

The first MANOVA specification is the list of variables to be used in the analyses. Dependent variables are named first, followed by the keyword BY and factor names and ranges. If there are covariates, list them last following keyword WITH. In a repeated measures design, list all variables that correspond to within-subjects factors as dependent variables. Between-subjects variables are considered factors.

For example, the command

```
MANOVA P2DIGIT P3DIGIT P4DIGIT.
```

specifies the three variables corresponding to number length when the probe digit is present as the dependent variable. To include the present/absent condition in the analysis as well, specify

```
MANOVA P2DIGIT P3DIGIT P4DIGIT NP2DIGIT NP3DIGIT NP4DIGIT.
```

To include the between-groups factor HAND with two levels coded as 1 and 2, specify

```
MANOVA P2DIGIT P3DIGIT P4DIGIT NP2DIGIT NP3DIGIT NP4DIGIT BY HAND(1,2).
```

When there are additional between-subjects factors, list them all after the BY keyword. Additional rules for specifying variables are given in Chapter 5.

6.29
Specifying A Constant Covariate

In a repeated measures design, you must specify as many covariate names as there are dependent variables on the MANOVA command. If there is a single covariate that is measured only once, for example before the experiment was conducted, use the COMPUTE command to replicate the covariate values. (A covariate that is measured once is called a *constant covariate*.) For example, the analysis of covariance described in Section 6.25, where REACT is the value of the reaction time can be specified as

```
COMPUTE C1=REACT.
COMPUTE C2=REACT.
COMPUTE C3=REACT.
COMPUTE C4=REACT.
COMPUTE C5=REACT.
COMPUTE C6=REACT.
MANOVA P2DIGIT P3DIGIT P4DIGIT NP2DIGIT NP3DIGIT NP4DIGIT BY HAND(1,2)
      WITH C1 C2 C3 C4 C5 C6.
```

6.30
Specifying the
Within-Subjects Factors

For a repeated measures design, you must also specify the structure of the design. For example, if there are six variables in the dependent variable list, they may have originated from a variety of repeated measures designs. There may be one within-subjects factor, say TREATMENT, which has six values representing six different agents administered to the same subject. Or there may be two within-subjects factors such as TREATMENT and DOSE, one having three levels and the other having two, e.g., each subject receives three different treatments at two dosage levels. Or, perhaps two treatments at each of three dosage levels are given.

The WSFACTORS subcommand identifies the correspondence between the variables list and the within-subjects factors. WSFACTORS supplies the name of each factor, followed by the number of levels in parentheses. The product of the number of levels of the factors must equal the number of dependent variables (except in doubly multivariate repeated measures; see Section 6.32). WSFACTOR must be the first subcommand after the variable list.

For example, to indicate that the three variables P2DIGIT, P3DIGIT, and P4DIGIT correspond to three levels of a within-subjects factor, which is to be assigned the name DIGIT, specify

```
MANOVA P2DIGIT P3DIGIT P4DIGIT
 /WSFACTORS=DIGIT(3).
```

The names assigned to the within-subjects factors must follow the SPSS/PC+ variable-naming conventions. Each within-subjects factor name must be unique. The within-subjects factor names exist only during the MANOVA analysis in which they are defined.

A name must be assigned to each within-subjects factor. For example, to define the two within-subjects factors for number length and presence/absence condition, specify

```
MANOVA P2DIGIT P3DIGIT P4DIGIT NP2DIGIT NP3DIGIT NP4DIGIT
 /WSFACTORS=COND(2) DIGIT(3).
```

Each variable named on the variables list corresponds to a particular combination of within-subjects factor levels. For example, variable P2DIGIT is the latency time for a two-digit number when the probe digit is present.

The order in which factors are named on WSFACTORS must correspond to the sequence of variables on the variable list. The first factor named on WSFACTORS changes most slowly. Thus, in the example above, values of the DIGIT factor change faster than values of the COND factor. For example, P2DIGIT is the response at the first level of CONDITION and the first level of DIGIT, and P3DIGIT is the response at the first level of CONDITION and the second level of DIGIT. If the order of the variables on the MANOVA command is changed, the order of factor names on the WSFACTORS subcommand must also be changed, as in

```
MANOVA P2DIGIT NP2DIGIT P3DIGIT NP3DIGIT P4DIGIT NP4DIGIT
 /WSFACTORS=DIGIT(3) COND(2).
```

In general, the variables must be arranged in the variable list in such a way that their structure can be represented on a WSFACTORS subcommand. For example, it is not possible to represent the following list of variables on a WSFACTORS subcommand, since the variables are not arranged in a predictable sequence:

```
MANOVA P2DIGIT P3DIGIT NP2DIGIT NP3DIGIT P4DIGIT NP4DIGIT
```

6.31
Renaming the
Transformed Variables

When a repeated measures design is specified, the original variables are transformed using an orthonormal transformation matrix, and the transformed variables are then analyzed. To make the SPSS/PC+ MANOVA output easier to interpret, it is a good idea to assign names to the new variables. This is done with the RENAME subcommand.

For example, the following command created the output shown in Figure 6.23c:

```
MANOVA P2DIGIT P3DIGIT P4DIGIT NP2DIGIT NP3DIGIT NP4DIGIT BY HAND(1,2)
 /WSFACTORS=COND(2) DIGIT(3)
 /RENAME=CONS TCONDIF TDIGIT1 TDIGIT2 TINT1 TINT2.
```

The name CONS is assigned to the CONSTANT effect, the name TCONDIF to the CONDITION effect, the names TDIGIT1 and TDIGIT2 to the two transformed variables for the DIGIT effect, and TINT1 and TINT2 to the two transformed variables that represent the interaction of condition and digit length.

The number of names listed on the RENAME subcommand must equal the number of dependent variables and covariates on the variables list. To retain a variable's original name, specify either the original name or an asterisk. For example, to retain the names of the covariates in the following command, specify:

```
MANOVA P2DIGIT P3DIGIT P4DIGIT NP2DIGIT NP3DIGIT NP4DIGIT BY HAND(1,2)
       WITH C1 C2 C3 C4 C5 C6
 /WSFACTORS=COND(2) DIGIT(3)
 /RENAME=CONS TCONDIF TDIGIT1 TDIGIT2 TINT1 TINT2 * * * * * *.
```

If you do not supply a RENAME subcommand in a situation where the variables are being transformed, as in repeated-measures analysis, MANOVA automatically assigns the names T1, T2, and so on, to the transformed variables. You must use the new names in all subsequent subcommands, whether you assigned them yourself or MANOVA supplied them. (The exception is the OMEANS subcommand, which uses the original variable names and produces tables of observed means of the untransformed variables.)

6.32
Labeling the Display of
Averaged Results

In a doubly multivariate repeated measures design (when more than one variable is measured at each combination of the factor levels), you can use the MEASURE subcommand to differentiate sets of dependent variables. In a doubly multivariate design, the arrangement of the within-subjects factors must be the same for all sets of variables. For example, if both systolic and diastolic blood pressure are measured at three points in time, you could specify

```
MANOVA SYS1 SYS2 SYS3 DIAS1 DIAS2 DIAS3
 /WSFACTORS=TIME(3)
 /MEASURE=SYSTOL DIASTOL.
```

This command names one factor, TIME, which has three levels for two sets of dependent variables. Variables SYS1, SYS2, and SYS3 are in the SYSTOL set, and DIAS1, DIAS2, and DIAS3 are DIASTOL. Note that the product of the number of variables named on MEASURE times the product of the levels of factors named on WSFACTORS equals the number of dependent variables on the variables list.

If you omit MEASURE from the above command, SPSS/PC+ MANOVA will automatically generate a doubly multivariate design based on the three levels of the TIME factor. The advantage of using MEASURE is that the display of averaged results (produced by SIGNIF(AVERF) on the PRINT subcommand)

will be labeled with the names you specify on MEASURE. If you do not use MEASURE, MANOVA prints the results but uses its own labeling. Thus the MEASURE subcommand is optional, but it is recommended for clarity.

6.33
Specifying the Contrasts

All of the CONTRASTS described in Chapter 5 can also be used for between-subjects factors in repeated measures designs. In the case of within-subjects factors, nonorthogonal contrasts such as deviation and simple are orthonormalized prior to the repeated measures analysis. If the contrast requested is not orthogonal, the parameter estimates obtained for terms involving the within-subjects factors will not correspond to the contrast requested. Therefore, it is recommended that only orthogonal contrasts be specified on the CONTRAST subcommand for within-subjects factors. Orthogonal contrast types are DIFFERENCE, HELMERT, and POLYNOMIAL.

If nonorthogonal contrasts are requested, the transformation matrix should always be printed to ascertain what orthonormalized contrasts are used. Since the default contrasts are deviation, they produce parameter estimates that are not easily interpreted.

6.34
Specifying the Design for Within-Subjects Factors

The WSDESIGN subcommand specifies the design for the within-subjects factors. Its specification is similar to the DESIGN subcommand discussed in Chapter 5. For example, to specify a complete factorial design for the DIGIT and COND within-subjects factors, specify

```
MANOVA P2DIGIT P3DIGIT P4DIGIT NP2DIGIT NP3DIGIT NP4DIGIT
 /WSFACTORS=COND(2) DIGIT(3)
 /WSDESIGN=COND DIGIT COND BY DIGIT.
```

As is the case for between-subjects factors, the complete factorial design is the default, and can be obtained by omitting the WSDESIGN command altogether, or by entering it with no specifications. To suppress estimation of the CONDITION by DIGIT interaction and specify a main-effects model, specify

```
MANOVA P2DIGIT P3DIGIT P4DIGIT NP2DIGIT NP3DIGIT NP4DIGIT
 /WSFACTORS=COND(2) DIGIT(3)
 /WSDESIGN=COND DIGIT.
```

The following specifications, which can be used on the DESIGN subcommand, are not permitted on the WSDESIGN subcommand:

• Error term references and definitions.
• The MUPLUS and CONSTANT keywords.
• Continuous variables.
• Between-subjects factors.

The WSDESIGN specification signals the beginning of within-subjects design processing, so if you explicitly enter a WSDESIGN subcommand, all other subcommands that affect the within-subjects design must appear before it. For example, if a POLYNOMIAL contrast is to be used for the DIGIT effect, this must be indicated prior to the WSDESIGN subcommand, as in

```
MANOVA P2DIGIT P3DIGIT P4DIGIT NP2DIGIT NP3DIGIT NP4DIGIT
 /WSFACTORS=COND(2) DIGIT(3)
 /CONTRAST(DIGIT)=POLY(1,2)
 /WSDESIGN COND DIGIT.
```

6.35
Repeated-Measures Processing

In a repeated measures analysis of variance, all dependent variables are not tested together as is usually done in MANOVA. Instead, sets of transformed variables that correspond to particular effects are tested. For example, in the memory experiment, the constant is tested first, then the variable that represents the CONDITION effect, then the two variables that represent the DIGIT effect, and finally the two variables that represent the DIGIT by CONDITION interaction. The cycling through the dependent variables is automatically accomplished when you enter a WSFACTORS subcommand.

For example, to obtain a test of the full-factorial within-subjects design, specify

```
MANOVA P2DIGIT P3DIGIT P4DIGIT NP2DIGIT NP3DIGIT NP4DIGIT
 /WSFACTORS=COND(2) DIGIT(3)
 /RENAME=CONS TCONDIF TDIGIT1 TDIGIT2 TINT1 TINT2.
```

6.36
Specifying the Between-Subjects Factors

Use the DESIGN subcommand according to the rules defined in Chapter 5 to list between-subjects effects to be tested. If no effects are listed on the DESIGN subcommand, the default is a full-factorial design. Thus, the complete memory experiment can be analyzed with the commands

```
MANOVA P2DIGIT P3DIGIT P4DIGIT NP2DIGIT NP3DIGIT NP4DIGIT BY HAND(1,2)
 /WSFACTORS=COND(2) DIGIT(3)
 /RENAME=CONS TCONDIF TDIGIT1 TDIGIT2 TINT1 TINT2
 /WSDESIGN=COND DIGIT COND BY DIGIT
 /DESIGN=HAND.
```

Here both the WSDESIGN and the DESIGN subcommands are optional, since complete factorial designs are the default.

6.37
Specifying Optional Output

All statistics and plots described in Chapter 5 are also available for repeated measures designs. However, some output is particularly useful for repeated measures designs. The orthonormalized transformation matrix used to generate the transformed variables is requested with the keyword TRANSFORM. The averaged univariate F tests are printed by default but can be explicitly requested with the keywords SIGNIF(AVERF).

For example, to print the transformation matrix specify

```
/PRINT=TRANSFORM
```

Homogeneity of variance tests and Mauchly's test of sphericity may be used to analyze departures from the symmetry assumptions necessary for a univariate (averaged F test) analysis. Use keyword HOMOGENEITY (BARTLETT, COCHRAN, and/or BOXM) to request the homogeneity tests, as in

```
/PRINT=TRANSFORM SIGNIF(AVERF) HOMOGENEITY(BARTLETT BOXM)
```

Mauchly's test is always displayed for a repeated measures analysis.

6.38
Annotated Example

The following SPSS/PC+ commands produced the output in Figures 6.7a, 6.7b, 6.8a, 6.8b, 6.8c, and 6.8d.

```
DATA LIST FREE
 /HAND P2DIGIT P3DIGIT P4DIGIT NP2DIGIT NP3DIGIT NP4DIGIT REACT.
BEGIN DATA.
lines of data
END DATA.
MANOVA P2DIGIT P3DIGIT P4DIGIT
 /WSFACTORS=DIGIT(3)
 /CONTRAST(DIGIT)=DIFFERENCE
 /RENAME=CONS DIF12 DIF12V3
 /WSDESIGN
 /PRINT=PARAMETERS(ESTIM) TRANSFORM
 /DESIGN.
FINISH.
```

- The DATA LIST command gives the variable names and tells SPSS/PC+ that the data will be found in freefield format.

- The MANOVA command specifies the three variables corresponding to number length when the probe digit is present as the dependent variables. The WSFACTORS subcommand indicates that the three variables P2DIGIT, P3DIGIT, and P4DIGIT correspond to three levels of a within-subject factor assigned the name DIGIT. The CONTRAST subcommand requests DIFFERENCE orthogonal contrasts. The RENAME subcommand gives new names to the transformed variables. The WSDESIGN requests a complete factorial design. The PRINT subcommand requests the parameter estimates and the transformation matrix as part of the display.

Contents

Chapter 7 Pursuing Happiness: Hierarchical Log-Linear Models

> There is only one way to achieve
>   happiness on this terrestrial ball,
> And that is to have either a clear
>   conscience or, none at all.
>
>   Ogden Nash

Ignoring Nash's warning, many of us continue to search for happiness in terrestrial institutions and possessions. Marriage, wealth, and health are all hypothesized to contribute to happiness. But do they really? And how would one investigate possible associations?

Consider Figure 7.0, which is a two-way classification of marital status and score on a happiness scale. The data are from the 1982 General Social Survey conducted by the National Opinion Research Center. Of the 854 currently married respondents, 92% indicated that they were very happy or pretty happy, while only 79% of the 383 divorced, separated, or widowed people classified themselves as happy.

Figure 7.0 Output from procedure CROSSTABS

```
CROSSTABS TABLES=HAPPY BY MARITAL
    /OPTIONS=4.
```

```
Crosstabulation:      HAPPY
                  By MARITAL

                 Count  |MARRIED |SINGLE |SPLIT  |
 MARITAL-->      Col Pct|        |       |       |  Row
                        |      1 |     2 |     3 |  Total
 HAPPY           -------+--------+-------+-------+
                     1  |    787 |   221 |   301 |  1309
 YES                    |   92.2 |  82.5 |  78.6 |  87.0
                        +--------+-------+-------+
                     2  |     67 |    47 |    82 |   196
 NO                     |    7.8 |  17.5 |  21.4 |  13.0
                        +--------+-------+-------+
                 Column |    854 |   268 |   383 |  1505
                 Total  |   56.7 |  17.8 |  25.4 | 100.0

 Number of Missing Observations =          1
```

Although the results in Figure 7.0 are interesting, they suggest many new questions. What role does income play in happiness? Are poor married couples happier than affluent singles? What about health? Determining the relationship among such variables is potentially complicated. If family income is recorded in three categories and condition of health in two, a separate two-way table of happiness score and marital status is obtained for each of the six possible combinations of health and income. As additional variables are included in the cross-classification tables, the number of cells rapidly increases and it is difficult, if not impossible, to unravel the associations among the variables by examining only the cell entries.

The usual response of researchers faced with crosstabulated data is to compute a chi-square test of independence for each subtable. This strategy is fraught with problems and usually does not result in a systematic evaluation of the relationship among the variables. The classical chi-square approach also does not provide estimates of the effects of the variables on each other, and its application to tables with more than two variables is complicated.

7.1
LOG-LINEAR MODELS

The advantages of statistical models that summarize data and test hypotheses are well recognized. Regression analysis, for example, examines the relationship between a dependent variable and a set of independent variables. Analysis of variance techniques provide tests for the effects of various factors on a dependent variable. But neither technique is appropriate for categorical data, where the observations are not from populations that are normally distributed with constant variance.

A special class of statistical techniques, called log-linear models, has been formulated for the analysis of categorical data (Haberman, 1978; Bishop, Feinberg, & Holland, 1975). These models are useful for uncovering the potentially complex relationships among the variables in a multiway crosstabulation. Log-linear models are similar to multiple regression models. In log-linear models, all variables that are used for classification are independent variables, and the dependent variable is the number of cases in a cell of the crosstabulation.

7.2
A Fully Saturated Model

Consider Figure 7.0 again. Using a log-linear model, the number of cases in each cell can be expressed as a function of marital status, degree of happiness, and the interaction between degree of happiness and marital status. To obtain a linear model, the natural logs of the cell frequencies, rather than the actual counts, are used. The natural logs of the cell frequencies in Figure 7.0 are shown in Table 7.2a. (Recall that the natural log of a number is the power to which the number e (2.718) is raised to give that number. For example, the natural log of the first cell entry in Figure 7.0 is 6.668, since $e^{6.668} = 787$.)

Table 7.2a   Natural logs

Happy	Married	Single	Split	Average
Yes	6.668	5.398	5.707	5.924
No	4.205	3.850	4.407	4.154
Average	5.436	4.624	5.057	5.039

The log-linear model for the first cell in Figure 7.0 is

$$\log(787) = \mu + \lambda_{yes}^{happy} + \lambda_{married}^{marital} + \lambda_{yes}^{happy} {}_{married}^{marital}$$

Equation 7.2a

The term denoted as μ is comparable to the grand mean in the analysis of variance. It is the average of the logs of the frequencies in all table cells. The lambda parameters represent the increments or decrements from the base value (μ) for particular combinations of values of the row and column variables.

Each individual category of the row and column variables has an associated lambda. The term $\lambda_{married}^{marital}$ indicates the effect of being in the married category of the marital-status variable, and similarly λ_{yes}^{happy} is the effect of being in the very happy category. The term $\lambda_{yes}^{happy} {}_{married}^{marital}$ represents the interaction of being very happy and married. Thus, the number of cases in a cell is a function of the values of the row and column variables and their interactions.

In general the model for the log of the observed frequency in the ith row and the jth column is given by

$$\ln F_{ij} = \mu + \lambda_i^H + \lambda_j^S + \lambda_{ij}^{HS}$$

Equation 7.2b

where F_{ij} is the observed frequency in the cell, λ_i^H is the effect of the ith happiness category, λ_j^S is the effect of the jth marital-status category, and λ_{ij}^{HS} is the interaction effect for the ith value of the happiness category, and the jth value of the marital status variable.

The lambda parameters and μ are estimated from the data. The estimate for μ is simply the average of the logs of the frequencies in all table cells. From Table 7.2a, the estimated value of μ is 5.039. Estimates for the lambda parameters are obtained in a manner similar to analysis of variance. For example, the effect of the very-happy category is estimated as

$$\lambda_{yes}^{happy} = 5.924 - 5.039 = 0.885$$

Equation 7.2c

where 5.924 is the average of the logs of the observed counts in the happy cells. The lambda parameter is just the average log of the frequencies in a particular category minus the grand mean. In general, the effect of the ith category of a variable, called a main effect, is estimated as

$$\lambda_i^{VAR} = \mu_i - \mu$$

Equation 7.2d

where μ_i is the mean of the logs in the ith category and μ is the grand mean. Positive values of lambda occur when the average number of cases in a row or a column is larger than the overall average. For example, since there are more married people in the sample than single or separated, the lambda for married is positive. Similarly, since there are fewer unhappy people than happy people, the lambda for not happy is negative.

The interaction parameters indicate how much difference there is between the sums of the effects of the variables taken individually and collectively. They represent the "boost" or "interference" associated with particular combinations of the values. For example, if marriage does result in bliss, the number of cases in the happy and married cell would be larger than the number expected based only on the frequency of married people ($\lambda_{married}^{marital}$) and the frequency of happy people (λ_{yes}^{happy}). This excess would be represented by a positive value for $\lambda_{yes\ married}^{happy\ marital}$. If marriage decreases happiness, the value for the interaction parameter would be negative. If marriage neither increases nor decreases happiness, the interaction parameter would be zero.

The estimate for the interaction parameter is the difference between the log of the observed frequency in a particular cell and the log of the predicted frequency using only the lambda parameters for the row and column variables. For example,

$$\lambda_{yes\ married}^{happy\ marital} = \ln F_{11} - (\mu + \lambda_{yes}^{happy} + \lambda_{married}^{marital})$$
$$= 6.668 - (5.039 + 0.885 + 0.397) = 0.347$$

Equation 7.2e

where F_{11} is the observed frequency in the married and happy cell. Table 7.2b contains the estimates of the λ parameters for the main effects (marital status and happiness) and their interactions.

Table 7.2b   Estimates of lambda parameters

$\lambda_{yes}^{happy} = 5.924 - 5.039 = 0.885$

$\lambda_{no}^{happy} = 4.154 - 5.039 = -0.885$

$\lambda_{married}^{marital} = 5.436 - 5.039 = 0.397$

$\lambda_{single}^{marital} = 4.624 - 5.039 = -0.415$

$\lambda_{split}^{marital} = 5.057 - 5.039 = 0.018$

$\lambda_{YM}^{HM} = 6.668 - (5.039 + 0.885 + 0.397) = 0.346$

$\lambda_{NM}^{HM} = 4.205 - (5.039 - 0.885 + 0.397) = -0.346$

$\lambda_{YSi}^{HM} = 5.398 - (5.039 + 0.885 - 0.415) = -0.111$

$\lambda_{NSi}^{HM} = 3.850 - (5.039 - 0.885 - 0.415) = 0.111$

$\lambda_{YSp}^{HM} = 5.707 - (5.039 + 0.885 + 0.018) = -0.235$

$\lambda_{NSp}^{HM} = 4.407 - (5.039 - 0.885 + 0.018) = 0.235$

To uniquely estimate the lambda parameters, we need to impose certain constraints on them. The lambdas must sum to zero across the categories of a variable. For example, the sum of the lambdas for marital status is 0.397 + (−0.415) +0.018 =0. Similar constraints are imposed on the interaction terms. They must sum to zero over all categories of a variable.

Each of the observed cell frequencies is reproduced exactly by a model that contains all main-effect and interaction terms. This type of model is called a *saturated* model. For example, the observed log frequency in Cell 1 of Figure 7.0 is given by

$$\ln F_{11} = \mu + \lambda_{yes}^{happy} + \lambda_{married}^{marital} + \lambda_{yes\ married}^{happy\ marital}$$
$$= 5.039 + 0.885 + 0.397 + 0.346 = 6.67$$

Equation 7.2f

All other observed cell frequencies can be similarly expressed as a function of the lambdas and the grand mean.

7.3
Output for the Cells

Consider Figure 7.3, which contains the observed and expected (predicted from the model) counts for the data shown in Figure 7.0. The first column gives the names of the variables used in the analysis, and the second contains the value labels for the cells in the table. The next column indicates the number of cases in each of the cells. For example, 787 people who classify themselves as happy are married, which is 52.29% of all respondents in the survey (787 out of 1505). This percentage is listed in the next column. Since the number of cases in each cell is expressed as a percentage of the total cases, the sum of all the percentages is 100. The saturated model reproduces the observed cell frequencies exactly, so the expected and observed cell counts and percentages are equal. For the same reason the next two columns, which compare the observed and expected counts, are all zeros. (Models that do not exactly reproduce the observed cells counts are examined later.)

Figure 7.3   Observed and expected frequencies for saturated model

```
HILOGLINEAR HAPPY(1,2) MARITAL(1,3)
  /DESIGN=HAPPY*MARITAL.
```

Observed, Expected Frequencies and Residuals.					
Factor	Code	OBS. count & PCT.	EXP. count & PCT.	Residual	Std. Resid.
HAPPY	YES				
MARITAL	MARRIED	787.00 (52.29)	787.00 (52.29)	0.0	0.0
MARITAL	SINGLE	221.00 (14.68)	221.00 (14.68)	0.0	0.0
MARITAL	SPLIT	301.00 (20.00)	301.00 (20.00)	0.0	0.0
HAPPY	NO				
MARITAL	MARRIED	67.00 (4.45)	67.00 (4.45)	0.0	0.0
MARITAL	SINGLE	47.00 (3.12)	47.00 (3.12)	0.0	0.0
MARITAL	SPLIT	82.00 (5.45)	82.00 (5.45)	0.0	0.0

**7.4
Parameter Estimates**

The estimates of the log-linear model parameters are also displayed as part of the HILOGLINEAR output. Figure 7.4 contains parameter estimates for the data in Figure 7.0. The parameter estimates are displayed in blocks for each effect.

Parameter estimates for the interaction effects are displayed first. Because estimates must sum to zero across the categories of each variable, only two parameter estimates need to be displayed for the interaction effects: those for $\lambda^{happy\ marital}_{yes\ married}$ and for $\lambda^{happy\ marital}_{yes\ single}$. All other interaction parameter estimates can be derived from these.

After the interaction terms, parameter estimates for the main effects of the variables are displayed. The first estimate is for λ^{happy}_{yes} and is identical to the value given in Table 7.2b (0.885). Again, only one parameter estimate is displayed, since we can infer that the parameter estimate for λ^{happy}_{no} is -0.885 (the two estimates must sum to zero). Two parameter estimates and associated statistics are displayed for the marital variable, since it has three categories. The estimate for the third parameter $\lambda^{marital}_{split}$ is the negative of the sum of the estimates for $\lambda^{marital}_{married}$ and $\lambda^{marital}_{single}$. Thus $\lambda^{marital}_{split}$ is estimated to be 0.0178, as shown in Figure 7.2b.

Since the individual parameter estimates in Figure 7.4 are not labeled, the following rules for identifying the categories to which they correspond may be helpful. For main effects, the parameter estimates correspond to the first $K-1$ categories of the variable, where K is the total number of categories. For interaction parameters, the number of estimates displayed is the product of the number of categories, minus one, of each variable in the interaction, multiplied together. For example, marital status has three categories and happiness has two, so the number of estimates displayed is $(3-1) \times (2-1) = 2$.

To identify individual parameters, first look at the order in which the variable labels are listed in the heading. In this case the heading is HAPPY*MARITAL. The first estimate corresponds to the first category of both variables, which is happy-yes and marital-married. The next estimate corresponds to the first category of the first variable (HAPPY) and the second category of the second variable (MARITAL). In general, the categories of the last variable rotate most quickly and those of the first variable most slowly. Terms involving the last categories of the variables are omitted.

Figure 7.4 Estimates for parameters

```
HILOGLINEAR HAPPY(1,2) MARITAL(1,3)
  /PRINT=ESTIM
  /DESIGN=HAPPY*MARITAL.
```

Estimates for Parameters.

HAPPY*MARITAL

Parameter	Coeff.	Std. Err.	Z-Value	Lower 95 CI	Upper 95 CI
1	.3464441901	.05429	6.38147	.24004	.45285
2	-.1113160745	.06122	-1.81833	-.23131	.00867

HAPPY

Parameter	Coeff.	Std. Err.	Z-Value	Lower 95 CI	Upper 95 CI
1	.8853236244	.03997	22.14946	.80698	.96367

MARITAL

Parameter	Coeff.	Std. Err.	Z-Value	Lower 95 CI	Upper 95 CI
1	.3972836534	.05429	7.31793	.29088	.50369
2	-.4150216289	.06122	-6.77930	-.53501	-.29503

Figure 7.4 also displays the standard error for each estimate. For the λ^{happy}_{yes} parameter, the standard error is 0.03997. The ratio of the parameter estimate to its standard error is given in the column labeled Z-Value. For sufficiently large sample sizes, the test of the null hypothesis that lambda is zero can be based on this Z value, since the standardized lambda is approximately normally distributed

with a mean of zero and a standard deviation of 1 if the model fits the data. Lambdas with Z values greater than 1.96 in absolute value can be considered significant at the 0.05 level. When tests for many lambdas are calculated, however, the usual problem of multiple comparisons arises. That is, when many comparisons are made, the probability that some are found to be significant when there is no effect increases rapidly. Special multiple-comparison procedures for testing the lambdas are discussed in Goodman (1964).

Individual confidence intervals can be constructed for each lambda. The 95% confidence interval for λ_{yes}^{happy} is $0.885 \pm (1.96 \times 0.03997)$, which results in a lower limit of 0.80698 and an upper limit of 0.96367. Since the confidence interval does not include zero, the hypothesis that the population value is zero can be rejected. These values are displayed in the last two columns of Figure 7.4.

7.5
The Independence Model

Representing an observed-frequency table with a log-linear model that contains as many parameters as there are cells (a saturated model) does not result in a parsimonious description of the relationship between the variables. It may, however, serve as a good starting point for exploring other models that could be used to represent the data. Parameters that have small values can be excluded from subsequent models.

To illustrate the general procedure for fitting a model that does not contain all possible parameters (an unsaturated model), consider the familiar independence hypothesis for a two-way table. If variables are independent they can be represented by a log-linear model that does not have any interaction terms. For example, if happiness and marital status are independent

$$\log \hat{F}_{ij} = \mu + \lambda_i^{happy} + \lambda_j^{marital}$$

Equation 7.5a

Note that $\hat{F}_{ij}$ is no longer the observed frequency in the (i,j)th cell, but is now the expected frequency based on the model. The estimates of the lambda parameters are obtained using an iterative algorithm (the previously described formulas, which provide direct estimates, apply only to saturated models). That is, the λ's are repeatedly estimated until successive estimates do not differ from each other by more than a preset amount. Each time an estimate is obtained it is called an iteration, while the preset amount is called the convergence criterion.

The message in Figure 7.5a gives the number of iterations required for convergence. For this example, two iterations were required for convergence. The observed and expected counts in each of the cells of the table are shown in Figure 7.5b.

**Figure 7.5a   HILOGLINEAR message:
iterations required for convergence**

```
HILOGLINEAR HAPPY(1,2) MARITAL(1,3)
 /DESIGN=MARITAL HAPPY.
```

```
DESIGN 1 has generating class

    MARITAL
    HAPPY

The Iterative Proportional Fit algorithm converged at iteration 2.
The maximum difference between observed and fitted marginal totals is      .000
and the convergence criterion is      .250
```

Figure 7.5b   Observed and expected frequencies for unsaturated model

```
Observed, Expected Frequencies and Residuals.

     Factor          Code        OBS. count  & PCT.    EXP. count  & PCT.    Residual    Std. Resid.

HAPPY              YES
  MARITAL          MARRIED       787.00 (52.29)        742.78 (49.35)         44.219         1.622
  MARITAL          SINGLE        221.00 (14.68)        233.10 (15.49)        -12.098         -.792
  MARITAL          SPLIT         301.00 (20.00)        333.12 (22.13)        -32.121        -1.760

HAPPY              NO
  MARITAL          MARRIED        67.00 ( 4.45)        111.22 ( 7.39)        -44.219        -4.193
  MARITAL          SINGLE         47.00 ( 3.12)         34.90 ( 2.32)         12.098         2.048
  MARITAL          SPLIT          82.00 ( 5.45)         49.88 ( 3.31)         32.121         4.548
```

The expected values are identical to those obtained from the usual formulas for expected values in a two-way crosstabulation, as shown in Figure 7.5c. For example, from Figure 7.0, the estimated probability of an individual being happy is 1309/1505, and the estimated probability of an individual being married is 854/1505. If marital status and happiness are independent, the probability of a happy, married person is estimated to be

$$1309/1505 \times 854/1505 = 0.4935 \qquad \text{Equation 7.5b}$$

The expected number of happy, married people in a sample of 1505 is then

$$0.4935 \times 1505 = 742.78 \qquad \text{Equation 7.5c}$$

This is the value displayed in the expected-count column in Figure 7.5b. Since the independence model is not saturated, the observed and expected counts are no longer equal, as was the case in Figure 7.3.

Figure 7.5c   Crosstabulation of happiness by marital status

```
CROSSTABS TABLE=HAPPY BY MARITAL
     /OPTIONS=14
     /STATISTICS=1.
```

```
Crosstabulation:      HAPPY
                   By MARITAL


                 Count  |MARRIED |SINGLE  |SPLIT
  MARITAL->      Exp Val|        |        |          Row
                        |     1  |     2  |     3    Total
  HAPPY                 +--------+--------+--------+
                    1   |   787  |   221  |   301  |  1309
     YES                | 742.8  | 233.1  | 333.1  |  87.0%
                        +--------+--------+--------+
                    2   |    67  |    47  |    82  |   196
      NO                | 111.2  |  34.9  |  49.9  |  13.0%
                        +--------+--------+--------+
                 Column     854     268      383     1505
                 Total     56.7%   17.8%    25.4%   100.0%


  Chi-Square      D.F.     Significance       Min E.F.      Cells with E.F.| 5
  ----------      ----     ------------       --------      ---------------

   48.81639         2         0.0000           34.902           None

  Number of Missing Observations =      1
```

7.6
Chi-square Goodness-of-Fit Tests

The test of the hypothesis that a particular model fits the observed data can be based on the familiar Pearson chi-square statistic, which is calculated as

$$\chi^2 = \sum_i \sum_j \frac{(F_{ij} - \hat{F}_{ij})^2}{\hat{F}_{ij}} \qquad \text{Equation 7.6a}$$

where the subscripts i and j include all cells in the table. An alternative statistic is the likelihood-ratio chi-square, which is calculated as

$$L^2 = 2 \sum_i \sum_j F_{ij} \, ln \, \frac{F_{ij}}{\hat{F}_{ij}}$$

Equation 7.6b

For large sample sizes these statistics are equivalent. The advantage of the likelihood-ratio chi-square statistic is that it, like the total sums of squares in analysis of variance, can be subdivided into interpretable parts that add up to the total (see Section 7.10).

Figure 7.6 shows that the value of the Pearson chi-square statistic is 48.82 and the likelihood-ratio chi-square is 48.01. The degrees of freedom associated with a particular model are the number of cells in the table minus the number of independent parameters in the model. In this example, there are six cells and four independent parameters to be estimated (the grand mean, λ_{yes}^{happy}, $\lambda^{married}$, λ^{split}), so there are two degrees of freedom. (There are only four independent parameters because of the constraint that parameter estimates must sum to zero over the categories of a variable. Therefore, the value for one of the categories is determined by the values of the others and is not, in a statistical sense, independent.)

The observed significance level associated with both chi-square statistics is very small (less than 0.0005), and the independence model is rejected. Note that the Pearson chi-square statistic displayed for independence model is identical to the chi-square value displayed by procedure CROSSTABS, as shown in Figure 7.5c.

Figure 7.6 Chi-square goodness-of-fit test

```
Goodness-of-fit test statistics

  Likelihood ratio chi square =     48.01198    DF = 2   P =   .000
           Pearson chi square =     48.81638    DF = 2   P =   .000
```

7.7 Residuals

Another way to assess how well a model fits the data is to examine the differences between the observed and expected cell counts based on the model. If the model fits the observed data well, these differences, called residuals, should be fairly small in value and not have any discernible pattern. The column labeled Residual in Figure 7.5b shows the differences between the observed and expected counts in each cell. For example, since 787 individuals were found to be very happy and married, while 742.78 are expected to fall into this category if the independence model is correct, the residual is $787 - 742.78 = 44.22$.

As in regression analysis, it is useful to standardize the residuals by dividing them by their standard error, in this case the square root of the expected cell count. For example, the standardized residual for the first cell in Figure 7.5b is

$$\text{Standardized Residual} = \frac{\text{Observed Count} - \text{Expected Count}}{\sqrt{\text{Expected Count}}}$$

Equation 7.7

This value is displayed in the column labeled Std. Resid. in Figure 7.5b. If the model is adequate, the standardized residuals are approximately normally distributed with a mean of zero and standard deviation of one. Standardized residuals greater than 1.96 or less than -1.96 suggest important discrepancies, since they are unlikely to occur if the model is adequate. Particular combinations of cells with large standardized residuals may suggest which other models might be more appropriate.

The same types of diagnostics for residuals used in regression analysis can be used in log-linear models. Figures 7.7a and 7.7b are plots of the standardized residuals against the observed and expected cell frequencies, respectively. If the model is adequate, there should be no discernible pattern in the plots. Patterns suggest that the chosen log-linear model, or the log-linear representation in general, may not be appropriate for the data.

Figure 7.7a   Plot of standardized residuals vs. observed cell frequencies

```
HILOGLINEAR HAPPY(1,2) MARITAL(1,3)
   /PLOT=RESID
   /DESIGN=MARITAL HAPPY
```

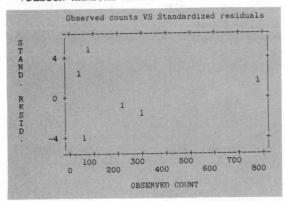

Figure 7.7b   Plot of standardized residuals vs. expected cell frequencies

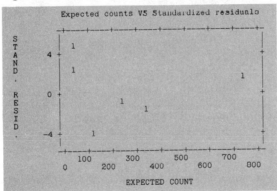

If the standardized residuals are normally distributed, the normal probability plot (Figure 7.7c) should be approximately linear. In this plot, the standardized residuals are plotted against "expected" residuals from a normal distribution.

Figure 7.7c   Plot of standardized residuals against expected residuals

```
HILOGLINEAR HAPPY(1,2) MARITAL(1,3)
   /PLOT=NORMPROB
   /DESIGN=MARITAL HAPPY.
```

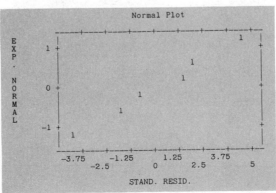

7.8
Hierarchical Models

A saturated log-linear model contains all possible effects. For example, a saturated model for a two-way table contains terms for the row main effects, the column main effects, and their interaction. Different models can be obtained by deleting terms from a saturated model. The independence model is derived by deleting the interaction effect. Although it is possible to delete any particular term from a model, in log-linear analysis attention is often focused on a special class of models which are termed *hierarchical*.

In a hierarchical model, if a term exists for the interaction of a set of variables, then there must be lower-order terms for all possible combinations of these variables. For a two-variable model, this means that the interaction term can only be included if both main effects are present. For a three-variable model, if the term λ^{ABC} is included in a model, then the terms λ^A, λ^B, λ^C, λ^{AB}, λ^{BC}, and λ^{AC} must also be included.

To describe a hierarchical model, it is sufficient to list the highest-order terms in which variables appear. This is called the *generating class* of a model. For example, the specification ABC indicates that a model contains the term λ^{ABC} and all its lower-order relations. (Terms are "relatives" if all variables that are included in one term are also included in the other. For example, the term λ^{ABCD} is a higher-order relative of the terms λ^{ABC}, λ^{BCD}, λ^{ACD}, λ^{BAD}, as well as all other lower-order terms involving variables A, B, C, or D. Similarly, λ^{AB} is a lower-order relative of both λ^{ABC} and λ^{ABD}.) The model

$$\ln F_{ijk} = \mu + \lambda_i^A + \lambda_j^B + \lambda_k^C + \lambda_{ij}^{AB}$$

Equation 7.8

can be represented by the generating class $(AB)(C)$, since AB is the highest-order term in which A and B occur, and C is included in the model only as a main effect.

7.9
Model Selection

Even if attention is restricted to hierarchical models, many different models are possible for a set of variables. How do you choose among them? The same guidelines used for model selection in regression analysis apply to log-linear models. A model should fit the data and be substantively interpretable and as simple (parsimonious) as possible. For example, if models with and without higher-order interaction terms fit the data well, the simpler models are usually preferable since higher-order interaction terms are difficult to interpret.

A first step in determining a suitable model might be to fit a saturated model and examine the standardized values for the parameter estimates. Effects with small estimated values can usually be deleted from a model. Another strategy is to systematically test the contribution to a model made by terms of a particular order. For example, you might fit a model with interaction terms and then a model with main effects only. The change in the chi-square value between the two models is attributable to the interaction effects.

7.10
Partitioning the Chi-Square Statistic

In regression analysis, the change in multiple R^2 when a variable is added to a model indicates the additional "information" conveyed by the variable. Similarly, in log-linear analysis the decrease in the value of the likelihood-ratio chi-square statistic when terms are added to the model signals their contribution to the model. (Remember R^2 increases when additional variables are added to a model, since large values of R^2 are associated with good models. Chi-square decreases when terms are added, since small values of chi-square are associated with good models.)

As an example, consider the happiness and marital-status data when two additional variables, total income in 1982 and the condition of one's health, are included. Figure 7.10a contains goodness-of-fit statistics for three different models. Design 3 contains all terms except the four-way interaction of HAPPY, MARITAL, INCOME82, and HEALTH. Design 2 contains main effects and second-order interactions only, and Design 1 is a main-effects-only model.

Design 1 has a large chi-square value and an observed significance level less than 0.0005, so it definitely does not fit well. To judge the adequacy of Designs 2 and 3, consider the changes in the chi-square goodness-of-fit statistic as terms are removed from the model.

Figure 7.10a   Goodness-of-fit statistics for three models

```
HILOGLINEAR HAPPY(1,2) MARITAL(1,3) INCOME82(1,3) HEALTH(1,2)
  /PRINT=ESTIM
  /DESIGN=HAPPY MARITAL INCOME82 HEALTH
  /PRINT=ESTIM
  /DESIGN=HAPPY*MARITAL  HAPPY*INCOME82  HAPPY*HEALTH   MARITAL*INCOME82
          MARITAL*HEALTH   INCOME82*HEALTH
  /PRINT=ESTIM
  /DESIGN=HAPPY*MARITAL*INCOME82  HAPPY*MARITAL*HEALTH
          MARITAL*INCOME82*HEALTH   HAPPY*INCOME82*HEALTH.
```

```
DESIGN 1 has generating class

    HAPPY
    MARITAL
    INCOME82
    HEALTH

The Iterative Proportional Fit algorithm converged at iteration 2.

  Goodness-of-fit test statistics

      Likelihood ratio chi square =    404.06381    DF = 29  P = 0.0
                Pearson chi square =    592.88247    DF = 29  P = 0.0


DESIGN 2 has generating class

    HAPPY*MARITAL
    HAPPY*INCOME82
    HAPPY*HEALTH
    MARITAL*INCOME82
    MARITAL*HEALTH
    INCOME82*HEALTH

The Iterative Proportional Fit algorithm converged at iteration 6.

  Goodness-of-fit test statistics

      Likelihood ratio chi square =     12.60130    DF = 16  P =  .702
                Pearson chi square =     12.31572    DF = 16  P =  .722


DESIGN 3 has generating class

    HAPPY*MARITAL*INCOME82
    HAPPY*MARITAL*HEALTH
    MARITAL*INCOME82*HEALTH
    HAPPY*INCOME82*HEALTH

The Iterative Proportional Fit algorithm converged at iteration 3.

  Goodness-of-fit test statistics

      Likelihood ratio chi square =      3.99256    DF = 4  P =  .407
                Pearson chi square =      3.97332    DF = 4  P =  .410
```

For a saturated model, the value of the chi-square statistic is always zero. Eliminating the fourth-order interaction (Design 3) results in a likelihood-ratio chi-square value of 3.99. The change in chi-square from zero to 3.99 is attributable to the fourth-order interaction. The change in the degrees of freedom between the two models equals 4, since a saturated model has zero degrees of freedom and the third-order interaction model has four. The change in the chi-square value can be used to test the hypothesis that the fourth-order interaction term is zero. If the observed significance level for the change is small, the hypothesis that the fourth-order term is zero is rejected, since this indicates that the model without the fourth-order term does not fit well. A chi-square value of 3.99 has an observed significance of 0.41, so the hypothesis that the fourth-order term is zero is not rejected.

The likelihood-ratio chi-square value for Design 2, the second-order interaction model, is 12.60. This value provides a test of the hypothesis that all third- and fourth-order interaction terms are zero. The difference between 12.60 and 3.99 (8.61) provides a test of the hypothesis that all third-order terms are zero. In general, the test of the hypothesis that the kth order terms are zero is based on

$$\chi^2 = \chi^2_{k-1} - \chi^2_k \qquad\qquad\qquad\qquad \textbf{Equation 7.10}$$

where χ^2_k is the value for the model that includes the kth-order effect or effects, and χ^2_{k-1} is the chi-squared value for the model without the kth-order effects.

The SPSS/PC+ HILOGLINEAR (hierarchical log-linear) procedure automatically calculates tests of two types of hypotheses: the hypothesis that all kth- and higher-order effects are zero and the hypothesis that the kth-order effects are zero. Figure 7.10b contains the test for the hypothesis that k- and higher-order effects are zero.

Figure 7.10b   Tests that k-way and higher-order effects are zero

```
HILOGLINEAR HAPPY(1,2) MARITAL(1,3) INCOME82(1,3) HEALTH(1,2)
  /PRINT=ASSOCIATION
  /DESIGN.
```

Tests that K-way and higher order effects are zero.

K	DF	L.R. Chisq	Prob	Pearson Chisq	Prob	Iteration
4	4	3.994	.4069	3.973	.4097	3
3	16	12.602	.7016	12.316	.7220	6
2	29	404.064	0.0	592.882	0.0	2
1	35	2037.779	.0000	2938.738	.0000	0

The first line of Figure 7.10b is a test of the hypothesis that the fourth-order interaction is zero. Note that the likelihood-ratio chi-square value of 3.99 is identical to the value displayed for Design 3 in Figure 7.10a. This is the goodness-of-fit statistic for a model without the fourth-order interaction. Similarly, the entry for the k of 3 is the goodness-of-fit test for a model without third- and fourth-order effects, like Design 2 in Figure 7.11. The last line, $k=1$, corresponds to a model that has no effects except the grand mean. That is, the expected value for all cells is the same—the average of the logs of the observed frequencies in all cells.

The column labeled Prob in Figure 7.10b gives the observed significance levels for the tests that k- and higher-order effects are zero. Small observed significance levels indicate that the hypothesis that terms of particular orders are zero should be rejected. Note in Figure 7.10b that the hypotheses that all effects are zero and that second-order and higher effects are zero should be rejected. Since the observed significance level for the test that third- and higher-order terms are zero is large (0.72), the hypothesis that third- and fourth-order interactions are zero should not be rejected. Thus, it appears that a model with first- and second-order effects is adequate to represent the data.

It is sometimes also of interest to test whether interaction terms of a *particular* order are zero. For example, rather than asking if all effects greater than two-way are zero, the question is whether two-way effects are zero. Figure 7.10c gives the tests for the hypothesis that k-way effects are zero.

Figure 7.10c   Tests that k-way effects are zero

Tests that K-way effects are zero.

K	DF	L.R. Chisq	Prob	Pearson Chisq	Prob	Iteration
1	6	1633.715	0.0	2345.856	0.0	0
2	13	391.462	0.0	580.567	0.0	0
3	12	8.608	.7360	8.343	.7578	0
4	4	3.994	.4069	3.973	.4097	0

From Figure 7.10b the likelihood-ratio chi-square for a model with only the mean is 2037.779. The value for a model with first-order effects is 404.064. The difference between these two values, 1633.715, is displayed on the first line of Figure 7.10c. The difference is an indication of how much the model improves when first-order effects are included. The observed significance level for a chi-square value of 1634 with six degrees of freedom (35−29) is small, less than 0.00005, so the hypothesis that first-order effects are zero is rejected. The remaining entries in Figure 7.10c are obtained in a similar fashion. The test that third-order effects are zero is the difference between a model without third-order terms ($\chi^2_{LR}=12.602$) and a model with third-order terms ($\chi^2_{LR}=3.994$). The resulting chi-square value of 8.608 with 12 degrees of freedom has a large observed significance level (0.736), so the hypothesis that third-order terms are zero is not rejected.

7.11
Testing Individual Terms in the Model

The two tests described in Section 7.10 provide an indication of the collective importance of effects of various orders. They do not, however, test the individual terms. That is, although the overall hypothesis that second-order terms are zero may be rejected, that does not mean that every second-order effect is present.

One strategy for testing individual terms is to fit two models differing only in the presence of the effect to be tested. The difference between the two likelihood-ratio chi-square values, sometimes called the partial chi-square, also has a chi-square distribution and can be used to test the hypothesis that the effect is zero. For example, to test that the HAPPY by MARITAL by INCOME effect is zero, a model with all three-way interactions can be fit. From Figure 7.10a, the likelihood-ratio chi-square value for this model is 3.99. When a model without the HAPPY by MARITAL by INCOME effect is fit (Figure 7.11a), the likelihood-ratio is 7.363. Thus the partial chi-square value with four (8−4) degrees of freedom is 3.37 (7.36−3.99).

Figure 7.11a   Model without HAPPY by MARITAL by INCOME

```
HILOGLINEAR HAPPY(1,2) MARITAL(1,3) INCOME82(1,3) HEALTH(1,2)
   /PRINT=ESTIM
   /DESIGN=HAPPY*MARITAL*HEALTH
           MARITAL*INCOME82*HEALTH
           HAPPY*INCOME82*HEALTH.
```

```
DESIGN 1 has generating class

    HAPPY*MARITAL*HEALTH
    MARITAL*INCOME82*HEALTH
    HAPPY*INCOME82*HEALTH

The Iterative Proportional Fit algorithm converged at iteration 4.

Goodness-of-fit test statistics

    Likelihood ratio chi square =      7.36257    DF = 8   P =  .498
                 Pearson chi square =      7.50541    DF = 8   P =  .483
```

Figure 7.11b contains the partial chi-square values and their observed significance levels for all effects in the HAPPY by MARITAL by HEALTH by INCOME table. Note that the observed significance levels are large for all three-way effects, confirming that first- and second-order effects are sufficient to represent the data. The last column indicates the number of iterations required to achieve convergence.

**Figure 7.11b Partial chi-squares
for HAPPY by MARITAL by HEALTH by INCOME**

```
HILOGLINEAR HAPPY(1,2) MARITAL(1,3) INCOME82(1,3) HEALTH(1,2)
  /PRINT=ASSOCIATION
  /DESIGN=HAPPY*MARITAL*HEALTH*INCOME82.
```

```
Tests of PARTIAL associations.

Effect Name                        DF   Partial Chisq    Prob   Iter

HAPPY*MARITAL*INCOME82              4          3.370     .4979    4
HAPPY*MARITAL*HEALTH               2           .458     .7954    4
HAPPY*INCOME82*HEALTH              2           .955     .6203    3
MARITAL*INCOME82*HEALTH            4          3.652     .4552    5
HAPPY*MARITAL                      2         15.050     .0005    5
HAPPY*INCOME82                     2         16.120     .0003    5
MARITAL*INCOME82                   4        160.739    0.0       4
HAPPY*HEALTH                       1         55.696     .0000    5
MARITAL*HEALTH                     2          8.391     .0151    5
INCOME82*HEALTH                    2         35.602     .0000    5
HAPPY                              1        849.539    0.0       2
MARITAL                           2        343.394    0.0       2
INCOME82                          2         86.114     .0000    2
HEALTH                            1        354.661    0.0       2
```

7.12
Model Selection Using Backward Elimination

As in regression analysis, another way to arrive at a "best" model is by using variable-selection algorithms. Forward selection adds effects to a model, while backward elimination starts with all effects in a model and then removes those that do not satisfy the criterion for remaining in the model. Since backward elimination appears to be the better procedure for model selection (Benedetti & Brown 1978), it is the only procedure described here.

The initial model for backward elimination need not be saturated but can be any hierarchical model. At the first step, the effect whose removal results in the least-significant change in the likelihood-ratio chi-square is eligible for elimination, provided that the observed significance level is larger than the criterion for remaining in the model. To ensure a hierarchical model, only effects corresponding to the generating class are examined at each step. For example, if the generating class is MARITAL*HAPPY*INCOME*HEALTH, the first step examines only the fourth-order interaction.

Figure 7.12a shows output at the first step. Elimination of the fourth-order interaction results in a chi-square change of 3.994, which has an associated significance level of 0.4069. Since this significance level is not less than 0.05 (the default HILOGLINEAR criterion for remaining in the model), the effect is removed. The new model has all three-way interactions as its generating class.

Figure 7.12a First step in backward elimination

```
HILOGLINEAR HAPPY(1,2) MARITAL(1,3) INCOME82(1,3) HEALTH(1,2)
  /METHOD=BACKWARD
  /MAXSTEPS=6
  /DESIGN=HAPPY*MARITAL*INCOME82*HEALTH.
```

```
Backward Elimination for DESIGN 1 with generating class

  HAPPY*MARITAL*INCOME82*HEALTH

Likelihood ratio chi square =      0.0      DF = 0  P = 1.000


If Deleted Simple Effect is        DF   L.R. Chisq Change   Prob  Iter

HAPPY*MARITAL*INCOME82*HEALTH       4          3.994        .4069   3

Step 1

  The best model has generating class

      HAPPY*MARITAL*INCOME82
      HAPPY*MARITAL*HEALTH
      HAPPY*INCOME82*HEALTH
      MARITAL*INCOME82*HEALTH

  Likelihood ratio chi square =    3.99354   DF = 4  P =   .407
```

Figure 7.12b contains the statistics for the second step. The effects eligible for removal are all three-way interactions. The HAPPY*MARITAL*HEALTH interaction has the largest observed significance level for the change in the chi-square if it is removed, so it is eliminated from the model. The likelihood-ratio chi-square for the resulting model is 4.45.

Figure 7.12b Statistics used to eliminate second effect

```
If Deleted Simple Effect is          DF   L.R. Chisq Change   Prob   Iter

  HAPPY*MARITAL*INCOME82               4         3.370        .4979    4
  HAPPY*MARITAL*HEALTH                 2          .458        .7954    4
  HAPPY*INCOME82*HEALTH                2          .955        .6203    3
  MARITAL*INCOME82*HEALTH              4         3.652        .4552    5

Step 2

  The best model has generating class

      HAPPY*MARITAL*INCOME82
      HAPPY*INCOME82*HEALTH
      MARITAL*INCOME82*HEALTH

  Likelihood ratio chi square =      4.45127    DF = 6  P =  .616
```

At the next three steps the remaining third-order interactions are removed from the model. The sixth step begins with all second-order items in the model, as shown in Figure 7.12c.

Figure 7.12c Sixth step in backward elimination

```
If Deleted Simple Effect is          DF   L.R. Chisq Change   Prob   Iter

  HAPPY*HEALTH                         1        55.697        .0000    5
  HAPPY*MARITAL                        2        15.052        .0005    5
  HAPPY*INCOME82                       2        16.121        .0003    5
  MARITAL*INCOME82                     4       160.739       0.0       5
  MARITAL*HEALTH                       2         8.392        .0151    5
  INCOME82*HEALTH                      2        35.603        .0000    4

Step 6

  The best model has generating class

      HAPPY*HEALTH
      HAPPY*MARITAL
      HAPPY*INCOME82
      MARITAL*INCOME82
      MARITAL*HEALTH
      INCOME82*HEALTH

  Likelihood ratio chi square =     12.60116    DF = 16  P =  .702


The final model has generating class

    HAPPY*HEALTH
    HAPPY*MARITAL
    HAPPY*INCOME82
    MARITAL*INCOME82
    MARITAL*HEALTH
    INCOME82*HEALTH

The Iterative Proportional Fit algorithm converged at iteration 0.
```

Since the observed significance level for removal of any of the two-way interactions is smaller than 0.05, no more effects are removed from the model. The final model contains all second-order interactions, and has a chi-square value of 12.60. This is the same model suggested by the partial-association table.

At this point it is a good idea to examine the residuals to see if any anomalies are apparent. The largest standardized residual is 1.34, which suggests that the model fits well. The residual plots also show nothing suspicious.

7.13 RUNNING PROCEDURE HILOGLINEAR

The SPSS/PC+ HILOGLINEAR procedure allows you to fit, test, and estimate parameters of hierarchical log-linear models. Using HILOGLINEAR, you can examine and compare a variety of hierarchical models, either by specifying tests of partial association or by requesting backward elimination. HILOGLINEAR also provides estimates of the parameters for saturated models.

HILOGLINEAR operates via a variables list and subcommands. None of the subcommands are required; the minimum specification on HILOGLINEAR is simply the variable list. The output for the minimum specification includes observed and expected frequencies for a k-way table and parameter estimates for the saturated model.

7.14
Specifying the Variables

The variables list identifies the categorical variables used in the model or models you fit. Variables must be numeric and integer. Each variable in the list must be accompanied by minimum and maximum values in parentheses, as in the command

```
HILOGLINEAR SEX(1,2) RACE(1,2) HAPPY(1,2) MARITAL(1,3) INCOME82(1,3).
```

If several consecutive variables in the variables list have the same ranges, the minimum and maximum values can be listed after the last variable with these values. Thus, the command

```
HILOGLINEAR SEX RACE HAPPY(1,2) MARITAL INCOME82(1,3).
```

is equivalent to the previous command.

The values of the variables should be consecutive positive integers because HILOGLINEAR assumes there is a category for every value in the specified range. For example, the values 1, 2, and 3 are preferable to the values 5, 10, and 15. If necessary, you can recode variables using the RECODE command prior to the HILOGLINEAR command.

7.15
Specifying the Generating Class

Use the DESIGN subcommand to specify the generating class for the terms in a model. Asterisks are used to specify the highest-order interactions in a generating class. For example, the command

```
HILOGLINEAR SEX RACE HAPPY(1,2) MARITAL INCOME82(1,3)
   /DESIGN=HAPPY*MARITAL*INCOME82 SEX.
```

specifies a hierarchical model with the main effects HAPPY, MARITAL, INCOME82, and SEX; all second-order effects involving HAPPY, MARITAL, and INCOME82; and the third-order interaction term HAPPY *MARITAL*INCOME82. The command

```
HILOGLINEAR HAPPY(1,2) MARITAL(1,3)
   /DESIGN=HAPPY*MARITAL.
```

specifies a hierarchical model with the main effects HAPPY and MARITAL and the second-order interaction of HAPPY and MARITAL, producing the output in Figures 7.3 and 7.4.

You can use multiple DESIGN subcommands on a HILOGLINEAR command. If you omit the DESIGN subcommand or use it without specifications, a default model is fit. SPSS/PC+ produces parameter estimates only if the saturated model is specified. If you request an unsaturated model, the output will contain only the goodness-of-fit test for the model, the observed and expected frequencies, and the residuals and standardized residuals.

7.16
Building a Model

Use the MAXORDER, CRITERIA, METHOD, and CWEIGHT subcommands to control computational and design aspects of a model and to perform model selection. Each of these subcommands remains in effect for any subsequent DESIGN subcommands unless overridden by new subcommand specifications.

7.17
Specifying the Order of the Model

The MAXORDER subcommand specifies the maximum order of terms in a model. If you specify MAXORDER=k, HILOGLINEAR fits a model with all terms of order k or less. Thus, MAXORDER provides an abbreviated way of specifying models. For example, the command

```
HILOGLINEAR MARITAL(1,3) HAPPY RACE SEX(1,2)
   /MAXORDER=2.
```

is equivalent to

```
HILOGLINEAR MARITAL(1,3) HAPPY RACE SEX(1,2)
  /DESIGN=MARITAL*HAPPY
          MARITAL*RACE
          MARITAL*SEX
          HAPPY*RACE
          HAPPY*SEX
          RACE*SEX.
```

If both MAXORDER and DESIGN are used, the MAXORDER subcommand restricts the model stated on the DESIGN subcommand. If MAXORDER specifies an order less than the total number of variables (i.e., if an unsaturated model is fit), HILOGLINEAR does not display parameter estimates but does produce a goodness-of-fit test and the observed and expected frequencies for the model.

7.18
Specifying the Estimation Criteria

HILOGLINEAR uses an iterative procedure to fit models. Use the CRITERIA subcommand to specify the values of constants in the iterative proportional-fitting and model-selection routines. The keywords available for CRITERIA are

CONVERGE(n)   *Convergence criterion.* The default is 0.25. Iterations stop when the change in fitted frequencies is less than the specified value.

ITERATE(n)   *Maximum number of iterations.* The default is 20.

P(p)   *Probability of chi-square for removal.* The default value is 0.05.

MAXSTEPS(n)   *Maximum number of steps.* The default is 10.

DEFAULT   *Default values.* Use DEFAULT to restore defaults altered by a previous CRITERIA subcommand.

The value for each keyword must be enclosed in parentheses. You can specify more than one keyword on a CRITERIA subcommand. Only those criteria specifically altered are changed. The keywords P and MAXSTEPS apply only to model selection and, therefore, must be used with an accompanying METHOD subcommand.

7.19
Requesting Backward Elimination

The METHOD subcommand requests a search for the "best" model through backward elimination of terms from the model. Use the subcommand METHOD alone or with the BACKWARD keyword.

If you omit the METHOD subcommand, HILOGLINEAR tests the model requested on the DESIGN subcommand but does not perform any model selection.

You can use the METHOD subcommand with DESIGN specifications (Section 7.15) or MAXORDER (Section 7.16) to obtain backward elimination that begins with the specified hierarchical model. For example, the command

```
HILOGLINEAR RACE SEX HAPPY(1,2) MARITAL INCOME82(1,3)
  /MAXORDER=3
  /METHOD=BACKWARD.
```

requests backward elimination beginning with a hierarchical model that contains all three-way interactions and excludes all four- and five-way interactions.

You can use the CRITERIA subcommand with METHOD to specify the removal criterion and maximum number of steps for a backward-elimination analysis. Thus, the command

```
HILOGLINEAR MARITAL INCOME(1,3) SEX HAPPY(1,2)
  /METHOD=BACKWARD
  /CRITERIA=P(.01) MAXSTEPS(25).
```

specifies a removal probability criterion of 0.01 and a maximum of 25 steps. The command

```
HILOGLINEAR HAPPY(1,2) MARITAL (1,3) INCOME82 (1,3) HEALTH (1,2)
  /METHOD=BACKWARD
  /CRITERIA=MAXSTEPS(6)
  /DESIGN=HAPPY*MARITAL*INCOME82*HEALTH.
```

requests a backward elimination of terms with a maximum of six steps. These commands produce the output in Figures 7.12a, 7.12b, and 7.12c.

7.20
Setting Structural Zeros

Use the CWEIGHT subcommand to specify cell weights for a model. Do not use CWEIGHT to weight aggregated input data (use the SPSS/PC+ WEIGHT command instead). CWEIGHT allows you to impose structural zeros on a model. HILOGLINEAR ignores the CWEIGHT subcommand with a saturated model.

There are two ways to specify cell weights. First, you can specify a numeric variable whose values are the cell weights. The command

```
HILOGLINEAR MARITAL(1,3) SEX HAPPY(1,2)
  /CWEIGHT=CELLWGT
  /DESIGN=MARITAL*SEX SEX*HAPPY MARITAL*HAPPY.
```

weights a cell by the value of the variable CELLWGT when a case containing the frequency for that cell is read.

Alternatively, you can specify a matrix of weights enclosed in parentheses on the CWEIGHT subcommand. You can use the prefix $n*$ to indicate that a cell weight is repeated n times in the matrix. The command

```
HILOGLINEAR MARITAL(1,3) INCOME(1,3)
  /CWEIGHT=(0 1 1 1 0 1 1 1 0)
  /DESIGN=MARITAL INCOME.
```

is equivalent to

```
HILOGLINEAR MARITAL(1,3) INCOME(1,3)
  /CWEIGHT=(0 3*1 0 3*1 0)
  /DESIGN=MARITAL INCOME.
```

You must specify a weight for every cell in the table. Cell weights are indexed by the levels of the variables in the order they are specified in the variables list. The index values of the rightmost variable change the most quickly.

7.21
Producing Optional Output

By default, HILOGLINEAR displays observed and expected cell frequencies, residuals and standardized residuals, and, for saturated models, parameter estimates. Use the following keywords on the PRINT command to obtain additional output:

FREQ	*Observed and expected cell frequencies.*
RESID	*Residuals and standardized residuals.*
ESTIM	*Parameter estimates, standard errors of estimates, and confidence intervals for parameters.* These are calculated only for saturated models.
ASSOCIATION	*Tests of partial association.* These are calculated only for saturated models.
DEFAULT	*Default display.* FREQ and RESID for all models plus ESTIM for saturated models.
ALL	*All available output.*

If you specify PRINT, only output explicitly requested is displayed. The PRINT subcommand affects all subsequent DESIGN subcommands unless a new PRINT subcommand is specified.

For example, the command

```
HILOGLINEAR HAPPY(1,2) MARITAL (1,3)
  /PRINT=ESTIM
  /DESIGN=HAPPY*MARITAL.
```

limits the display to parameter estimates, standard errors of estimates, and confidence intervals for the saturated model. This command produces the output in Figure 7.4.

7.22
Requesting Plots

To obtain plots of residuals, you must specify the PLOT subcommand. The following keywords are available on PLOT:

RESID   *Plot of standardized residuals against observed and expected counts.*

NORMPLOT   *Normal and detrended normal probability plots of the standardized residuals.*

NONE   *No plots.* Suppresses any plots requested on a previous PLOT subcommand. This is the default if the subcommand is omitted.

DEFAULT   *Default plots.* RESID and NORMPLOT are plotted when PLOT is used without keyword specifications or with keyword DEFAULT. No plots are produced if the subcommand is omitted entirely.

ALL   *All available plots.*

The PLOT subcommand affects all subsequent DESIGN subcommands unless a new PLOT subcommand is specified.

7.23
Missing Values

By default, HILOGLINEAR deletes cases with missing values for any variable named on the variables list from the analysis. Use the MISSING subcommand to include cases with user-missing values or to specify the default explicitly. The keywords are

LISTWISE   *Delete cases with missing values listwise.* This is the default.

INCLUDE   *Include cases with user-missing values.*

DEFAULT   *Same as LISTWISE.*

The MISSING subcommand can be specified only once on each HILOGLINEAR command and applies to all the designs specified on that command.

7.24
Annotated Example

The following SPSS/PC+ commands produced the output in Figures 7.10b, 7.10c, 7.12a, 7.12b, and 7.12c:

```
DATA LIST
   /  MARITAL 8 AGE 15-16 RACE 24 INCOME82 31-32
      SEX 40 HAPPY 48 HEALTH 56.
RECODE MARITAL (1=1)(5=2)(2 THRU 4=3)(ELSE=SYSMIS)/
       INCOME82 (1 THRU 10=1)(11 THRU 14=2)(15 THRU 17=3)(ELSE=SYSMIS)/
       SEX (1=2)(2=1)/HAPPY (1 THRU 2=1)(3=2)(ELSE=SYSMIS)/
       HEALTH (1 THRU 2=1)(3 THRU 4=2)(ELSE=SYSMIS).
VALUE LABELS MARITAL 1 'MARRIED' 2 'SINGLE' 3 'SPLIT'/
             INCOME82 1 'LOW' 2 'MIDDLE' 3 'HIGH'/
             SEX 1 'FEMALE' 2 'MALE'/
             HAPPY 1 'YES' 2 'NO'/
             HEALTH 1 'GOOD+' 2 'FAIR-'.
BEGIN DATA.
lines of data
END DATA.
HILOGLINEAR HAPPY(1,2) MARITAL (1,3) INCOME82 (1,3) HEALTH (1,2)
   /PLOT=ALL
   /METHOD=BACKWARD
   /MAXSTEPS=6
   /DESIGN=HAPPY*MARITAL*INCOME82*HEALTH.
FINISH.
```

• The DATA LIST command gives the variable names and column locations of the variables used in the analysis.

• The RECODE command recodes the variables into consecutive integers to assure efficient processing.

• The VALUE LABELS command assigns descriptive labels to the recoded values of variables MARITAL, INCOME82, SEX, HAPPY, and HEALTH.

• The HILOGLINEAR command requests a backward elimination of the model with a maximum number of six steps. It also requests plots of the standardized residuals against observed and expected counts, as well as the normal and detrended normal probability plots of the standardized residuals.

Contents

Chapter 8   Measuring Scales: Reliability Analysis

From the moment we're born, the world begins to "score" us. One minute after birth, we're rated on the 10-point Apgar scale, followed closely by the 5-minute Apgar scale, and then on to countless other scales that will track our intelligence, credit worthinesss, likelihood of hijacking a plane, and so forth. A dubious mark of maturity is when we find ourselves administering these scales.

8.1
CONSTRUCTING A SCALE

When we wish to measure characteristics such as driving ability, mastery of course materials, or the ability to function independently, we must construct some type of measurement device. Usually we develop a scale or test that is composed of a variety of related items. The responses to each of the items can be graded and summed, resulting in a score for each case. A question that frequently arises is, How good is our scale? In order to answer this question, let's consider some of the characteristics of a scale or test.

When we construct a test to measure how well college students have learned the material in an introductory psychology course, the questions actually included in the test are a small sample from all of the items that may have been selected. Though we have selected a limited number of items for inclusion in a test, we want to draw conclusions about the students' mastery of the entire course contents. In fact, we'd like to think that even if we changed the actual items on the test, there would be a strong relationship between students' scores on the test actually given and the scores they would have received on other tests we could have given. A good test is one which yields stable results. That is, it's *reliable*.

8.2
Reliability and Validity

Everyone knows the endearing qualities of a reliable car. It goes anytime, anywhere, for anybody. It behaves the same way under a wide variety of circumstances. Its performance is repeatable. A reliable measuring instrument behaves similarly: the test yields similar results when different people administer it and when alternative forms are used. When conditions for making the measurement change, the results of the test should not.

A test must be reliable to be useful. But it's not enough for a test to be reliable; it must also be *valid*. That is, the instrument must measure what it is intended to measure. A test that requires students to do mirror drawing and memorize nonsense syllables may be quite reliable, but it is a poor indicator of mastery of the concepts of psychology. The test has poor validity.

There are many different ways to assess both reliability and validity. In this chapter, we will be concerned only with measures of reliability.

8.3
Describing Test Results

Before embarking on a discussion of measures of reliability, let's take a look at some of the descriptive statistics that are useful for characterizing a scale. We will be analyzing a scale of the physical activities of daily living in the elderly.* The goal of the scale is to assess an elderly person's competence in the physical activities of daily living. Three hundred and ninety-five people were rated on the eight items shown in Figure 8.3a. For each item, a score of 1 was assigned if the patient was unable to perform the activity, 2 if the patient was able to perform the activity with assistance, and 3 if the patient required no assistance to perform the activity.

Figure 8.3a   Physical activity items

```
RELIABILITY /VARIABLES = ITEM1 TO ITEM8
  ...
```

```
1.    ITEM1    Can eat
2.    ITEM2    Can dress and undress
3.    ITEM3    Can take care of own appearance
4.    ITEM4    Can walk
5.    ITEM5    Can get in and out of bed
6.    ITEM6    Can take a bath or shower
7.    ITEM7    Can get to bathroom on time
8.    ITEM8    Has been able to do tasks for 6 months
```

When we summarize a scale, we want to look at the characteristics of the individual items, the characteristics of the overall scale, and the relationship between the individual items and the entire scale. Figure 8.3b contains descriptive statistics for the individual items.

Figure 8.3b   Univariate descriptive statistics

```
RELIABILITY /VARIABLES = ITEM1 TO ITEM8
   /STATISTICS DESCRIPTIVES
  ...
```

		MEAN	STD DEV	CASES
1.	ITEM1	2.9266	.3593	395.0
2.	ITEM2	2.8962	.4116	395.0
3.	ITEM3	2.9165	.3845	395.0
4.	ITEM4	2.8684	.4367	395.0
5.	ITEM5	2.9114	.3964	395.0
6.	ITEM6	2.8506	.4731	395.0
7.	ITEM7	2.7873	.5190	395.0
8.	ITEM8	1.6582	.4749	395.0

You see that the average scores for the items range from 2.93 for item 1 to 1.66 for item 8. Item 7 has the largest standard deviation, .5190.

Figure 8.3c   Interitem correlation coefficients

```
RELIABILITY /VARIABLES = ITEM1 TO ITEM8
   /STATISTICS DESCRIPTIVES CORRELATIONS
  ...
```

```
                   CORRELATION MATRIX

            ITEM1      ITEM2      ITEM3      ITEM4      ITEM5

ITEM1      1.0000
ITEM2       .7893     1.0000
ITEM3       .8557      .8913     1.0000
ITEM4       .7146      .7992      .7505     1.0000
ITEM5       .8274      .8770      .8173      .8415     1.0000
ITEM6       .6968      .8326      .7684      .8504      .7684
ITEM7       .5557      .5736      .5340      .5144      .5497
ITEM8       .0459      .1427      .0795      .2108      .0949

            ITEM6      ITEM7      ITEM8

ITEM6      1.0000
ITEM7       .5318     1.0000
ITEM8       .2580      .1883     1.0000
```

---

* Thanks to Dr. Michael Counte of Rush-Presbyterian-St. Lukes Medical Center, principal investigator of the National Institute of Aging panel study of elderly health beliefs and behavior, for making these data available.

The correlation coefficients between the items are shown in Figure 8.3c. The only item that appears to have a small correlation with the other items is item 8. Its highest correlation is .26, with item 6.

Additional statistics for the scale as a whole are shown in Figure 8.3d and 8.3e.

Figure 8.3d   Scale statistics

```
RELIABILITY /VARIABLES = ITEM1 TO ITEM8
  /STATISTICS DESCRIPTIVES CORRELATIONS SCALE
  ...
```

STATISTICS FOR SCALE	MEAN	VARIANCE	STD DEV	# OF VARIABLES
	21.8152	7.3896	2.7184	8

Figure 8.3e   Summary statistics for items

```
RELIABILITY /VARIABLES = ITEM1 TO ITEM8
  /STATISTICS DESCRIPTIVES CORRELATIONS SCALE
  /SUMMARY = MEANS VARIANCES CORRELATIONS
  ...
```

	MEAN	MINIMUM	MAXIMUM	RANGE	MAX/MIN	VARIANCE
ITEM MEANS	2.7269	1.6582	2.9266	1.2684	1.7649	.1885
ITEM VARIANCES	.1891	.1291	.2694	.1403	2.0864	.0022
INTER-ITEM CORRELATIONS	.5843	.0459	.8913	.8454	19.4033	.0790

The average score for the scale is 21.82, and the standard deviation is 2.7 (Figure 8.3d). The average score on an item (Figure 8.3e) is 2.73, with a range of 1.27. Similarly, the average of the item variances is .19, with a minimum of .13 and a maximum of .27. The correlations between items range from .046 to .891. The ratio between the largest and smallest correlation is .891/.046, or 19.4. The average correlation is .584.

8.4
Relationship Between the Scale and the Items

Now let's take a look at the relationship between the individual items and the composite score.

Figure 8.4   Item-total summary statistics

```
RELIABILITY /VARIABLES = ITEM1 TO ITEM8
  /STATISTICS DESCRIPTIVES CORRELATIONS SCALE
  /SUMMARY = MEANS VARIANCES CORRELATIONS TOTAL
  ...
```

ITEM-TOTAL STATISTICS	SCALE MEAN IF ITEM DELETED	SCALE VARIANCE IF ITEM DELETED	CORRECTED ITEM-TOTAL CORRELATION	SQUARED MULTIPLE CORRELATION	ALPHA IF ITEM DELETED
ITEM1	18.8886	5.8708	.7981	.7966	.8917
ITEM2	18.9190	5.5061	.8874	.8882	.8820
ITEM3	18.8987	5.7004	.8396	.8603	.8873
ITEM4	18.9468	5.4718	.8453	.8137	.8848
ITEM5	18.9038	5.6202	.8580	.8620	.8852
ITEM6	18.9646	5.3084	.8520	.8029	.8833
ITEM7	19.0278	5.6414	.5998	.3777	.9095
ITEM8	20.1570	6.7316	.1755	.1331	.9435

For each item, the first column of Figure 8.4 shows what the average score for the scale would be if the item were excluded from the scale. For example, we know from Figure 8.3d that the average score for the scale is 21.82. If item 1 were eliminated from the scale, the average score would be 18.89. This is computed by simply subtracting the average score for the item from the scale mean. In this case it's $21.82 - 2.93 = 18.89$. The next column is the scale variance if the item were eliminated. The column labeled "CORRECTED ITEM-TOTAL CORRELA-TION" is the Pearson correlation coefficient between the score on the individual item and the sum of the scores on the remaining items. For example, the correlation between the score on item 8 and the sum of the scores of items 1 through 7 is only .176. This indicates that there is not much of a relationship between the eighth item and the other items. On the other hand, item 2 has a very high correlation, .887, with the other items.

Another way to look at the relationship between an individual item and the rest of the scale is to try to predict a person's score on the item based on the scores obtained on the other items. We can do this by calculating a multiple regression equation with the item of interest as the dependent variable and all of the other items as independent variables. The multiple R^2 from this regression equation is displayed for each of the items in the column labeled "SQUARED MULTIPLE CORRELATION." We can see that almost 80% of the observed variability in the responses to item 1 can be "explained" by the other items. As expected, item 8 is poorly predicted from the other items. Its multiple R^2 is only .13.

8.5
THE RELIABILITY COEFFICIENT

By looking at the statistics shown above, we've learned quite a bit about our scale and the individual items of which it is composed. However, we still haven't come up with an index of how reliable the scale is. There are several different ways to measure reliability:

- You can compute an estimate of reliability based on the observed correlations or covariances of the items with each other.
- You can correlate the results from two alternate forms of the same test or split the same test into two parts and look at the correlation between the two parts.

(See Lord and Novick, 1968, and Nunnally, 1978.)

One of the most commonly used reliability coefficients is *Cronbach's Alpha*. Alpha (or α) is based on the "internal consistency" of a test. That is, it is based on the average correlation of items within a test, if the items are standardized to a standard deviation of 1; or on the average covariance among items on a scale, if the items are not standardized. We assume that the items on a scale are positively correlated with each other because they are measuring, to a certain extent, a common entity. The average correlation of an item with all other items in the scale tells us about the extent of the common entity. If items are not positively correlated with each other, we have no reason to believe that they are correlated with other possible items we may have selected. In this case, we do not expect to see a positive relationship between this test and other similar tests.

8.6
Interpreting Cronbach's Alpha

Cronbach's α has several interpretations. It can be viewed as the correlation between this test or scale and all other possible tests or scales containing the same number of items, which could be constructed from a hypothetical universe of items that measure the characteristic of interest. In the physical activities scale, for example, the eight questions actually selected for inclusion can be viewed as a sample from a universe of many possible items. The patients could have been asked whether they can walk up a flight of stairs, or get up from a chair, or cook a meal, or whether they can perform a myriad of other activities related to daily living. Cronbach's α tells us how much correlation we expect between our scale and all other possible 8-item scales measuring the same thing.

Another interpretation of Cronbach's α is the squared correlation between the score a person obtains on a particular scale (the observed score) and the score he would have obtained if questioned on *all* of the possible items in the universe (the true score).

Since α can be interpreted as a correlation coefficient, it ranges in value from 0 to 1. (Negative α values can occur when items are not positively correlated among themselves and the reliability model is violated.)

Figure 8.6 Cronbach's Alpha

```
RELIABILITY /VARIABLES = ITEM1 TO ITEM8
   /STATISTICS DESCRIPTIVES CORRELATIONS SCALE
   /SUMMARY = MEANS VARIANCES CORRELATIONS TOTAL
   /SCALE (ALPHA) = ALL </MODEL = ALPHA.>
```

```
RELIABILITY COEFFICIENTS      8 ITEMS

ALPHA =    .9089           STANDARDIZED ITEM ALPHA =    .9183
```

Cronbach's α for the physical activity scale is shown in Figure 8.6. Note that the value, .91, is large, indicating that our scale is quite reliable. The other entry in Figure 8.6, labeled "STANDARDIZED ITEM ALPHA," is the α value that would be obtained if all of the items were standardized to have a variance of 1. Since the items in our scale have fairly comparable variances, there is little difference between the two αs. If items on the scale have widely differing variances, the two αs may differ substantially.

Cronbach's α can be computed using the following formula:

$$r = \frac{k\,\overline{cov}/\overline{var}}{1 + (k-1)\overline{cov}/\overline{var}}$$

Equation 8.6a

where k is the number of items in the scale, $\overline{cov}$ is the average covariance between items, and $\overline{var}$ is the average variance of the items. If the items are standardized to have the same variance, the formula can be simplified to

$$r = \frac{k\,\overline{r}}{1 + (k-1)\overline{r}}$$

Equation 8.6b

where $\overline{r}$ is the average correlation between items.

Looking at Equation 8.6b, we can see that Cronbach's α depends on both the length of the test (k in the formula) and the correlation of the items on the test. For example, if the average correlation between items is .2 on a 10 item scale, α is .71. If the number of items is increased to 25, α is .86. You can have large reliability coefficients even when the average interitem correlation is small, if the number of items on the scale is large enough.

8.7
Alpha If Item Deleted

When we are examining individual items, as in Figure 8.4, we may wish to know how each of the items affects the reliability of the scale. This can be accomplished by calculating Cronbach's α when each of the items is removed from the scale. These αs are shown in the last column of Figure 8.4. You can see that eliminating item 8 from the physical activity scale causes α to increase from .9089 (as in Figure 8.4) to .9435 (Figure 8.3d). From the correlation matrix in Figure 8.3c we saw that item 8 is not strongly related to the other items, so we would expect that eliminating it from the scale would increase the overall reliability of the scale. Elimination of any of the other items from the scale causes little change in α.

8.8
THE SPLIT-HALF RELIABILITY MODEL

Cronbach's α is based on correlations of items on a single scale. It's a measure based on the internal consistency of the items. Other measures of reliability are based on splitting the scale into two parts and looking at the correlation between the two parts. Such measures are called *split-half* coefficients. One of the disadvantages of this method is that the results depend on the allocation of items to halves. The coefficient you get depends on how you split your scale. Sometimes split-half methods are applied to situations in which two tests are administered, or the same test is administered twice.

Figure 8.8a Split-half statistics

```
RELIABILITY /VARIABLES = ITEM1 TO ITEM8
   /STATISTICS DESCRIPTIVES CORRELATIONS SCALE
   /SUMMARY = MEANS VARIANCES CORRELATIONS TOTAL
   /SCALE (SPLIT) = ALL /MODEL = SPLIT.
```

```
         # OF CASES =        395.0

                                                # OF
STATISTICS FOR      MEAN      VARIANCE   STD DEV VARIABLES
       PART 1     11.6076     2.1527     1.4672      4
       PART 2     10.2076     1.8959     1.3769      4
       SCALE      21.8152     7.3896     2.7184      8

ITEM MEANS          MEAN      MINIMUM    MAXIMUM    RANGE     MAX/MIN   VARIANCE
       PART 1      2.9019     2.8684     2.9266     .0582     1.0203     .0007
       PART 2      2.5519     1.6582     2.9114    1.2532     1.7557     .3575
       SCALE       2.7269     1.6582     2.9266    1.2684     1.7649     .1885

ITEM VARIANCES      MEAN      MINIMUM    MAXIMUM    RANGE     MAX/MIN   VARIANCE
       PART 1       .1593      .1291      .1907     .0616     1.4774     .0007
       PART 2       .2190      .1571      .2694     .1123     1.7147     .0021
       SCALE        .1891      .1291      .2694     .1403     2.0864     .0022

INTER-ITEM
CORRELATIONS        MEAN      MINIMUM    MAXIMUM    RANGE     MAX/MIN   VARIANCE
       PART 1       .8001      .7146      .8913     .1768     1.2474     .0039
       PART 2       .3985      .0949      .7684     .6735     8.0973     .0606
       SCALE        .5843      .0459      .8913     .8454    19.4033     .0790


ITEM-TOTAL STATISTICS

                 SCALE       SCALE     CORRECTED
                 MEAN       VARIANCE    ITEM-       SQUARED       ALPHA
                 IF ITEM    IF ITEM    TOTAL        MULTIPLE      IF ITEM
                 DELETED    DELETED    CORRELATION  CORRELATION   DELETED

ITEM1           18.8886     5.8708      .7981        .7966         .8917
ITEM2           18.9190     5.5061      .8874        .8882         .8820
ITEM3           18.8987     5.7004      .8396        .8603         .8873
ITEM4           18.9468     5.4718      .8453        .8137         .8848
ITEM5           18.9038     5.6202      .8580        .8620         .8852
ITEM6           18.9646     5.3084      .8520        .8029         .8833
ITEM7           19.0278     5.6414      .5998        .3777         .9095
ITEM8           20.1570     6.7316      .1755        .1331         .9435
```

Figure 8.8a contains summary statistics that would be obtained if we split the physical ability scale into two equal parts. The first 4 items are part 1, while the second 4 items are part 2. Note that separate descriptive statistics are given for each of the parts, as well as for the entire scale. Reliability statistics for the split model are shown in Figure 8.8b.

Figure 8.8b Split-half reliability

```
RELIABILITY /VARIABLES = ITEM1 TO ITEM8
   /STATISTICS DESCRIPTIVES CORRELATIONS SCALE
   /SUMMARY = MEANS VARIANCES CORRELATIONS TOTAL
   /SCALE (SPLIT) = ALL /MODEL = SPLIT.
```

```
RELIABILITY COEFFICIENTS    8 ITEMS

CORRELATION BETWEEN FORMS =    .8269    EQUAL LENGTH SPEARMAN-BROWN =      .9052

GUTTMAN SPLIT-HALF =           .9042    UNEQUAL-LENGTH SPEARMAN-BROWN =    .9052

ALPHA FOR PART 1 =             .9387    ALPHA FOR PART 2 =                 .7174

   4 ITEMS IN PART 1                       4 ITEMS IN PART 2
```

The correlation between the two halves, labeled on the output as "CORRELATION BETWEEN FORMS', is .8269. This is an estimate of the reliability of the test if it has 4 items. The equal length Spearman-Brown coefficient, which has a value of .9052 in this case, tells us what the reliability of the 8-item test would be if it was made up of two equal parts that have a 4-item reliability of .8269.

(Remember, the reliability of a test increases as the number of items on the test increase, provided that the average correlation between items does not change.) If the number of items on each of the two parts is not equal, the unequal length Spearman-Brown coefficient can be used to estimate what the reliability of the overall test would be. In this case, since the two parts are of equal length, the two Spearman-Brown coefficients are equal. The Guttman split-half coefficient is another estimate of the reliability of the overall test. It does not assume that the two parts are equally reliable or have the same variance. Separate values of Cronbach's α are also shown for each of the two parts of the test.

8.9 OTHER RELIABILITY MODELS

In the previous models we've considered, we didn't make any assumptions about item means or variances. If we have information about item means and variances, we can incorporate this additional information in the estimation of reliability coefficients. Two commonly used models are the *strictly parallel* model and the *parallel* model. In the strictly parallel model, all items are assumed to have the same means, the same variances for the true (unobservable) scores, and the same error variances over replications. When the assumption of equal means is relaxed, we have what's known as a parallel model.

Additional statistics can be obtained from a strictly parallel or parallel model. Figure 8.9a contains a test of the goodness-of-fit for the parallel model applied to the physical activity data. (This model is not appropriate for these data. We'll use it, however, to illustrate the output for this type of model.)

Figure 8.9a Goodness-of-fit for parallel model

```
RELIABILITY /VARIABLES = ITEM1 TO ITEM8
    /STATISTICS DESCRIPTIVES CORRELATIONS SCALE
    /SUMMARY = MEANS VARIANCES CORRELATIONS TOTAL
    /SCALE (ML) = ALL /MODEL - PARALLEL.
```

```
TEST FOR GOODNESS OF FIT OF MODEL          PARALLEL

CHI SQUARE =      1660.1597       DEGREES OF FREEDOM =       34
LOG OF DETERMINANT OF UNCONSTRAINED MATRIX =     -21.648663
LOG OF DETERMINANT OF CONSTRAINED MATRIX    =     -17.403278
PROBABILITY =    .0000
```

As you can see, the chi-square value is very large and we must reject the hypothesis that the parallel model fits. If the parallel model were appropriate we could consider the results, which are shown in Figure 8.9b.

Figure 8.9b Maximum-likelihood reliability estimate

```
    PARAMETER ESTIMATES

ESTIMATED COMMON VARIANCE =        0.1891
            ERROR VARIANCE =        0.0842
             TRUE VARIANCE =        0.1049
ESTIMATED COMMON INTERITEM CORRELATION =    0.5549

ESTIMATED RELIABILITY OF SCALE    = .9089
UNBIASED ESTIMATE OF RELIABILITY = .9093
```

The first entry is an estimate of the common variance for an item. It is the sum of the true variance and the error variance, which are displayed below it. An estimate of the common interitem correlation, based on the model, is also shown. Figure 8.9b also shows two reliability coefficients. The first is a maximum likelihood estimate of the reliability coefficient, while the second is the maximum likelihood estimate corrected for bias. If either the parallel or the strictly parallel model fits the data, then the best linear combination of the items is simply their sum.

8.10
RUNNING
PROCEDURE
RELIABILITY

Use RELIABILITY to analyze *additive* scales: scales formed by simply adding a number of component variables, or items. RELIABILITY can efficiently analyze different groups of items to help you choose the best scale. RELIABILITY does not create the scale for you. After choosing the items that you want, on the basis of the reliability analysis, use the COMPUTE command to form the scale as the sum of the items.

8.11
Specifying Variables

The VARIABLES subcommand specifies a group of variables for subsequent analysis. It must be the first subcommand. You can enter more than one VARIABLES subcommand; each one specifies variables for the following SCALE subcommands, up to the next VARIABLES subcommand (if any). You can specify VARIABLES=ALL to use all variables in your active file as scale components.

8.12
Specifying a Scale

After a VARIABLES subcommand, enter one or more SCALE subcommands. Each SCALE subcommand defines a scale for analysis. Specifications on SCALE consist of a scale name of up to eight characters, in parentheses, and a list of the variables making up the scale. Specify ALL to use all the variables on the VARIABLES subcommand. For example:

```
RELIABILITY VARIABLES=ITEM1 TO ITEM8 /SCALE (SUM) = ALL.
```

• The scale name SUM will be used to label the reliability analysis.
• The scale includes all the variables from ITEM1 to ITEM8.

You can use more than one SCALE subcommand to analyze the items on the preceding VARIABLES subcommand:

```
RELIABILITY VARIABLES=ITEM1 TO ITEM8
/SCALE (ALL) = ALL
/SCALE (ALLBUT8) = ITEM1 TO ITEM7
/SCALE (FIRST4) = ITEM1 TO ITEM4.
```

When you use the keyword TO on the SCALE subcommand, as in this example, it refers to the order that variables were listed on the preceding VARIABLES subcommand, and not to their order in the active file.

8.13
Choosing a Model

The default model for reliability analysis is ALPHA, which calculates Cronbach's α coefficient for each SCALE subcommand. To use a different model, specify the MODEL subcommand after the SCALE to which the model applies. Available models are:

ALPHA   *Cronbach's α.* This is the default.

SPLIT (n)   *Split-half coefficients.* A split-half reliability analysis is performed, based on the order in which you named the items on the preceding SCALE subcommand. The first half of the items (rounding up if the number of items is odd) form the first part, and the remaining items form the second part.
After the keyword SPLIT, you can specify in parentheses the number of items to be placed in the *second* part. Thus /MODEL= SPLIT(5) indicates that the last five items on the SCALE subcommand should form the second part, and the items that precede them should form the first part.

GUTTMAN   *Guttman's lower bounds for true reliability.*

PARALLEL   *Maximum likelihood reliability estimate under parallel assumptions.* This model assumes that the items all have equal variance.

STRICTPARALLEL *Maximum likelihood reliability estimate under strictly parallel assumptions.* This model assumes that the items have the same variance and the same mean.

You can only specify MODEL once after a single SCALE subcommand. To use more than one model on the same scale, specify several SCALE subcommands, each followed by MODEL:

```
RELIABILITY VARIABLES=ITEM1 TO ITEM8
/SCALE (ALPHA)=ALL  /MODEL=ALPHA
/SCALE (SPLIT)=ALL  /MODEL=SPLIT
/SCALE (ML)=ALL     /MODEL=PARALLEL.
```

8.14
Obtaining Statistics

Use the STATISTICS and SUMMARY subcommands for additional statistics from RELIABILITY. Use these subcommands only once; they apply to all the SCALE subcommands that you enter.

SUMMARY provides comparisons of various statistics over all items in a scale, as well as comparisons of each item to the others taken as a group. Available keywords are:

MEANS *Summary statistics for item means.* The average item mean, the largest, smallest, range, and variance of item means, and the ratio of the largest to the smallest item mean.

VARIANCES *Summary statistics for item variances.* Same statistics as those displayed for MEANS.

COVARIANCES *Summary statistics for interitem covariances.* Same statistics as those displayed for MEANS.

CORRELATIONS *Summary statistics for interitem correlations.* Same statistics as those displayed for MEANS.

TOTAL *Summary statistics comparing each item to the scale composed of the other items.* Scale mean and variance if the item were deleted; correlation between the item and the scale if it were deleted; squared multiple correlation with the other items; Cronbach's α if the item were deleted.

ALL *All available summary statistics.*

For example, Figures 8.3e and 8.4 were obtained by specifying

```
RELIABILITY /VARIABLES = ITEM1 TO ITEM8
  /SUMMARY = MEANS VARIANCES CORRELATIONS TOTAL
  ...
```

The STATISTICS command computes a variety of descriptive and diagnostic statistics. The keywords for it are:

DESCRIPTIVES *Item means and standard deviations.*

COVARIANCES *Interitem variance-covariance matrix.*

CORRELATIONS *Interitem correlation matrix.*

SCALE *Scale mean and variance.*

ANOVA *Repeated-measures analysis of variance table.*

TUKEY *Tukey's estimate of the power to which the scale must raised to achieve additivity.* This tests the assumption that there is no multiplicative interaction among the items.

HOTELLING *Hotelling's T^2.* This tests for violations of the assumption that item means are equal, for scales with more than two items.

FRIEDMAN *Friedman's chi-square and Kendall's coefficient of concordance.* Request this in addition to ANOVA if your items have the form of ranks. The chi-square test replaces the usual F test in the ANOVA table.

COCHRAN *Cochran's Q.* You can request this in addition to ANOVA if your items are all dichotomies. The Q statistic replaces the usual F test in the ANOVA table.

ALL *All available statistics.*

For example, Figures 8.3b, 8.3c, and 8.3d were obtained by specifying

```
RELIABILITY /VARIABLES = ITEM1 TO ITEM8
  /STATISTICS DESCRIPTIVES CORRELATIONS SCALE
  ...
```

8.15
Annotated Example

The following commands produced the output in Figures 8.3a through 8.9b.

```
DATA LIST FREE/ ID ITEM1 TO ITEM8.
VARIABLE LABELS ITEM1 'Can eat'
 ITEM2 'Can dress and undress'
 ITEM3 'Can take care of own appearance'
 ITEM4 'Can walk'
 ITEM5 'Can get in and out of bed'
 ITEM6 'Can take a bath or shower'
 ITEM7 'Can get to bathroom on time'
 ITEM8 'Has been able to do tasks for 6 months'.
VALUE LABELS ITEM1 TO ITEM8 1 'Unable to perform'
 2 'Needs assistance'        3 'Needs no assistance'.
BEGIN DATA.
3433 3 3 3 3 3 2 2
1418 3 3 3 3 3 3 2
2180 3 2 3 2 3 2 3 1
  ...
END DATA.
RELIABILITY VARIABLES = ITEM1 TO ITEM8
 /STATISTICS = DESCRIPTIVES CORRELATIONS SCALE
 /SUMMARY = MEANS VARIANCES CORRELATIONS TOTAL
 /SCALE (DEFAULT) ALL /MODEL ALPHA
 /SCALE (SPLIT) ALL    /MODEL SPLIT
 /SCALE (ML) ALL       /MODEL PARALLEL.
```

- The DATA LIST command indicates that the variables ID and ITEM1 to ITEM8 are to be read in free format.
- The VARIABLE LABELS and VALUE LABELS commands provide descriptive labels.
- The RELIABILITY command names all eight items on the VARIABLES subcommand.
- The STATISTICS subcommand requests descriptive statistics (Figure 8.3b), the correlation matrix (Figure 8.3c), and scale statistics (Figure 8.3d).
- The SUMMARY subcommand requests summary tables of means, variances, and correlations (Figure 8.3e), as well as item-total summary statistics (Figure 8.4).
- A series of SCALE subcommands follow. Each provides a scale name (in parentheses) and specifies that all eight variables should be included in the scale. Scale names are arbitrary (although limited to 8 letters or numbers); these were chosen to indicate the model used for each scale.
- Each SCALE subcommand is followed by a MODEL subcommand that specifies the model for that scale.

Bibliography

Afifi, A. A., and V. Clark. *Computer-aided Multivariate Analysis.* Belmont, California: Lifetime Learning Publications, 1984.

Anderberg, M. R. *Cluster Analysis for Applications.* New York: Academic Press, 1973.

Andrews, D.F., R. Gnanadesikan, and J. L. Warner. Methods for assessing multivariate normality. In: *Multivariate Analysis III.* ed. P. R. Krishnaiah. New York: Academic Press, 1973.

Bacon, L. Unpublished data, 1980.

Barcikowski, R. S., and R. R. Robey. Decisions in single group repeated measures analysis: statistical tests and three computer packages. *American Statistician,* 38:2 (1984), 148-50.

Barnard, R. M. *Field-dependent Independence and Selected Motor Abilities,* Ph.D. diss. School of Education of New York University, 1973.

Benedetti, J. K., and M. B. Brown. Strategies for the selection of log-linear models. *Biometrics,* 34 (1978), 680-686.

Bishop, Y. M. M., S. E. Feinberg, and P. W. Holland. *Discrete Multivariate Analysis: Theory and Practice.* Cambridge, Mass: MIT Press, 1975.

Bock, R. D. *Multivariate Statistical Methods in Behavioral Research.* New York: McGraw-Hill, 1975.

Burns, P R. *Multiple Comparison Methods in MANOVA.* Proceedings 7th SPSS Users and Coordinators Conference, 1984.

Cattell, R. B. The meaning and strategic use of factor analysis. In *Handbook of Multivariate Experimental Psychology,* ed. R. B. Catell. Chicago: Rand McNally, 1966.

Churchill, G. A., Jr. *Marketing Research: Methodological Foundations.* Hinsdale, Illinois: Dryden Press, 1979

Cochran, W. G., and G. M. Cox. *Experimental Designs.* 2nd ed. New York: John Wiley and Sons, 1957.

Consumer Reports, July 1983.

Everitt, B. S. *The Analysis of Contingency Tables.* London: Chapman and Hall, 1977.

____. *Cluster Analysis.* 2nd ed. London: Heineman Educational Books Ltd., 1980.

____. *Graphical Techniques for Multivariate Data.* New York: North-Holland, 1978.

Eysenck, M.W. *Human Memory: Theory, Research and Individual Differences.* New York: Pergamon Press, 1977.

Feinberg, S. E. *The Analysis of Cross-Classified Categorical Data.* Cambridge, Mass: MIT Press, 1977.

Finn, J. D. *A General Model for Multivariate Analysis.* New York: Holt, Rinehart, and Winston, 1974.

Freund, R. J. The case of the missing cell. *The American Statistician,* 34 (1980), 94-98.

Gilbert, E. S. On discrimination using qualitative variables. *Journal of the American Statistical Association,* 63 (1968), 1399-1412.

Goldstein, M., and W. R. Dillon. *Discrete Discriminant Analysis.* New York: Wiley and Sons, 1978.

Goodman, L. A. *The Analysis of Cross-Classified Data Having Ordered Categories.* Cambridge: Harvard University Press, 1984.

Green, B. F. The two kinds of linear discriminant functions and their relationship. *Journal of Educational Statistics,* 4:3 (1979), 247-263.

Green, P. E. *Analyzing Multivariate Data.* Hinsdale, Illinois: Dryden Press, 1978.

Greenhouse, S. W., and S. Geisser. On methods in analysis of profile data. *Psychometrika,* 24 (1959), 95-112.

Haberman, S. J. *Analysis of Qualitative Data,* Vol 1. London: Academic Press, 1978.

Hand, D. J. *Discrimination and Classification.* New York: Wiley and Sons, 1981.

Harman, H. H. *Modern Factor Analysis.* 2nd ed. Chicago: University of Chicago Press, 1967.

Horton, R. L. *The General Linear Model.* New York: McGraw-Hill, 1978.

Huynh, H., and L. S. Feldt. Estimation of the Box correction for degrees of freedom from sample data in randomized block and split-plot designs. *Journal of Educational Statistics, 1 (1976), 69-82.*

Jonassen, C. T., and S. H. Peres. *Interrelationships of Dimensions of Community Systems.* Columbus: Ohio State University Press, 1960.

Kaiser, H. F. An index of factorial simplicity. *Psychometrika* 39 (1974), 31-36.

Kim, J. O., and C. W. Mueller. *Introduction to Factor Analysis.* Beverly Hills: Sage Press, 1978.

Kshirsagar, A. M., and E. Arseven. A note on the equivalency of two discrimination procedures. *The American Statistician,* 29 (1975), 38-39.

Lachenbruch, P. A. *Discriminant Analysis.* New York: Hafner Press, 1975.

Lord, F. M. and M. R. Novick. *Statistical Theories of Mental Test Scores.* Reading, MA: Addison-Wesley. 1968.

Miller, R. G. *Simultaneous Statistical Inference.* 2nd ed. New York: Springer-Verlag, 1981.

Milligan, G. W. An examination of the effect of six types of error perturbation on fifteen clustering algorithms. *Psychometrika,* 45 (1980), 325-42.

Milligan, G. W., and P. D. Isaac. The validation of four ultrametric clustering algorithms. *Pattern Recognition,* 12 (1980), 41-50.

Milliken, G. W., and D. E. Johnson. *Analysis of Messy Data.* Belmont, California: Lifetime Learning Publications, 1984.

Moore, D. H. Evaluation of five discrimination procedures for binary variables. *Journal of the American Statistical Association,* 68 (1973), 399.

Morrison, D. F. *Multivariate Statistical Methods.* New York: McGraw-Hill, 1967.

Norusis, M. J. *SPSS^X Advanced Statistics Guide.* New York: McGraw-Hill, 1985.

———. *SPSS^X Introductory Statistics Guide.* New York: McGraw-Hill, 1983.

Nunnally, J. *Psychometric Theory.* 2nd ed. New York: McGraw-Hill, 1978.

Olsen, C. L. On choosing a test statistic in multivariate analysis of variance. *Psychological Bulletin,* 83 (1976), 579-586.

Romesburg, H. C. *Cluster Analysis for Researchers.* Belmont, California: Lifetime Learning Publications, 1984.

Searle, S. R. *Linear Models.* New York: John Wiley and Sons, 1971.

Sneath, P. H. A., and R. R. Sokal. *Numerical Taxonomy.* San Francisco: W.H. Freeman and Co., 1973.

SPSS Inc. *SPSS^X User's Guide.* 2nd ed. New York: McGraw-Hill, 1986.

———. *SPSS Statistical Algorithms.* Chicago: SPSS Inc., 1985.

SPSS Inc., M. J. Norusis. *SPSS/PC+ for the IBM PC/XT/AT.* Chicago: SPSS Inc., 1986.

Stoetzel, J. A factor analysis of liquor preference of French consumers. *Journal of Advertising Research,* 1:1 (1960), 7-11.

Tatsuoka, M. M. *Multivariate Analysis.* New York: John Wiley and Sons, 1971.

Timm, N. H. *Multivariate Analysis with Applications in Education and Psychology.* Monterey: Brooks/Cole, 1975.

Tucker, L. R. Relations of factor score estimates to their use. *Psychometrika,* 36 (1971), 427-436.

Tucker, R. F., R. F. Koopman, and R. L. Linn. Evaluation of factor analytic research procedures by means of simulated correlation matrices. *Psychometrika,* 34 (1969), 421-459.

Van Vliet, P. K. J., and J. M. Gupta. *THAM v. sodium bicarbonate in idiopathic Respiratory Distress Syndrome* Archives of Disease in Childhood, 48 (1973), 249-255.

Wahl, P. W. and R. A. Kronmal. Discriminant functions when covariances are unequal and sample sizes are moderate. *Biometrics,* 33 (1977), 479-484.

Winer, B. J. *Statistical Principles in Experimental Design.* New York: McGraw-Hill, 1971.

Witkin, H. A., et al. *Personality Through Perception.* New York: Harper and Brothers, 1954.

Command Reference

Commands

Contents

CLUSTER

```
CLUSTER {varlist} [/MISSING={LISTWISE**} {INCLUDE}]
        {ALL    }          {DEFAULT** }

        [/READ=[SIMILAR] [{TRIANGLE}]]  [/WRITE=[DISTANCE]]
                         {LOWER   }

        [/MEASURE={SEUCLID**}] [/METHOD={BAVERAGE**}[(rootname)]
                 {DEFAULT** }          {DEFAULT** }
                 {EUCLID    }          {WAVERAGE  }
                 {COSINE    }          {SINGLE    }
                 {POWER(p,r)}          {COMPLETE  }
                 {BLOCK     }          {CENTROID  }
                 {CHEBYCHEV }          {MEDIAN    }
                                       {WARD      }

        [/SAVE=CLUSTER({level  })]   [/ID=varname]
                      {min,max}

        [/PRINT=[CLUSTER({level  })]  [{SCHEDULE**}]]
                        {min,max}      {DEFAULT** }

            [DISTANCE]  [NONE]

        [/PLOT=[VICICLE** [({1,n-1,1       })]]  [DENDROGRAM]]
                          {min[,max[,inc]]}

            [HICICLE [({1,n-1,1       })]]  [NONE]
                     {min[,max[,inc]]}
```

**Default if subcommand is omitted.

Example:

```
CLUSTER VARA TO VARD
 /PLOT=DENDROGRAM
 /PRINT=CLUSTER (2 4).
```

Overview   The CLUSTER procedure produces hierarchical clusters of items based on their dissimilarity or similarity on one or more variables. Cluster analysis is discussed in Anderberg (1973).

Defaults   By default, CLUSTER assumes that the items being clustered are cases and uses the squared Euclidean distances between cases on the variables in the analysis as the measure of distance. Cases are clustered using the method of average linkage between groups. The default display includes the number of cases in the analysis, the agglomeration schedule for the clustering, and a vertical icicle plot. Cases are identified by case number. By default, CLUSTER reads cases for the analysis and omits cases with missing values for any variable in the analysis.

Tailoring   **Cluster Measures and Methods.** You can use one of six similarity or distance measures and can cluster items using any one of seven methods: single, complete, or between- or within-groups average linkage, or the median, centroid, or Ward method. You can request more than one clustering method on a single CLUSTER command. Some clustering methods are restricted to particular distance metrics.

Display and Plots. You can display cluster membership, the distance or similarity matrix used to cluster variables or cases, and the agglomeration schedule for the cluster solution. You can request either a horizontal or vertical icicle plot or a dendrogram of the cluster solution, and you can control the cluster levels displayed on the icicle plot. You can also specify a variable to be used as a case identifier in the display.

Adding Variables to the Active File. You can save cluster membership for specified solutions as new variables in the active file.

Writing and Reading Matrices. You can write out the distance matrix and use it in subsequent CLUSTER analyses. You can also read in matrices produced by other procedures (e.g., CORRELATION) to cluster other items, such as variables.

Missing Values. You can include cases with user-missing values for the clustering variables in the analysis.

Syntax

- The minimum specification is a list of variables.
- The variables list must come first. Other subcommands can be specified in any order.
- Subcommands must be separated by slashes.
- The variables list and subcommands can each be specified once.
- More than one clustering method can be used on a matrix.

Operations

- CLUSTER causes the data to be read.
- The CLUSTER procedure involves four steps:

  First, CLUSTER obtains distance measures of similarities between or distances separating initial clusters (individual cases or variables being clustered).

  Next, it combines the two nearest clusters to form a new cluster.

  Third, it recomputes similarities or distances of existing clusters to the new cluster.

  CLUSTER then returns to the second step until all items are combined in one cluster.

- Clustering requires that valid values be present for most items.
- CLUSTER identifies clusters in solutions by sequential integers (1, 2, 3, and so on).
- When a narrow width is defined on the SET command, plots exceeding the defined width are broken into two sections and are printed one after the other.
- The BLOCK specification on the SET command controls the character used in the dendrogram.

Limitations

- The number of variables allowed on the variables list is the same as the system limit.
- CLUSTER stores both items and a lower-triangular matrix of similarities or distances in memory. Storage requirements increase rapidly with the number of items (cases). You should be able to cluster about 100 items using a small number of variables in a 64K workspace.
- Maximum 1 variables list and 1 each of the optional subcommands.

Example

```
CLUSTER VARA TO VARD
/PLOT=DENDROGRAM
/PRINT=CLUSTER (2 4).
```

- This example clusters cases based on their values for all variables between and including VARA and VARD on the active file.
- The analysis uses the default measure of distance (squared Euclidean) and the default clustering method (average linkage between groups).
- The PLOT subcommand requests a dendrogram.
- The PRINT subcommand requests a table that gives the cluster membership of each case for the two-, three-, and four-cluster solutions.

Variables List   When cases are read, the variables list identifies the variables used to compute similarities or distances between cases. When a distance or similarity matrix is read, the variables list uses the names for the items in the matrix.

- The variables list is required and must be specified before the optional subcommands.
- You can use keyword ALL to refer to all user-defined variables in the active file.
- You can use keyword TO to refer to consecutive variables in the active file.

MEASURE   The MEASURE subcommand specifies the distance or similarity measure to be
Subcommand   used in clustering cases.

- If the MEASURE subcommand is omitted or included with no specifications, squared Euclidean distances are used.
- Only one measure can be specified.

The following measures are available:

SEUCLID   *Squared Euclidean distances.* The distance between two cases is the sum of the squared differences in values on each variable. Use SEUCLID with centroid, median, and Ward's methods of clustering. SEUCLID is the default and can also be requested with the keyword DEFAULT.

EUCLID   *Euclidean distances.* The distance between two cases is the square root of the sum of the squared differences in values on each variable.

COSINE   *Cosine of vectors of variables.* This is a pattern similarity measure.

BLOCK   *City-block or Manhattan distances.* The distance between two cases is the sum of the absolute differences in values on each variable.

CHEBYCHEV   *Chebychev distance metric.* The distance between two cases is the maximum absolute difference in values for any variable.

POWER(p,r)   *Distances in an absolute power metric.* The distance between two cases is the rth root of the sum of the absolute differences to the pth power of values on each variable. Appropriate selection of integer parameters p and r yields Euclidean, squared Euclidean, Minkowski, city-block, minimum, maximum, and many other distance metrics.

METHOD Subcommand   The METHOD subcommand specifies one or more clustering methods.

- If the METHOD subcommand is omitted or included with no specifications, the method of average linkage between groups is used.
- Only one METHOD subcommand can be used, but more than one method can be specified on it.
- When you have a large number of items (cases), CENTROID and MEDIAN require significantly more CPU time than other methods.

The following methods can be specified:

BAVERAGE   *Average linkage between groups (UPGMA).* BAVERAGE is the default and can also be requested with the keyword DEFAULT.

WAVERAGE   *Average linkage within groups.*

SINGLE   *Single linkage or nearest neighbor.*

COMPLETE   *Complete linkage or furthest neighbor.*

CENTROID   *Centroid clustering (UPGMC).* Squared Euclidean distances should be used with this method.

MEDIAN   *Median clustering (WPGMC)*. Squared Euclidean distances should be used with this method.

WARD   *Ward's method*. Squared Euclidean distances should be used with this method.

Example

```
CLUSTER AVAR BVAR CVAR
/METHOD=SINGLE COMPLETE WARDS.
```

- This example clusters cases based on their values for variables AVAR, BVAR, and CVAR, and uses three clustering methods: single linkage, complete linkage, and Ward's method.

PRINT Subcommand

The PRINT subcommand controls the display of cluster output (except plots, which are controlled by the PLOT subcommand).

- If the PRINT subcommand is omitted or included with no specifications, an agglomeration schedule is displayed. If other keywords are specified on PRINT, the agglomeration schedule is displayed only if explicitly requested.
- CLUSTER automatically displays summary information (the clustering method and measure used and the number of cases) for each method named on the METHOD subcommand. This summary is displayed regardless of specifications on PRINT.

You can specify any or all of the following on the PRINT subcommand:

SCHEDULE   *Agglomeration schedule*. Displays the order in which and distances at which items and clusters combine to form new clusters. It also shows the last cluster level at which an item joined the cluster. SCHEDULE is the default and can also be requested with keyword DEFAULT.

CLUSTER(min,max)   *Cluster membership*. For each item, the display includes the value of the case identifier (or the variable name if matrix input is used), the case sequence number, and a value (1, 2, 3, etc.) identifying the cluster to which that case belongs in a given cluster solution. Specify either a single integer value in parentheses indicating the number of cluster solutions or a minimum and maximum value in parentheses indicating a range of solutions for which display is desired. If the number of clusters specified exceeds the number produced, the largest number of clusters is used (number of items minus 1). If CLUSTER is specified more than once, the last specification is taken.

DISTANCE   *Matrix of distances or similarities between items*. DISTANCE displays the matrix read or computed. The type of matrix produced (similarities or dissimilarities) depends upon the measure selected. DISTANCE produces a large volume of output and uses significant CPU time when the number of cases to cluster is large.

NONE   *None of the above*. NONE overrides any other keywords specified on PRINT.

Example

```
CLUSTER AVAR BVAR CVAR/ PRINT=CLUSTER(3,5).
```

- This example requests the display of cluster membership for each case for the three-, four-, and five-cluster solutions.

PLOT Subcommand

The PLOT subcommand controls the plots produced for each method specified on the METHOD subcommand. For icicle plots, PLOT allows you to control the cluster solution at which the plot begins and ends and the increment for displaying intermediate cluster solutions.

- If the PLOT subcommand is omitted or included with no specifications, a vertical icicle plot is produced.
- If keywords are specified on the PLOT subcommand, only those plots requested are produced.

- If there is not enough memory for a dendrogram or an icicle plot, the plot is skipped and a warning is issued.

- A large plot can be avoided by specifying range values or an increment for VICICLE or HICICLE. Smaller plots require significantly less workspace and time.

VICICLE(min,max,inc)   *Vertical icicle plot.* This is the default. The range specifications are optional. If used, they must be integer and must be enclosed in parentheses. *min* is the cluster solution at which to start the display (the default is 1) and *max* is the cluster solution at which to end the display (the default is the number of cases minus 1). If max is greater than the number of cases minus 1, the default is used. *inc* is the increment to use between cluster solutions (the default is 1). If max is specified, min must be specified, and if inc is specified, both min and max must be specified. If VICICLE is specified more than once, the last specification is used.

HICICLE(min,max,inc)   *Horizontal icicle plot.* All specifications for VICICLE apply to HICICLE. If both VICICLE and HICICLE are specified, the last one specified is used.

DENDROGRAM   *Tree diagram.* The dendrogram is scaled by the joining distances of the clusters.

NONE   *No plots.*

Example   `CLUSTER AVAR BVAR CVAR/PLOT=VICICLE(1,20).`

- This example produces a vertical icicle plot for the one-cluster through the twenty-cluster solution.

Example   `CLUSTER AVAR BVAR CVAR`
`/PLOT=VICICLE(1,151,5).`

- This example produces a vertical icicle plot for every fifth cluster solution starting with 1 and ending with 151 (1 cluster, 6 clusters, 11 clusters, and so on).

- In this example, the vertical dimension of the icicle plot fits on a single printed page.

ID Subcommand

The ID subcommand names a string variable to be used as the case identifier in cluster membership tables, icicle plots, and dendrograms. If the ID subcommand is omitted, cases are identified by case number.

SAVE Subcommand

The SAVE subcommand allows you to save cluster membership at specified solution levels as new variables on the active file.

- The only specification on SAVE is the CLUSTER keyword, followed by an equals sign and either the number of a single cluster solution or a range of solutions separated by a comma or blank. The solution number or range must be enclosed in parentheses.

- Both the CLUSTER keyword and a solution number or range are required. There are no default specifications.

- For each method for which you want to save cluster membership you must specify a rootname on the METHOD subcommand. The METHOD subcommand is therefore required when you use the SAVE subcommand. The rootname is specified in parentheses after the method keyword.

- The solution number or range applies to all methods for which you supply a rootname on METHOD.

- The new variables derive their names from the rootname and the number of the cluster solution.

- If the variables created by SAVE cause you to exceed the 200-variable limit, the entire CLUSTER command is not executed.

Example
```
CLUSTER A B C
/METHOD=BAVERAGE (CLUSMEM)
/SAVE=CLUSTERS(3,5).
```

• This command creates three new variables, CLUSMEM5, CLUSMEM4, and CLUSMEM3, containing the cluster membership for each case at the five-, four-, and three-cluster solutions.

• The order of the new variables on the active file will be CLUSMEM5, CLUSMEM4, and CLUSMEM3, since this is the order in which the solutions are obtained.

WRITE Subcommand

The WRITE subcommand allows you to write a computed distance or similarity matrix based on a measure of similarity or dissimilarity to the results file named on the SET command.

• If the WRITE subcommand is omitted, no file is written.

• If the WRITE subcommand is included without specifications, a square distance matrix of similarities or dissimilarities (depending on the measure selected) is written.

• Matrix elements are written in fixed 16-column fields with 5 decimal places. Thus, there are 5 matrix elements on each 80-character record.

• The dimensions of the matrix depend on the number of items clustered. If cases are read, the distance matrix is dimensioned by the number of cases clustered.

• Each row of the matrix begins on a new line.

• The WRITE subcommand writes the matrix to the results file named on the SET command or to the default results file (SPSS.PRC). Any existing contents of the results file are overwritten.

DISTANCE *Write a distance or similarity matrix.* This is the default.

Example
```
SET RESULTS='GSS80.MAT'.
DATA LIST FILE='GSS80.DAT'/SUICIDE1 TO SUICIDE4 2-9.
N 35.
CLUSTER  SUICIDE1 TO SUICIDE4
/WRITE DISTANCE.
```

• This example produces a default clustering of 35 cases. It uses all variables between and including SUICIDE1 to SUICIDE4 on the active file.

• A matrix of squared Euclidean distances is written to the file GSS80.MAT.

READ Subcommand

By default, CLUSTER assumes that the data file it uses contains cases. Use the READ subcommand to indicate that the data file contains a matrix. The general conventions for matrix materials are described in DATA LIST: Matrix Materials.

• If the READ subcommand is included without specifications, the matrix is assumed to be a square distance matrix. This is the default matrix written by CLUSTER.

• If any keywords are specified on READ, only the defaults that are specifically changed are altered.

• If you use the READ subcommand on CLUSTER, you must first use a DATA LIST command specifying matrix input. The DATA LIST command also assigns a variable name to each item that dimensions the matrix.

• All items named on the CLUSTER variables list must be defined on the DATA LIST command.

• The order in which items are named on the variables list must be the same as their order in the matrix.

• The MEASURE subcommand is ignored with matrix input.

• All methods specified on METHOD will accept either similarity or dissimilarity distance matrices as input. Incorrect results will be obtained for all methods if a similarity matrix is read and not identified as such.

• CLUSTER can read more than one distance matrix from the same file. Each matrix must be of the same type (similarity or dissimilarity) and must have the same dimensions.

• CLUSTER can also read other matrices such as a correlation matrix created by CORRELATION or another SPSS/PC+ procedure. This allows you to cluster variables as well as cases or to use a distance or similarity measure not available in CLUSTER.

Use the following keywords to read a matrix other than the default. TRIANGLE and LOWER are alternatives.

SIMILAR *Distance matrix based on a similarity measure.* By default, the distance matrix is assumed to be based on a measure of dissimilarity, or distance.

TRIANGLE *Lower-triangular matrix.* Same as LOWER but includes the diagonal elements. By default, the matrix is assumed to be square.

LOWER *Lower-subdiagonal matrix.* Same as TRIANGLE but without the diagonal elements. By default, the matrix is assumed to be square.

Example
```
DATA LIST MATRIX FILE='GSS80.MAT'/CASE1 TO CASE35.
CLUSTER CASE1 TO CASE35/READ.
```

• The DATA LIST command names the file and the items in the matrix. The matrix is assumed to be in the fixed format written by CLUSTER.

• The variables list indexes the matrix to be read by naming the variable that stands for each matrix item. In this case, the items are the cases on which the matrix was calculated.

• The READ subcommand specifies that a matrix is to be read. By default, CLUSTER will assume that the matrix was based on a measure of distance.

Example This example will read a matrix that was produced by the following commands:
```
SET RESULTS='VARS.MAT'.
DATA LIST FILE='VARS.DAT'/VA VB VC 1-3.
CORRELATION VARIABLES=VA VB VC/OPTIONS=2 4.
```

• The CORRELATION procedure computes correlations among the three variables and writes the matrix to the file VARS.MAT.

The commands to read this matrix into CLUSTER are
```
DATA LIST MATRIX FREE FILE='VARS.MAT'/VA VB VC.
CLUSTER VA VB VC
/PRINT=DISTANCE/READ=SIMILAR.
```

• The DATA LIST command specifies that a matrix will be read in freefield format (keyword FREE) from the VARS.MAT file and assigns variable names to the items in the matrix. FREE is specified because the matrix to be read is not in the default format produced by CLUSTER. In this example, the items being clustered are variables.

• The variables list on CLUSTER names the same variables as the DATA LIST command and in the same order. This identifies the entries of the input matrix.

• The PRINT subcommand allows you to verify that the matrix is being read properly.

• The READ subcommand specifies that a matrix will be read instead of cases. The matrix is a square matrix and contains a measure of similarity.

• CLUSTER will read both the correlation matrix and the matrix of *n*'s written by CORRELATION. You should ignore the warning message and analysis produced by the matrix of *n*'s.

• This analysis clusters variables across cases by the default between-groups average-linkage method.

MISSING Subcommand

The MISSING subcommand controls the treatment of cases with missing values. By default, a case that has a missing value for any variable in the variable list is omitted from the analysis.

LISTWISE *Delete cases with missing values listwise.* Only cases with nonmissing values on all variables in the variables list are used. LISTWISE is the default and can also be requested with keyword DEFAULT.

INCLUDE *Include cases with user-missing values.* Only cases with system-missing values are excluded.

Reference

Anderberg, M. J. *Cluster analysis for applications.* New York: Academic Press, 1973.

DATA LIST: Matrix Materials

```
DATA LIST [FILE='filename'] MATRIX [{FIXED}]
                                    {FREE }

            /varlist
```

Example:

```
DATA LIST FILE='FAC.MAT' MATRIX / X1 X2 X3 X4 X5.
N 100.
FACTOR READ=CORRELATION TRIANGLE
 /VARIABLES-X1 TO X5.
```

Overview

The DATA LIST command with keyword MATRIX provides variable names and a dictionary for matrix materials used as input in CLUSTER, FACTOR, ONEWAY, REGRESSION, and MANOVA. The matrix materials can include correlation coefficients, covariance coefficients, a matrix of n's, or group distance measures. Matrix materials can be read in fixed or freefield format but must conform to the requirements of the individual procedures (see below and the discussion of each procedure in this Command Reference). The matrix input can be inline or read from an external file. For general information on defining matrix materials on DATA LIST, refer to DATA LIST: Matrix Materials in the Command Reference of the *SPSS/PC+* manual.

Matrix Data

The SPSS/PC+ procedures CORRELATION, CLUSTER, ONEWAY, FACTOR, and REGRESSION write matrix materials in a fixed format that automatically conforms to the requirements of the various procedures that read matrix materials. Some materials, such as factor matrices written by FACTOR and matrices written by MANOVA, are specially formatted for a specific procedure. If you enter your own matrix materials, they must conform to these formats as well as to the following requirements:

- Matrix materials can be arranged in fixed or freefield format.
- Each cell of the matrix must contain a value.
- Each element in a row in freefield format matrix materials is separated by at least one space or a comma.
- Each row vector of a matrix begins on a new line.
- Each type of matrix material begins on a new line.
- In fixed format, there is a maximum number of elements that can be entered in a row (see discussion of individual procedures below). The format must confirm to the requirements of the procedure that reads the matrix.
- If the elements for a vector do not fit in one row, the elements can be continued on the next row. Each row must be filled before continuing to the next.
- Matrix elements cannot be split across input lines.
- Decimal points must be entered with the data. You cannot specify implied decimal places.

Matrix Input for Procedure CLUSTER

- Procedure CLUSTER reads matrix materials in both fixed and freefield format.
- Fixed-format matrix materials for CLUSTER must be arranged so that each matrix cell is 16 columns wide with up to 5 decimal places. You can have only 5 elements of a vector in each row.
- Freefield format matrix materials, such as a correlation matrix written by procedure CORRELATION, must conform to the requirements listed under "Matrix Data" above.

C

Command Reference

Example
```
DATA LIST MATRIX  FREE /
 ABDEFECT ABHLTH ABNOMORE ABPOOR ABRAPE ABSINGLE.
BEGIN DATA.
 1.0000000  .6118418   .3936668   .3743177   .6284106   .3820830
  .6118418 1.0000000   .2870408   .3098805   .6097969   .2935045
  .3936668  .2870408  1.0000000   .7658386   .3806726   .7881280
  .3743177  .3098805   .7658386  1.0000000   .3847740   .7379326
  .6284106  .6097969   .3806726   .3847740  1.0000000   .3909586
  .3820830  .2935045   .7881280   .7379326   .3909586  1.0000000
END DATA.
CLUSTER ABDEFECT ABHLTH ABNOMORE ABPOOR ABRAPE ABSINGLE/
 READ=SIMILAR.
```

- The DATA LIST command specifies inline matrix materials in freefield format. The active file dictionary contains six variable names.

- In this case, the matrix is a correlation matrix. Each row vector begins on a new line.

- The READ subcommand on CLUSTER indicates that a square matrix based on a measure of similarity will be read (see "READ Subcommand" under CLUSTER).

- Since this matrix is from the CORRELATION procedure, it is read in freefield format. The final record written by CORRELATION, containing the number of cases, has been edited out of the matrix.

Example
```
DATA LIST MATRIX/CASE1 TO CASE19.
BEGIN DATA
       0.0         19062.00391    17697.00781    17545.00781    19038.00781
 19050.00781       17742.00781    17964.00781    19125.00391      111.99998
 19230.00391       18041.00781    17693.00781    19023.00781     9635.00781
  9860.00781        9899.00781     9901.00781    10028.00781
 19062.00391           0.0        18485.00000    17867.00000    17904.00000
 17890.00000       18484.00000    18508.00000       49.00000    18536.00391
   109.99998       18537.00000    18193.00000    18009.00000     9427.00000
  9228.00000        9657.00000     9885.00000     9726.00000
     :                 :              :              :
 10028.00781        9726.00000     9929.00000     9659.00000     9502.00000
  9435.99609        9589.99609     9737.99609     9537.00000     9730.00781
  9476.00000        9660.99609     9449.00000     9261.00000       87.00000
    46.00000          40.99998       52.99998        0.0
END DATA.
CLUSTER ALL /MISSING INCLUDE/READ.
```

- The DATA LIST commands specifies inline matrix materials in fixed format (the default). The active file dictionary contains 19 variable names.

- The distance matrix to be read was produced using procedure CLUSTER with the MISSING=INCLUDE and WRITE=DISTANCE subcommands. Cases, not variables, are going to be clustered.

- The data are automatically arranged in the format required by CLUSTER. Each column vector is 16 characters wide with 5 decimal values. There are 4 rows for each vector. Only the first two and last vectors are shown.

- The READ subcommand on CLUSTER indicates that a distance matrix will be read (see "The READ Subcommand" under CLUSTER).

Matrix Input for Procedure FACTOR

- Procedure FACTOR can use matrix materials in either fixed or freefield format.

- Fixed-format matrix materials for FACTOR must be arranged so that each column vector entry is 10 columns wide with up to 3 decimal places. You can enter up to 8 values in each row.

- Matrix materials in freefield format must conform to requirements noted above under "Matrix Data."

Example
```
DATA LIST MATRIX / X1 X2 X3 X4 X5.
N 100.
BEGIN DATA.
1.000
0.945     1.000
0.840     0.720     1.000
0.735     0.630     0.560     1.000
0.630     0.540     0.480     0.420     1.000
END DATA.
FACTOR READ=CORRELATION TRIANGLE
 /VARIABLES=X1 TO X5
 /ANALYSIS=X1 TO X5
 /PRINT=ALL
 /CRI=FAC(1)
 /EXT=ULS.
```

- The DATA LIST command specifies inline matrix materials in fixed format (the default). The active file dictionary contains five variable names.
- The N command tells SPSS/PC+ that the matrix input is based on 100 cases.
- The matrix data conform to the fixed-format requirements of FACTOR. Each row vector starts on a new line and each column entry occupies 10 columns.
- The READ subcommand on FACTOR indicates that a lower-triangular correlation matrix will be read (see FACTOR: Matrix Materials).
- This example takes advantage of spelling permitted by three-character truncation of keywords.

Example
```
DATA LIST FREE MATRIX /X1 TO X5.
N 100.
BEGIN DATA.
1.000
0.945,1.000
0.840,0.720,1.000
0.735,0.630,0.560,1.000
0.630,0.540,0.480,0.420,1.000
END DATA.
FACTOR READ=CORRELATION TRIANGLE
 /VARIABLES=X1 TO X5
 /ANALYSIS=X1 TO X5
 /PRINT=ALL
 /CRI=FAC(1)
 /EXT=ULS.
```

- The DATA LIST command specifies inline matrix materials in freefield format. The active file dictionary contains five variable names (X1, X2, X3, X4, and X5).
- The correlation matrix is entered with each coefficient separated by a comma.
- The READ subcommand on FACTOR indicates that a lower-triangular correlation matrix will be read (see FACTOR: Matrix Materials).

Matrix Input for Procedure MANOVA

- Procedure MANOVA reads matrix materials in either fixed or freefield format.
- For complete information on the contents and format of matrix materials used by MANOVA, refer to "The WRITE Subcommand" under Univariate MANOVA.
- Because of the special requirements of MANOVA, this procedure cannot use matrix materials written by another procedure, nor can another procedure use the matrix materials written by MANOVA.

Example
```
DATA LIST MATRIX /Y1 Y2 Y3 EDUC SEX.
BEGIN DATA.
            6         54         2          3
       1        1
    2.09000000E+00  4.53000000E+00  3.56000000E+00
       1        2
    1.38000000E+00  4.17000000E+00  3.38000000E+00
       2        1
    2.12000000E+00  5.35000000E+00  3.59000000E+00
       2        2
    1.47000000E+00  4.89000000E+00  3.12000000E+00
       3        1
    2.13000000E+00  5.94000000E+00  3.51000000E+00
       3        2
    1.74000000E+00  5.37000000E+00  3.27000000E+00
            8        10        11          8        9        8
     1.00000
      .25689   1.00000
     -.07085    .13390   1.00000
    3.80000000E-01  6.30000000E-01  3.90000000E-01
END DATA.
MANOVA Y1 Y2 Y3 BY EDUC(1,3) SEX(1,2)
 /READ
 /ANALYSIS Y1 Y2 WITH Y3
 /DISCRIM
 /PRINT=ERROR(SSCP COR)
 /DESIGN.
```

- The DATA LIST command specifies inline matrix materials in fixed format (the default). The active file contains five variables (data from Tatsuoka, 1971).
- The matrix materials were produced by a WRITE subcommand in MANOVA, using the same variables specification as that used here to read the materials.
- The READ subcommand indicates that matrix materials should be read from the location specified or implied on the DATA LIST MATRIX command (inline, in this example).
- The ANALYSIS subcommand allows you to drop continuous variables that are in the matrix materials from the analysis or, as in this example, redefine them as covariates or dependent variables.
- The DISCRIM subcommand requests discriminant analysis, and the PRINT subcommand requests that two error matrices be displayed.

Reference   Tatsuoka, M.M. *Multivariate Analysis*. New York: John Wiley and Sons, 1971.

DSCRIMINANT

```
DSCRIMINANT GROUPS=varname(min,max) /VARIABLES=varlist

[/SELECT=varname(value)] [/ANALYSIS=varlist(level) [varlist...]]


[/METHOD={DIRECT  }] [/TOLERANCE={0.001}] [/MAXSTEPS={2v}]
         {WILKS   }              {t    }             {m }
         {MAHAL   }
         {MAXMINF }
         {MINRESID}
         {RAO     }

[/FIN={1.0}] [/FOUT={1.0}] [/PIN={1.0}] [/POUT={1.0}] [/VIN={0 }]
      {fi }        {fo }        {pi }         {po }        {vi}

[/FUNCTIONS={g-1,100.0,1.0}] [/PRIORS={EQUAL     }]
            {nf , cp  ,sig}          {SIZE      }
                                     {value list}

[/SAVE=[CLASS varname] [PROBS rootname] [SCORES rootname]]

[/ANALYSIS=...]

[/OPTIONS=option numbers]

[/STATISTICS={statistic numbers}]
             {ALL              }
```

Options:

1	Include missing values	8	Include cases with missing values during classification
4	Suppress step output		
5	Suppress summary table	9	Classify only unselected cases
6	Varimax rotation of function matrix	10	Classify only unclassified cases
7	Varimax rotation of structure matrix	11	Use individual covariance matrices for classification

Statistics:

1	Group means	8	Group covariance matrices
2	Group standard deviations	9	Total covariance matrix
3	Pooled within-groups covariance matrix	10	Territorial map
		11	Unstandardized function coefficients
4	Pooled within-groups correlation matrix	12	Classification function coefficients
		13	Classification results table
5	Matrix of pairwise F ratios	14	Casewise materials
6	Univariate F ratios	15	Combined plot
7	Box's M	16	Separate plot

Example:

```
DSCRIMINANT GROUPS=OUTCOME (1,4)
/VARIABLES=VAR1 TO VAR7
/SAVE CLASS=PREDOUT.
```

Overview   Procedure DSCRIMINANT performs discriminant analysis and allows great flexibility in the method used and in the output displayed. Linear discriminant analysis is a technique in which one finds the best possible linear combination of variables to predict which of several groups or categories will contain cases. This combination can then be used to classify cases whose group membership is unknown. The grouping variable must be categorical, and the independent (predictor) variables must be interval or dichotomous, since they will be used in a regression-type equation.

Defaults   By default, DSCRIMINANT enters all variables simultaneously into the discriminating equation (the DIRECT method) provided that they are not so highly correlated that collinearity problems arise. Default output consists of counts of cases in the groups, the method used and associated parameters, and a summary of results including eigenvalues, standardized discriminant function coefficients, and within-groups correlations between the discriminant functions and the predictor variables.

Tailoring

Variable Selection Method. In addition to the direct entry method, you can specify any of several stepwise methods for entering variables into the discriminant analysis, based on different statistical criteria. You can also specify the numerical parameters for these methods.

Case Selection. You can select a subset of cases for analysis within the DSCRIMINANT command.

Prior Probabilities. You can specify prior probabilities for membership in the different groups. These are used in classifying cases but not in the analysis leading to the discriminant functions.

Discriminant Statistics. You can add new variables to the active file containing the predicted group membership, the probabilities of membership in each of the groups, and the scores on the discriminant functions.

Classification Options. You can request that DSCRIMINANT classify only those cases that were not selected for inclusion in the discriminant analysis, or only those cases whose code on the grouping variable fell outside the range analyzed. In addition, you can classify cases on the basis of the separate-group covariance matrices rather than the pooled within-groups covariance matrix.

Statistical Display. You can request any of a variety of statistics. You can rotate the pattern or structure matrices. You can compare actual with predicted group membership using a classification results table or any of several types of plots or histograms. In addition, you can print the discriminant scores and the actual and predicted group membership for each case.

Missing Values. You can include user-defined missing values in the analysis. During the classification phase, you can substitute means for missing values so that cases with missing data will be classified.

Syntax

- The only required subcommands are GROUPS and VARIABLES.
- The GROUPS, VARIABLES, and SELECT subcommands must precede any other subcommands and may be entered in any order.
- An ANALYSIS subcommand specifies the predictor variables to be used in a single analysis. The variables must first have been named on the VARIABLES subcommand.
- All other subcommands may be entered in any order and apply only to the preceding ANALYSIS subcommand. If any of these subcommands are entered before the first ANALYSIS subcommand or if there is no ANALYSIS subcommand, the entire set of variables named on VARIABLES is analyzed as requested.
- Optional output is controlled by the OPTIONS and STATISTICS subcommands.
- Subcommands are separated by slashes.

Operations

- DSCRIMINANT causes the data to be read.
- The procedure first determines one or more discriminant functions that best distinguish between the groups.
- Using these functions, the procedure then classifies cases into the group predicted by the predictor variables.
- If more than one ANALYSIS command is supplied, these steps are repeated for each requested group of variables.

Limitations

- Only one each of the GROUPS, VARIABLES, and SELECT subcommands may be used.
- The number of predictor variables that may be used is limited by available memory.
- A maximum of 10 ANALYSIS subcommands may be entered.
- Pairwise deletion of missing data is not available.

Example

```
DSCRIMINANT GROUPS=OUTCOME (1,4)
/VARIABLES=VAR1 TO VAR7
/STATISTICS=3 8 9 11
/SAVE CLASS=PREDOUT.
```

- Only cases for which the grouping variable GROUPS has values 1, 2, 3, or 4 will be used in computing the discriminant functions.
- The variables on the active file between and including VAR1 and VAR7 will be used to compute the discriminant functions and to classify cases.
- In addition to the default output, the STATISTICS subcommand requests the display of the pooled within-groups covariance matrix, the group and total covariance matrices, and the unstandardized discriminant function coefficients.
- Predicted group membership will be saved in the variable PREDOUT, which will be added to the active file if it does not already exist.

The Analysis Phase

DSCRIMINANT first calculates the discriminant function(s) that best distinguish the groups you have specified. This process is called the analysis phase. It is followed by the classification phase (see below).

GROUPS Subcommand

The GROUPS subcommand specifies the name of the grouping variable, which defines the categories or groups among which the discriminant function should distinguish. Along with the variable name, you must specify a range of categories. The discriminant analysis will attempt to predict membership in the categories of this variable.

- The GROUPS subcommand is required and may be used only once.
- The specification consists of a variable name followed by a range of values in parentheses.
- You can specify only one grouping variable, and its values must be integers.
- Empty groups are ignored and do not affect calculations. For example, if there are no cases in Group 2, the value range (1,5) will define only four groups.
- Cases with values outside the value range or with missing values, are ignored during the analysis phase but will be classified during the classification phase.

VARIABLES Subcommand

The VARIABLES subcommand identifies the predictor variables, which are used to classify cases into the groups defined on the GROUPS subcommand. The list of variables follows the usual SPSS/PC+ conventions for variable lists.

- The VARIABLES subcommand is required and may be used only once. Use the ANALYSIS subcommand to obtain multiple analyses.
- Only numeric variables may be used.
- Variables should be suitable for use in a regression-type equation: either measured at the interval level, or dichotomous.

ANALYSIS Subcommand

Use the ANALYSIS subcommand to request several different discriminant analyses using the same grouping variable, or to control the order in which variables are entered into a stepwise analysis.

- The ANALYSIS subcommand is optional. By default all variables on the VARIABLES subcommand are included in the analysis.
- The variables named on ANALYSIS must first be specified on the VARIABLES subcommand.
- The keyword ALL includes all variables on the VARIABLES subcommand.
- If you use the TO convention to specify a list of variables on an ANALYSIS subcommand, it refers to the order of variables on the VARIABLES subcommand, which is not necessarily that in the active file.

Example

```
DSCRIMINANT GROUPS=SUCCESS(0,1)
/VARIABLES=VAR10 TO VAR15, AGE, VAR5
/ANALYSIS=VAR15 TO VAR5
/ANALYSIS=ALL.
```

- The first ANALYSIS will use variables VAR15, AGE, and VAR5 to discriminate between cases where SUCCESS=0 and the cases where SUCCESS=1.

- The second ANALYSIS will use all variables on the VARIABLES subcommand.

Inclusion Levels. When you specify a stepwise method (any method other than the default METHOD=DIRECT), you can control the order in which variables are considered for entry or removal by specifying *inclusion levels* on the ANALYSIS subcommand. By default, all variables in the analysis are entered according to the criterion requested on the METHOD subcommand.

- An inclusion level is an integer between 0 and 99, specified in parentheses after a variable or list of variables on an ANALYSIS subcommand.

- The default inclusion level is 1.

- Variables with higher inclusion levels are considered for entry before variables with lower inclusion levels.

- Variables with even inclusion levels are entered as a group.

- Variables with odd inclusion levels are entered individually, according to the stepwise method specified on the METHOD subcommand.

- Only variables with an inclusion level of 1 are considered for removal. To make a variable with a higher inclusion level eligible for removal, name it twice on the ANALYSIS subcommand, first specifying the desired inclusion level and then an inclusion level of 1.

- Variables with an inclusion level of 0 are never entered. However, the statistical criterion for entry is computed and printed.

- Variables which fail the TOLERANCE criterion are not entered regardless of their inclusion level.

The following are some common methods of entering variables along with the ANALYSIS subcommand and inclusion levels that could be used to achieve them. These examples assume that one of the stepwise methods is specified on the METHOD subcommand (otherwise inclusion levels have no effect).

- *Direct.* ANALYSIS=ALL(2) forces all variables into the equation. (This is the default and can be requested with METHOD=DIRECT or simply by omitting the METHOD and ANALYSIS subcommands.)

- *Stepwise.* ANALYSIS=ALL(1) yields a stepwise solution in which variables are entered and removed in stepwise fashion. (This is the default when anything other than DIRECT is specified on the METHOD subcommand.)

- *Forward.* ANALYSIS=ALL(3) enters variables into the equation stepwise, but does not ever remove variables.

- *Backward.* ANALYSIS=ALL(2) ALL(1) forces all variables into the equation and then allows them to be removed stepwise if they satisfy the criterion for removal.

Example
```
DSCRIMINANT GROUPS=SUCCESS(0,1)
/VARIABLES=A, B, C, D, E
/ANALYSIS=A TO C (2) D, E (1)
/METHOD=WILKS.
```

- A, B, and C are entered into the analysis first, assuming that they pass the tolerance criterion. Since their inclusion level is even, they are entered together.

- D and E are then entered stepwise. Whichever of the two minimizes the overall value of Wilks' lambda is entered first.

- After entering D and E, SPSS/PC+ checks whether the partial F for either one justifies removal from the equation (see the discussion under FOUT and POUT).

Example
```
DSCRIMINANT GROUPS=SUCCESS(0,1)
/VARIABLES=A, B, C, D, E
/ANALYSIS=A TO C (2) D, E (1).
```

- Since no stepwise method is specified, inclusion levels have no effect and all variables are entered into the model at once.

SELECT Subcommand

With the SELECT subcommand you can limit the discriminant analysis to cases with a specified value on any one variable.

- Only one SELECT subcommand is allowed. It may follow the GROUPS and VARIABLES subcommands but must precede any other subcommands.
- Specifications for the SELECT subcommand consist of a variable name and a single value in parentheses. Multiple variables or values are not permitted.
- The selection variable need not have been named on the GROUPS (or VARIABLES) subcommand.
- Only cases with the specified value on the selection variable are used in the analysis phase.
- By default all cases, whether selected or not, will be classified. You can use Option 9 to classify only the unselected cases.
- When you use the SELECT subcommand, classification statistics are reported separately for selected and unselected cases, unless you use Option 9 to restrict classification.

Example

```
DSC GRO=APPROVAL(1,5)
/VAR=Q1 TO Q10
/SEL=COMPLETE(1)
/OPT=9.
```

- This example uses three-letter truncation of keywords.
- Using only the cases where variable COMPLETE = 1, DSCRIMINANT will form a discriminant function out of Q1 TO Q10 that discriminates between the categories 1 to 5 of the grouping variable APPROVAL.
- Because Option 9 is requested, the discriminant function will be used to classify only the unselected cases, namely the cases for which COMPLETE does not equal 1.

METHOD Subcommand

Use the METHOD subcommand to select any of six methods for entering variables into the analysis phase.

- A variable will never be entered into the analysis if it does not pass the tolerance criterion specified on the TOLERANCE subcommand (or the default).
- A METHOD subcommand applies to the *preceding* ANALYSIS subcommand or to an analysis using all predictor variables if no ANALYSIS subcommand has been specified.
- Only one METHOD command may be entered per ANALYSIS.

Any one of the following methods may be entered on the METHOD subcommand:

DIRECT   *All variables passing the tolerance criteria are entered simultaneously.* This is the default method.

WILKS   *The variable that minimizes the overall Wilks' lambda is entered.*

MAHAL   *The variable that maximizes the Mahalanobis' distance between the two closest groups is entered.*

MAXMINF   *The variable that maximizes the smallest F ratio between pairs of groups is entered.*

MINRESID   *The variable that minimizes the sum of the unexplained variation for all pairs of groups is entered.*

RAO   *The variable that produces the largest increase in Rao's V is entered.*

Statistical Criteria for Entry or Removal

In addition to naming a method for variable selection on the METHOD subcommand, you can specify a number of optional subcommands to set other parameters controlling the selection algorithm.

- These subcommands must follow the METHOD subcommand to which they apply and may be entered in any order.

C

Command Reference

• All of these subcommands except TOLERANCE apply only to the stepwise methods. Therefore, the METHOD subcommand is not required when you specify TOLERANCE.

TOLERANCE Subcommand

The tolerance of a variable that is a candidate for inclusion in the analysis is the proportion of its within-group variance that is not accounted for by other variables currently in the analysis. A variable with very low tolerance is nearly a linear function of the other variables; its inclusion in the analysis would make the calculations unstable. The TOLERANCE subcommand specifies the minimum tolerance a variable can have and still be entered into the analysis.

• The default tolerance is 0.001.

• You can specify any decimal value between 0 and 1 as the minimum tolerance.

FIN Subcommand

FIN specifies the minimum partial F value a variable must have to enter the analysis.

• The default is FIN=1.

• You can set FIN to any nonnegative number.

• PIN overrides FIN if both are specified.

• FIN is ignored if the METHOD subcommand is omitted or if METHOD specifies DIRECT.

PIN Subcommand

PIN specifies the minimum probability of F a variable must have to enter the analysis. Since the probability of F depends upon the degrees of freedom and the variables in the equation, it can change at each step. Use the PIN subcommmand to keep the minimum F's at a minimum significance level.

• If the PIN subcommand is omitted, the value of FIN is used.

• You can set PIN to any decimal value between 0 and 1.

• If PIN is specified, FIN is ignored.

• PIN is ignored if the METHOD subcommand is omitted or if METHOD specifies DIRECT.

FOUT Subcommand

As additional variables are entered into the analysis, the partial F for variables already in the equation changes. FOUT is the maximum partial F a variable can have before it is removed from the analysis.

• The default is FOUT=1.0.

• You can set FOUT to any nonnegative number. However, FOUT should be less than FIN if FIN is also specified.

• To be removed, variables must also have an inclusion level of 1 (the default).

• POUT overrides FOUT if both are specified.

• FOUT is ignored if the METHOD subcommand is omitted or if METHOD specifies DIRECT.

POUT Subcommand

POUT is the maximum probability of F a variable can have before it is removed from the analysis.

• By default, a variable is removed if its partial F falls below the FOUT specification.

• You can set POUT to any decimal value between 0 and 1. However, POUT should be greater than PIN if PIN is also specified.

• To be removed, variables must also have an inclusion level of 1 (the default).

• POUT overrides FOUT if both are specified.

• POUT is ignored if the METHOD subcommand is omitted or if METHOD specifies DIRECT.

VIN Subcommand

The VIN subcommand specifies the minimum Rao's V a variable must have to enter the analysis. When you use METHOD=RAO, variables satisfying one of the other criteria for entering the equation may actually cause a decrease in Rao's V for the equation. The default VIN prevents this, but does not prevent variables which provide no additional separation between groups from being added.

- The default is VIN=0.
- You can specify any value for VIN.
- VIN should be used only when you have specified METHOD=RAO. Otherwise, it is ignored.

MAXSTEPS Subcommand

By default, the maximum number of steps allowed in a stepwise analysis is the number of variables with inclusion levels greater than 1 plus twice the number of variables with inclusion levels equal to 1. This is the maximum number of steps possible without a loop in which a variable is repeatedly cycled in and out. Use the MAXSTEPS subcommand to decrease the maximum number of steps allowed.

- MAXSTEPS applies only to the stepwise methods.
- MAXSTEPS should be specified after the METHOD subcommand to which it applies.
- The format is MAX=*n*, where *n* is the maximum number of steps desired.

FUNCTIONS Subcommand

By default, DSCRIMINANT computes the maximum number of functions that are mathematically possible. This is either the number of groups minus 1 or the number of predictor variables, whichever is less. Use the FUNCTIONS subcommand to set more restrictive criteria for the extraction of functions. The FUNCTIONS subcommand has three parameters:

nf   *Maximum number of functions.* The default is the number of groups minus one or the number of predictor variables, whichever is less.

cp   *Cumulative percentage of eigenvalues.* The default is 100%.

sig   *Significance level of function.* The default is 1.0.

- You can restrict the number of functions with only one parameter at a time.
- The parameters must always be specified in the following order: *nf*, *cp*, *sig*. Thus, if you specify *cp*, you must explicitly specify the default for *nf*. If you specify *sig*, you must specify defaults for *nf* and *cp*. Since *nf* is first, it can be specified without *cp* and *sig*.
- If more than one nondefault restriction is specified on the FUNCTIONS subcommand, SPSS/PC+ uses the first one encountered.

Example
```
DSCRIMINANT  GROUPS=CLASS(1,5)
/VARIABLES = SCORE1 TO SCORE20
/FUNCTIONS=4,100,.80.
```

- The first two specifications on the FUNCTIONS subcommand are defaults: the default for *nf* is 4 (5, the number of groups, minus 1), and the default for *cp* is always 100.
- The third specification tells DSCRIMINANT to use fewer than four discriminant functions if the significance level of a function is greater than 0.80.

Statistical Display for the Analysis Phase

By default, the following statistics are produced during the analysis phase:

- *Summary table.* A table showing the action taken at every step (for stepwise methods only).
- *Summary statistics.* Eigenvalues, percent of variance, cumulative percent of variance, canonical correlations, Wilks' lambda, chi-square, degrees of freedom, and significance of chi-square are reported for the functions. (Can be suppressed with Option 5.)
- *Step statistics.* Wilks' lambda, equivalent *F*, degrees of freedom, and significance of *F* are reported for each step. Tolerance, *F*-to-remove, and the stepping criterion value are reported for each variable in the equation. Tolerance, minimum tolerance, *F*-to-enter, and the stepping criterion value are reported for each variable not in the equation. (Can be suppressed with Option 4.)
- *Final statistics.* Standardized canonical discriminant function coefficients, the structure matrix of discriminant functions and all variables named in the

analysis (whether they were entered into the equation or not), and functions evaluated at group means, are reported following the last step. (These statistics cannot be suppressed.)

In addition, you can request the following optional statistics on the STATISTICS subcommand:

Statistic 1   *Means.* Prints overall and group means for all variables named on the ANALYSIS subcommand.

Statistic 2   *Standard deviations.* Prints overall and group standard deviations for all variables named on the ANALYSIS subcommand.

Statistic 3   *Pooled within-groups covariance matrix.*

Statistic 4   *Pooled within-groups correlation matrix.*

Statistic 5   *Matrix of pairwise* F *ratios.* Displays the *F* ratio for each pair of groups. This *F* is the significance test for the Mahalanobis' distance between groups. This statistic is available only with the stepwise methods.

Statistic 6   *Univariate* F *ratios.* Displays *F* for each variable. This is a one-way analysis of variance test for equality of group means on a single predictor variable.

Statistic 7   *Box's* M *test.* This is a test for equality of group covariance matrices.

Statistic 8   *Group covariance matrices.*

Statistic 9   *Total covariance matrix.*

Statistic 11   *Unstandardized canonical discriminant functions.*

Statistic 12   *Classification function coefficients.* Although DSCRIMINANT does not directly use the Fisher linear discriminant functions to classify cases, you can use these coefficients to classify other samples.

Rotation Options

The pattern and structure matrices printed during the analysis phase may be rotated to facilitate interpretation of results. To obtain a VARIMAX rotation, specify either Option 6 or 7 on the associated OPTIONS command.

Option 6   *Rotate pattern matrix.*

Option 7   *Rotate structure matrix.*

Neither Option 6 nor Option 7 affects the classification of cases since the rotation is orthogonal.

Display Format

Two options are available to reduce the amount of output produced during stepwise analysis:

Option 4   *Suppress printing of step-by-step output.*

Option 5   *Suppress printing of the summary table.*

These two options only affect display output, not the computation of intermediate results.

The Classification Phase

Once DSCRIMINANT has completed the analysis phase, you can use the results to classify your cases. DSCRIMINANT provides a variety of statistics for evaluating the ability of a particular model to classify cases, along with several subcommands and options to control the classification phase.

PRIORS Subcommand

By default, DSCRIMINANT assumes equal probabilities for group membership when classifying cases. You can provide different prior probabilities with the PRIORS subcommand.

Any one of the following can be specified on PRIORS:

EQUAL   *Equal prior probabilities.* This is the default specification.

SIZE   *Proportion of the cases analyzed that fall into each group.* If 50% of the cases included in the analysis fall into the first group, 25% in the second, and 25% in the third, the prior probabilities are 0.5, 0.25, and 0.25, respectively. Group size is determined after cases with missing values for the predictor variables are deleted.

Value list   *User-specified prior probabilities.* A list of probabilities summing to 1.0 is specified.

- Prior probabilities are used only during classification.

- If you provide unequal prior probabilities, DSCRIMINANT adjusts the classification coefficients to reflect this prior knowledge.

- If adjacent groups have the same prior probability, you can use the notation *n*c* in the value list to indicate that *n* adjacent groups have the same prior probability *c*.

- The value list must name or imply as many prior probabilities as groups.

- You can specify a prior probability of 0. No cases are classified into such a group.

- If the sum of the prior probabilities is not 1, SPSS/PC+ rescales the probabilities to sum to 1 and issues a warning.

Example
```
DSCRIMINANT  GROUPS=TYPE(1,5)
/VARIABLES=A TO H
/PRIORS = 4*.15,.4.
```

- The PRIORS subcommand establishes prior probabilities of 0.15 for the first four groups and 0.4 for the fifth group.

Example   Specifying a list of prior probabilities is often used to produce classification coefficients for samples with known group membership. For example, if you have five groups, the value list might look like the following:
```
DSCRIMINANT  GROUPS=TYPE(1,5)
/VARIABLES=A TO H
/PRIORS = .25 .2 .3 .1 .15.
```

Classification Options

Three options relating to the classification phase may be requested on the OPTIONS subcommand.

Option 9   *Classify only unselected cases.* If you use the SELECT subcommand, DSCRIMINANT will by default classify all cases with valid data for the predictor variables. Option 9 suppresses the classification phase for cases selected for the analysis, classifying only the unselected cases.

Option 10   *Classify only unclassified cases.* The analysis phase includes only cases with values for the grouping variable within the range specified. With Option 10 you can suppress classification of cases used to derive the discriminant functions. Only cases with missing or out-of-range values on the grouping variable will be classified.

Option 11   *Use individual-group covariance matrices of the discriminant functions for classification.* By default, DSCRIMINANT uses the pooled within-groups covariance matrix to classify cases; if you specify Option 11 it will instead use the individual-group covariance matrices.

Display Output

You can request a classification results table and three types of plots to help you examine the effectiveness of the discriminant analysis. You can also print discriminant scores and related information for each case. Consult the Statistics Guide (Part B) and Examples (Part D) in this manual for examples of this output.

Statistic 10   *Territorial map.* A territorial map uses the first two discriminant functions as its axes and displays the boundaries between the territories predicted to fall into each group. It is not available for an analysis producing a single discriminant function. Only the first two discriminant functions can be used as axes. Group centroids are plotted as asterisks. Individual cases are not plotted on this map.

Statistic 13 *Classification results table.* This table reports the proportion of cases that are classified correctly and enables you to judge whether cases are systematically misclassified. If you include a SELECT subcommand, two tables are produced—one for selected cases and one for unselected cases.

Statistic 14 *Casewise classification information.* Displays the following information for each case classified: case sequence number; number of missing values in the case; value on SELECT variable, if any; actual group; highest group classification (G); the probability of a case which is in group G being that far from the group centroid $(P(D|G))$; the probability of a case with these discriminant scores being in group G $(P(G|D))$; the second-highest group classification and its $P(G|D)$; and the discriminant scores.

Statistic 15 *All-groups plot.* Cases in all groups are plotted on a single scatter plot, using the first two discriminant functions as axes. The plotting symbol for each case is the group number. Group centroids are plotted as asterisks. If the analysis yields only one discriminant function, a stacked histogram is plotted instead.

Statistic 16 *Separate-groups plots.* Cases in each group are plotted separately on plots that are otherwise the same as those produced by Statistic 15. If the analysis yields only one discriminant function, a histogram is plotted for each group.

Missing Values

By default, cases missing on any of the predictor variables named on the VARIABLES subcommand are used during neither phase. Cases out-of-range or missing on the grouping variable are not used during the analysis phase but are classified in the classification phase.

Two options are available for cases which are missing on the predictor variables:

Option 1 *Include missing values.* User-missing values are treated as valid values. Only the system-missing value is excluded.

Option 8 *Substitute means for missing values during classification.* Cases with missing values are not used during analysis. Cases with missing values on the classification variables are classified, using the mean as a substitute for the missing data.

SAVE Subcommand

The SAVE subcommand allows you to add much of the casewise information produced by Statistic 14 to the active file and to specify new variable names for this information. The following keywords may be specified on the SAVE subcommand:

CLASS *Save a variable containing the predicted group membership.* Specify a name for this variable after the keyword CLASS.

SCORES *Save the discriminant scores.* One score is saved for each discriminant function derived. Specify a *rootname* up to seven characters long after the SCORES keyword. DSCRIMINANT will use the rootname to form new variable names for the discriminant scores.

PROBS *Save each case's probabilities of membership in each group.* As many variables are added to each case as there are groups. Specify a *rootname* up to seven characters long after the PROBS keyword. DSCRIMINANT will use the rootname to generate variable names for the new variables.

• Request only the keywords for the results you want saved.

• SAVE applies to the previous ANALYSIS subcommand (or to an analysis of all variables if no ANALYSIS subcommand precedes SAVE).

- To save casewise results from more than one analysis, enter a SAVE command after each, using different rootnames.
- You can specify the keywords CLASS, SCORES, and PROBS in any order, but the new variables are always added to the end of the active file in the following order: first class, then discriminant scores, then probabilities.
- Appropriate variable labels are generated automatically for the new variables.
- The CLASS variable will use the value labels (if any) from the GROUP variable specified for the analysis.

Example
```
DSCRIMINANT GROUPS = WORLD(1,3)
 / VARIABLES = FOOD TO FSALES
 / SAVE CLASS=PRDCLASS SCORES=SCORE PROBS=PRB.
```

- With three groups, the following variables are added to each case:

Name	Description
PRDCLASS	Predicted group
SCORE1	Discriminant score for Function 1
SCORE2	Discriminant score for Function 2
PRB1	Probability of being in Group 1
PRB2	Probability of being in Group 2
PRB3	Probability of being in Group 3

FACTOR

```
FACTOR VARIABLES={varlist} [/MISSING=[{LISTWISE**}] [INCLUDE]]
                 {ALL    }          {PAIRWISE }
                                    {MEANSUB  }
                                    {DEFAULT  }

        [/WIDTH=[{width on SET**}] ]
                 {n             }

        [/ANALYSIS={varlist}...]
                   {ALL**  }

        [/FORMAT=[SORT] [BLANK(n)] [DEFAULT**]]

        [/PRINT=[DEFAULT**] [INITIAL] [EXTRACTION] [ROTATION]
                [UNIVARIATE] [CORRELATION] [DET] [INV] [REPR] [AIC]
                [KMO] [FSCORE] [SIG] [ALL] ]

        [/PLOT=[EIGEN] [ROTATION (n1,n2) (n3,n4)...]]

        [/DIAGONAL={DEFAULT** }]
                   {value list}

        [/CRITERIA=[FACTORS(n)] [MINEIGEN({1.0})] [ITERATE({25})]
                                          {eig}             {ni}

                   [RCONVERGE({0.0001})] [DELTA({0})]
                             {rl    }           {d}

                   [ECONVERGE({0.001})] [{KAISER }]
                             {el    }    {NOKAISER}
                   [DEFAULT**]]

        [/EXTRACTION={PC**    }]
                     {DEFAULT**}
                     {PA1**   }
                     {PAF     }
                     {ALPHA   }
                     {IMAGE   }
                     {ULS     }
                     {GLS     }
                     {ML      }
                     {PA2     }

        [/SAVE={REG    } ({ALL} rootname)]
               {BART   }  {n }
               {AR     }
               {DEFAULT}

        [/ROTATION={VARIMAX**}]
                   {DEFAULT**}
                   {EQUAMAX  }
                   {QUARTIMAX}
                   {OBLIMIN  }
                   {NOROTATE }

        [/ANALYSIS...]

        [/CRITERIA...]              [/EXTRACTION...]

        [/SAVE...]                  [/ROTATION...]
```

**Default if subcommand is omitted.

Example:

```
FACTOR VARIABLES=VAR1 TO VAR12.
```

Overview   Procedure FACTOR performs factor analysis using one of seven extraction
methods. For information on writing and reading matrices, see FACTOR:
Matrix Materials.

Defaults   By default, FACTOR performs principal components analysis with a varimax
rotation on all variables in the analysis using default criteria. A case that has a
missing value for any variable on the FACTOR command is omitted from all
analyses.
    The default display includes the initial communalities, eigenvalues of the
correlation matrix, and percent of variance associated with each; communalities, eigenvalues, and unrotated factor loadings; the rotated factor pattern
matrix; and the factor transformation matrix. If you specify an oblique rotation
(oblimin), the display also includes the factor structure matrix and the factor
correlation matrix.

Tailoring   **Analysis Block Display.** You can tailor the statistical display for an analysis block
to include correlation matrices, reproduced correlation matrices, and other
statistics. You can control the order of entries in the factor pattern and structure
matrices. You can also request scree plots and plots of the variables in factor
space for all analyses within an analysis block.

    Extraction Phase Options. You can choose among six extraction methods in
addition to the default principal components extraction: principal axis factoring,
alpha factoring, image factoring, unweighted least squares, generalized least
squares, and maximum likelihood. You can supply initial diagonal values for
principal axis factoring. You can also select the statistical criteria used in the
extraction.

    Rotation Phase Options. You can control the criteria for factor rotation. You can
also choose among three rotation methods (equamax, quartimax, and oblimin)
in addition to the default varimax rotation, or specify no rotation.

    Factor Scores. You can save factor scores as new variables on the active file,
using any of three methods.

    Display Format. You can control the width of the display within FACTOR.

    Writing and Reading Matrices. The optional subcommands used to write and
read matrices are discussed in FACTOR: Matrix Materials.

    Missing Values. You can request pairwise deletion of cases with missing values or
assign the variable mean to cases with missing values. You can also include cases
with user-missing values.

Syntax   • The minimum specification is the VARIABLES subcommand with a variables
list.

    • Subcommands are separated by slashes.

    • The global subcommands VARIABLES, MISSING, and WIDTH can be
specified only once and are in effect for the entire FACTOR procedure.
WIDTH can be specified anywhere, while VARIABLES and MISSING must
precede any of the other subcommands.

    • The subcommands ANALYSIS, PRINT, PLOT, DIAGONAL, and FORMAT
are *analysis block* subcommands. ANALYSIS specifies a subset of variables;
the other subcommands apply to all analyses performed on those variables
until another ANALYSIS subcommand is entered.

    • You can request more than one analysis block within a FACTOR procedure.

    • The subcommands CRITERIA and EXTRACTION are *extraction block*
subcommands. EXTRACTION triggers the extraction of factors according to a
specified method. CRITERIA can be used one or more times in an extraction
block to set parameters governing any *subsequent* EXTRACTION and ROTA-
TION subcommands.

- You can request more than one extraction block within an analysis block.
- The subcommands SAVE and ROTATION are *rotation block* subcommands. ROTATION triggers a rotation of the factors in the current extraction block, and SAVE adds factor scores for the following rotation to the active file.
- You can request more than one rotation block within an extraction block.
- You can save factor scores more than once within a rotation block.

Some subcommands (VARIABLES, ANALYSIS, EXTRACTION, SAVE, ROTATION) perform or initiate an action. For any specific analysis, you should enter these subcommands, or as many of them as you need, in the following order:

- VARIABLES causes the calculation of a correlation matrix, which is the basis for all further analysis.
- ANALYSIS initiates an analysis block, in which specifications for the analysis of a subset of variables are collected.
- EXTRACTION triggers the actual extraction of factors.
- SAVE defines new variables containing factor scores and adds them to the active file.
- ROTATION rotates the most recently extracted factors.

Other subcommands set specifications which remain in effect thereafter:

- The FORMAT and CRITERIA subcommands remain in effect until you explicitly change them.
- The PRINT, PLOT, and DIAGONAL subcommands remain in effect for the current analysis block. However, defaults are restored when an ANALYSIS subcommand is subsequently specified.

Operations
- FACTOR causes the data to be read.
- FACTOR builds a correlation matrix of variables named on the VARIABLES subcommand before it produces any factor results.
- The width specified on the WIDTH subcommand, if any, overrides the width defined on SET.

Limitations
- The number of variables allowed on the VARIABLES subcommand is the same as the system limit. However, the size of the correlation matrix that can actually be computed is limited by the memory available for workspace.
- Maximum 1 VARIABLES subcommand.
- Maximum 1 MISSING subcommand.
- Maximum 1 WIDTH subcommand.
- Maximum 10 ANALYSIS subcommands.
- Maximum 1 DIAGONAL subcommand within an analysis block.
- There is no fixed limit on other subcommands.

Example `FACTOR VARIABLES=VAR1 TO VAR12.`
- This example produces the default principal components analysis of twelve variables. Those with eigenvalues greater than 1 (the default criterion for extraction) are rotated using varimax (the default rotation method).

Subcommand Order   • The standard subcommand order is illustrated in Figure A.

A   Subcommand order

```
FACTOR VARIABLES=...
/MISSING=...
/WIDTH=...
/READ
```

Analysis Blocks

```
/ANALYSIS=...
/PRINT=...
/PLOT=...
/DIAGONAL=...
/FORMAT=...
/WRITE=...
```

Extraction Blocks

```
/CRITERIA=(extraction criteria)
/EXTRACTION=...
```

Rotation Blocks

```
/CRITERIA=(rotation criteria)
/ROTATION=...
/SAVE=...
```

• Subcommands listed in the ANALYSIS block apply to all EXTRACTION and ROTATION blocks within that ANALYSIS block. Subcommands listed in the EXTRACTION block apply to all ROTATION blocks within that EXTRACTION block.

• Each ANALYSIS block can contain multiple EXTRACTION blocks, and each EXTRACTION block can contain multiple ROTATION blocks.

• The CRITERIA and FORMAT subcommands remain in effect until explicitly overridden. Other subcommands affect only the block in which they are contained.

• The order of subcommands can be different from the order shown in Figure A. However, any analysis that can be performed with procedure FACTOR can be performed using this order, repeating ROTATION, EXTRACTION, and ANALYSIS blocks as needed.

Because of this structured syntax, which allows rotation blocks nested within extraction blocks nested within analysis blocks, you can get unexpected results if you specify commands out of order.

• If you enter any subcommand other than the global subcommands (VARIABLES, MISSING, WIDTH, READ) before the first ANALYSIS subcommand, an implicit analysis block including all variables on the variables subcommand is activated. Factors are extracted and rotated for this implicit block before any explicitly requested analysis block is activated.

• If you enter a SAVE or ROTATION subcommand before the first EXTRACTION in any analysis block, an implicit extraction block using the default method (PC) is activated. Factors are extracted and rotated for this implicit block before any explicitly requested extraction block is activated.

• If you enter CRITERIA *after* an EXTRACTION or ROTATION subcommand, the criteria do not affect that extraction or rotation.

Example
```
FACTOR VAR=VAR1 TO VAR12
/CRITERIA=FACTORS(3)
/ANALYSIS=VAR1 TO VAR8
/EXTRACTION=PAF
/ROTATION=QUARTIMAX.
```

- The CRITERIA subcommand activates an analysis block of all twelve variables. FACTOR extracts three factors using the default extraction method (principal components) and rotation (varimax) before entering the analysis block with VAR1 to VAR8, where different extraction and rotation methods are requested.

Example
```
FACTOR VARIABLES=VAR1 TO VAR12
/SAVE DEFAULT (ALL,FAC)
/EXTRACTION=PAF
/ROTATION=OBLIMIN.
```

- The SAVE subcommand activates an extraction block using the default extraction method (principal components) and rotation (varimax). These factors are saved on the active file as FAC1, FAC2, and so on.
- The next extraction block uses principal axis factoring and oblimin rotation but does not contain a SAVE subcommand, so no factor scores are saved in the active file.

Example
```
FACTOR VAR1 TO VAR12
/EXTRACTION PAF
/CRITERIA FACTORS(5).
```

- Since no CRITERIA subcommand precedes EXTRACTION, default criteria are used, and the CRITERIA subcommand is ignored.

VARIABLES Subcommand

The required VARIABLES subcommand names all the variables to be used in the FACTOR procedure. FACTOR computes a correlation matrix that includes all the variables named. This matrix is used by all analysis blocks that follow.

- The specification on VARIABLES is a list of variables.
- There can be only one VARIABLES subcommand and only the MISSING and WIDTH subcommands can precede it.
- Variables must be numeric.
- Keyword ALL on VARIABLES refers to all variables on the active file.
- All variables named on subsequent subcommands must first be named on the VARIABLES subcommand.

MISSING Subcommand

Use the MISSING subcommand to control the treatment of cases with missing values.

- The MISSING subcommand can be specified only once.
- If the MISSING subcommand is omitted or included without specifications, listwise deletion is in effect.
- The MISSING subcommand must precede any analysis block subcommands.
- The MISSING specification controls all analyses requested on the FACTOR command.
- The LISTWISE, PAIRWISE, and MEANS keywords on MISSING are alternatives describing how missing data should be treated in computing the correlation matrix. Any of these may be requested in combination with INCLUDE, which specifies whether user-missing data should be treated as missing or valid.

The following keywords can be specified on MISSING:

LISTWISE *Delete cases with missing values listwise.* Only cases with nonmissing values for all variables named on the VARIABLES subcommand are used. Listwise deletion may also be requested with keyword DEFAULT.

PAIRWISE   *Delete cases with missing values pairwise.* All cases with nonmissing values for each pair of variables correlated are used to compute that correlation, regardless of whether the cases have missing values on any other variable.

MEANSUB   *Replace missing values with the variable mean.* All cases are used after the substitution is made. If INCLUDE is also specified, user-missing values are included in the computation of the means, and means are substituted only for the system-missing value.

INCLUDE   *Include user-missing values.* Cases with user-missing values are treated as valid, regardless of whether LISTWISE, PAIRWISE, or MEANSUB is in effect.

WIDTH Subcommand

Use the WIDTH subcommand to control the width of the display.

- WIDTH can be specified anywhere and affects all FACTOR displays. If more than one width is specified, the last is in effect.
- The only specification on WIDTH is an integer ranging from 72 to 132.
- If the WIDTH subcommand is omitted, the width specified on the SET command is used.
- If the WIDTH subcommand is entered without specifications, a width of 132 is used.

ANALYSIS Subcommand

The optional ANALYSIS subcommand specifies a subset of the variables named on VARIABLES for use in subsequent analyses. It can also be used to perform different analyses on the same set of variables.

- The specification for ANALYSIS is a list of variables, all of which must have been named on the VARIABLES subcommand.
- Each use of ANALYSIS explicitly initiates an analysis block. The analysis block ends when another ANALYSIS subcommand or the end of the FACTOR procedure is reached.
- Within an analysis block, only those variables named on the ANALYSIS subcommand are available.
- If the ANALYSIS subcommand is omitted, all variables named on the VARIABLES subcommand are used in all extractions.
- The keyword TO on the ANALYSIS subcommand refers to the order of variables on the VARIABLES list, not the order in the active file.
- Keyword ALL refers to all variables named on the VARIABLES subcommand.

Example
```
FACTOR VARIABLES=VAR1 VAR2 VAR3 VAR4 VAR5 VAR6
/ANALYSIS=VAR1 TO VAR4
/ANALYSIS=VAR4 TO VAR6.
```

- This example specifies two analysis blocks. Variables VAR1, VAR2, VAR3, and VAR4 are included in the first analysis block. Variables VAR4, VAR5, and VAR6 are in the second analysis block.
- The keyword TO on the ANALYSIS subcommands refers to the order of variables on the VARIABLES list, not the order in the active file.
- A default principal components analysis with a varimax rotation will be performed for each analysis block.

FORMAT Subcommand

Use the FORMAT subcommand to reformat the display of factor pattern and structure matrices to increase interpretability.

- FORMAT can be specified once in each analysis block. If more than one FORMAT is encountered in an analysis block, the last is in effect.

• If the FORMAT subcommand is omitted or included without specifications, variables appear in the order in which they are named and all matrix entries are printed.

• Once specified, FORMAT stays in effect until it is overridden.

The following keywords may be specified on FORMAT:

SORT *Order the factor loadings in descending order by the magnitude of the first factor.*

BLANK(n) *Suppress coefficients lower in absolute value than threshold* n.

DEFAULT *Turn off keywords SORT and BLANK.*

Example

```
FACTOR VARIABLES=VAR1 TO VAR12
/MISSING=MEANSUB
/FORMAT=SORT BLANK(.3)
/EXTRACTION=ULS
/ROTATION=NOROTATE.
```

• This example specifies a single analysis block. All variables between and including VAR1 and VAR12 on the active file are included.

• The MISSING subcommand requests that variable means be substituted for missing values.

• The FORMAT subcommand requests that variables be ordered in factor pattern matrices by descending value of loadings. Factor loadings with an absolute value less than 0.3 will be omitted.

• Factors are extracted using unweighted least squares.

• The factors are not rotated.

PRINT Subcommand

Use the PRINT subcommand to control the statistical display for an analysis block, and all extraction and rotation blocks within it.

• If the PRINT subcommand is omitted or included without keywords, the displays indicated by the keywords INITIAL, EXTRACTION, and ROTATION are produced for the current analysis block.

• If any keywords are specified, only those displays specifically requested are produced for the current analysis block.

• The defaults are reinstated when an ANALYSIS subcommand is encountered.

• The statistics requested include only the variables in the analysis block.

• PRINT can be placed anywhere within the analysis block. If more than one PRINT subcommand is specified, the last encountered is in effect.

The following keywords can be specified on PRINT:

UNIVARIATE *Valid n's, means, and standard deviations.*

INITIAL *Initial communalities for each variable, eigenvalues of the unreduced correlation matrix for each factor, and percent of variance for each.*

CORRELATION *Correlation matrix.*

SIG *Matrix of significance levels of correlations.*

DET *The determinant of the correlation matrix.*

INV *The inverse of the correlation matrix.*

AIC *The anti-image covariance and correlation matrices* (Kaiser, 1970). The measure of sampling adequacy for the individual variable is printed on the diagonal of the anti-image correlation matrix.

KMO *The Kaiser-Meyer-Olkin measure of sampling adequacy and Bartlett's test of sphericity.* Tests of significance are not computed with matrix input if an N command is not used.

EXTRACTION *Factor pattern matrix, revised communalities, the eigenvalue of each factor retained, and the percent of variance each eigenvalue represents.*

REPR	*Reproduced correlations and residual correlations.*
ROTATION	*Rotated factor pattern and factor transformation matrices.* Displayed for all rotations except OBLIMIN. For OBLIMIN rotations, the factor pattern, factor structure, and factor correlation matrices are displayed.
FSCORE	*The factor score coefficient matrix.* Factor score coefficients are calculated using the regression method.
ALL	*All available statistics.*
DEFAULT	*INITIAL, EXTRACTION, and ROTATION.*

Example
```
FACTOR VARS=VAR1 TO VAR12
/MISS=MEANS
/PRINT=DEF AIC KMO REPR
/EXTRACT=ULS
/ROTATE=VARIMAX.
```

• This example specifies a single analysis block that includes all variables between and including VAR1 and VAR12 on the active file.

• Variable means are substituted for missing values.

• In addition to the default display, the display includes the anti-image correlation and covariance matrices, the Kaiser-Meyer-Olkin measure of sampling adequacy, and the reproduced residual and correlation matrix.

• Factors are extracted using unweighted least squares.

• The factor pattern matrix is rotated using the varimax rotation.

PLOT Subcommand

Use the PLOT subcommand to request scree plots or plots of variables in rotated factor space.

• If the PLOT subcommand is omitted, no plots are produced.

• If the PLOT subcommand is used without specifications, it is ignored.

• PLOT is in effect only for analyses in the analysis block where it is specified. The default (no plots) is reinstated when the next ANALYSIS subcommand is encountered.

• PLOT can be placed anywhere within an analysis block. If more than one PLOT subcommand is specified, the last one encountered is in effect.

The following keywords may be specified on PLOT:

EIGEN	*Display the scree plot* (Cattell, 1966). The eigenvalues from each extraction are plotted in descending order.
ROTATION(n1 n2) (n3 n4)...	*Plot the variables in factor space for each rotation.* Specify a pair of factor numbers in parentheses for each plot desired. Always enter the ROTATION subcommand explicitly when you enter this keyword on the PLOT subcommand.

DIAGONAL Subcommand

The DIAGONAL subcommand specifies values for the diagonal in conjunction with principal axis factoring.

• Only one DIAGONAL subcommand can be specified in each analysis block.

• DIAGONAL is in effect for all PAF extractions within the analysis block.

• DIAGONAL is ignored with extraction methods other than PAF.

• If the DIAGONAL subcommand is omitted or included without specifications, FACTOR uses the default method for specifying the diagonal.

• Default communality estimates for PAF (and for other methods, except principal components) are squared multiple correlations. If these cannot be computed, the maximum absolute correlation between the variable and any other variable in the analysis is used.

The following may be specified on DIAGONAL:

valuelist *Diagonal values.* The number of values supplied must equal the number of variables in the analysis block. Use the notation n* before a value to indicate the value is repeated *n* times.

DEFAULT *Initial communality estimates.*

Example
```
FACTOR VARIABLES=VAR1 TO VAR12
/DIAGONAL=.56 .55 .74 2*.56 .70 3*.65 .76 .64 .63
/EXTRACTION=PAF
/ROTATION=VARIMAX.
```

• A single analysis block includes all variables between and including VAR1 and VAR12 on the active file.

• DIAGONAL specifies 12 values to use as initial estimates of communalities in principal axis factoring.

• The factor pattern matrix is rotated using varimax rotation.

CRITERIA Subcommand

Use the CRITERIA subcommand to control extraction and rotation criteria.

• CRITERIA can be specified before any implicit or explicit request for an extraction or rotation.

• Only defaults specifically altered are changed.

• Any criterion that is altered remains in effect for *all* subsequent analysis blocks until it is explicitly overridden. CRITERIA subcommands thus have cumulative effects.

The keywords listed below may be specified on CRITERIA.

• The FACTORS, MINEIGEN, and ECONVERGE keywords apply to extractions.

• The RCONVERGE, KAISER, NOKAISER, and DELTA keywords apply to rotations.

• ITERATE applies to both extrations and rotations.

FACTORS(nf) *Number of factors extracted.* The default is the number of eigenvalues greater than MINEIGEN.

MINEIGEN(eg) *Minimum eigenvalue used to control the number of factors extracted.* The default is 1.

ECONVERGE(e1) *Convergence criterion for extraction.* The default is 0.001.

ITERATE(ni) *Number of iterations for the solutions in the extraction or rotation phases.* The default is 25.

RCONVERGE(e2) *Convergence criterion for rotation.* The default is 0.0001.

KAISER *Kaiser normalization in the rotation phase.* This is the default. The alternative is NOKAISER.

NOKAISER *No Kaiser normalization.*

DELTA(d) *Delta for direct oblimin rotation.* DELTA affects the ROTATION subcommand only when OBLIMIN rotation is requested. The default is 0.

DEFAULT *Reestablish default values for all criteria.*

Example
```
FACTOR VARIABLES=VAR1 TO VAR12
/CRITERIA=FACTORS(6)
/EXTRACTION=PC
/ROTATION=NOROTATE
/CRITERIA=DEFAULT
/EXTRACTION=ML
/ROTATION=VARIMAX
/PLOT=ROTATION(1 2) (1 3).
```

• This example initiates a single analysis block that analyzes all variables between and including VAR1 and VAR12 on the active file.

• Six factors are extracted in the first extraction. The extraction uses the default principal components method and the factor pattern matrix is not rotated.

• The default criteria are reinstated for the second extraction, which uses the maximum likelihood method. The second factor pattern matrix is rotated using the varimax rotation.

• The PLOT subcommand requests plots of the variables in the factor space defined by the first and second factors and of variables in the factor space defined by the first and third factors. The PLOT subcommand applies to both extractions, since there is only a single ANALYSIS block.

EXTRACTION Subcommand

Use the EXTRACTION subcommand to specify the factor extraction technique to be used.

• Multiple EXTRACTION subcommands can be specified within an analysis block.

• If EXTRACTION is not specified or if it is included without specifications, the default principal components extraction is used.

• If you specify criteria for EXTRACTION, the CRITERIA subcommand must precede the EXTRACTION subcommand.

• When you specify EXTRACTION, you should always explicitly specify a rotation method (or ROTATION=NOROTATE).

The following extraction techniques may be specified on EXTRACTION:

PC   *Principal components analysis* (Harman, 1967). This is the default. PC can also be requested with keyword PA1 or DEFAULT.

PAF   *Principal axis factoring.* PAF can also be requested with keyword PA2.

ALPHA   *Alpha factoring* (Kaiser, 1963).

IMAGE   *Image factoring* (Kaiser & Caffry, 1963).

ULS   *Unweighted least squares* (Harman & Jones, 1966).

GLS   *Generalized least squares.*

ML   *Maximum likelihood* (Jörcskog & Lawley, 1968).

Example

```
FACTOR VARIABLES=VAR1 TO VAR12
/EXTRACTION=ULS
/ROTATE=NOROTATE
/ANALYSIS=VAR1 TO VAR6
/EXTRACTION=ULS
/ROTATE=NOROTATE
/EXTRACTION=ML
/ROTATE=NOROTATE.
```

• This example specifies two analysis blocks.

• In the first analysis block, variables VAR1 through VAR12 are analyzed using unweighted least-squares extraction. The factor pattern matrix is not rotated.

• In the second analysis block, variables VAR1 through VAR6 are analyzed first with an unweighted least-squares extraction and then with a maximum likelihood extraction. No rotation is performed for either extraction.

ROTATION Subcommand

The ROTATION subcommand specifies the factor rotation method. It can also be used to suppress the rotation phase entirely.

• You can specify multiple ROTATION subcommands after each extraction.

• Rotations are performed on the matrix resulting from the previous extraction.

• If you omit both the EXTRACTION and ROTATION subcommands, you implicitly initiate a rotation phase with a varimax rotation.

• If you include the ROTATION subcommand without specifications, the default VARIMAX rotation is used.

• If you include an EXTRACTION subcommand but omit the ROTATION subcommand, the rotation phase may be suppressed.

• Keyword NOROTATE on the ROTATION subcommand produces a plot of variables in unrotated factor space if the PLOT subcommand is also included in the analysis block.

The following can be specified on ROTATION:

VARIMAX   *Varimax rotation*. This is the default if EXTRACTION and ROTATION are both omitted or if EXTRACTION is omitted and ROTATION is entered without specifications. Varimax can also be specified with keyword DEFAULT.

EQUAMAX   *Equamax rotation.*

QUARTIMAX   *Quartimax rotation.*

OBLIMIN   *Direct oblimin rotation.*

NOROTATE   *No rotation.*

Example

```
FACTOR VARIABLES=VAR1 TO VAR12
/EXTRACTION=ULS
/ROTATION
/ROTATION=OBLIMIN.
```

• The first ROTATION subcommand specifies the default varimax rotation.

• The second ROTATION subcommand specifies an oblimin rotation based on the same extraction of factors.

SAVE Subcommand

The SAVE subcommand allows you to save factor scores from any rotated or unrotated extraction as new variables on the active file. You can use any of three methods for computing the factor scores.

• SAVE must follow the ROTATE subcommand specifying the rotation for which factor scores are to be saved. If no ROTATE subcommand precedes SAVE, factor scores are saved for the unrotated factors, regardless of whether they have previously been rotated.

• Specifications for SAVE consist of a keyword specifying a method for computing the scores and, in parentheses, the number of scores to save and a rootname with which to form variable names.

• You can specify SAVE more than once in a rotation block. Thus, you can calculate factor scores using different methods for a single rotation.

• Each specification applies to the next rotation or to the unrotated factors if no rotation follows.

• The new variables are added to the end of the active file.

• If adding the new variables results in an active file with more than 200 variables, SPSS/PC+ prints an error message and stops processing the FACTOR command.

Keywords to specify the method of computing factor scores are:

REG   *The regression method.*

BART   *The Bartlett method.*

AR   *The Anderson-Rubin method.*

DEFAULT *The default is the regression method.*

After one of the above keywords, specify in parentheses the number of scores to save and a rootname to use in naming the variables.

• You can specify either an integer or the keyword ALL.

• The maximum number of scores you can specify is the number of factors retained in the solution.

• SPSS/PC+ forms variable names by appending sequential numbers to the rootname you specify.

• The rootname must begin with a letter and otherwise conform to the rules for SPSS/PC+ variable names.

• The rootname must be no longer than seven characters. If ten or more scores are being saved, the rootname must be short enough that the variable names formed will not exceed eight characters.

• The new names formed must be unique within the active file.

• FACTOR automatically generates variable labels for the new variables.

Example
```
FACTOR VARIABLES=VAR1 TO VAR12
/CRITERIA FACTORS(4)
/ROTATION
/SAVE REG (4,PCOMP)
/CRITERIA DEFAULT
/EXTRACTION PAF
/ROTATION
/SAVE DEF (ALL,FACT).
```

- Since there is no EXTRACTION subcommand before the first ROTATION, the first extraction will be the default principal components.

- The first CRITERIA subcommand specifies that four principal components should be extracted.

- The first SAVE subcommand requests that scores be calculated by the regression method. Four scores will be added to the file, and they be named PCOMP1, PCOMP2, PCOMP3, and PCOMP4.

- The first ROTATION subcommand requests the default varimax rotation for the principal components. The varimax-rotated scores will be saved as PCOMP1, PCOMP2, PCOMP3, and PCOMP4.

- The next CRITERIA subcommand restores default criteria. Here it implies that subsequent extractions should extract all factors with eigenvalues greater than 1.

- The second EXTRACTION subcommand specifies principal axis factoring.

- The second SAVE subcommand requests that scores be calculated by the default method (which is the regression method, as before). The number of scores added to the file is the number extracted, and their names are FACT1, FACT2, and so on.

- The final ROTATION subcommand requests varimax rotation for PAF factors, so the varimax-rotated factor scores are saved. If this subcommand had been omitted, the rotation phase would have been skipped, and scores for unrotated factors would then be added to the file.

References

Cattell, R. B. The meaning and strategic use of factor analysis. In R. B. Cattell (ed.), *Handbook of Multivariate Experimental Psychology*. Chicago: Rand McNally, 1966.

Harman, H. H. *Modern Factor Analysis*. Chicago: University of Chicago Press, 1967.

Harman, H. H., and W. H. Jones. Factor analysis by minimizing residuals (Minres). *Psychometrika*, 31, 351-368, 1966.

Jöreskog, K. G., and D. N. Lawley. New methods in maximum likelihood factor analysis. *British Journal of Mathematical and Statistical Psychology*, 21, 85-96, 1968.

Kaiser, H. F. A second-generation Little Jiffy. *Psychometrika*, 35, 401-415, 1970.

Kaiser, H. F. Image analysis. In C. W. Harris (ed.), *Problems in Measuring Change*. Madison: University of Wisconsin Press, 1963.

Kaiser, H. F., and J. Caffry. Alpha factor analysis. *Psychometrika*, 30, 1-14, 1965.

C

Command Reference

FACTOR: Matrix Materials

```
FACTOR VARIABLES=varlist

    [/READ=[{CORRELATION [TRIANGLE]}]]
           {DEFAULT              }
           {FACTOR(n)            }


    [/WRITE=[{CORRELATION}]]
            {DEFAULT    }
            {FACTOR     }
```

Examples:
```
SET RESULTS 'FACT.MAT'.
FACTOR VARIABLES=SUICIDE1 TO SUICIDE4
/WRITE.

DATA LIST MATRIX FILE='FACT.MAT' / SUICIDE1 TO SUICIDE4.
FACTOR VARIABLES=SUICIDE1 TO SUICIDE4
/READ
/ROTATION=OBLIMIN.
```

Overview

The FACTOR procedure can write a correlation matrix or a factor loading matrix to the results file named on SET for use in subsequent SPSS/PC+ sessions. It can also read either type of matrix, instead of a case file, for further analysis. Matrix materials to be read can be in either fixed or freefield format but must conform to certain record and format specifications (see DATA LIST: Matrix Materials). Matrices written by the FACTOR procedure are suitable for input under either format.

When reading matrix input, FACTOR only performs analyses that are possible with that type of matrix input. Subcommands that cannot be executed are ignored.

Syntax

- WRITE is an analysis block subcommand. With WRITE=CORRELATION (or simply WRITE), a correlation matrix is written once for the analysis block in which the WRITE subcommand appears. With WRITE=FACTOR, a factor matrix is written once for each extraction performed in the analysis block.

- The READ subcommand must be specified before the first analysis block. Only VARIABLES, MISSING, and WIDTH can precede the READ subcommand.

- READ and WRITE cannot be used in the same FACTOR procedure.

- Any of the other FACTOR subcommands can be used when READ= CORRELATION (or simply READ) is specified.

- When READ=FACTOR(n) is specified, the VARIABLES subcommand must precede the READ subcommand.

- When READ=FACTOR(n) is specified, factor rotation is the only analysis that can be performed.

Operations

- FACTOR writes fixed-column matrices, with each matrix entry in a 10-column field. There are thus up to 8 entries on each record. Each row of the matrix begins on a new record.

- If the results file named on SET is not empty when you specify WRITE, FACTOR will overwrite the contents of the file. Use the SET command to specify the name of the results file before you execute FACTOR. The default is SPSS.PRC.

- When FACTOR reads correlation matrices written by other procedures such as CORRELATION, it skips the record or matrix of n's and prints a message for each line of the matrix of n's.

- When a correlation matrix is read, the MISSING subcommand and the UNIV specification on the PRINT subcommand are ignored (see FACTOR).

- When a factor matrix is read, the MISSING, ANALYSIS, DIAGONAL, and EXTRACTION subcommands are ignored. Only rotation plots are available on the PLOT subcommand. The only printed output available is the communalities and ROTATION information, requests for other output are ignored (see FACTOR).

Limitations

• Only one matrix can be read.

WRITE Subcommand

Use the WRITE subcommand to write a correlation or factor matrix to the results file.

• WRITE is an analysis block subcommand and can be specified within any analysis block.
• The variables in the analysis block are the only variables included in the matrix.
• When WRITE is included without keywords, FACTOR writes a correlation matrix.
• The matrix is written to the results file specified on the SET command (by default, SPSS.PRC).
• If FACTOR writes a correlation matrix, the matrix is indexed by the number and order of variables on the ANALYSIS subcommand immediately preceding WRITE. If no ANALYSIS subcommand precedes WRITE, the list on the VARIABLES subcommand is used.
• If FACTOR writes a factor matrix, each variable in the analysis defines a row and each factor extracted defines a column.
• One factor matrix is written for each extraction in the analysis block.
• The factor matrix that is written is unrotated.
• Unless you edit the results file, only the first factor matrix written to the file can be read into a subsequent FACTOR procedure.

The following can be specified on WRITE:

CORRELATION   *Write a correlation matrix.* The correlation matrix can also be requested with keyword DEFAULT.

FACTOR   *Write an unrotated factor matrix for each EXTRACTION in the analysis block.*

Example

```
DATA LIST FREE FILE='GSS80.DAT'
/ABANY,ABDEFECT,ABHLTH,ABNOMORE,ABPOOR,ABRAPE,ABSINGLE.
SET RESULTS='GSS80.MAT'.
FACTOR VAR=ABANY TO ABSINGLE
/WRITE FACTOR.
```

• The DATA LIST command requests that data be read from the file GSS80.DAT. DATA LIST also specifies that the data will be read in freefield format and provides names for the variables.
• The SET command identifies GSS80.MAT as the results file.
• In the first analysis block, all variables in the active file are analyzed. The default principal components extraction and varimax rotation are performed.
• The WRITE subcommand writes out a factor matrix of the unrotated factors.

READ Subcommand

Use the READ subcommand to indicate that a correlation or factor matrix is to be read.

• READ is a global subcommand and can be specified only once on the FACTOR subcommand.
• The VARIABLES subcommand must be the first subcommand specified when you use READ.
• READ must be specified before the first analysis block.
• When READ is included without specifications, FACTOR assumes that it is reading a correlation matrix that is in the same format as the matrices FACTOR writes.

- When you specify READ on FACTOR, you must first specify a DATA LIST MATRIX command that points to the file containing the matrix materials and names the variables that will be read (see the example below).

- Only a single factor matrix can be read from a file, regardless of how many matrices were written (by multiple EXTRACTION commands) in the ANALYSIS block containing the WRITE command.

- The number and order of variables named on DATA LIST MATRIX must match the number and order of variables in the correlation or factor matrix.

- You can analyze a subset of variables when you read a correlation matrix but not when you read a factor matrix.

- Because FACTOR does not read the number of cases with matrix materials, specify an N command before FACTOR to obtain significance levels for extraction techniques using a chi-square test or when PRINT KMO is specified.

The following can be specified on the READ subcommand:

CORRELATION   *Read a correlation matrix.* A correlation matrix can also be specified with keyword DEFAULT or by entering the READ subcommand with no specifications.

TRIANGLE   *Read a correlation matrix in lower-triangular form.* TRIANGLE can be specified only after the CORRELATION keyword.

FACTOR(nf)   *Read a factor matrix. nf* is the number of factors (columns) in the matrix.

Example
```
DATA LIST MATRIX FREE
/ABANY,ABDEFECT,ABHLTH,ABNOMORE,ABPOOR,ABRAPE,ABSINGLE.
BEGIN DATA
   .6747329   .2183443
   .6522527   .1644450
   .3511271   .8334249
 -.0181689   .8180816
   .6998996  -.0986098
   .6363841  -.1623558
   .7479211  -.4813617
END DATA.
FACTOR VAR=ABANY TO ABSINGLE
/READ FAC (2)
/ROTATE EQUAMAX
/ROTATE QUARTIMAX.
```

- This example reads a factor matrix computed on seven variables. Two factors were extracted when the matrix was computed.

- The DATA LIST MATRIX command is required in order to read matrix input. Here the matrix is inline.

- The matrix is analyzed using equamax and quartimax rotations.

HILOGLINEAR

```
HILOGLINEAR {varlist} (min,max) [varlist (min,max)...]
            {ALL    }

[/METHOD=BACKWARD]

[/MAXORDER=k]

[/CRITERIA=[CONVERGE({0.25**})] [ITERATE({20**})]
                     {n     }            {n   }

         [P(([0.05**])] [MAXSTEPS({10**})] [DEFAULT**]]
            {prob  }             {n   }

[/CWEIGHT={varname }]
          {(matrix)}

[/PRINT=[DEFAULT**] [FREQ**] [RESID**] [ESTIM**]
        [NONE] [ASSOCIATION] [ALL]]

[/PLOT=[{DEFAULT}] [RESID] [NORMPLOT] [NONE**]]
        {ALL    }

[/MISSING={LISTWISE**} {INCLUDE}]
          {DEFAULT** }

[/DESIGN=[effectname effectname*effectname ...]]
[/DESIGN=...]
```

**Default if subcommand is omitted.

Example:

```
HILOGLINEAR AVAR(1,2) BVAR(1,2) CVAR(1,3) DVAR(1,3)
/DESIGN=AVAR*BVAR*CVAR, DVAR.
```

Overview   HILOGLINEAR fits hierarchical log-linear models to multidimensional contingency tables using iterative proportional-fitting algorithms. HILOGLINEAR also estimates parameters for saturated models. These techniques are described in Everitt (1977), Bishop, Fienberg, and Holland (1975), and Goodman (1978).

Defaults   By default, HILOGLINEAR estimates a saturated model for all variables in the analysis. The default display includes raw and expected cell counts, raw and standardized residuals, and parameter estimates. A case that has a missing value for any variable in the analysis is omitted.

Tailoring   **Design Specification.** You can request automatic model selection using backward elimination with the METHOD subcommand. You can also specify any hierarchical design and request multiple designs using the DESIGN subcommand.

Design Control. You can control the criteria used in the iterative proportional-fitting and model-selection routines with the CRITERIA subcommand. You can also limit the order of effects in the model with MAXORDER and specify structural zeros for cells in the tables you analyze with CWEIGHT.

Display and Plots. With the PRINT subcommand, you can limit the display for a design or include partial associations or tests for orders of effects for saturated models. You can request residuals plots or normal probability plots of residuals with the PLOT subcommand.

Missing Values. You can control the handling of user-missing values with the MISSING subcommand.

Syntax   • The minimum specification is a variables list with at least two variables followed by their minimum and maximum values.

• The variables list must be specified first.

- The DESIGN subcommand is optional. If no DESIGN subcommand is specified or DESIGN is not the last subcommand, a default model is estimated.
- The METHOD, PRINT, PLOT, CRITERIA, MAXORDER, and CWEIGHT subcommands should be placed before the designs to which they apply. Other than this, they can appear in any order.
- You can specify multiple PRINT, PLOT, CRITERIA, MAXORDER, and CWEIGHT subcommands. The last of each type specified is in effect for subsequent designs.
- The PRINT, PLOT, CRITERIA, MAXORDER and CWEIGHT subcommands remain in effect until they are overridden by new subcommands.
- You can specify multiple METHOD subcommands, but each one affects only the next design.
- The MISSING subcommand can be specified only once and can be placed anywhere after the variables list.
- Subcommands must be separated by slashes.

Operations

- HILOGLINEAR causes the data to be read.
- HILOGLINEAR builds a contingency table using all variables on the variables list. The table contains a cell for each possible combination of values within the ranges specified for each of the variables.
- HILOGLINEAR assumes there is a category for every integer value in the range of each variable. Empty categories waste space and can cause computational problems. If there are empty categories, you should use the RECODE command to create consecutive integer values for categories.
- Cases with values outside the range specified for any variable are excluded.
- If the last subcommand is not a DESIGN subcommand, HILOGLINEAR prints a warning and generates the default model. This is the saturated model unless MAXORDER is specified. This model is in addition to any that are explicitly requested.
- Only hierarchical log-linear models can be specified.
- If the model is not saturated (for example, when MAXORDER is less than the number of factors), only a goodness-of-fit and the observed and expected frequencies are given.
- The display uses the WIDTH defined on SET. If the defined width is less than 132, some portions of the display may be deleted.

Limitations

- Maximum 10 factors.
- Maximum 1 variables list.
- Maximum 1 MISSING subcommand.

Example

```
HILOGLINEAR AVAR(1,2) BVAR(1,2) CVAR(1,3) DVAR(1,3)
/DESIGN=AVAR*BVAR*CVAR, DVAR.
```

- This example builds a $2 \times 2 \times 3 \times 3$ contingency table for analysis.
- The DESIGN subcommand specifies the generating class for a hierarchical model. This model consists of main effects for all four variables, two-way interactions among AVAR, BVAR, and CVAR, and the three-way interaction term AVAR by BVAR by CVAR.

Variables List

The required variables list specifies the variables in the analysis.

- Variables must have integer values. If a variable has a fractional value, the fractional portion is truncated.

- Keyword ALL can be used to refer to all user-defined variables in the active file. If ALL is specified, all variables must have the same range.
- A range must be specified for each variable, with the minimum and maximum values separated by a comma and are enclosed in parentheses.
- If the same range applies to several variables, the range can be specified once after the last variable to which it applies.
- The variables list must precede all other subcommands.

METHOD Subcommand

By default, HILOGLINEAR tests the model specified on the DESIGN subcommand (or the default model) and does not perform any model selection. All variables are entered and none are removed. Use the METHOD subcommand to specify automatic model selection using backward elimination for the next design specified.

- You must specify the keyword BACKWARD on the METHOD subcommand.
- The METHOD subcommand affects only the next design.

BACKWARD *Backward elimination.* Perform backward elimination of terms in the model. All terms are entered. Those that do not meet the P criteria specified on the CRITERIA subcommand (or the default P) are removed.

MAXORDER Subcommand

The MAXORDER subcommand controls the maximum order of terms in the model estimated for subsequent designs. If MAXORDER is specified, HILOGLINEAR will test a model only with terms of that order or less.

- MAXORDER specifies the highest-order term that will be considered from the next design. MAXORDER can thus be used to abbreviate computations for the BACKWARD method.
- If the integer on MAXORDER is less than the number of factors, parameter estimates and measures of partial association are not available. Only goodness-of-fit and the observed and expected frequencies are displayed.

Example

```
HILOGLINEAR VARA VARB VARC(1 2)
/MAXORDER=2
/DESIGN=VARA*VARB*VARC
/DESIGN=VARA VARB VARC.
```

- This example builds a $2 \times 2 \times 2$ contingency table for VARA, VARB, and VARC.
- The MAXORDER subcommand restricts the terms in the model specified on the first DESIGN subcommand to two-way interactions or less.
- The MAXORDER subcommand has no effect on the second DESIGN subcommand, since the design requested considers only main effects.

CRITERIA Subcommand

Use the CRITERIA subcommand to change the values of constants in the iterative proportional-fitting and model-selection routines for subsequent designs.

- The default criteria are in effect if the CRITERIA subcommand is omitted (see below).
- You cannot specify the CRITERIA subcommand without any keywords.
- Specify each criteria keyword followed by a criterion value in parentheses.
- Only those criteria specifically altered are changed.
- You can specify more than one keyword on CRITERIA, and they can be in any order.

The following criteria can be specified:

CONVERGE(n) *Convergence criterion.* The default is .25. Iterations stop when the change in fitted frequencies is less than the specified value.

ITERATE(n) *Maximum number of iterations.* The default is 20.

P(prob) *Probability of chi-square for model.* P is in effect only when method BACKWARD is specified. The default is .05.

MAXSTEPS(n) *Maximum number of steps.* MAXSTEPS is in effect only when method BACKWARD is specified. The default is 10.

DEFAULT *Default criteria.* Use DEFAULT to restore defaults changed by a previous CRITERIA subcommand.

CWEIGHT Subcommand

The CWEIGHT subcommand specifies cell weights for a model. CWEIGHT is typically used to specify structural zeros in the table.

• You can specify the name of a variable whose values are cell weights or provide a matrix of cell weights enclosed in parentheses.

• You must specify a weight for every cell in the contingency table, where the number of cells equals the product of the number of values of all variables.

• Cell weights are indexed by the values of the variables in the order in which they are specified on the variables list. The index values of the rightmost variable change the most quickly.

• A variable named on CWEIGHT must be numeric.

• You can use the notation $n*cw$ to indicate that cell weight cw is repeated n times in the matrix.

• CWEIGHT does not weight aggregated input data (see Command Reference: WEIGHT in the *SPSS/PC+* manual).

• CWEIGHT is ignored with saturated models.

Example
```
HILOGLINEAR AVAR(1,2) BVAR(1,2) CVAR(1,3)
/CWEIGHT=CELLWGT
/DESIGN AVAR*BVAR, BVAR*CVAR, AVAR*CVAR.
```

• This example weights a cell by the value of the variable CELLWGT when a case containing the frequency for that cell is read.

Example
```
HILOGLINEAR DVAR(1,3) EVAR(1,3)
/CWEIGHT=(0 1 1  1 0 1  1 1 0)
/DESIGN=DVAR, EVAR.

HILOGLINEAR DVAR(1,3) EVAR(1,3)
/CWEIGHT=(0 3*1 0 3*1 0)
/DESIGN=DVAR,EVAR.
```

• These two equivalent HILOGLINEAR commands set the diagonal cells in the model to structural zeros. This type of model is known as a quasi-independence model.

• Because both DVAR and EVAR have three values, weights must be specified for nine cells.

• The first HILOGLINEAR command specifies cell weights explicitly.

• The second HILOGLINEAR command uses the $n*cw$ notation to indicate that the cell weight is repeated.

• The first cell weight is applied to the cell in which DVAR is 1 and EVAR is 1; the second weight is applied to the cell in which DVAR is 1 and EVAR is 2, and so forth.

Example
```
TITLE AMERICAN BLADDER NUT SEPARABILITY  HARRIS(1910).
SUBTITLE AN INCOMPLETE RECTANGULAR TABLE.
DATA LIST FREE / LOCULAR RADIAL FREQ.
WEIGHT BY FREQ.
BEGIN DATA.
1 1 462
1 2 130
1 3 2
1 4 1
2 1 103
2 2 35
2 3 1
2 4 0
3 5 614
3 6 138
3 7 21
3 8 14
3 9 1
4 5 443
4 6 95
4 7 22
4 8 8
4 9 5
END DATA.
HILOGLINEAR LOCULAR (1,4) RADIAL (1,9)
/CWEIGHT=(4*1 5*0   4*1 5*0   4*0 5*1   4*0 5*1)
/DESIGN LOCULAR RADIAL.
```

- This example uses aggregated table data as input.
- The DATA LIST command defines three variables. The values of LOCULAR and RADIAL index the levels of those variables, so that each case defines a cell in the table. The values of FREQ are the cell frequencies.
- The WEIGHT command weights each case (cell) by the value of the variable FREQ. Since each case represents a cell, the cell frequency will have the value of FREQ for that case.
- The BEGIN DATA and END DATA commands enclose the lines of data.
- The HILOGLINEAR variables list specifies two variables. LOCULAR has values 1, 2, 3, and 4. RADIAL has integer values 1 through 4.
- The CWEIGHT subcommand identifies a block rectangular pattern of cells that are logically empty. There is one weight specified for each cell of the 36-cell table.
- The DESIGN subcommand specifies only main effects only for LOCULAR and RADIAL. Lack of fit for this model indicates an interaction of the two variables.
- Since there is no PRINT or PLOT subcommand, HILOGLINEAR produces the default output for an unsaturated model.

PRINT Subcommand

The PRINT subcommand controls the display produced for the following designs.

- If the PRINT subcommand is omitted or included with no specifications, the default display is produced.
- If any keywords are specified on PRINT, only output specifically requested is displayed.

The following can be specified on PRINT:

FREQ   *Frequencies.* Display observed and expected cell frequencies. If the defined width is wide enough, HILOGLINEAR also prints cell percentages.

RESID   *Residuals.* Display raw and standardized residuals.

C

Command Reference

ESTIM   *Parameter estimates for a saturated model.* ESTIM is included in the default display for saturated models. ESTIM is not available for unsaturated models (including when MAXORDER is less than the number of factors).

ASSOCIATION *Partial associations of effects for a saturated model.* ASSOCIATION is not available for unsaturated models (including when MAXORDER is less than the number of factors). This option is computationally expensive for tables with many factors.

DEFAULT   *Default display.* Includes FREQ and RESID for all models and ESTIM for saturated models. This is the default if PRINT is omitted or included without any specifications.

ALL   *All available displays.*

NONE   *Design information and goodness-of-fit statistics only.* This option overrides all other specifications on the PRINT subcommand.

PLOT Subcommand

Use the optional PLOT subcommand to request residuals plots for the following designs.

• No plots are displayed for saturated models.

• If the PLOT subcommand is omitted, no plots are produced.

• If PLOT is included without specifications, standardized residuals and normal probability plots are produced.

• Plots use the box characters specified on the BOXSTRING subcommand of the SET command (see Command Reference: SET in the *SPSS/PC+* manual).

RESID   *Standardized residuals by observed and expected counts.*

NORMPLOT   *Normal probability plots of adjusted residuals.*

NONE   *No plots.* Specify NONE to suppress plots requested on a previous PLOT subcommand. This is the default if the PLOT subcommand is omitted.

DEFAULT   *Default plots.* Includes RESID and NORMPLOT. This is the default when PLOT is specified without keywords.

ALL   *All available plots.*

MISSING Subcommand

By default, a case with missing values for any variable named on the variables list is omitted from the analysis. Use the MISSING subcommand to change the treatment of cases with user-missing values.

• The MISSING subcommand can be named only once and can be placed anywhere following the variables list.

• The MISSING subcommand cannot be used without specifications.

• A case with a system-missing value for any variable named on the variables list is always excluded from the analysis.

The following specifications are available for MISSING:

LISTWISE   *Delete cases with missing values listwise.* This is the default if the subcommand is omitted. You can also request listwise deletion with keyword DEFAULT.

INCLUDE   *Include user-missing values as valid.* Only cases with system-missing values are deleted.

DESIGN Subcommand

The default model is a saturated model that includes all variables in the variables list. A saturated model contains all main effects and interactions for those variables. Use the DESIGN subcommand to specify a different generating class for the model. In a hierarchical model, higher-order interaction effects imply lower-order interaction and main effects. The highest-order effects to be estimated are the generating class.

• If the DESIGN subcommand is omitted or included without specifications, the default model is estimated.

- To specify a design, list the the highest-order terms, using variable names and asterisks (*) to indicate interaction effects.
- Higher-order interaction terms specified on DESIGN imply all lower-order interaction and main effect terms. AVAR*BVAR*CVAR implies the three-way interaction AVAR by BVAR by CVAR, two-way interactions AVAR by BVAR, AVAR by CVAR, and BVAR by CVAR, and main effects for AVAR, BVAR, and CVAR.
- One model is estimated for each DESIGN subcommand.
- If the last subcommand on HILOGLINEAR is not DESIGN, the default model will be estimated in addition to models explictly requested.
- Any PRINT, PLOT, CRITERIA, METHOD, and MAXORDER subcommands that apply to a DESIGN subcommand must appear before it.
- All variables named on the DESIGN subcommand must be named or implied on the variables list.
- You can specify more than one DESIGN subcommand.

References

Bishop, Y., S. Fienberg, P. Holland. *Discrete multivariate analysis: Theory and practice.* Cambridge: MIT Press, 1975.

Everitt, B. S. *The analysis of contingency tables.* New York: Halsted Press, 1977.

Goodman, L. A. *Analyzing qualitative/categorical data.* Cambridge: Abt Books, 1978.

C

Command Reference

MANOVA

```
MANOVA dependent varlist [BY factor list (min,max) [factor list...]

                         [WITH covariate list]]

[/WSFACTORS=name (levels) name...]

[/READ[=SUMMARY]]

[/TRANSFORM [(varlist[/varlist])]=[ORTHONORM] [{DEVIATIONS (refcat) }]]
                                             {DIFFERENCE          }
                               [{CONTRAST}] {HELMERT             }
                                {BASIS   } {SIMPLE (refcat)     }
                                            {REPEATED            }
                                            {POLYNOMIAL[(metric)]}
                                            {SPECIAL (matrix)    }

[/WSDESIGN=effect effect...]

[/MEASURE=newname newname...]

[/RENAME={newname} {newname}...]
         {*      } {*      }

[/MISSING={LISTWISE}
          {INCLUDE }

            {[CELLINFO ([MEANS**] [SSCP] [COV] [COR] [ALL])]              }
            {                                                             }
            {[HOMOGENEITY ([BARTLETT**] [COCHRAN**] [BOXM**] [ALL])]      }
            {                                                             }
            {[DESIGN ([ONEWAY] [OVERALL**] [DECOMP] [BIAS] [SOLUTION])]   }
[/{PRINT  }={[ERROR ([SSCP] [COV**] [COR**] [STDDEV])]                    }]
  {NOPRINT} {                                                             }
            {[SIGNIF ([MULTIV**] [EIGEN] [DIMENR] [UNIV**] [HYPOTH]       }
            {         [STEPDOWN] [{AVERF }] [BRIEF] [SINGLEDF] [ALL])]     }
            {                     {AVONLY}                                }
            {[PARAMETERS ([ESTIM**] [ORTHO] [COR] [NEGSUM] [ALL])]        }
            {                                                             }
            {[TRANSFORM]                                                  }

[/PLOT=[CELLPLOTS] [STEMLEAF] [ZCORR]
       [NORMAL] [BOXPLOTS] [SIZE{(width,height)}]]
                                 {(40,15)       }

[/PCOMPS[=[COR**] [NCOMP(n)] [MINEIGEN(eigencut)]
         [COV] [ROTATE(rottype)]            ]]

[/OMEANS[=[VARIABLES(varlist)] [TABLES ({factor name     })]]]
                                        {factor BY factor}
                                        {CONSTANT        }

[/PMEANS[=[VARIABLES(varlist)] [TABLES ({factor name     })]]]
                                        {factor BY factor}
              [ERROR(errorno)] [PLOT]   {CONSTANT        }

[/DISCRIM[=[ROTATE(rottype)] [ALPHA(alpha)] [ALL]]]
          [RAW**] [STAN**] [ESTIM**] [COR**]

[/RESIDUALS[=[CASEWISE**] [ERROR(errorno)] [PLOT] ]]
```

```
[/METHOD=[MODELTYPE ({MEANS       })]
                     {OBSERVATIONS}


        [ESTIMATION ({QR      } {NOLASTRES} {NOBALANCED} {CONSTANT  })]
                     {CHOLESKY} {LASTRES  } {BALANCED  } {NOCONSTANT}


        [SSTYPE ({UNIQUE    })]]
                 {SEQUENTIAL}


[/WRITE[=SUMMARY]]


[/ANALYSIS [({CONDITIONAL  })]=dependent varlist
             {UNCONDITIONAL}    [WITH covariate varlist]
                                [/dependent varlist...]]


[/PARTITION (factorname)[=({1,1...   })]]
                          {df,df...}


                          {DEVIATION [(refcat)]        }
                          {SIMPLE [[(refcat)]]          }
                          {DIFFERENCE                  }
[/CONTRAST (factorname)={HELMERT                       }]
                          {REPEATED                     }
                          {POLYNOMIAL[({1,2,3...})]]    }
                          {            {metric }         }
                          {SPECIAL (matrix)             }


         {WITHIN            }   {W }
[/ERROR={RESIDUAL          } or {R }]
         {WITHIN + RESIDUAL}   {WR}
         {n                 }


         {[CONSTANT...]                                            }
         {[effect effect...]                                       }
         {[effects BY effects...]                                  }
         {[POOL (varlist)...]                                      }
[/DESIGN={[effects {WITHIN} effects...]                            }]
         {         {W     }                                        }
         {[effect + effect...]                                     }
         {[factor (level)... [WITHIN factor (partition)...]]       }
         {[MUPLUS...]                                              }
         {[MWITHIN...]                                             }
         {[{term-to-be-tested } {AGAINST} {WITHIN   }   {W }]     }
         {  {term=n           } {VS     } {RESIDUAL } or {R }     }
         {                                {WR       }   {RW}     }
         {                                {n        }             }
```

**Defaults if subcommands are entered without specifications. In repeated measures, SIGNIF(AVERF), not SIGNIF(MULTIV), is printed by default.

Example 1: Analysis of Variance

```
MANOVA RESULT BY TREATMNT(1,4) GROUP(1,2).
```

Example 2: Analysis of Covariance

```
MANOVA RESULT BY TREATMNT(1,4) GROUP(1,2) WITH RAINFALL.
```

Example 3: Repeated-Measures Analysis

```
MANOVA SCORE1 TO SCORE4 BY CLASS(1,2)
/WSFACTORS=MONTH(4).
```

Example 4: Parallelism Test with Crossed Factors

```
MANOVA YIELD BY PLOT(1,4) TYPEFERT(1,3) WITH FERT
/ANALYSIS YIELD
/METHOD SSTYPE(SEQUENTIAL)
/DESIGN FERT, PLOT, TYPEFERT,
    FERT BY PLOT + FERT BY TYPEFERT
    + FERT BY PLOT BY TYPEFERT.
```

Overview   MANOVA (multivariate analysis of variance) is a generalized analysis of
variance and covariance procedure. You can use MANOVA to analyze a wide
variety of univariate and multivariate designs, including analysis of repeated
measures. MANOVA is *not* restricted to multivariate analysis of variance. Some
univariate designs, such as those involving mixed models, partitioned effects,
nested factors, or factor-by-covariate interactions, can only be analyzed in
SPSS/PC+ by this procedure.

To simplify the presentation, reference material on MANOVA is divided
into three sections: *univariate* designs with one dependent variable; *multivariate*
designs with several interrelated dependent variables; and *repeated-measures*
designs in which the dependent variables represent the same types of measurements taken at more than one time.

If you are unfamiliar with the models, assumptions, and statistics used in
MANOVA, consult the Statistics Guide in Part B of this manual.

The full syntax diagram for MANOVA is presented here. The MANOVA
sections that follow include partial syntax diagrams showing the subcommands
and specifications discussed in that section. Individually, those diagrams are
incomplete. Subcommands listed for univariate designs are available for any
analysis, and subcommands listed for multivariate designs can be used in any
multivariate analysis, including repeated measures.

MANOVA was designed and programmed by Philip Burns of Northwes-
tern University.

MANOVA:
Univariate

```
MANOVA dependent var [BY factor list (min,max) [factor list...]
                       [WITH covariate list]    ]

[/MISSING={LISTWISE}
          {INCLUDE }

             {[CELLINFO ([MEANS**] [SSCP] [COV] [COR] [ALL])]       }
             {                                                       }
             {[HOMOGENEITY ([BARTLETT**] [COCHRAN**] [ALL])]        }
[/{PRINT  }={[DESIGN ([ONEWAY] [OVERALL**] [DECOMP] [BIAS] [SOLUTION])] }
  {NOPRINT} {                                                       }
             {[PARAMETERS ([ESTIM**] [ORTHO] [COR] [NEGSUM] [ALL])] }
             {                                                       }
             {[SIGNIF(SINGLEDF)]                                    }

[/PLOT=[CELLPLOTS] [STEMLEAF] [NORMAL] [BOXPLOTS] ]
       [SIZE{(width,height)}]
            {(40,15)        }

[/OMEANS[=[VARIABLES(varlist)] [TABLES ({factor name    })]]]]
                                        {factor BY factor}
                                        {CONSTANT        }

[/PMEANS[=[VARIABLES(varlist)] [TABLES ({factor name    })]]]]
                                        {factor BY factor}
              [ERROR(errorno)] [PLOT]   {CONSTANT        }

[/RESIDUALS=[CASEWISE**] [ERROR(errorno)] [PLOT] ]

[/METHOD=[MODELTYPE ({MEANS       })]
                     {OBSERVATIONS}

          [ESTIMATION ({QR      } {NOLASTRES} {NOBALANCED} {CONSTANT  })]
                       {CHOLESKY} {LASTRES  } {BALANCED  } {NOCONSTANT}

          [SSTYPE ({UNIQUE    })]]
                   {SEQUENTIAL}

[/READ[=SUMMARY]]  [/WRITE[=SUMMARY]]

[/ANALYSIS=dependent var [WITH covariate list]]

[/PARTITION (factorname)[=({1,1...   })]]
                          {df,df...}

                              {DEVIATION [(refcat)]      }
                              {SIMPLE [(refcat)]         }
                              {DIFFERENCE                }
[/CONTRAST (factorname)={HELMERT                   }]
                              {REPEATED                  }
                              {POLYNOMIAL[({1,2,3...})]} }
                              {            {metric  }    }
                              {SPECIAL (matrix)          }

         {WITHIN            }    {W }
[/ERROR={RESIDUAL          } or {R }]
         {WITHIN + RESIDUAL}    {WR}
         {n                }

         {[CONSTANT...]                                          }
         {[effect effect...]                                     }
         {[POOL (varlist)...]                                    }
         {[effects BY effects...]                                }
[/DESIGN={[effects {WITHIN} effects...]                          }]
         {         {W     }                                      }
         {[effect + effect...]                                   }
         {[factor (level)... [WITHIN factor (partition)...]]     }
         {[CONPLUS...]                                           }
         {[MWITHIN...]                                           }
         {[{term-to-be-tested} {AGAINST} {WITHIN  }    {W }]}    }
         {[{term=n          } {VS     } {RESIDUAL} or {R }]}    }
         {                              {WR       }    {WR}}    }
         {                              {n        }    {RW}}    }
```

**Defaults if subcommands are entered without specifications.

Example:

```
MANOVA YIELD BY SEED(1,4) FERT(1,3) WITH RAIN
/PRINT=CELLINFO(MEANS COV) PARAMETERS(ESTIM)
/DESIGN.
```

Overview

MANOVA is the most powerful of the analysis of variance procedures in SPSS/PC+ and can be used for both univariate and multivariate designs. Only MANOVA allows you to

- Specify nesting of effects.
- Specify individual error terms for effects in mixed model analyses.
- Estimate covariate-by-factor interactions to test the assumption of homogeneity of regression lines.
- Obtain parameter estimates for a variety of contrast types, including irregularly-spaced polynomial contrasts with multiple factors.
- Test user-specified special contrasts with multiple factors.
- Partition effects in models.
- Pool effects in models.

This section describes the use of MANOVA for univariate analyses. However, the subcommands described here can be used in any type of analysis with MANOVA. See MANOVA: Multivariate and MANOVA: Repeated Measures for additional subcommands used for those types of analysis. If you are unfamiliar with the models, assumptions, and statistics used in MANOVA, consult the Statistics Guide in Part B of this manual.

Defaults

If you do not specify a DESIGN subcommand, MANOVA will use a full factorial model, which includes all main effects and all possible interactions among factors. Estimation is performed, by default, using the cell-means model and UNIQUE (regression-type) sums of squares, adjusting each effect for all other effects in the model. Factors are tested using *deviation* contrasts to determine if their categories significantly differ from the mean. Default output for a univariate design consists of the number of cases processed, the effects included (explicitly or implicitly) in the model, and an analysis of variance table.

Tailoring

Design Specification. You can specify which terms to include in the design. This allows you to estimate a model other than the full factorial model, incorporate factor-by-covariate interactions, indicate nesting of effects, and indicate specific error terms for each effect in mixed models.

Contrast Types. You can specify contrasts other than the default deviation contrasts.

Parameter Estimation. You can request parameter estimates for the model. You can also control the manner in which the model is estimated by requesting the observations model rather than the cell means model; by specifying sequential decomposition of the sums of squares; and by choosing among alternative methods of parameter estimation.

Optional Output. You can choose from a wide variety of optional output. Output appropriate to univariate designs includes cell means, design or other matrices, parameter estimates, tests for homogeneity of variance across cells, tables of observed and/or predicted means, and various plots useful in checking assumptions.

Matrix Materials. You can write matrices of intermediate results to the results file, and you can read such matrices to perform further analyses.

Syntax

MANOVA begins with a variables list identifying the dependent variable, the factors (if any), and the covariates (if any). This is followed by a slash and any optional subcommands.

- Subcommands are separated from one another by slashes.
- Most subcommands include additional specifications, which can be separated by spaces or commas. Some of these specifications, in turn, have parenthetical sub-specifications.

- For many analyses, the MANOVA variables list and the DESIGN subcommand are the only specifications needed. If a full factorial design is desired, the DESIGN subcommand can be omitted.
- The DESIGN subcommand triggers the estimation of a specific model. An analysis of one model is produced for each DESIGN subcommand.
- All other subcommands apply only to designs that *follow* them. If you do not enter a DESIGN subcommand or if you enter any subcommand after the last DESIGN subcommand, MANOVA will use a full factorial model for the last DESIGN.
- MANOVA subcommands other than DESIGN remain in effect for all subsequent models unless replaced.
- The MISSING subcommand can only be specified once.
- The following keywords cannot be used as factor names: BY, CONSTANT, WITHIN, W, MUPLUS, AGAINST, VS, MWITHIN, or POOL.

Limitations

- Memory requirements depend primarily on the number of cells in the design. For the default saturated model, this equals the product of the number of levels or categories in each factor.
- MANOVA does not calculate covariate-by-covariate interaction terms. You must calculate these using the COMPUTE statement before invoking MANOVA.

Example

```
MANOVA YIELD BY SEED(1,4) FERT(1,3) WITH RAINFALL
/PRINT=CELLINFO(MEANS) PARAMETERS(ESTIM)
/DESIGN.
```

- YIELD is the dependent variable; SEED (with values 1, 2, 3, and 4) and FERT (with values 1, 2, and 3) are factors; RAINFALL is a covariate.
- The means of the dependent variable for each cell are requested with PRINT = CELLINFO(MEANS).
- The parameter estimates have been requested with PRINT − PARAMETERS(ESTIM).
- The default design, a full factorial model, will be estimated. This statement could have been omitted, or could have been specified in full as DESIGN = SEED, FERT, SEED BY FERT.

MANOVA Variables List

The variables list specifies all variables that will be used in any subsequent analyses.

- The dependent variable must be the first specification on MANOVA.
- The names of the factors follow the dependent variable. Use the keyword BY to separate the dependent variable from the factors.
- Factors must have adjacent integer values, and you must supply the minimum and maximum values in parentheses after the factor name(s).
- Enter the covariates, if any, following the factors and their ranges. Use the keyword WITH to separate covariates from factors (if any) and the dependent variable.
- MANOVA will remove the linear effect of the covariates from your dependent variable before performing analysis of variance.

Example

```
MANOVA DEPENDNT BY FACTOR1 (1,3) FACTOR2, FACTOR3 (1,2).
```

- In this example three factors are specified.
- FACTOR1 has values 1, 2, and 3, while FACTOR2 and FACTOR3 have values 1 and 2.

DESIGN Subcommand

The DESIGN subcommand specifies the effects included in a specific model. It must be the last subcommand entered for any model.

    The *cells* in a design are defined by all of the possible combinations of levels of the factors in that design. The number of cells equals the product of the number of levels of all the factors. A design is *balanced* if each cell contains the same number of cases.

- The specifications on the DESIGN subcommand consist of a list of terms to be included in the model, separated by spaces or commas.

- The default design, which may be specified with a DESIGN subcommand with no specifications, is a saturated model containing all main effects and all orders of factor-by-factor interaction.

- If no DESIGN subcommand is entered or if any other subcommand is entered after the last DESIGN subcommand, a default (saturated) design is estimated.

- To include a term for the main effect of a factor, enter the name of the factor on the DESIGN statement.

- To include a term for an interaction between factors, specify FACT1 BY FACT2, where FACT1 and FACT2 are the names of the factors involved in the interaction.

- Terms are entered into the model in the order you list them on the DESIGN subcommand. This order affects the significance tests if you have specified METHOD = SSTYPE(SEQUENTIAL) to partition the sums of squares in a hierarchical fashion.

- You can specify other types of terms in the model, as described in the following sections.

Example

```
MANOVA Y BY A(1,2) B(1,2) C(1,3)
/DESIGN
/DESIGN A, B, C
/DESIGN A, B, C, A BY B, A BY C.
```

- The first DESIGN subcommand produces the default full factorial design, with all main effects and interactions for factors A, B, and C.

- The second DESIGN subcommand produces an analysis with main effects only for A, B, and C.

- The third DESIGN subcommand produces an analysis with main effects and the interactions between A and the other two factors. The interaction between B and C is not in the design, nor is the interaction between all three factors.

Example

```
MANOVA Y BY A(1,3) WITH X
/DESIGN.
```

- The linear effect of the covariate X is removed from the dependent variable Y before any other effects are estimated.

- The default full factorial design in this case is simply the factor A.

Nesting Effects (WITHIN Keyword)

The effects of a factor are nested within those of another factor if the levels of the nested factor are substantively different within each level of the second factor. In the example at the beginning of this section, the two factors were type of seed (SEED) and type of fertilizer (FERT). If different fertilizers were used for each type of seed, the effects of FERT would be nested within the effects of SEED.

- Indicate a nested effect with the keyword WITHIN, for example, FERT WITHIN SEED.

- An effect can be nested within an interaction term, for example, FERT WITHIN SEED BY PLOT. Here the levels of FERT are considered distinct for each combination of levels of SEED and PLOT.

- A factor may be nested within one specific level of another factor by indicating the level in parentheses. The term FERT WITHIN SEED(2) indicates that the levels of FERT are defined only within the second level of SEED.

MWITHIN Keyword

A term of the form MWITHIN factor (level) tests whether the dependent variable is zero within the specified level of the factor.

- MWITHIN is followed by the name of a factor and, in parentheses, the number of one of its levels.

- The level is indicated by ordinal position, not value. If you have specified TIME(3,6) on the MANOVA variables list, the term MWITHIN TIME(1) refers to the first level of TIME, which is the level associated with the value 3.

• You can form an interaction with an MWITHIN term. For example, the term GROUP BY MWITHIN TIME(1) tests whether the means of the dependent variable are significantly different for different levels of GROUP, *within only the first level of TIME*. This allows you to estimate "simple effects."

Pooled Effects

Different effects can be "pooled" for the purpose of significance testing.

• To pool effects, connect them with a plus sign, for example, FERT + FERT BY SEED. A single test will be made for the combined effect of FERT and the FERT by SEED interaction.

• The keyword BY is evaluated before effects are pooled together. Syntactically, A + B BY C is evaluated as A + (B BY C). Parentheses are not allowed in this context. To get the equivalent of (A + B) BY C, specify A BY C + B BY C.

MUPLUS Keyword

If a term is preceded by keyword MUPLUS, the constant term (MU) in the model is combined with that term. The normal use of this specification is to obtain parameter estimates that represent weighted means for the levels of some factor. For example, the term MUPLUS SEED represents the constant, or overall mean, plus the effect for each level of SEED. The significance of such effects is usually uninteresting, but the parameter estimates represent the weighted means for each level of SEED, adjusted for any covariates in the model.

• MUPLUS cannot appear more than once on a given DESIGN subcommand.

• MUPLUS (factor) is the only way to get standard errors for the predicted means for each level of that factor. The predicted means themselves can be obtained with the PMEANS subcommand.

• Parameter estimates are not displayed by default; you must explicitly request them on the PRINT subcommand.

Partitioned Effects

To identify individual degrees of freedom or partitions of the degrees of freedom associated with an effect, enter a number in parentheses on the DESIGN subcommand.

• If you specify the PARTITION subcommand, the number refers to a partition.

• If you do not use the PARTITION subcommand, the number refers to a single degree of freedom associated with the effect. For example, if SEED is a factor with four levels, you can treat its three degrees of freedom as independent effects by naming them SEED(1), SEED(2), and SEED(3) on the DESIGN subcommand.

• The number in parentheses always refers to an individual degree of freedom for a factor if that factor follows keyword WITHIN or MWITHIN, regardless of how or whether you have partitioned the degrees of freedom.

• Partitions can include more than one degree of freedom provided that you use the PARTITION subcommand. If the first partition of SEED includes two degrees of freedom, the term SEED(1) on a DESIGN subcommand tests both degrees of freedom.

• A factor has one fewer degrees of freedom than it has levels or values.

Effects of Continuous Variables

Usually you name factors but not covariates on the DESIGN subcommand. The linear effects of covariates are removed from the dependent variable before the design is tested. However, the design can include variables measured at the interval level and originally named as covariates or as additional dependent variables.

• Continuous variables on a DESIGN subcommand must be named as dependents or covariates on the MANOVA variables list.

• Before you can name a continuous variable on a DESIGN subcommand, you must supply an ANALYSIS subcommand that does *not* name the variable. This excludes it from the analysis as a dependent variable or covariate and makes it eligible for inclusion on DESIGN.

• More than one continuous variable can be pooled into a single effect (provided that they are all excluded on an ANALYSIS subcommand) with the keyword POOL(varlist). For a single continuous variable, POOL(VAR) is equivalent to VAR.

- The TO convention in the variables list for POOL refers to the order of continuous variables (dependent variables and covariates) on the original MANOVA variables list, which is not necessarily their order on the active file. This is the *only* allowable use of the keyword TO on a DESIGN subcommand.

- You can specify interaction terms between factors and continuous variables. If FAC is a factor and COV is a covariate that has been omitted from an ANALYSIS subcommand, FAC BY COV is a valid term on a DESIGN statement.

- You cannot specify an interaction between two continuous variables. Use the COMPUTE command to create a variable representing the interaction prior to MANOVA.

Example

This example tests whether the regression line of the dependent variable Y on the two variables X1 and X2 has the same slope across all the categories of the factors AGE and TREATMNT.

```
MANOVA Y BY AGE(1,5) TREATMNT(1,3) WITH X1, X2
/ANALYSIS = Y
/METHOD = SSTYPE(SEQUENTIAL)
/DESIGN = POOL(X1,X2),
          AGE, TREATMNT, AGE BY TREATMNT,
          POOL(X1,X2) BY AGE + POOL(X1,X2) BY TREATMNT
             + POOL(X1,X2) BY AGE BY TREATMNT.
```

- The ANALYSIS subcommand excludes X1 and X2 from the standard treatment of covariates, so that they can be used in the design.

- The METHOD subcommand requests a sequential (or hierarchical) decomposition of the sums of squares.

- The DESIGN subcommand includes five terms. POOL(X1,X2), the overall regression of the dependent variable on X1 and X2, is entered first, followed by the two factors and their interaction.

- The last term is the test for equal regressions. It consists of three factor-by-continuous-variable interactions pooled together. POOL(X1,X2) BY AGE is the interaction between AGE and the combined effect of the continuous variables X1 and X2. It is combined with similar interactions between TREATMNT and the continuous variables and between the AGE BY TREATMNT interaction and the continuous variables.

- If the last term is not statistically significant, there is no evidence that the regression of Y on X1 and X2 is different across any combination of the categories of AGE and TREATMNT.

Error Terms for Individual Effects

The "error" sum of squares against which terms in the design are tested is specified on the ERROR subcommand. For any particular term on a DESIGN subcommand, you can specify a different error term to be used in the analysis of variance.

- To test a term against only the within-cells sum of squares, specify the term followed by VS WITHIN on the DESIGN subcommand. For example, GROUP VS WITHIN tests the effect of the factor GROUP against only the within-cells sum of squares. For most analyses this is the default error term.

- To test a term against only the residual sum of squares (the sum of squares for all terms not included in your DESIGN), specify the term followed by VS RESIDUAL.

- To test against the combined within-cells and residual sums of squares, specify the term followed by VS WITHIN+RESIDUAL.

- To test against any other sum of squares in the analysis of variance, include a term corresponding to the desired sum of squares in the design and assign it to a number between 1 and 10. You can then test against the number of the error term. It is often convenient to test against the term before you define it. This is perfectly acceptable, so long as you define the error term on the same DESIGN subcommand.

Example

```
MANOVA DEP BY A, B, C (1,3)
/DESIGN=A VS 1,
        B WITHIN A = 1 VS 2,
        C WITHIN B WITHIN A = 2 VS WITHIN.
```

- In this example the factors A, B, and C are completely nested; levels of C occur within levels of B, which occur within levels of A. Each factor is tested against everything within it.
- A, the outermost factor, is tested against the B WITHIN A sum of squares, to see if it contributes anything beyond the effects of B within each of its levels. The B WITHIN A sum of squares is defined as "error term" number 1.
- B nested within A, in turn, is tested against "error term" number 2, which is defined as the C WITHIN B WITHIN A sum of squares.
- Finally, C nested within B nested within A is tested against the within-cells sum of squares.

User-defined error terms are specified "on the fly" by simply inserting = n after a term. Keywords used in building a design term, such as BY or WITHIN, are evaluated first. For example, error term number 2 in the above example consists of the entire term C WITHIN B WITHIN A. An error-term *number,* but not an error-term *definition,* can follow the keyword VS.

CONSTANT Keyword

By default, the constant term is included as the first term in the model.

- If you have specified NOCONSTANT on the METHOD subcommand, a constant term will not be included in any design unless you request it with the CONSTANT keyword on DESIGN.
- You can specify an error term for the constant.
- A factor named CONSTANT will not be recognized on the DESIGN subcommand.

ERROR Subcommand

The ERROR subcommand allows you to specify or change the error term used to test all effects for which you do not explicitly specify an error term on DESIGN. The ERROR subcommand affects all terms in all subsequent designs, except terms for which you explicitly provide an error term.

WITHIN	*Terms in the model are tested against the within-cell sum of squares.* This is the default unless there is no variance within cells or unless the observations model is used (see the MODELTYPE parameter under METHOD Subcommand).
RESIDUAL	*Terms in the model are tested against the residual sum of squares.* This includes all terms not named on the DESIGN statement.
WITHIN+RESIDUAL	*Terms are tested against the pooled within-cells and residual sum of squares.* This is the default for designs processed using the observations model.
error number	*Terms are tested against a numbered error term.* The error term must be defined on each DESIGN subcommand (see the discussion of error terms under DESIGN Subcommand).

- If you specify ERROR=WITHIN+RESIDUAL and one of the components does not exist, MANOVA uses the other component alone.
- If you specify your own error term by number, you must define a term with that number on each DESIGN subcommand. If a design does not have an error term with the specified number, MANOVA does not carry out significance tests. It will, however, display hypothesis sums of squares and, if requested, parameter estimates.

Example

```
MANOVA DEP BY A(1,2) B(1,4)
/ERROR = 1
/DESIGN = A, B, A BY B = 1 VS WITHIN
/DESIGN = A, B.
```

- The ERROR subcommand defines error term 1 as the default error term.

• In the first design, A by B is defined as error term 1 and is therefore used to test the A and B effects. The A by B effect itself is explicitly tested against the within-cells error.

• In the second design, no term is defined as error term 1, so no significance tests are carried out. Hypothesis sums of squares are displayed for A and B.

CONTRAST Subcommand

Use the CONTRAST subcommand to specify the type of contrast desired among the levels of a factor. For a factor with k levels or values, the contrast type determines the meaning of its $(k-1)$ degrees of freedom.

• Specify the factor name in parentheses following the subcommand CONTRAST.

• You can specify only one factor per CONTRAST subcommand, but you can enter multiple CONTRAST subcommands.

• After closing the parentheses, enter an equals sign followed by one of the CONTRAST keywords.

• To obtain significance levels for individual degrees of freedom for the specified contrast, enter the factor name followed by a number in parentheses on the DESIGN subcommand. The number refers to a partition of the factor's degrees of freedom. If you do not use the PARTITION subcommand, each degree of freedom is a distinct partition.

Example

```
MANOVA DEP BY FAC(1,5)
/CONTRAST(FAC)=DIFFERENCE
/PRINT=PARAM(ESTIM)
/DESIGN=FAC(1) FAC(2) FAC(3) FAC(4).
```

• The factor FAC has five categories and therefore four degrees of freedom.

• The CONTRAST subcommand requests DIFFERENCE contrasts, which compare each level (except the first) with the mean of the previous levels.

• Each of the four degrees of freedom is tested individually on the DESIGN subcommand.

• Parameter estimates for each degree of freedom will be displayed.

Orthogonal contrasts are particularly useful. In a balanced design, contrasts are orthogonal if the sum of the coefficients in each contrast row is zero and if for any pair of contrast rows, the products of corresponding coefficients sum to zero. Difference, Helmert, and polynomial contrasts always meet these criteria in balanced designs.

The available contrast types are

DEVIATION   *Deviations from the grand mean.* This is the default. Each level of the factor except one is compared to the grand mean. One category (by default the last) must be omitted so that the effects will be independent of one another. To omit a category other than the last, specify the number of the omitted category (which is not necessarily the same as its *value*) in parentheses after the DEVIATION keyword. For example,

```
MANOVA A BY B(2,4)
/CONTRAST(B)=DEVIATION(1)
```

omits the first category, in which B has the value 2. Deviation contrasts are not orthogonal.

DIFFERENCE   *Difference or reverse Helmert contrasts.* Each level of the factor except the first is compared to the mean of the previous levels. In a balanced design, difference contrasts are orthogonal.

HELMERT   *Helmert contrasts.* Each level of the factor except the last is compared to the mean of subsequent levels. In a balanced design, Helmert contrasts are orthogonal.

SIMPLE   *Each level of the factor except the last is compared to the last level.* To use a category other than the last as the omitted reference category, specify its number (which is not necessarily the same as its *value*) in parentheses following the keyword SIMPLE. For example,

```
MANOVA A BY B(2,4)
/CONTRAST(B)=SIMPLE(1)
```

compares the other levels to the first level of B, in which B has the value 2. Simple contrasts are not orthogonal.

POLYNOMIAL   *Polynomial contrasts.* The first degree of freedom contains the linear effect across the levels of the factor; the second contains the quadratic effect; and so on. In a balanced design, polynomial contrasts are orthogonal. By default, the levels are assumed to be equally spaced; you can specify unequal spacing by entering a *metric* consisting of one integer for each *level* of the factor in parentheses after the keyword POLYNOMIAL. For example, CONTRAST(STIMULUS) = POLYNOMIAL(1,2,4) indicates that the three levels of STIMULUS are actually in the proportion 1:2:4. The default metric is always $(1,2,...,k)$, where k variables are involved. Only the relative differences between the terms of the metric matter: (1,2,4) is the same metric as (2,3,5) or (20,30,50), because in each instance the difference between the second and third numbers is twice the difference between the first and second.

REPEATED   *Comparison of adjacent levels.* Each level of the factor except the first is compared to the previous level. Repeated contrasts are not orthogonal.

SPECIAL   *A user-defined contrast.* After this keyword enter a square matrix in parentheses with as many rows and columns as there are levels in the factor. The first row represents the mean effect of the factor and is generally a vector of *1*'s. It represents a set of weights indicating how to collapse over the categories of this factor in estimating parameters for *other* factors. The other rows of the contrast matrix contain the special contrasts indicating the desired comparisons between levels of the factor. If the special contrasts are linear combinations of each other, MANOVA reports the linear dependency and stops processing.

PARTITION Subcommand

The PARTITION subcommand subdivides the degrees of freedom associated with a factor. This permits you to test the significance of the effect of a specific contrast or group of contrasts of the factor instead of the overall effect of all contrasts of the factor.

- Specify the factor name in parentheses following the PARTITION subcommand.

- After closing the parentheses, you can enter an equals sign followed by a parenthetical list of integers indicating the degrees of freedom for each partition or subdivision.

- If you omit the list specifying degrees of freedom, MANOVA partitions the factor into single degrees of freedom.

- Each value in the partition list must be a positive integer and the sum of the values cannot exceed the degrees of freedom for the factor.

- The degrees of freedom available for a factor are one less than the number of levels of the factor.

- The meaning of each degree of freedom depends upon the contrast type for the factor. For example, with deviation contrasts (the default), each degree of freedom represents the deviation of the dependent variable in one level of the factor from its grand mean over all levels. With polynomial contrasts, the degrees of freedom represent the linear effect, the quadratic effect, and so on.

- If your list does not account for all the degrees of freedom, MANOVA adds one final partition containing the remaining degrees of freedom.

• You can use a repetition factor of the form $n*$ to specify a series of partitions with the same number of degrees of freedom. PARTITION(TREATMNT) = (3*2,1) builds three partitions with two degrees of freedom each followed by a fourth partition with a single degree of freedom. If any degrees of freedom remain, they will be placed in a fifth partition.

• Include the effect of a specific partition of a factor in your design with a number in parentheses on the DESIGN subcommand (see example below).

• If you want the default single-degree-of-freedom partition, you can omit the PARTITION subcommand and simply enter the appropriate term on the DESIGN subcommand.

Example
```
MANOVA OUTCOME BY TREATMNT(1,12)
/PARTITION(TREATMNT) = (3,2,6)
/DESIGN TREATMNT(2).
```

• The factor TREATMNT has twelve categories and therefore eleven degrees of freedom.

• The PARTITION subcommand divides the effect of TREATMNT into three partitions, containing respectively 3, 2, and 6 degrees of freedom. The specification (3,2) would have produced the same division, since MANOVA would have supplied a final partition to contain the remaining six degrees of freedom.

• The DESIGN subcommand specifies a model in which only the second partition of TREATMNT is tested. This partition contains the fourth and fifth degrees of freedom.

• Since the default contrast type is DEVIATION (see the CONTRAST subcommand), this second partition represents the deviation of the fourth and fifth levels of TREATMNT from the grand mean.

ANALYSIS Subcommand

The ANALYSIS subcommand allows you to work with a subset of the continuous variables (dependent variable and covariates) you have named on the MANOVA variables list. In univariate analysis of variance, you can use the ANALYSIS subcommand to allow factor-by-covariate interaction terms in your model. (see DESIGN Subcommand). You can also use it to switch the roles of the dependent variable and a covariate.

• In general, the ANALYSIS subcommand gives you complete control over which continuous variables are dependent variables, which are covariates, and which are to be neither.

• ANALYSIS specifications are like the MANOVA variables specification except that factors are not named. Enter the dependent variable and, if there are covariates, the keyword WITH and the covariates.

• Only variables listed as dependent variables or covariates on the MANOVA variables specification can be entered on an ANALYSIS subcommand.

• In a univariate analysis of variance, the most important use of ANALYSIS is to *omit* covariates altogether from the analysis list, thereby making them available for inclusion on DESIGN (see examples below and under DESIGN Subcommand).

• For more information on the ANALYSIS subcommand, refer to MANOVA: Multivariate.

Example
```
MANOVA DEP BY FACTOR(1,3) WITH COV
/ANALYSIS DEP
/DESIGN FACTOR, COV, FACTOR BY COV.
```

• COV, a continuous variable, is included on the MANOVA variables list as a covariate.

• COV is not mentioned on the ANALYSIS subcommand so it will not be included in the model as a dependent variable or covariate. It can, therefore, be explicitly included on the DESIGN subcommand.

• The DESIGN subcommand includes the main effects of FACTOR and COV, and the FACTOR by COV interaction.

PRINT and NOPRINT Subcommands

Use the PRINT and NOPRINT subcommands to control the display of optional output. (Additional output can be obtained on the PCOMPS, DISCRIM, OMEANS, PMEANS, PLOT, and RESIDUALS subcommands.) PRINT specifications appropriate for univariate MANOVA are described below. For information on PRINT specifications appropriate for other MANOVA models, see MANOVA: Multivariate, and MANOVA: Repeated Measures.

- Specifications on PRINT subcommand remain in effect for all subsequent designs.
- Some PRINT output, such as CELLINFO, applies to the entire MANOVA procedure and is displayed only once.
- You can "turn off" optional output that you request on the PRINT subcommand by entering a NOPRINT subcommand with the specifications originally used on the PRINT subcommand.
- Some optional output greatly increases the processing time. Request only the output you want to see.

CELLINFO	*Basic information about each cell in the design.*
PARAMETERS	*Parameter estimates.*
HOMOGENEITY	*Tests for homogeneity of variance.*
DESIGN	*Design information.*
ERROR	*Error standard deviations* (in univariate analysis).

CELLINFO Keyword

Use the CELLINFO keyword on PRINT to request any of the following.

- Enclose CELLINFO specifications in parentheses after the CELLINFO keyword.
- Since output from CELLINFO is displayed once before the analysis of any particular design, specify CELLINO only once.

MEANS	*Cell means, standard deviations, and counts for the dependent variable and covariates.* Confidence intervals for the cell means are displayed if you have SET WIDTH WIDE.
SSCP	*Within-cell sum-of-squares and cross-products matrices for the dependent variable and covariates.*
COV	*Within-cell variance-covariance matrices for the dependent variable and covariates.*
COR	*Within-cell correlation matrices, with standard deviations on the diagonal, for the dependent variable and covariates.*

- When you specify SSCP, COV, or COR, the cells are numbered for identification, beginning with Cell 1.
- The levels vary most rapidly for the factor named last on the MANOVA variables specification.
- Empty cells are neither displayed nor numbered.
- A table showing the levels of each factor corresponding to each cell number is displayed at the beginning of MANOVA output.

Example

```
MANOVA DEP BY A(1,4) B(1,2) WITH COV
/PRINT=CELLINFO(MEANS COV)
/DESIGN.
```

- For each combination of levels of A and B, MANOVA displays separately the means and standard deviations of DEP and COV. Beginning with Cell 1, it will then display the variance-covariance matrix of DEP and COV within each non-empty cell.
- A table of cell numbers will be displayed to show the factor levels corresponding to each cell.
- The keyword COV, as a parameter of CELLINFO, is not confused with the variable COV.

PARAMETERS Keyword

The PARAMETERS keyword displays information relating to the estimated size of the effects in the model.

• Specify any of the following in parentheses on PARAMETERS.

• There is no default specification for PARAMETERS.

ESTIM *The estimated parameters themselves, along with their standard errors, t tests, and confidence intervals.* Only nonredundant parameters are displayed.

NEGSUM *The negative of the sum of parameters for each effect.* For main effects this equals the parameter for the omitted (redundant) contrast. NEGSUM is displayed along with the parameter estimates.

ORTHO *The orthogonal estimates of parameters used to produce the sums of squares.*

COR *Covariances and correlations among the parameter estimates.*

SIGNIF Keyword

The SIGNIF keyword requests special significance tests, most of which apply to multivariate designs (see MANOVA: Multivariate). The following specification is useful in univariate applications of MANOVA:

SINGLEDF *Significance tests for the single degrees of freedom making up each effect* for ANOVA tables in univariate designs. When orthogonal contrasts are being applied, these degrees of freedom correspond to the degrees of freedom in the contrast. This output is therefore particularly useful for orthogonal contrasts. You can always see the exact linear combinations being tested by requesting the solution matrix with PRINT = DESIGN(SOLUTION).

Example

```
MANOVA DEP BY FAC(1,5)
/CONTRAST(FAC)=POLY
/PRINT=SIGNIF(SINGLEDF) DESIGN(SOLUTION)
/DESIGN.
```

• POLYNOMIAL contrasts are applied to FAC, testing the linear, quadratic, cubic, and quartic components of its five levels. POLYNOMIAL contrasts are orthogonal in balanced designs.

• The SINGLEDF specification on PRINT=SIGNIF requests significance tests for each of these four components.

• The SOLUTION matrix is also requested to verify the linear combinations tested with SIGNIF(SINGLEDF).

HOMOGENEITY Keyword

The HOMOGENEITY keyword requests tests for the homogeneity of variance of the dependent variable and covariates across the cells of the design. Enter one or more of the following specifications in parentheses:

BARTLETT *Bartlett-Box F test.*

COCHRAN *Cochran's C.*

DESIGN Keyword

You can request the following by entering one or more of the specifications in parentheses following the keyword DESIGN. See Bock (1975) for discussion of these matrices.

ONEWAY *The one-way basis matrix (not the contrast matrix) for each factor.*

OVERALL *The overall reduced-model basis (design) matrix (not the contrast matrix).*

DECOMP *The QR/CHOLESKY decomposition of the design.*

BIAS *Contamination coefficients displaying the bias present in the design.*

SOLUTION *Coefficients of the linear combinations of the cell means used in significance testing.* These are *not* the coefficients used in estimating parameters, unless the parameters are orthogonal.

• The DECOMP and BIAS matrices can provide valuable information on the confounding of the effects and the estimability of the chosen contrasts. If two effects are confounded, the entry corresponding to them in the BIAS matrix will be nonzero; if they are orthogonal, the entry will be zero. This is particularly useful in designs with unpatterned empty cells.

• The SOLUTION matrix shows the exact linear combination of cell means used to test effects and can be useful in interpreting those tests.

ERROR Keyword   Generally, the ERROR keyword on PRINT produces error matrices. In univariate analyses, the only valid specification for ERROR is STDDEV.

STDDEV   *The error standard deviation.* Normally this is the within-cells standard deviation of the dependent variable. If you specify multiple error terms on DESIGN (a mixed model), this specification will display the standard deviation of each.

OMEANS Subcommand

The OMEANS (observed means) subcommand displays tables of the means of continuous variables for levels or combinations of levels of the factors.

• Use keywords VARIABLES and TABLES to indicate which observed means you want to display.
• With no specifications, the OMEANS subcommand is equivalent to PRINT = CELLINFO(MEANS).
• OMEANS displays confidence intervals for the cell means if you have SET WIDTH WIDE.
• Since output from OMEANS is displayed once before the analysis of any particular design, this subcommand should be specified only once.

VARIABLES   *The continuous variables for which you want means.* Specify the variables in parentheses after the VARIABLES keyword. You can request means for the dependent variable or any covariates. If you omit the VARIABLES keyword, observed means are displayed for the dependent variable and all covariates. If you enter the VARIABLES keyword, you must also enter the TABLES keyword discussed below.

TABLES   *The factors for which you want the observed means displayed.* List the factors, or combinations of factors separated with BY, in parentheses. Observed means are displayed for each level, or combination of levels, of the factors named (see example below). Both weighted means (based on all cases) and unweighted means (where all cells are weighted equally regardless of the number of cases they contain) are displayed. If you enter the keyword CONSTANT, the grand mean is displayed.

Example
```
MANOVA DEP BY A(1,3) B(1,2)
/OMEANS=TABLES(A,B)
/DESIGN.
```

• Since there is no VARIABLES specification in the OMEANS subcommand, observed means are displayed for all continuous variables. DEP is the only dependent variable here, and there are no covariates.
• The TABLES specification in the OMEANS subcommand requests tables of observed means for each of the three categories of A (collapsing over B) and for both categories of B (collapsing over A).
• MANOVA displays both weighted means, in which all cases count equally, and unweighted means, in which all cells count equally.

PMEANS Subcommand

The PMEANS (predicted means) subcommand displays a table of the predicted cell means of the dependent variable, both adjusted for the effect of covariates in the cell and unadjusted for covariates. For comparison, it also displays the observed cell means.

• Output from PMEANS can be computationally expensive.
• PMEANS without any additional specifications displays a table showing for each cell the observed mean of the dependent variable, the predicted mean adjusted for the effect of covariates in that cell (ADJ. MEAN), the predicted mean unadjusted for covariates (EST. MEAN), and the raw and standardized residuals from the estimated means.

C

Command Reference

- Cells are numbered in output from PMEANS, so that the levels vary most rapidly on the factor named last in the MANOVA variables specification (as in output from PRINT=CELLINFO). A table showing the levels of each factor corresponding to each cell number is displayed at the beginning of the MANOVA output.

- Predicted means are suppressed if the last term is being calculated by subtraction because of METHOD = ESTIM(LASTRES).

- Predicted means are also suppressed for any design in which the MUPLUS keyword appears.

- Covariates are not predicted.

The following keywords are available to modify the output of the PMEANS subcommand:

VARIABLES   *The dependent variables for which you want tables of predicted means.* Used in multivariate MANOVA. If you enter the VARIABLES keyword, you must also enter the TABLES keyword.

TABLES   *Additional tables showing adjusted predicted means for specified factors or combinations of factors.* Enter the names of factors or combinations of factors in parentheses after this keyword. For each factor or combination, MANOVA displays the predicted means (adjusted for covariates) collapsed over all other factors.

ERROR   *The error term used in standardizing the residuals, when more than one error term is specified.* MANOVA normally uses the default error term (see ERROR Subcommand) to standardize the residuals for PMEANS. When the DESIGN subcommand specifies more than one error term, you must specify which is to be used in standardizing PMEANS residuals by entering the ERROR keyword on a PMEANS subcommand and the desired error term in parentheses. Specify either WITHIN, RESIDUAL, WITHIN + RESIDUAL, or an error number you define for a term on the DESIGN subcommand.

PLOT   *A plot of the predicted means for each cell.* The SIZE keyword on the PLOT subcommand controls the size of this plot.

- No predicted means will be produced for a design with multiple error terms unless you use the ERROR keyword on the PMEANS subcommand to indicate which term should be used in standardizing the residuals.

- If you specify a defined error number on the ERROR keyword for PMEANS, no predicted means will be produced for designs in which you do not define that error term.

Example
```
MANOVA DEP BY A(1,4) B(1,3)
/PMEANS TABLES(A, B, A BY B)
/DESIGN = A, B.
```

- The PMEANS subcommand displays the default table of observed and predicted (both adjusted for covariates and unadjusted) means for DEP and raw and standardized residuals in each of the twelve cells in the model.

- The TABLES specification on PMEANS displays tables of predicted means for A (collapsing over B), for B (collapsing over A), and all combinations of A and B.

- Since A and B are the only factors in the model, the means for A by B in the TABLES specification come from every cell in the model. They are identical to the adjusted predicted means in the default PMEANS table, which always includes all nonempty cells.

- Predicted means for A by B can be requested in the TABLES specification, even though the A by B effect is not in the design.

Example
```
MANOVA DEP BY A B C(1,3)
/PMEANS ERROR(1)
/DESIGN A VS 1, B WITHIN A = 1, C.
```

- Two error terms are used in this design: the B within A sum of squares, which is defined as error term 1 (to test the A effect), and the usual within-cells sum of squares (to test B within a itself as well as the C effect).

- Consequently, the PMEANS subcommand *requires* an ERROR specification. If the keyword ERROR is omitted from the PMEANS subcommand, MANOVA does not display the means.
- Since there is no TABLES keyword on the PMEANS subcommand, the default table of predicted means for each cell is produced.

PLOT Subcommand

MANOVA can display a variety of plots useful in checking the assumptions needed in the analysis. Plots are produced only once in the MANOVA procedure, regardless of how many DESIGN subcommands you enter. Use the following keywords on the PLOT subcommand to request plots:

CELLPLOTS   *Cell statistics, including a plot of cell means vs. cell variances, a plot of cell means vs. cell standard deviations, and a histogram of cell means.* Plots are produced for each continuous variable (dependent or covariate) named on the MANOVA variables list. The first two plots aid in detecting heteroscedasticity (nonhomogeneous variances) and in determining an appropriate data transformation if one is needed. The third plot gives distributional information for the cell means.

BOXPLOTS   *Boxplots.* Plots are displayed for each continuous variable (dependent or covariate) named on the MANOVA variables list. Boxplots provide a simple graphical means of comparing the cells in terms of mean location and spread. The data must be stored in memory for these plots; if there is not enough memory, boxplots are not produced and a warning message is issued.

NORMAL   *Normal and detrended normal plots.* Plots are produced for each continuous variable (dependent or covariate) named on the MANOVA variables list. MANOVA ranks the scores and then plots the ranks against the expected normal deviate, or detrended expected normal deviate, for that rank. These plots aid in detecting non-normality and outlying observations. All data must be held in memory to compute ranks. If not enough memory is available, MANOVA displays a warning and skips the plots.

STEMLEAF   *A stem-and-leaf display.* Plots are produced for each continuous variable (dependent or covariate) named on the MANOVA variables list. This display details the distribution of each continuous variable as a whole, not for each cell. The plots are not produced if there is insufficient memory.

- An additional plot available on the PLOT subcommand, ZCORR, is described in under MANOVA: Multivariate.
- You can request other plots on the PMEANS and RESIDUALS subcommands.

The following keyword is available on the plot subcommand to control the size of these plots.

SIZE   *The dimensions of MANOVA plots.* Includes plots specified on the PMEANS and RESIDUALS subcommands. The default size is 40 horizontal spaces by 15 vertical lines. If you enter SIZE(80,20) on the PLOT subcommand, plots will be 80 horizontal spaces by 20 vertical lines. Large plots require more memory.

RESIDUALS Subcommand

Use the RESIDUALS subcommand to display and plot casewise values and residuals for your models.

- In a saturated design (the default), there are no residuals. Unless you specify a design with residual error, the RESIDUALS subcommand produces no output.
- In designs with multiple error terms, you must specify the ERROR keyword, as described below, on the RESIDUALS subcommand.

- If a designated error term does not exist for a given design, no predicted values or residuals are calculated.
- If you specify RESIDUALS without any specifications, CASEWISE output is displayed.

The following keywords are available.

CASEWISE   *A case-by-case listing of the observed, predicted, residual, and standardized residual values for each dependent variable.*

PLOT   *A plot of observed values, predicted values, and case numbers vs. the standardized residuals, plus normal and detrended normal probability plots for the standardized residuals (5 plots in all). Keyword SIZE on the PLOT subcommand controls the size of these plots.*

ERROR   *The error term that will be used to calculate the standardized residuals that you display or plot in a model containing multiple error terms. Specify WITHIN, RESIDUAL, or WITHIN + RESIDUAL in parentheses after the keyword ERROR, or specify the number of an error term defined on the DESIGN subcommand. When the same error term is used in testing all effects, that is the term used to calculate residuals. See ERROR Subcommand for the specification of a default error term.*

METHOD Subcommand

Use the METHOD subcommand to control computational aspects of your MANOVA analysis. You can specify any or all of three keywords:

SSTYPE   *The method of partitioning sums of squares.*

MODELTYPE   *The model for parameter estimation.*

ESTIMATION   *How parameters are to be estimated.*

SSTYPE Keyword

MANOVA offers two different methods of partitioning the sums of squares. Specify either one in parentheses following keyword SSTYPE.

UNIQUE   *Regression approach.* Each term is corrected for every other term in the model. With this approach, sums of squares for various components of the model do not add up to the total sum of squares unless the design is balanced. SSTYPE(UNIQUE) is the default.

SEQUENTIAL   *Hierarchical decomposition of the sums of squares.* Each term is adjusted only for the terms that precede it in the DESIGN statement. This is an orthogonal decomposition, and the sums of squares in the model add up to the total sum of squares.

MODELTYPE Keyword

This keyword specifies the model for parameter estimation. You can specify either of the following in parentheses after the keyword MODELTYPE:

MEANS   *The cell means model.* This model requires significantly less processing time and is the default unless you specify continuous variables on the DESIGN subcommand.

OBSERVATIONS   *The observations model.* This more costly model is used by default when you specify one or more continuous variables on the DESIGN subcommand.

ESTIMATION Keyword

Four different aspects of parameter estimation are controlled by keyword ESTIMATION. You can enter one choice from each of the following pairs of alternatives in parentheses after ESTIMATION. In each case, the default is listed first.

QR   QR uses Householder transformations to effect a QR (orthogo-
CHOLESKY   nal) decomposition of the design matrix. This method bypasses the normal equations and the inaccuracies that can result from

creating the cross-products matrix, and it generally results in extremely accurate parameter estimates. The CHOLESKY method is computationally less expensive but sometimes less accurate.

NOBALANCED By default, MANOVA assumes that your design is not bal-
BALANCED anced. If you are analyzing a balanced, orthogonal design, specifying the BALANCED keyword can result in substantial savings in processing time. Use BALANCED only if 1) all cell sizes are equal; 2) you are using the cell-means model; and 3) the contrast type for each factor is orthogonal. If you specify balanced processing but your design does not conform to these requirements, MANOVA reverts to the more general unbalanced processing mode. If you have specified METHOD = ESTIMATION(BALANCED), you can revert to unbalanced estimation in a later design with METHOD = ESTIMATION(NOBALANCED).

NOLASTRES By default MANOVA explicitly calculates all effects in the
LASTRES design. You can sometimes save processing time by suppressing the calculation of the last effect in the model with the LASTRES keyword. Do this only if 1) you have specified SSTYPE(SEQUENTIAL) in a METHOD subcommand; 2) you do not want parameter estimates for the last effect in the model (you can get a significance test for this effect); and 3) the last effect in the model does not contain any continuous variables. With LASTRES, the sum of squares for the last effect in the DESIGN statement is calculated as the residual sum of squares, by subtraction from the total sum of squares. This is particularly economical when the last effect is a high-order interaction term, a common situation. If you have specified LASTRES, you can revert to normal direct estimation with METHOD = ESTIMATION(NOLASTRES).

CONSTANT CONSTANT requests that all models include a constant (grand
NOCONSTANT mean) term, even if none is explicitly specified on the DESIGN subcommand. NOCONSTANT excludes constant terms from models that do not include the keyword CONSTANT on the DESIGN subcommand. If you have specified ESTIMATION (NOCONSTANT), you can revert to the default on later models by entering ESTIMATION (CONSTANT).

Example
```
MANOVA DEP BY A B C (1,4)
/METHOD=SSTYPE(SEQUENTIAL) ESTIMATION(CHOLESKY BALANCED LASTRES)
/DESIGN
/METHOD=ESTIMATION(NOLASTRES)
/PRINT=PARAM(ESTIM)
/DESIGN=A, B, C, A BY B, A BY C, B BY C.
```

• For the first design, a fully saturated model, the METHOD options are chosen to reduce processing costs as much as possible.

• Results will not be satisfactory unless the conditions detailed above are met.

• Parameter estimates are not requested for the first design, so it does not matter that estimates for the last effect are unavailable.

• The second METHOD subcommand turns off LASTRES so that in subsequent designs all terms are estimated directly. Other parameters from the first METHOD subcommand remain in effect.

• The PRINT subcommand requests parameter estimates for subsequent designs.

• The second DESIGN omits the third-order interaction. If no METHOD subcommand had been entered to restore NOLASTRES, the final term (B by C) would have been estimated by subtraction and no parameter estimates would have been possible.

C

Command Reference

MISSING Subcommand

By default, cases with missing values for any of the variables on the MANOVA variables list are excluded from the analysis. The MISSING subcommand allows you to include cases with user-missing values. Available specifications are

LISTWISE *Cases with missing values for any variable named on the MANOVA variables list are excluded from the analysis.* This is the default.

INCLUDE *User-missing values are treated as valid.* For factors, you must include the missing-value codes within the range specified on the MANOVA variables list. It may be necessary to recode these values so that they will be adjacent to the other factor values. System-missing values may not be included in the analysis.

- The same missing-value treatment is used to process all designs in a single execution of MANOVA.

- If you enter more than one MISSING subcommand, the last one entered will be in effect for the entire procedure, including for designs specified before the MISSING subcommand.

- Pairwise deletion of missing data is not available in MANOVA.

WRITE Subcommand

MANOVA allows you to write intermediate results to the results file and then read them back into a later run for further analysis. This can significantly reduce processing time when you are analyzing large numbers of cases or variables.

- The WRITE subcommand writes matrix materials to the results file (by default, SPSS.PRC) in a format that can be read in by the MANOVA READ subcommand.

- WRITE requires no specifications.

- Six types of records are written to the results file.

The formats of the output records are as follows:

Type 1 *Design information.* Four 10-character fields containing, respectively, the number of nonempty cells, the number of observations, the number of factors, and the number of continuous variables (dependent variables and covariates).

Type 2 *Factor codes for cells.* For each nonempty cell, a Type 2 record lists the value of each factor. These values are written in 8-character fields. Each Type 2 record is followed by the corresponding Type 3 records.

Type 3 *Cell means for continuous variables.* Each number occupies 16 characters. Means for continuous variables are written in the order variables were named on the MANOVA variables specification.

Type 4 *Cell n's.* Following the pairs of Type 2 and 3 records, MANOVA writes out case counts for all cells on Type 4 records, using 10 characters per count.

Type 5 *Within-cell error correlation matrix for continuous variables.* The matrix is written in lower-triangular form, with ones on the diagonal and correlations in F10.6 format. The order of variables is that on the MANOVA variables specification.

Type 6 *Within-cell standard deviations for continuous variables.* Standard deviations are written in the order variables were named on the MANOVA variables specification.

READ Subcommand

The READ subcommand reads matrix materials formatted as described for the WRITE subcommand. Starting an analysis with these intermediate results can significantly reduce processing time.

- READ requires no specifications.

- READ must be used with a DATA LIST MATRIX command, as shown in the example below.

• Since a matrix, rather than a case file, must be active when you use the READ subcommand, residuals analysis cannot be performed. You cannot use the RESIDUALS subcommand with READ.

• The only plot that can be obtained with matrix input is ZCORR.

• You cannot specify continuous variables or factor-by-covariate interactions on the DESIGN subcommand when using matrix input.

• The homogeneity-of-variance tests specified by PRINT = HOMOGENEITY are not available with matrix input.

Example   When using the READ subcommand in MANOVA, you must precede the MANOVA command by a DATA LIST of this form:

```
DATA LIST MATRIX FILE='filename.ext' / varlist .
```

• You do not need to use the same names that were used when the matrix materials were written.

• The order in which you list variables on DATA LIST MATRIX does not matter, except in determining the order of variables on the active file created by MANOVA.

• The active file created by MANOVA when it reads these matrix materials cannot be used by any procedure other than MANOVA.

Example
```
GET FILE='MYFILE.SYS'.
SET RESULTS 'MANOVA.MAT'.
MANOVA V1 V2 V3 V4 BY SEX(1,2) CLASS(1,3)
/WRITE
/DESIGN SEX CLASS.

DATA LIST MATRIX FILE='MANOVA.MAT'
/X1 TO X4 SEX CLASS.

MANOVA X1 X2 X3 X4 BY SEX(1,2) CLASS(1,3)
/READ
/ANALYSIS X1 WITH X2 X3
/PRINT=PARAM(ESTIM)
/DESIGN=SEX, CLASS, SEX BY CLASS.
```

• The SET RESULTS command specifies that matrix materials should be written to the file MANOVA.MAT.

• In the first MANOVA procedure, the WRITE subcommand sends formatted matrix materials to MANOVA.MAT. These materials describe the four continuous variables V1 TO V4 in the six cells defined by SEX and CLASS.

• The DATA LIST MATRIX command names the MANOVA.MAT file and assigns names to the variables. The names X1 TO X4 will now be used for the variables originally known as V1 TO V4. The order in which variables are named on DATA LIST MATRIX does not matter.

• The second MANOVA command uses the new names. The variables specification defines four continuous variables and two factors. The number and order of continuous variables, the number and order of factors, and the levels of each factor must be the same as those in the MANOVA command that wrote the matrix materials. The names of the six variables must be chosen from among the names on the DATA LIST MATRIX command.

• The ANALYSIS subcommand redefines X2 and X3 as covariates and omits X4 entirely from the analysis.

• The DESIGN subcommand specifies a different design than the one in the original analysis.

• Any analysis using these four continuous variables and two factors can be performed. However, the RESIDUALS subcommand, most plots, the homogeneity-of-variance tests, and continuous variables on the DESIGN subcommand cannot be specified.

Reference   Bock, R. D. *Multivariate statistical methods in behavioral research.* New York: McGraw-Hill, 1975.

MANOVA: Multivariate

```
MANOVA dependent varlist [BY factor list (min,max) [factor list...]

                          [WITH covariate varlist]]

[/TRANSFORM [(varlist [/varlist])]=[ORTHONORM] [{DEVIATIONS (refcat)  }]]
                                                {DIFFERENCE           }
                                  [{CONTRAST}] {HELMERT              }
                                  {BASIS    } {SIMPLE (refcat)       }
                                              {REPEATED              }
                                              {POLYNOMIAL [(metric)] }
                                              {SPECIAL (matrix)      }

[/RENAME={newname} {newname}...]
         {*      } {*      }

           {[HOMOGENEITY ([BOXM**])]                                    }
[/{PRINT  }={[ERROR ([SSCP] [COV**] [COR**] [STDDEV])]                  }]
  {NOPRINT} {[SIGNIF [([MULTIV] [EIGEN] [DIMENR] [UNIV] [HYPOTH]        }
           {         [STEPDOWN] [{AVERF }]  [BRIEF] [SINGLEDF])]}       }
           {                     {AVONLY}                               }
           {[TRANSFORM]                                                 }

[/PCOMPS=[COR**] [NCOMP(n)] [MINEIGEN(eigencut)] ]
         [COV] [ROTATE(rottype)]

[/PLOT=[ZCORR]]

[/DISCRIM[=[RAW**] [STAN**] [ESTIM**] [COR**] [ALL]]]
          [ROTATE(rottype)] [ALPHA(alpha)]

[/ANALYSIS [({CONDITIONAL  })]=dependent varlist
             {UNCONDITIONAL}
                               [WITH covariate varlist]

                               [/dependent varlist...]]
```

**Defaults if subcommands are entered without specifications. In repeated measures, SIGNIF(AVERF) is printed by default instead of SIGNIF(UNIV).

Example:

```
MANOVA SCORE1 TO SCORE4 BY METHOD(1,3).
```

Overview

This section discusses the subcommands that are used in *multivariate* analysis of variance and covariance designs with several interrelated dependent variables. It does not contain information on all subcommands you will need to specify the design. For subcommands not covered here, refer to MANOVA: Univariate.

Syntax

- Multivariate syntax for MANOVA is identical to univariate syntax, except that two or more dependent variables are named before the keyword BY in the MANOVA variables specification.

- Several subcommands are available in multivariate analysis that do not apply to univariate analysis. Additional keywords for some subcommands are also available.

- If you enter one of the multivariate specifications in a univariate analysis, MANOVA will ignore it.

MANOVA Variables List

The basic syntax for the MANOVA variables specification in multivariate designs is

```
MANOVA dependent varlist BY factors(range) WITH covariates
```

- Multivariate MANOVA calculates statistical tests that are valid for analyses of dependent variables that are correlated with one another.

- If the dependent variables are uncorrelated, *univariate* significance tests (also available in MANOVA) have greater statistical power.

ANALYSIS Subcommand

The ANALYSIS subcommand is discussed in MANOVA: Univariate as a means of obtaining factor-by-covariate interaction terms. In multivariate analyses it is considerably more useful.

- The ANALYSIS subcommand specifies a subset of the continuous variables (dependent variables and covariates) listed on the MANOVA variables list and completely *redefines* which variables are dependent and which are covariates.
- All variables named on an ANALYSIS subcommand must have been named on the MANOVA variables list. It does not matter whether they were named as dependent variables or as covariates.
- Factors cannot be named on an ANALYSIS subcommand.
- After the keyword ANALYSIS, specify the names of one or more dependent variables and, optionally, the keyword WITH followed by one or more covariates.
- An ANALYSIS specification remains in effect for all designs until you enter another ANALYSIS subcommand.
- Continuous variables named on the MANOVA variables list but *omitted* from the ANALYSIS subcommand currently in effect can be specified on the DESIGN subcommand.
- You can use an ANALYSIS subcommand to request analyses of several groups of variables, provided that the groups do not overlap. Separate the groups of variables with slashes and enclose the entire ANALYSIS specification in parentheses.

When you specify multiple analyses on a single subcommand, you can specify keyword CONDITIONAL in parentheses after the subcommand but before the equals sign.

- If you specify CONDITIONAL on an ANALYSIS subcommand, the variables in an analysis group will be used as covariates in subsequent analysis groups.
- The default is to process each list of variables separately, without regard to other lists. The keyword UNCONDITIONAL can be used to request this treatment explicitly.
- CONDITIONAL analysis is not carried over from one ANALYSIS subcommand to another.

Example
```
MANOVA A B C BY FAC(1,4) WITH D, E
/ANALYSIS = (A, B / C / D WITH E)
/DESIGN.
```

- The first analysis uses A and B as dependent variables and no covariates.
- The second analysis uses C as a dependent variable and no covariates.
- The third analysis uses D as the dependent variable and E as a covariate.

Example
You can share one or more covariates among all the ANALYSIS groups by "factoring them out" from the parentheses, as in the following:
```
MANOVA A, B, C, D, E BY FAC(1,4) WITH F G
/ANALYSIS = (A, B / C / D WITH E) WITH F G
/DESIGN.
```

- The first analysis uses A and B with F and G as covariates.
- The second analysis uses C with F and G as covariates.
- The third analysis uses D with E, F, and G as covariates.
- Factoring out F and G is the only way to use them as covariates in all three analyses, since no variable can be named more than once on an ANALYSIS subcommand.

Example
```
MANOVA A B C BY FAC(1,3)
/ANALYSIS(CONDITIONAL) = (A WITH B / C)
/DESIGN.
```

- In the first analysis, A is the dependent variable, B is a covariate, and C is not used.
- In the second analysis, C is the dependent variable, and both A and B are covariates.

TRANSFORM Subcommand

The TRANSFORM subcommand performs linear transformations of some or all of the continuous variables (dependent variables and covariates).

- Transformations apply to all subsequent designs unless replaced by another TRANSFORM subcommand.
- TRANSFORM subcommands are not cumulative. Only the transformation specified most recently is in effect at any time. You can restore the original variables in later designs by requesting TRANSFORM=SPECIAL with an identity matrix.
- You should *not* use TRANSFORM when you use the WSFACTORS subcommand to request repeated measures analysis; a transformation is automatically performed in repeated measures analysis (see MANOVA: Repeated Measures).
- Transformations are in effect only for the duration of the MANOVA procedure. After the procedure is complete, the original variables remain on the active file.
- The transformation matrix is not printed by default. Use PRINT= TRANSFORM to see the matrix generated by the TRANSFORM subcommand.
- If you do not use the RENAME subcommand with TRANSFORM, the continuous variables listed in the MANOVA variables specification are renamed temporarily (for the duration of the procedure) as T1, T2, etc. Explicit use of RENAME is recommended.
- Subsequent references to transformed variables must use the new names. The only exception is when you supply a VARIABLES specification on the OMEANS subcommand after using TRANSFORM. In this case, specify the original names. OMEANS prints observed means of original variables.

Specifications on the TRANSFORM subcommand include an optional list of variables to be transformed; optional keywords to describe how to generate a transformation matrix from the specified contrasts; and a required keyword specifying the transformation contrasts.

Variable Lists

- By default MANOVA applies the transformation you request to all continuous variables (dependent variables and covariates) *together*.
- You can enter a variable list in parentheses following the TRANSFORM keyword; if you do, only the listed variables are transformed.
- You can enter multiple variable lists, separated by slashes, within a single set of parentheses. Each list must have the same number of variables, and the lists must not overlap. The transformation is applied separately to the variables in each list.
- In designs with covariates it is usually inappropriate to transform them together with the dependent variables. Transform only the dependent variables, or, in some designs, apply the same transformation to the dependent variables and the covariates.

Optional Keywords

- You can enter the optional keywords CONTRAST, BASIS, and ORTHONORM following the subcommand TRANSFORM, the variable list(s), if any, and an equals sign. CONTRAST and BASIS are alternatives; ORTHONORM can be requested along with either CONTRAST or BASIS.
- By default, the transformation matrix is generated directly from the contrast matrix of the given type (see CONTRAST Subcommand under MANOVA: Univariate). You can request this method explictly with keyword CONTRAST.
- If you enter keyword BASIS, the transformation matrix is generated from the one-way basis matrix corresponding to the specified contrast. This only makes a difference if the transformation contrasts are not orthogonal.
- Keyword ORTHONORM requests that the transformation matrix be orthonormalized by rows before use. MANOVA eliminates redundant rows. Orthonormalization is not done by default.
- ORTHONORM is independent of the CONTRAST/BASIS choice; you can enter it before or after either of those keywords.

Transformation Methods   You must enter one of the keywords listed below on the TRANSFORM subcommand to indicate the type of transformation contrasts you want. There is no default.

- The transformation keyword (and its specifications, if any) must follow all other specifications on the TRANSFORM subcommand.

Note that these are identical to the keywords available for the CONTRAST subcommand (see MANOVA: Univariate). However, in univariate designs, they are applied to the different *levels* of a factor. Here they are applied to the *continuous variables* in the analysis. This reflects the fact that the different dependent variables in a multivariate MANOVA setup can often be thought of as corresponding to different levels of some factor.

DEVIATION   *Deviations from the mean of the variables being transformed.* The first transformed variable is the mean of all variables in the transformation. Other transformed variables represent deviations of individual variables from the mean. One of the original variables (by default the last) is omitted as redundant. To omit a variable other than the last, specify the number of the variable to be omitted in parentheses after the DEVIATION keyword. For example, TRANSFORM (A B C) = DEVIATION(1) omits A and creates variables representing the mean, the deviation of B from the mean, and the deviation of C from the mean. A deviation transformation is not orthogonal.

DIFFERENCE   *Difference or reverse Helmert transformation.* The first transformed variable is the mean of the original variables. Each of the original variables except the first is then transformed by subtracting the mean of those (original) variables which precede it. A difference transformation is orthogonal.

HELMERT   *Helmert transformation.* The first transformed variable is the mean of the original variables. Each of the original variables except the last is then transformed by subtracting the mean of those (original) variables that follow it. A Helmert transformation is orthogonal.

SIMPLE   *Each original variable, except the last, is compared to the last of the original variables.* To use a variable other than the last as the omitted reference variable, specify its number in parentheses following the keyword SIMPLE. For example, TRANSFORM(A B C) = SIMPLE(2) specifies the second variable, B, as the reference variable. The three transformed variables represent the mean of A, B, and C; the difference between A and B; and the difference between C and B. A simple transformation is not orthogonal.

POLYNOMIAL   *Orthogonal polynomial transformation.* The first transformed variable represents the mean of the original variables. Other transformed variables represent the linear, quadratic, and higher-degree components. By default, values of the original variables are assumed to represent equally spaced points. You can specify unequal spacing by entering a *metric* consisting of one integer for each variable in parentheses after the keyword POLYNOMIAL. For example, TRANSFORM(RESP1 RESP2 RESP3) = POLYNOMIAL(1,2,4) might indicate that three response variables correspond to levels of some stimulus that are in the proportion 1:2:4. The default metric is always $(1,2,...,k)$, where k variables are involved. Only the relative differences between the terms of the metric matter: (1,2,4) is the same metric as (2,3,5) or (20,30,50), because in each instance the difference between the second and third numbers is twice the difference between the first and second.

REPEATED   *Comparison of adjacent variables.* The first transformed variable is the mean of the original variables. Each additional transformed variable is the difference between one of the original variables and the original variable that followed it. Such transformed variables are often called *difference scores*. A repeated transformation is not orthogonal.

SPECIAL *A user-defined transformation*. After keyword SPECIAL, enter a square matrix in parentheses with as many rows and columns as there are variables to transform. MANOVA multiplies this matrix by the vector of original variables to obtain the transformed variables (see examples below).

Example
```
MANOVA X1 TO X3 BY A(1,4)
/TRANSFORM(X1 X2 X3) = SPECIAL( 1  1 -1,
                                2  0  1,
                                1  0 -1 )
/DESIGN.
```

- The given matrix will be multiplied by the three continuous variables (considered as a column vector) to yield the transformed variables. The first transformed variable will therefore equal $X1 + X2 - X3$, the second will equal $2X1 + X3$, and the third will equal $X1 - X3$.

- The variable list is optional in this example, since all three interval-level variables are transformed.

- You do not need to enter the matrix one row at a time, as shown here. TRANSFORM = SPECIAL(1 1 −1 2 0 1 1 0 −1) is fully equivalent.

- You can specify a repetition factor, followed by an asterisk, to indicate multiple consecutive elements of a SPECIAL transformation matrix. TRANSFORM = SPECIAL (2*1 −1 2 0 2*1 0 −1) is equivalent to the above matrix.

Example
```
MANOVA X1 TO X3, Y1 TO Y3 BY A(1,4)
/TRANSFORM(X1 X2 X3/Y1 Y2 Y3) = SPECIAL( 1  1 -1
                                         2  0  1
                                         1  0 -1 )
/DESIGN.
```

- Here the same transformation as in the previous example is applied to X1, X2, X3 and also to Y1, Y2, Y3.

RENAME Subcommand

Use the RENAME subcommand to assign new names to transformed variables. Renaming variables after a transformation is strongly recommended. If you transform but do not rename the variables, the names T1, T2, ..., Tn are used as names for the transformed variables.

- Follow the RENAME subcommand with a list of new variable names.

- You must enter a new name for each dependent variable and covariate on the MANOVA variables specification.

- Enter the new names in the order the original variables appeared in the MANOVA variables specification.

- To retain the original name for one or more of the interval variables, you can either enter an asterisk or reenter the old name as the new name.

- References to dependent variables and covariates on subcommands following RENAME *must* use the new names. The original names will not be recognized within the MANOVA procedure. The only exception is the OMEANS subcommand, which prints observed means of the original (untransformed) variables. Use the original names on OMEANS.

- The new names exist only during the MANOVA procedure that created them. They do not remain in the active file after the procedure is complete.

Example
```
MANOVA A, B, C, V4, V5 BY TREATMNT(1,3)
/TRANSFORM(A, B, C) = REPEATED
/RENAME = MEANABC, AMINUSB, BMINUSC, *, *
/DESIGN.
```

- The REPEATED transformation produces three transformed variables, which are then assigned mnemonic names MEANABC, AMINUSB, and BMINUSC.

- V4 and V5 retain their original names.

Example
```
MANOVA WT1, WT2, WT3, WT4 BY TREATMNT(1,3) WITH COV
/TRANSFORM (WT1 TO WT4) = POLYNOMIAL
/RENAME = MEAN, LINEAR, QUAD, CUBIC, *
/ANALYSIS = MEAN, LINEAR, QUAD WITH COV
/DESIGN.
```

- After the polynomial transformation of the four WT variables, RENAME assigns appropriate names to the various trends.

- Even though only four variables were transformed, the RENAME subcommand applics to all five continuous variables. An asterisk is required to retain the original name for COV.

- The ANALYSIS subcommand following RENAME refers to the interval variables by their new names. A reference to WT1, for example, would produce a syntax error.

PRINT and NOPRINT Subcommands

All of the PRINT specifications described under MANOVA: Univariate are available in multivariate analyses. The following additional output can also be requested. To suppress any optional output, specify the appropriate keyword on NOPRINT.

ERROR	*Error matrices.* Three types of matrices are available (see below).
SIGNIF	*Significance tests.*
TRANSFORM	*Transformation matrix.* Available if you have transformed the dependent variables with the TRANSFORM subcommand.
HOMOGENEITY	*A test for multivariate homogeneity of variance, BOXM, is available.*

ERROR Keyword

In multivariate analysis, error terms consist of entire matrices, not single values. You can print any of the following error matrices on a PRINT subcommand by requesting them in parentheses following the keyword ERROR. If you enter PRINT=ERROR without further specifications, COV and COR are printed.

SSCP	*Error sums-of-squares and cross-products matrix.*
COV	*Error variance-covariance matrix.*
COR	*Error correlation matrix with standard deviations on the diagonal.* This also prints the determinant of the matrix and Bartlett's test of sphericity, a test of whether the error correlation matrix is significantly different from an identity matrix.

SIGNIF Keyword

You can request any of the optional output listed below by entering the appropriate specification in parentheses after the SIGNIF keyword on the PRINT subcommand. Further specifications for SIGNIF are described under MANOVA: Repeated Measures.

- By default MANOVA prints the display corresponding to MULTIV and UNIV for a multivariate analysis not involving repeated measures.

- If you enter any specification for SIGNIF on the PRINT subcommand, the default output is suppressed and MANOVA displays only what you have explicitly requested.

MULTIV	*Multivariate F tests for group differences.* This is displayed by default.
EIGEN	*Eigenvalues of the $S_h S_e^{-1}$ matrix.* This matrix is the product of the hypothesis sums-of-squares and cross-products (SSCP) matrix and the inverse of the error SSCP matrix.
DIMENR	*A dimension-reduction analysis.*
UNIV	*Univariate F tests.* This is displayed by default, except in repeated measures analysis. If the dependent variables are uncorrelated, univariate tests have greater statistical power.
HYPOTH	*The hypothesis SSCP matrix.*
STEPDOWN	*Roy-Bargmann stepdown F tests.*

BRIEF   *Abbreviated multivariate output.* This is similar to a univariate analysis of variance table but with Wilks' multivariate *F* approximation (lambda) replacing the univariate *F*. BRIEF overrides any of the SIGNIF specifications listed above.

The SINGLEDF keyword described under MANOVA: Univariate does not apply to analysis of variance tables in multivariate designs, except for the averaged *F*-tests described in MANOVA: Repeated Measures.

TRANSFORM Keyword   PRINT = TRANSFORM prints the transposed transformation matrix in use for each subsequent design. This matrix is helpful in interpreting a multivariate analysis in which you have transformed the interval-level variables with either TRANSFORM or WSFACTORS.

- The matrix printed by this option is the *transpose* of the transformation matrix.
- Original variables correspond to the rows of the matrix, and transformed variables to the columns.
- A transformed variable is a linear combination of the original variables, using the coefficients printed in the column corresponding to that transformed variable.

HOMOGENEITY Keyword   In addition to the BARTLETT and COCHRAN specifications described under MANOVA: Univariate, the following test for homogeneity is available for multivariate analyses.

BOXM *Box's M statistic.*

PLOT Subcommand

In addition to the plots described under MANOVA: Univariate, the following is available for multivariate analyses:

ZCORR *A half-normal plot of the within-cells correlations among the dependent variables.* MANOVA first transforms the correlations using Fisher's *Z* transformation. If errors for the dependent variables are uncorrelated, the plotted points should lie close to a straight line.

PCOMPS Subcommand

The PCOMPS subcommand requests a principal components analysis of each error sum-of-squares and cross-product matrix in a multivariate analysis. You can print the principal components of the error correlation matrix, the error variance-covariance matrix, or both. These principal components are corrected for differences due to the factors and covariates in the MANOVA analysis. They tend to be more useful than principal components extracted from the raw correlation or covariance matrix when there are significant group differences between the levels of the factors or when a significant amount of error variance is accounted for by the covariates. You can specify any of the keywords listed below on PCOMPS.

- You must specify either COR or COV (or both). Otherwise, MANOVA will not produce any principal components.

COR   *Principal components analysis of the error correlation matrix.*

COV   *Principal components analysis of the error variance-covariance matrix.*

ROTATE   *Rotate the principal components solution.* By default no rotation is performed. Specify a rotation type (either VARIMAX, EQUAMAX, QUARTIMAX, or NOROTATE) in parentheses after keyword ROTATE. Specify PCOMPS = ROTATE (NOROTATE) to cancel a rotation specified for a previous design.

NCOMP   *The number of principal components to rotate.* Specify a number in parentheses. The default is the number of dependent variables.

MINEIGEN *The minimum eigenvalue for principal component extraction.* Specify a cutoff value in parentheses. Components with eigenvalues below the cutoff will not be retained in the solution. The default is 0: all components (or the number specified on NCOMP) are extracted.

- Both NCOMP and MINEIGEN limit the number of components that are rotated.

- If the number specified on NCOMP is less than two, two components are rotated (provided that at least two components have eigenvalues greater than any value specified on MINEIGEN).

- Principal components analysis is computationally expensive if the number of dependent variables is large.

DISCRIM Subcommand

The DISCRIM subcommand produces a canonical discriminant analysis for each effect in a design. (For covariates, DISCRIM produces a canonical correlation analysis.) These analyses aid in the interpretation of multivariate effects. You can request the following statistics by entering the appropriate keywords after the subcommand DISCRIM:

RAW   *Raw discriminant function coefficients.*

STAN   *Standardized discriminant function coefficients.*

ESTIM   *Effect estimates in discriminant function space.*

COR   *Correlations between the dependent variables and the canonical variables defined by the discriminant functions.*

ROTATE   *Rotation of the matrix of correlations between dependent and canonical variables.* Specify VARIMAX, EQUAMAX, or QUARTIMAX in parentheses after this keyword.

ALPHA   *Set the significance level required before a canonical variable is extracted.* The default is 0.25. To change the default, specify a decimal number between 0 and 1 in parentheses after ALPHA.

- The correlations between dependent variables and canonical discriminant functions are not rotated unless at least two discriminant functions are significant at the level defined by ALPHA.

- If you set ALPHA to 1.0, all discriminant functions are reported (and rotated, if you so request).

- If you set ALPHA to 0, no discriminant functions are reported.

MANOVA: Repeated Measures

```
MANOVA dependent varlist [BY factor list (min,max)
       [factor list...] [WITH covariate list]]

    /WSFACTORS=name (levels) [name...]

  [/MEASURE=newname newname...]

  [/WSDESIGN=effect effect...]

  [/{PRIN  }=[SIGNIF({AVERF }) (MULTIV)] ]
    {NOPRINT}         {AVONLY}
```

Example:

```
MANOVA Y1 TO Y4 BY GROUP(1,2)
/WSFACTORS=YEAR(4).
```

Overview

This section discusses the subcommands that are used in *repeated measures* designs on MANOVA, in which the dependent variables represent measurements of the same variable (or variables) at different times. This section does not contain information on all subcommands you will need to specify the design. For some subcommands not covered here, such as DESIGN and PRINT, refer to MANOVA: Univariate. For information on optional output and the multivariate significance tests available, refer to MANOVA: Multivariate.

- In a simple repeated-measures analysis, all dependent variables represent different measurements of the same variable for different values (or levels) of a *within-subjects factor*. Between-subjects factors and covariates can also be included in the model, just as in analyses not involving repeated measures.

- A within-subjects factor is simply a factor that distinguishes measurements made on the same subject or case, rather than distinguishing different subjects or cases.

- MANOVA permits more complex analyses, in which the dependent variables represent levels of two or more within-subjects factors.

- MANOVA also permits analyses in which the dependent variables represent measurements of several variables for the different levels of the within-subjects factors. These are known as *doubly multivariate* designs.

- A repeated-measures analysis includes a within-subjects design describing the model to be tested with the within-subjects factors, as well as the usual between-subjects design describing the effects to be tested with between-subjects factors. The default for both types of design is a full factorial model.

- MANOVA always performs an orthonormal transformation of the dependent variables in a repeated-measures analysis. By default, MANOVA renames them as T1, T2, and so forth.

Defaults

Whenever you enter the WSFACTORS command, MANOVA performs special repeated-measures processing. Default output includes SIGNIF(AVERF) but not SIGNIF(UNIV). In addition, for any within-subjects effect involving more than one transformed variable, the Mauchly test of sphericity is displayed to test the assumption that the covariance matrix of the transformed variables is constant on the diagonal and zero off the diagonal. The Greenhouse-Geiser epsilon and the Huynh-Feldt epsilon are also displayed for use in correcting the significance tests in the event that the assumption of sphericity is violated. These tests are discussed in Part B: Statistics Guide.

Syntax

- The WSFACTORS (within-subject factors), WSDESIGN (within-subjects design), and MEASURE subcommands are used only in repeated-measures analysis.

- WSFACTORS is required for any repeated-measures analysis. A default WSDESIGN consisting of all main effects and interactions among within-subjects factors is used if you do not enter a WSDESIGN subcommand. The MEASURE subcommand is used for *doubly multivariate* designs, in which the dependent variables represent repeated measurements of more than one variable.

- WSFACTORS must be the first subcommand you enter, following the list of dependent variables, factors, and covariates on the MANOVA variables specification.

- The WSFACTORS subcommand automatically triggers special repeated-measures analysis and implies a full factorial within-subjects design (unless you specify the WSDESIGN subcommand).

- Do not use the TRANSFORM subcommand with the WSFACTORS subcommand, since WSFACTORS automatically causes an orthonormal transformation of the dependent variables.

- The WSFACTORS subcommand determines how the dependent variables on the MANOVA variables list will be interpreted.

- The number of cells in the within-subjects design is the product of the number of levels for each within-subjects factor.

- The number of dependent variables on the MANOVA variables list must be a multiple of the number of cells in the within-subjects design. If there are six cells in the within-subjects design, each group of six dependent variables represents a single variable that has been measured in each of the six cells.

- Normally, the number of dependent variables should equal the number of cells in the within-subjects design multiplied by the number of variables named on the MEASURE subcommand (if one is used). If you have more groups of dependent variables than are accounted for by the MEASURE subcommand, MANOVA will choose variable names to label the output, which may therefore be difficult to interpret.

- If you use covariates in a repeated-measures analysis, there must be one covariate for each cell in the within-subjects design. Normally the covariates should be identical copies of one another (you can create these with the COMPUTE command).

Example
```
MANOVA Y1 TO Y4 BY GROUP(1,2)
 /WSFACTORS=YEAR(4)
 /CONTRAST(YEAR)=POLYNOMIAL
 /RENAME=CONST, LINEAR, QUAD, CUBIC
 /PRINT=TRANSFORM PARAM(ESTIM)
 /WSDESIGN=YEAR
 /DESIGN=GROUP.
```

- The WSFACTORS subcommand immediately follows the MANOVA variables list and specifies a repeated-measures analysis in which the four dependent variables represent a single variable measured at four levels of the within-subjects factor. The within-subjects factor is called YEAR for the duration of the MANOVA procedure.

- The CONTRAST subcommand requests polynomial contrasts for the levels of YEAR. Since the four variables Y1, Y2, Y3, Y4 in the active file represent the four levels of YEAR, the effect is to perform an orthonormal polynomial transformation of these variables.

- The RENAME subcommand assigns names to the dependent variables to reflect the transformation.

- The PRINT subcommand requests that the transformation matrix and the parameter estimates be displayed.

- The WSDESIGN subcommand specifies a within-subjects design that includes only the effect of the YEAR within-subjects factor. Since YEAR is the only within-subjects factor specified, this is the default design and WSDESIGN could have been omitted.

- The DESIGN subcommand specifies a between-subjects design that includes only the effect of the GROUP between-subjects factor. This subcommand could have been omitted.

Example
```
COMPUTE SES1 = SES.
COMPUTE SES2 = SES.
COMPUTE SES3 = SES.
COMPUTE SES4 = SES.
MANOVA SCORE1 TO SCORE4 BY METHOD(1,2) WITH SES1 TO SES4
/WSFACTORS=SEMESTER(4)
/CONTRAST(SEMESTER)=DIFFERENCE
/RENAME=MEAN,DIF2 TO DIF4,*,*,*,*.
```

- The four dependent variables represent a score measured four times (corresponding to the four levels of SEMESTER).

- The four COMPUTE commands create four copies of the constant covariate SES so that there will be one covariate for each of the within-subjects cells.

- The RENAME subcommand supplies names for the difference transformation of the within-subjects factor SEMESTER. Since the MANOVA variables specification includes eight continuous variables, eight names are specified. The four asterisks indicate that the existing names are kept for the covariates.

- Covariates are transformed in the same way as the dependent variables. However, since these covariates are identical, the orthonormal transformation does not affect them.

WSFACTORS Subcommand

The WSFACTORS subcommand names the within-subjects factors and specifies the number of levels for each.

- For repeated-measures designs, WSFACTORS must be the first subcommand after the MANOVA variables list.

- Only one WSFACTORS subcommand is permitted per execution of MANOVA.

- Names for the within-subjects factors are specified on the WSFACTORS subcommand. Factor names must not duplicate any of the dependent variables, factors, or covariates named on the MANOVA variables list.

- If there is more than one within-subjects factor, they must be named in the order corresponding to the order of the dependent variables on the MANOVA variables list. MANOVA varies the levels of the last-named WSFACTOR most rapidly when assigning dependent variables to within-subjects cells (see example below).

- Levels of the factors must be represented in the data by the dependent variables named on the MANOVA variables list.

- Enter a number in parentheses after each factor to indicate how many levels the factor has. If two or more adjacent factors have the same number of levels, you can enter the number of levels in parentheses after all of them.

- You enter only the number of levels for WSFACTORs, not a range of values.

Example
```
MANOVA X1Y1 X1Y2 X2Y1 X2Y2 X3Y1 X3Y2 BY TREATMNT(1,5) GROUP(1,2)
/WSFACTORS=X(3) Y(2)
/DESIGN.
```

- The MANOVA variables list names six dependent variables and two between-subjects factors, TREATMNT and GROUP.

- The WSFACTORS subcommand identifies two within-subjects factors whose levels distinguish the six dependent variables. X has three levels and Y has two. Thus, there are 3 * 2 = 6 cells in the within-subjects design, corresponding to the six dependent variables.

- Variable X1Y1 corresponds to levels 1,1 of the two WSFACTORS; variable X1Y2 corresponds to levels 1,2; X2Y1 to levels 2,1; and so on up to X3Y2, which corresponds to levels 3,2. The first within-subjects factor named, X, varies most slowly, and the last within-subjects factor named, Y, varies most rapidly in the list of dependent variables.

- Since there is no WSDESIGN subcommand, the within-subjects design will include all main effects and interactions: X, Y, and X by Y.

- Likewise, the between-subjects design includes all main effects and interactions: TREATMNT, GROUP, TREATMNT by GROUP.

• In addition, repeated-measures analysis *always* includes interactions between the within subjects factors and the between-subjects factors. There are three such interactions for each of the three within-subjects effects.

WSDESIGN Subcommand

The WSDESIGN subcommand specifies the design for within-subjects factors. Its specifications are like those of the DESIGN subcommand, but it uses the within-subjects factors rather than the between-subjects factors.

• The default WSDESIGN is a full factorial design, which includes all main effects and all interactions for within-subjects factors. The default is in effect whenever a design is processed without a preceding WSDESIGN or when the preceding WSDESIGN subcommand has no specifications.

• A WSDESIGN specification can include main effects for WS factors; factor-BY-factor interactions among WS factors; nested terms (term WITHIN term) involving WS factors and their interactions; terms using the MWITHIN keyword; and combinations of the above pooled together with the plus sign.

• A WSDESIGN specification can *not* include between-subjects factors or terms based on them; interval-level variables; the MUPLUS or CONSTANT keywords; or error-term definitions or references.

• The WSDESIGN specification applies to all subsequent between-subjects designs until another WSDESIGN subcommand is encountered.

Example

```
MANOVA JANLO,JANHI,FEBLO,FEBHI,MARLO,MARHI BY SEX(1,2)
/WSFACTORS MONTH(3) STIMULUS(2)
/WSDESIGN MONTH, STIMULUS
/DESIGN SEX
/WSDESIGN.
```

• There are six dependent variables, corresponding to three months and two different levels of stimulus.

• The dependent variables are named on the MANOVA variables list in such an order that the level of stimulus varies more rapidly than the month. Thus, STIMULUS is named last on the WSFACTORS subcommand.

• The first WSDESIGN subcommand specifies only the main effects for within-subjects factors. There is no MONTH by STIMULUS interaction term.

• The second WSDESIGN subcommand has no specifications and therefore invokes the default within-subjects design, which includes the main effects and their interaction.

• Since the last subcommand is not DESIGN, MANOVA generates a full factorial design at the end. In this example there is only one between-subjects factor, SEX, so the last design is identical to the one specified by DESIGN =SEX. The last design, however, will include the MONTH BY STIMULUS within-subjects interaction. It will *automatically* include the interaction between SEX and MONTH BY STIMULUS; you do not need to specify, and indeed cannot specify, such interactions between elements of the within-subjects and the between-subjects designs.

PRINT Subcommand

Two additional specifications on the PRINT subcommand are useful in repeated-measures analysis: SIGNIF (AVERF) and SIGNIF (AVONLY).

• SIGNIF (AVERF) and SIGNIF (AVONLY) are mutually exclusive.

• When you request repeated-measures analysis with the WSFACTORS subcommand, the default display includes SIGNIF(AVERF) but does not include the usual SIGNIF(UNIV).

• The averaged *F* tests are appropriate in repeated measures because the dependent variables that are averaged actually represent the same variable at different times. When the analysis is not *doubly multivariate,* as discussed below, you can specify PRINT = SIGNIF (AVERF UNIV) to obtain significance tests for each degree of freedom, just as in univariate MANOVA.

SIGNIF(AVERF)   *An averaged* F *test* for use with repeated measures. This is the default display in repeated measures analysis. The averaged *F* test in the multivariate setup for repeated measures is equivalent to the univariate (or split-plot or mixed-model) approach to repeated measures.

SIGNIF(AVONLY) *Only the averaged F test* for repeated measures. AVONLY produces the same output as AVERF and suppresses all other PRINT=SIGNIF output.

MEASURE Subcommand

In a *doubly multivariate* analysis, the dependent variables represent multiple variables measured under the different levels of the within-subjects factors. Use the MEASURE subcommand to assign names to the variables that you have measured for the different levels of within-subjects factors.

• Specifications on MEASURE consist of a list of one or more variable names to be used in labeling the output of PRINT=SIGNIF(HYPOTH AVERF) and PRINT=SIGNIF(UNIV).

• The number of dependent variables on the DESIGN subcommand should equal the product of the number of cells in the within-subjects design and the number of names on the MEASURE subcommand.

• If you do not enter a MEASURE subcommand and there are more dependent variables than cells in the within-subjects design, MANOVA assigns names (normally MEAS.1, MEAS.2, etc.) to the different measures.

• All of the dependent variables corresponding to each measure should be listed together and ordered so that the within-subjects factor named last on the WSFACTORS subcommand varies most rapidly.

Example
```
MANOVA TEMP1 TO TEMP6, WEIGHT1 TO WEIGHT6 BY GROUP(1,2)
/WSFACTORS=DAY(3) AMPM(2)
/MEASURE=TEMP WEIGHT
/WSDESIGN=DAY, AMPM, DAY BY AMPM
/PRINT=SIGNIF(HYPOTH AVERF)
/DESIGN.
```

• There are twelve dependent variables: six temperatures and six weights, corresponding to morning and afternoon measurements on three days.

• The WSFACTORS subcommand identifies the two factors (DAY and AMPM) that distinguish the temperature and weight measurements for each subject. These factors define six within-subjects cells.

• The MEASURE subcommand indicates that the first group of six dependent variables correspond to TEMP and the second group of six dependent variables correspond to WEIGHT.

• These labels, TEMP and WEIGHT, are used on the output requested by PRINT = SIGNIF (HYPOTH AVERF).

• The WSDESIGN subcommand requests a full factorial within-subjects model. Since this is the default, WSDESIGN could have been omitted.

CONTRAST Subcommand for WSFACTORS

The levels of a within-subjects factor are represented by different dependent variables. Therefore, contrasts between levels of such a factor compare these dependent variables. Specifying the type of contrast amounts to specifying a transformation to be performed on the dependent variables.

• An orthonormal transformation is automatically performed on the dependent variables in a repeated-measures analysis.

• To specify the type of orthonormal transformation, use the CONTRAST subcommand for the within-subjects factors.

• Regardless of the contrast type you specify, the transformation matrix is orthonormalized before use.

• If you do not specify a contrast type for within-subjects factors, the default contrast type (deviation) is orthonormalized and used to form a transformation matrix. Parameter estimates based on this transformation are not particularly suited to repeated-measures analysis. The contrast types that are intrinsically orthogonal are recommended for within-subjects factors. These are difference, Helmert, and polynomial.

- When you implicitly request a transformation of the dependent variables with CONTRAST for within-subjects factors, the same transformation is applied to any covariates in the analysis. There must be as many covariates as dependent variables. Normally the covariates are identical copies of one another, in which case the orthonormal transformation does not have any effect.

- You can display the transpose of the transformation matrix generated by your within-subjects contrast by using the TRANSFORM keyword on the PRINT subcommand.

Example
```
MANOVA SCORE1 SCORE2 SCORE3 BY GROUP(1,4)
/WSFACTORS=ROUND(3)
/CONTRAST(ROUND)=DIFFERENCE
/CONTRAST(GROUP)=DEVIATION
/PRINT=TRANSFORM PARAM(ESTIM).
```

- This analysis has one between-subjects factor, GROUP, with levels 1, 2, 3, and 4, and one within-subjects factor, ROUND, with three levels that are represented by the three dependent variables.

- The first CONTRAST subcommand specifies difference contrasts for ROUND, the within-subjects factor. Since this subcommand applies to the within-subjects analysis, it must precede the CONTRAST subcommand for GROUP.

- There is no WSDESIGN subcommand, so a default full factorial within-subjects design is assumed. This could also have been specified as WSDESIGN =ROUND, or simply WSDESIGN.

- The second CONTRAST subcommand specifies deviation contrasts for GROUP, the between-subjects factor. This subcommand could have been omitted since deviation contrasts are the default.

- The PRINT subcommand requests the display of the transformation matrix generated by the within-subjects contrast and the parameter estimates for the model.

- There is no DESIGN subcommand, so a default full factorial between-subjects design is assumed. This could also have been specified as DESIGN = GROUP, or simply DESIGN.

Example
```
COMPUTE COV2=COV.
COMPUTE COV3=COV.
COMPUTE COV4=COV.
MANOVA DEP1 DEP2 DEP3 DEP4 BY FAC(1,2) WITH COV COV2 COV3 COV4
/WSFACTOR=MONTH(4)
/CONTRAST(MONTH)=POLYNOMIAL
/RENAME=CONST,LINEAR,QUAD, CUBIC,*,*,*,*
/PRINT=TRANSFORM PARAM(ESTIM)
/DESIGN.
```

- Since there are four dependent variables, four copies of the covariate are needed. Three COMPUTE commands create the extra copies.

- The MANOVA variables list names four dependent variables representing the levels of the within-subjects factor MONTH; a single between-subjects factor with two categories; and the four copies of the covariate.

- The CONTRAST subcommand specifies an orthonormalized polynomial transformation of the dependent variables. This transformation will also be applied, separately, to the covariates.

- The PRINT subcommand requests the display of the transformation matrix and the parameter estimates.

RENAME Subcommand

Since any repeated-measures analysis involves a transformation of the dependent variables, it is *always* a good idea to rename the dependent variables. Choose appropriate names depending on the type of contrast specified for within-subjects factors. This is easier to do if you are using one of the orthogonal contrasts; the most reliable way to assign new names is to inspect the transformation matrix.

C

Command Reference

Example
```
MANOVA LOW1 LOW2 LOW3 HI1 HI2 HI3
/WSFACTORS=LEVEL(2) TRIAL(3)
/CONTRAST(TRIAL)=DIFFERENCE
/RENAME=CONST LEVELDIF TRIAL2 TRIAL3 HITRIAL2 HITRIAL3
/PRINT=TRANSFORM
/DESIGN.
```

- This analysis has two within-subjects factors and no between-subjects factors.

- Difference contrasts are requested for TRIAL, which has three levels.

- Since all orthonormal contrasts are equivalent for a factor with two levels, there is no point in specifying a contrast type for LEVEL.

- New names are assigned to the transformed variables based on the transformation matrix, which was displayed in a previous trial. These names correspond to the meaning of the transformed variables: the mean or constant, the average difference between levels, the average effect of Trial 2 compared to 1, the average effect of Trial 3 compared to 1 and 2; and the two interactions between LEVEL and TRIAL.

Transformation matrix

	CONST	LEVELDIF	TRIAL2	TRIAL3	HITRIAL2	HITRIAL3
LOW1	0.408	0.408	−0.500	−0.289	−0.500	−0.289
LOW2	0.408	0.408	0.500	−0.289	0.500	−0.289
LOW3	0.408	0.408	0.000	0.577	0.000	0.577
HI1	0.408	−0.408	−0.500	−0.289	0.500	0.289
HI2	0.408	−0.408	0.500	−0.289	−0.500	0.289
HI3	0.408	−0.408	0.000	0.577	0.000	−0.577

QUICK CLUSTER

```
QUICK CLUSTER {varlist} [/INITIAL = [{SELECT**    }]]
              {ALL     }             {FIRST       }
                                     {(value list)}

[/CRITERIA = [CLUSTERS({   2   })] [NOUPDATE]]
                       {number }

[/PRINT = [CLUSTER] [ID(varname)] [INITIAL**]]
          [DISTANCE] [ANOVA]

[/WRITE]

[/SAVE = [CLUSTER(varname)] [DISTANCE(varname)]]

[/MISSING = {LISTWISE**}
            {PAIRWISE  }
            {INCLUDE   }]
            {DEFAULT** }
```

**Default if subcommand is omitted.

Example:

```
QUICK CLUSTER VARA TO VARD
/CRITERIA=CLUSTERS(4)
/SAVE=CLUSTER(GROUP).
```

Overview   The QUICK CLUSTER procedure groups cases efficiently into clusters, when the desired number of clusters is known. It is not as flexible as CLUSTER, but it uses considerably less processing time and memory, especially when the number of cases is large.

Defaults   By default, QUICK CLUSTER forms two clusters, and chooses well-spaced cases as initial cluster centers. It then assigns each case to the nearest cluster, updating the cluster center every time a case is added, so that the center will be at the mean value of all the cases included in the cluster. After all cases have been used to update the cluster centers, each case is assigned to the nearest of the updated centers. (This will often, but not always, be the one to which it was joined during the updating phase.)

Default output consists of the initial cluster centers, the centers used for the final assignment of cases, the actual centers of the final clusters, and the number of cases in each cluster. By default, cases are deleted from the analysis if they have any missing values on the variables used in clustering.

Tailoring   **Clustering Criteria.** You can specify the number of clusters to be formed. You can suppress the updating phase and simply assign cases to the initial cluster centers to classify cases very rapidly into clusters whose centers have already been determined.

Initial Cluster Centers. You can specify the points to be used as initial cluster centers. Alternatively, you can use the first k cases in the file that have nonmissing data as initial centers (where k is the number of clusters requested) to avoid the search for widely spaced cases.

Saving Cluster Centers. You can write the final cluster centers to the results file, possibly for use as initial cluster centers in a later run.

Adding Results to the Active File. You can add a new variable to your active file to indicate the cluster membership of each case. You can also add a variable indicating the distance of each case from its cluster center.

Display Output. You can display cluster membership and distance from the final cluster center for each case. Cases are identified either by sequential numbers or by the values of any variable in your file. You can ask to see the distances between each final cluster center and the other final centers. You can also request descriptive F tests for each variable used in the clustering and a covariance matrix.

C

Command Reference

Missing Values. You can request pairwise deletion of missing data, in which a case is assigned to the nearest cluster on the basis of variables for which the case has valid data. You can also include user-missing values in the calculation of distances.

Syntax
- The minimum specification is a list of variables.
- The variable list must be specified first. Other subcommands can be specified in any order.
- Subcommands must be separated from each other and from the variable list by slashes.

Operations
- QUICK CLUSTER causes the data to be read.
- The procedure involves three steps. These steps are as follows:

  First, QUICK CLUSTER selects initial cluster centers according to the method specified on the INITIAL subcommand.

  Second, the cluster centers are updated by joining each case to the nearest center. After each case is joined, the cluster center is updated to the (new) mean value of all cases in the cluster plus the initial cluster center.

  Third, the cases are examined again, and each is assigned to the cluster whose final updated center location is closest to it.

- By default, initial cluster centers are formed by choosing one case (with valid data for the clustering variables) for each cluster requested. These cases are chosen to be well separated from one another, so this initial selection requires a pass through the data.
- Two other methods are available for choosing initial cluster centers (see INITIAL Subcommand).
- If CRITERIA=NOUPDATE is specified, the updating of cluster centers is suppressed and cases are simply assigned to the nearest initial cluster center.
- Variables measured on different scales should be standardized prior to their use in QUICK CLUSTER. Otherwise, the scale on which different variables are measured will affect the distances used in forming clusters.

Limitations
- The number of variables allowed on the variable list is the same as the system limit.
- Since QUICK CLUSTER processes cases sequentially rather than storing them in memory, memory requirements depend on the number of variables and the number of clusters, but not on the number of cases.
- Only 1 variable list and 1 each of the optional subcommands can be specified.

Example
```
QUICK CLUSTER VARA TO VARD
/CRITERIA=CLUSTERS(4)
/WRITE.
```
- This example clusters cases based on their values for all variables between and including VARA and VARD on the active file.
- Four clusters, rather than the default two, will be formed.
- Initial cluster centers will be chosen by the default method, by finding four widely spaced cases.
- The four final cluster centers will be written to the results file specified on the SET command (SPSS.PRC by default).

Variables List
The variables list identifies the variables on which cases are to be clustered.

- The variable list is required and must be the first specification on QUICK CLUSTER.
- You can use the keyword ALL to refer to all user-defined variables in the active file.
- You can use the keyword TO to refer to consecutive variables in the active file.

CRITERIA Subcommand Use the CRITERIA subcommand to specify the number of clusters desired or to suppress the updating of initial cluster centers. If updating is suppressed, QUICK CLUSTER simply assigns cases to the initial centers.

- If you do not specify the number of clusters on a CRITERIA subcommand, cases will be grouped into two clusters.
- QUICK CLUSTER uses the squared Euclidean distance measure in assigning cases to the nearest cluster center. In this algorithm, the unsquared Euclidean measure would assign cases in the same way.

The following criteria may be specified:

CLUSTERS(number) *Number of clusters to create.* If you do not specify a number, two clusters are formed.

NOUPDATE *Do not update the initial cluster centers.* Cases are simply assigned to the nearest of the initial cluster centers. This specification is normally used only if the initial centers are specified on the INITIAL subcommand.

INITIAL Subcommand Use the INITIAL subcommand to specify the method by which initial cluster centers are chosen.

SELECT *Select widely spaced cases from the data file as initial centers.* QUICK CLUSTER searches through the data for cases that are widely separated on the clustering variables. This normally produces a good clustering solution. However, it requires that the data file be read an extra time in order to select the initial centers. SELECT is the default.

FIRST *Use the first* k *cases in the data file as initial centers,* where *k* is the number of clusters requested. This method saves the initial pass through the data and may be appropriate when a large number of clusters are to be formed and the order of cases in the data file is essentially random. It should *not* be used if the file is sorted on any of the clustering variables.

(value list) *Take cluster centers directly from the INITIAL subcommand.* Specify one value for each clustering variable for each of the requested clusters. For example, if there are five clustering variables and four clusters are requested, you should enter twenty values: five for the first initial center, then five for the second, and so on. Values must be separated by spaces or commas and the entire list should be enclosed in parentheses.

Example
```
QUICK CLUSTER A B
/CRITERIA=CLUSTERS(3)
/INITIAL=(1 6 7 7 22 9).
```

- This example forms three clusters of cases based on their values for variables A and B.
- The initial cluster centers will be at the points (A=1,B=6), (A=7,B=7), and (A=22,B=9).

PRINT Subcommand QUICK CLUSTER always displays the initial cluster centers, the updated centers used to classify cases (classification cluster centers), the mean values of the cases in each cluster (final cluster centers), and the number of cases in each cluster. Use the PRINT subcommand to request additional output.

- Some PRINT options will markedly increase the volume of output or the processing time required for large cluster problems.

CLUSTER *Cluster membership for each case.* Each case displays an identifying number or value, the number of the cluster to which it was assigned, and its distance from the center of that cluster. This output is extensive when you process a large number of cases.

C

Command Reference

ID(varname) *Case identification in output.* SPSS/PC+ will use the value of the variable named to identify cases in output. By default, cases are identified by their sequential number in the active file.

DISTANCE *Pairwise distances between all final cluster centers.* When a very large number of clusters are requested, this output can consume a great deal of processing time.

ANOVA *Descriptive univariate F tests for the clustering variables.* Since cases are assigned to clusters so as to maximize differences between the clusters, it is not legitimate to interpret the *F* tests as tests of the null hypothesis that there are no differences between clusters. The tests are descriptive only.

Example
```
QUICK CLUSTER A B C D E
/CRITERIA=CLUSTERS(6)
/PRINT=CLUSTER ID(CASEID) DISTANCE.
```

• Six clusters are formed on the basis of the five variables A, B, C, D, and E.

• Cluster membership and distance from cluster center are displayed for each case in the file.

• Cases are identified by the values of the variable CASEID.

• Distances between all cluster centers are printed.

WRITE Subcommand

Use the WRITE subcommand to write the final cluster centers to the results file (SPSS.PRC by default). The file will include the values of all cluster variables for each final cluster center. By editing this file with REVIEW, you can use these cluster centers on an INITIAL subcommand in a subsequent execution of QUICK CLUSTER.

• The WRITE subcommand does not have any specifications.

• Cluster centers are written to the current results file and replace any existing data in that file.

SAVE Subcommand

Use the SAVE subcommand to save results of the cluster analysis as new variables in your active file.

• The SAVE subcommand affects only the active file. To preserve the clustering results for analysis in later sessions, you must use the SAVE command to save a system file on disk.

The following variables can be saved on the active file:

CLUSTER(varname) *The cluster number of each case.* Specify a variable name in parentheses. The value of this variable will be set to an integer from 1 to the number of clusters.

DISTANCE(varname) *The distance of each case from its cluster center.* Specify a variable name in parentheses. For each case, the value of this variable will be the distance of that case from its cluster center.

Example
```
QUICK CLUSTER A B C D
/CRITERIA=CLUSTERS(6)
/SAVE=CLUSTER(CLUSNUM) DISTANCE(DISTCNTR).
```

• Six clusters of cases are formed on the basis of variables A, B, C, and D.

• The variable CLUSNUM will be set to an integer between 1 and 6 to indicate cluster membership for each case.

• The variable DISTCNTR will be set to the Euclidean distance between a case and the center of the cluster to which it is assigned.

MISSING Subcommand   Use the MISSING subcommand with the following keywords to specify the treatment of cases with missing values.

LISTWISE   *Delete cases with missing values listwise.* A case with a missing value on any of the clustering variables is deleted from the analysis and will not be assigned to a cluster. This is the default.

PAIRWISE   *Assign each case to the nearest cluster on the basis of the clustering variables for which the case has nonmissing values.* Cases are deleted if they have missing values on all clustering variables.

INCLUDE   *Treat user-missing values as valid.*

DEFAULT   *Same as LISTWISE.*

Example   This example uses QUICK CLUSTER twice to classify cases in a very large data file.

```
GET FILE='BIGFILE.SYS'.
COMPUTE TEST = UNIFORM(100).
PROCESS IF (TEST < 1).
QUICK CLUSTER V1 TO V5
/CRITERIA CLUSTERS(4)
/WRITE.
```

This first QUICK CLUSTER procedure processes a sample of cases to reduce processing time.

- For each case, TEST is calculated as a random number between 0 and 100. The PROCESS IF command then selects approximately 1% of the cases for the first QUICK CLUSTER procedure.

- Using the default method of selecting initial centers, QUICK CLUSTER processes this small group of cases and writes the final centers to the procedure output file (SPSS.PRC by default).

```
QUICK CLUSTER V1 TO V5
/INITIAL= (23.6  11.3 -2.71  55.0   19.2
            6.75  4.1  0.24  91.2   29.1
           10.2  -1.2  9.25   3.1   10.9
            2.0  10.0 -8.1   12.0   22    )
/CRITERIA CLUSTERS(4) NOUPDATE
/SAVE CLUSTER(CLUSNUM).
SAVE OUTFILE='CLUSTERD.SYS'.
```

- This QUICK CLUSTER procedure begins with the centers from the first procedure. A text editor was used to edit the contents of SPSS.PRC into a file for this run.

- Since NOUPDATE is specified on the CRITERIA subcommand, SPSS/PC+ simply classifies all cases to the nearest center.

- The cluster number (in this case, an integer from 1 to 4) is added to the active file as variable CLUSNUM.

- The SAVE command saves a system file containing CLUSNUM on disk.

C

Command Reference

RELIABILITY

This command available since the release of SPSS/PC+ V2.0.

```
RELIABILITY VARIABLES=varlist

 [/SCALE(scalename)=varlist [/SCALE... ]]

 [/MODEL={ALPHA         }] [/VARIABLES...]
         {SPLIT[(n)]    }
         {GUTTMAN       }
         {PARALLEL      }
         {STRICTPARALLEL}

 [/MISSING={EXCLUDE}]
           {INCLUDE}

 [/FORMAT={LABELS  }]
          {NOLABELS}

 [/METHOD=COV]

 [/STATISTICS=[DESCRIPTIVE] [SCALE    ]  [{ANOVA   }]  [ALL]]
              [COV        ] [TUKEY    ]   {FRIEDMAN}
              [CORR       ] [HOTELLING]   {COCHRAN }

 [/SUMMARY=[MEANS   ]  [COV ]  [TOTAL]]
           [VARIANCE]  [CORR]  [ALL  ]
```

Example:
```
RELIABILITY /VARIABLES=SCORE1 TO SCORE10
 /SCALE (OVERALL) = ALL
 /MODEL = ALPHA
 /SUMMARY = MEANS TOTAL.
```

Overview

RELIABILITY estimates reliability statistics for the components of multiple-item additive scales. It uses any of five models for reliability analysis and offers a great variety of statistical displays.

Defaults

By default, RELIABILITY displays the number of cases, number of items, and Cronbach's α. Whenever possible, it uses an algorithm that does not require the calculation of the covariance matrix. Cases with a missing value for any variable in the analysis are excluded.

Tailoring

Model type. You can specify any of five models.

Statistical display. Available statistics include descriptive statistics, correlation and covariance matrices, a repeated-measures analysis of variance table, Hotelling's T^2, Tukey's test for additivity, Friedman's chi-square for the analysis of ranked data, and Cochran's Q.

Computational method. You can force RELIABILITY to use the covariance method, even when you are not requesting any output that requires it.

Missing data. You can include user-missing values in the computations.

Syntax

- The minimum specifications are the VARIABLES subcommand, and a SCALE subcommand that provides a name for the scale, and either the names of the variables in that scale or ALL.

- You must enter the VARIABLES subcommand first. You can enter it more than one time.

- Other subcommands can be specified in any order and must be separated by slashes.

- The STATISTICS and SUMMARY subcommands are cumulative. You can enter them at any point after the VARIABLES subcommand. If you enter them more than once, all statistics that you request are produced for each scale.

Operations
- RELIABILITY causes the data to be read.
- If you request output that is not available for your model or for your data, RELIABILITY ignores the request.
- RELIABILITY uses an economical algorithm whenever possible but calculates a covariance matrix when necessary; see the METHOD subcommand for details.

Limitations
- Maximum 10 VARIABLES subcommands.
- Maximum 50 SCALE subcommands.
- Maximum 200 variables (the system limit) on any scale.

Example
```
RELIABILITY /VARIABLES=SCORE1 TO SCORE10
  /SCALE (OVERALL) = ALL
  /SCALE (ODD) = SCORE1 SCORE3 SCORE5 SCORE7 SCORE9
  /SUMMARY = MEANS TOTAL.
```
- This example analyzes two additive scales composed of the variables (or "items") from SCORE1 to SCORE10.
- One scale (labeled OVERALL in the display output) is composed of all 10 items. Another (labeled ODD) is composed of every other item.
- Summary statistics are displayed for each scale, showing item means and the relation of each item to the total scale.

VARIABLES Subcommand

The VARIABLES subcommand specifies the variables to be used in the analysis.

- The VARIABLES subcommand is required and must be specified first.
- You can use keyword ALL to refer to all user-defined variables in the active file.
- You can use keyword TO to refer to consecutive variables in the active file.
- You can specify VARIABLES more than once in a single RELIABILITY command.

SCALE Subcommand

The SCALE subcommand defines a scale for analysis, providing a name for the scale, and specifying its component variables. After SCALE, specify:

- A name for the scale, in parentheses. This name is used only to label the output from RELIABILITY. The RELIABILITY command does *not* add any new variables to your active file. If the analysis is satisfactory, use COMPUTE to create a new variable containing the sum of the component items.
- A list of variables to be used as components for the additive scale. The keyword ALL refers to all variables named on the preceding VARIABLES subcommand.

RELIABILITY analyzes the scale formed by adding the component variables.

- Variables named on SCALE must have been named on the previous VARIABLES subcommand.
- You can specify the keyword TO to reference consecutive variables *from the VARIABLES subcommand.*
- You can specify SCALE more than once following a VARIABLES subcommand, to analyze different groups of the component variables.

Example
```
RELIABILITY VARIABLES = ITEM1 TO ITEM20
  /SCALE (A) = ITEM1 TO ITEM10
  /SCALE (B) = ITEM1 ITEM3 ITEM5 ITEM16 TO ITEM20
  /SCALE (C) = ALL.
```
- This command analyzes three different scales: scale A has 10 items, scale B has 8 items, and scale C has 20 items.

MODEL Subcommand

The MODEL subcommand specifies the type of reliability analysis for the scale on the preceding SCALE subcommand. If you do not specify MODEL, ALPHA is the default.

Available models are:

ALPHA	*Cronbach's* α. Standardized item α is also displayed if you specify METHOD COV. This is the default.
SPLIT	*Split-half coefficients.* By default, the first half of the items is compared with the last half of the items (with the odd item, if any, going to the first half). You can specify a number in parentheses to override this default division, indicating how many items should be in the *second* half. For example, MODEL SPLIT (6) takes the last 6 variables for the second half, with all others in the first half.
GUTTMAN	*Guttman's lower bounds for true reliability.*
PARALLEL	*Maximum likelihood reliability estimate under parallel assumptions.* This model assumes that items have the same variance, but not necessarily the same mean.
STRICTPARALLEL	*Maximum likelihood reliability estimate under strictly parallel assumptions.* This model assumes that items have the same means, the same true score variances over a set of objects being measured, and the same error variance over replications.

STATISTICS Subcommand

The STATISTICS subcommand displays optional statistics. After STATISTICS, you can specify one or more of the following:

DESC	*Item means and standard deviations.*
COV	*Inter-item variance-covariance matrix.*
CORR	*Inter-item correlation matrix.*
SCALE	*Scale mean(s) and scale variance(s).*
TUKEY	*Tukey's test for additivity.* This helps determine whether a transformation of the items in your scale is needed to reduce non-additivity. The test prints an estimate of the power to which the items should be raised in order to be additive.
HOTEL	*Hotelling's* T^2. This is a test for equality of means among the items.
ANOVA	*Repeated-measures analysis of variance table.*
FRIEDMAN	*Friedman's chi-square and Kendall's coefficient of concordance.* These apply to ranked data. You must request ANOVA in addition to FRIEDMAN; the Friedman chi-square appears in place of the usual *F* test.
COCHRAN	*Cochran's Q.* This applies when all of the items are dichotomies. You must request ANOVA in addition to COCHRAN; the *Q* statistic appears in place of the usual *F* test.
ALL	*All applicable statistics.*

The STATISTICS subcommand is cumulative. If you enter it more than once, all statistics that you request are produced for each scale.

SUMMARY Subcommand

The SUMMARY subcommand displays summary statistics for each individual item in the scale. After SUMMARY, you can specify one or more of the following:

MEANS	*Statistics on item means.* The average, minimum, maximum, range, ratio of maximum to minimum, and variance of the item means.
VARIANCE	*Statistics on item variances.* Same statistics as for MEANS.
COV	*Statistics on item covariances.* Same statistics as for MEANS.
CORR	*Statistics on item correlations.* Same statistics as for MEANS.

TOTAL   *Statistics comparing each individual item to the scale composed of the other items.* Includes the scale mean, variance, and Cronbach's α without the item, and the correlation between the item and the scale without it.

ALL   *All applicable summary statistics.*

The SUMMARY subcommand is cumulative. If you enter it more than once, all statistics that you request are produced for each scale.

METHOD Subcommand

Two computational methods are available with the RELIABILITY procedure. The "space-saver" method does not require the calculation of a covariance matrix and is used whenever possible. RELIABILITY does compute the covariance matrix for all variables on each VARIABLES subcommand if *any* of the following is true:

- You specify a model other than ALPHA or SPLIT.
- You request COV, CORR, FRIEDMAN, or HOTELLING on the STATISTICS subcommand.
- You request anything other than TOTAL on the SUMMARY subcommand.

Even if none of these conditions applies, you can force RELIABILITY to use the covariance matrix with the METHOD subcommand. Only a single specification applies:

COVARIANCE.   *Calculate and use the covariance matrix,* even if it is not needed.

FORMAT Subcommand

By default, RELIABILITY prints the variable label of each variable in the scale before reporting on the analysis. The FORMAT subcommand lets you suppress this initial display of variable names and labels. The available keywords on FORMAT are:

LABELS   *Display names and labels for all items* before the analysis. This is the default.

NOLABELS   *Do not display names and labels.*

MISSING Subcommand

RELIABILITY deletes cases from analysis if they have a missing value for any variable named on the current VARIABLES subcommand. By default, both system-missing and user-missing values are excluded. You can use the MISSING subcommand to control deletion of missing data. Specify one of the following after MISSING:

EXCLUDE   *Exclude user-missing as well as system-missing values.* This is the default.

INCLUDE   *Treat user-missing values as valid,* excluding only system-missing values.

RELIABILITY was designed and programmed by David A. Specht of Monsanto Agricultural Products, with the assistance of Thomas A. Bubolz of Iowa State University.

C

Command Reference

Examples

Contents

Examples

CLUSTER   This example clusters cities using data from the 1982 *Information Please Almanac*. These are the 25 most populous cities in the U.S. in 1980. The variables are

- CITY—the city in question.
- CHURCHES—number of churches.
- PARKS—number of parks. Some cities only report total acreage and have a missing-value code of 9999 for number of parks.
- PHONES—number of telephones.
- TVS—number of television sets.
- RADIOST—number of radio stations.
- TVST—number of television stations.
- POP80—city population in 1980.
- TAXRATE—property tax rate in city.

We use these variables to cluster cities into groups that are relatively homogeneous with respect to these variables. Cities differ on these variables simply as a function of their population. We therefore rescale the variables to number of parks, etc., per person. The data are in an external file named ACLUS.DAT.

The SPSS/PC+ commands in the command file named on the INCLUDE command are

```
DATA LIST FILE='ACLUS.DAT'
 / CITY 6-18(A) POP80 53-60
 / CHURCHES 10-13 PARKS 14-17 PHONES 18-25 TVS 26-32
   RADIOST 33-35 TVST 36-38 TAXRATE 52-57(2)
 / .
MISSING VALUE PARKS (9999).
COMPUTE CHURCHES=CHURCHES/POP80.
COMPUTE PARKS=PARKS/POP80.
COMPUTE PHONES=PHONES/POP80.
COMPUTE TVS=TVS/POP80.
COMPUTE RADIOST=RADIOST/POP80.
COMPUTE TVST=TVST/POP80.
CLUSTER CHURCHES TO TAXRATE
 /METHOD=BAVERAGE
 /ID=CITY
 /PRINT=CLUSTER(3,5) DISTANCE SCHEDULE
 /PLOT=VICICLE HICICLE DENDROGRAM.
FINISH.
```

- DATA LIST names the file that contains the data and gives variable names and column locations. There are three records per case. No variables are read from the third record, so an extra slash is included to skip the unread record for each case.
- The MISSING VALUE command tells SPSS/PC+ to treat the value 9999 as a user-missing value for variable PARKS.
- The COMPUTE commands divide each measure by the population of the city in 1980. This yields the number of churches, phones, etc., per person.
- The CLUSTER variable specification names six variables using the TO convention.
- METHOD clusters cases by the method of average linkage between groups. It uses the default squared Euclidean distances over the six specified variables.

- The ID subcommand requests that the string variable CITY be used to label CLUSTER output.
- The cluster membership table is part of the default display (Figure A).
- PRINT requests the computed distances between cases, the cluster to which each case belongs for the 3-, 4-, and 5-cluster solutions, and the cluster agglomeration schedule (Figure B).
- PLOT presents the cluster solution as both a horizontal (Figure C) and a vertical icicle plot (Figure D), as well as a dendrogram (Figure E).

The display is shown in Figures A through E. The exact appearance of the printed display will depend on the characters available on the printer used.

A Cluster membership of cases

```
Data Information

        22 unweighted cases accepted.
         3 cases rejected because of missing value.

Squared Euclidean measure used.

1 Agglomeration method specified.


Cluster Membership of Cases using Average Linkage (Between Groups)

                               Number of Clusters

     Label         Case    5    4    3

     Baltimore      1       1    1    1
     Chicago        2       2    2    2
     Cleveland      3       1    1    1
     Columbus       4       3    1    1
     Dallas         5       4    3    3
     Denver         6       4    3    3
     Detroit        7       3    1    1
     Houston        8       4    3    3
     Indianapolis   9       5    4    2
     Jacksonville  10       4    3    3
     Los Angeles   11       4    3    3
     Memphis       12       3    1    1
     Nashville     13       1    1    1
     New Orleans   14       2    2    2
     New York      15       2    2    2
     Philadelphia  16       1    1    1
     Phoenix       17       4    3    3
     San Diego     18       3    1    1
     San Francisco 19       3    1    1
     San Jose      20       4    3    3
     Seattle       21       4    3    3
     Washington    22       4    3    3
```

B Agglomeration schedule for clustering

```
Agglomeration Schedule using Average Linkage (Between Groups)

           Clusters Combined                      Stage Cluster 1st Appears   Next
  Stage   Cluster 1  Cluster 2    Coefficient     Cluster 1    Cluster 2     Stage

     1        5         20         .213571            0            0           8
     2       17         22         .261159            0            0           6
     3        4         18         .292620            0            0          11
     4        8         21         .656814            0            0           8
     5        3         13        3.067433            0            0          14
     6       10         17        3.173483            0            2          16
     7        1         16        5.655860            0            0          14
     8        5          8        8.083633            1            4          12
     9        7         12       13.270877            0            0          11
    10       14         15       16.843185            0            0          13
    11        4          7       33.221954            3            9          15
    12        5         11       38.605591            8            0          17
    13        2         14       48.604095            0           10          19
    14        1          3       73.268372            7            5          18
    15        4         19       88.134521           11            0          18
    16        6         10       97.164627            0            6          17
    17        5          6      250.892181           12           16          20
    18        1          4      651.010742           14           15          20
    19        2          9     1026.891846           13            0          21
    20        1          5     1710.032959           18           17          21
    21        1          2     5559.281250           20           19           0
```

C Horizontal icicle plot

```
Horizontal Icicle Plot Using Average Linkage (Between Groups)

                            Number of Clusters

                            111111111122
       C A S E              12345678901234567890l
       Label         Seq    ++++++++++++++++++++++

       Indianapolis    9    XXXXXXXXXXXXXXXXXXXXXX
                            XXX
                            XXX
       New York       15    XXXXXXXXXXXXXXXXXXXXXX
                            XXXXXXXXXXX
                            XXXXXXXXXXX
       New Orleans    14    XXXXXXXXXXXXXXXXXXXXXX
                            XXXXXXXX
                            XXXXXXXX
       Chicago         2    XXXXXXXXXXXXXXXXXXXXXX
                            X
                            X
       Washington     22    XXXXXXXXXXXXXXXXXXXXXX
                            XXXXXXXXXXXXXXXXXXX
                            XXXXXXXXXXXXXXXXXXX
       Phoenix        17    XXXXXXXXXXXXXXXXXXXXXX
                            XXXXXXXXXXXXXX
                            XXXXXXXXXXXXXX
       Jacksonville   10    XXXXXXXXXXXXXXXXXXXXXX
                            XXXXX
                            XXXXX
       Denver          6    XXXXXXXXXXXXXXXXXXXXXX
                            XXXX
                            XXXX
       Los Angeles    11    XXXXXXXXXXXXXXXXXXXXXX
                            XXXXXXXXX
                            XXXXXXXXX
       Seattle        21    XXXXXXXXXXXXXXXXXXXXXX
                            XXXXXXXXXXXXXXX
                            XXXXXXXXXXXXXXX
       Houston         8    XXXXXXXXXXXXXXXXXXXXXX
                            XXXXXXXXXXXX
                            XXXXXXXXXXXX
       San Jose       20    XXXXXXXXXXXXXXXXXXXXXX
                            XXXXXXXXXXXXXXXXXX
                            XXXXXXXXXXXXXXXXXX
       Dallas          5    XXXXXXXXXXXXXXXXXXXXXX
                            XX
                            XX
       San Francisco  19    XXXXXXXXXXXXXXXXXXXXXX
                            XXXXXXX
                            XXXXXXX
       Memphis        12    XXXXXXXXXXXXXXXXXXXXXX
                            XXXXXXXXXXXXX
                            XXXXXXXXXXXXX
       Detroit         7    XXXXXXXXXXXXXXXXXXXXXX
                            XXXXXXXXXX
                            XXXXXXXXXX
       San Diego      18    XXXXXXXXXXXXXXXXXXXXXX
                            XXXXXXXXXXXXXXXXX
                            XXXXXXXXXXXXXXXXX
       Columbus        4    XXXXXXXXXXXXXXXXXXXXXX
                            XXXX
                            XXXX
       Nashville      13    XXXXXXXXXXXXXXXXXXXXXX
                            XXXXXXXXXXXXXXX
                            XXXXXXXXXXXXXXX
       Cleveland       3    XXXXXXXXXXXXXXXXXXXXXX
                            XXXXXXXX
                            XXXXXXXX
       Philadelphia   16    XXXXXXXXXXXXXXXXXXXXXX
                            XXXXXXXXXXXXXX
                            XXXXXXXXXXXXXX
       Baltimore       1    XXXXXXXXXXXXXXXXXXXXXX
```

D Vertical icicle plot

```
Vertical Icicle Plot using Average Linkage (Between Groups)

 (Down) Number of Clusters  (Across) Case Label and number

     I  N  N  C  W  P  J  D  L  S  H  S  D  S  M  D  S  C  N  C  P  B
     n  e  e  h  a  h  a  e  o  e  o  a  a  a  e  e  a  l  a  l  h  a
     d  w  w  i  s  o  c  n  s  a  u  n  n  n  m  t  n  u  s  e  i  l
     i     Y  c  h  e  k  v  e  t  s  l  F  m  p  r  D  m  h  v  l  t
     a  Y  r  a  i  n  s  e  A  t  o  J  r  p  h  o  i  b  v  e  a  i
     n  o  l  g  n  i  o  r  n  l  n  a  a  h  o  i  e  u  i  l  d  m
     a  r  e  o  g  x  n     g  e     o  n  i  e  t  g  s  l  a  e  o
     p  k  a     t     v     e  s     s  c  s  n  r  o     l  n  l  r
     o     n     o     i     l        e  i     i     o     e  d  p  e
     l     s     n     l     e        s  s           x        h  h
     i                 l                 c                          i
     s                 e                 o                          a

     1  1        2  1  1     1  2     2     1  1     1     1     1
     9  5  4  2  2  7  0  6  1  8  0  5  9  2  7  8  4  3  6  1

 1 +XXXXXXXXXXXXXXXXXXXXXXXXXXXXXXXXXXXXXXXXXXXXXXXXXXXXXXXXXXXXXXXX
 2 +XXXXXXXXX   XXXXXXXXXXXXXXXXXXXXXXXXXXXXXXXXXXXXXXXXXXXXXXXXXXXX
 3 +XXXXXXXXX   XXXXXXXXXXXXXXXXXXXXXXX   XXXXXXXXXXXXXXXXXXXXXXXXXXX
 4 +X XXXXXXX   XXXXXXXXXXXXXXXXXXXXXXX   XXXXXXXXXXXXXXXXXXXXXXXXXXX
 5 +X XXXXXX    XXXXXXXXXXX   XXXXXXXXXXX   XXXXXXXXXXXX    XXXXXXXXX
 6 +X XXXXXX    XXXXXXXXX     XXXXXXXXXXX   XXXXXXXXXXXX    XXXXXXXXX
 7 +X XXXXXX    XXXXXXXXX     XXXXXXXXXXX   XXXXXXXXXXXX    XXXXXXXXX
 8 +X XXXXXX    XXXXXXX   X   XXXXXXXXXXX   X XXXXXXXXXX    XXXXXXXXX
 9 +X XXXXXX    XXXXXXX   X   XXXXXXXXXXX   X XXXXXXXXXX    XXXX XXXX
10 +X XXXX  X   XXXXXXX   X   XXXXXXXXXXX   X XXXXXXXXXX    XXXX XXXX
11 +X XXXX  X   XXXXXXX   X X XXXXXXXXXXX   X XXXXXXXXXX    XXXX XXXX
12 +X XXXX  X   XXXXXXX   X   X XXXXXXXXX   X XXXX  XXXX    XXXX XXXX
13 +X X  X  X   XXXXXXX   X   X XXXXXXXXX   X XXXX  XXXX    XXXX XXXX
14 +X X  X  X   XXXXXXX   X X X X XXXXXXX   X X  X  XXXX    XXXX XXXX
15 +X X  X  X   XXXXXXX   X X XXXX  XXXX    X X  X  XXXX    XXXX XXXX
16 +X X  X  X   XXXX   X  X X XXXX  XXXX    X X  X  XXXX    XXXX X  X
17 +X X  X  X   XXXX   X  X X XXXX  XXXX    X X  X  XXXX    XXXX X  X
18 +X X  X  X   XXXX   X  X X XXXX  XXXX    X X  X  XXXX  X X  X X  X
19 +X X  X  X   XXXX   X  X X X  X  XXXX    X X  X  XXXX  X X  X X  X
20 +X X  X  X   XXXX   X  X X X  X  XXXX    X X  X  X  X  X X  X X  X
21 +X X  X  X   X  X   X  X X X  X  XXXX    X X  X  X  X  X X  X X  X
```

E Dendrogram

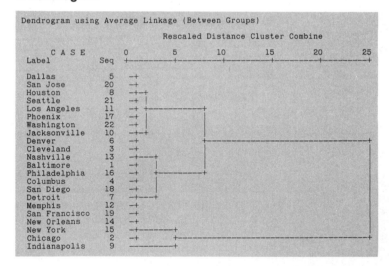

```
Dendrogram using Average Linkage (Between Groups)

                             Rescaled Distance Cluster Combine

        C A S E         0    5    10   15   20   25
Label            Seq    +----+----+----+----+----+

Dallas            5     -+
San Jose         20     -+
Houston           8     -+-+
Seattle          21     -+ |
Los Angeles      11     -+ +---------------+
Phoenix          17     -+ |               |
Washington       22     -+-+               |
Jacksonville     10     -+-+               |
Denver            6     -+  +------------------------------------+
Cleveland         3     -+                                       |
Nashville        13     -+---+                                   |
Baltimore         1     -+   |                                   |
Philadelphia     16     -+   +-+                                 |
Columbus          4     -+                                       |
San Diego        18     -+                                       |
Detroit           7     -+---+                                   |
Memphis          12     -+                                       |
San Francisco    19     -+                                       |
New Orleans      14     -+                                       |
New York         15     -+-------+                               |
Chicago           2     -+       +-----------------------------+ |
Indianapolis      9     ---------+
```

DSCRIMINANT

This example analyzes 1979 prices and earnings in 45 cities around the world, compiled by the Union Bank of Switzerland. The variables are

- FOOD—the average net cost of 39 different food and beverage items in the city, expressed as a percentage above or below that of Zurich, where Zurich equals 100%.
- SERVICE—the average cost of 28 different goods and services in the city, expressed as a percentage above or below that of Zurich, where Zurich equals 100%.
- BUS, MECHANIC, CONSTRUC, COOK, MANAGER, FSALES—the average gross annual earnings of municipal bus drivers, automobile mechanics, construction workers, cooks, managers, and female sales workers, working from five to ten years in their respective occupations. Each variable is expressed as a percentage above or below that of Zurich, where Zurich equals 100%.
- WORLD—economic development status of the country in which the city is located, divided into three groups: economically advanced nations, such as the United States and most European nations; nations that are members of the Organization for Petroleum Exporting Countries (OPEC); and nations that are economically under-developed. The groups are labeled 1ST WORLD, PETRO WORLD, and 3RD WORLD, respectively.

There are two objectives to this analysis. First, we discriminate between cities in different categories by examining their wage and price structures. Secondly, we predict a city's economic class category from coefficients calculated using wages and prices as predictors. The data are in an external file named ADSC.DAT.

The SPSS/PC+ commands in the command file named on the INCLUDE command are

```
DATA LIST FREE FILE='ADSC.DAT'
 /WORLD FOOD SERVICE BUS MECHANIC CONSTRUC
  COOK MANAGER FSALES.
MISSING VALUE ALL (0).
VALUE LABELS WORLD 1 '1ST WORLD' 2 'PETRO WORLD' 3 '3RD WORLD'.
DSCRIMINANT GROUPS=WORLD(1.3)
 /VARIABLES=FOOD SERVICE BUS MECHANIC CONSTRUC COOK MANAGER FSALES
 /PRIORS=SIZE
 /SAVE=CLASS=PRDCLAS SCORES=DISCSCR
 /STATISTICS=11 13.
FINISH.
```

- The DATA LIST command names the file that contains the data and assigns variable names. The FREE keyword indicates that the data are in freefield format.
- The MISSING VALUE command assigns 0 as a user-missing value to all the variables.
- The VALUE LABELS command assigns descriptive labels to the values of variable WORLD.
- The DSCRIMINANT command requests a three-group discriminant analysis. The variable WORLD named on the GROUPS subcommand defines the groups.
- The variables FOOD, SERVICE, BUS, MECHANIC, CONSTRUC, COOK, MANAGER, and FSALES, named on the VARIABLES subcommand, are used as predictor variables during the analysis phase.
- The PRIORS subcommand tells SPSS/PC+ that during the classification phase, prior probabilities are equal to the known size of the groups (Figure A).
- The SAVE subcommand saves three variables on the active file: the predicted group for each of the classified cases (variable PRDCLAS) and the two discriminant scores (variables DISCSCR1 and DISCSCR2). The saved variables are shown in Figure B.
- The STATISTICS subcommand requests the display of the unstandardized discriminant functions (Figure C) and the classification results table (Figure D).

D

Examples

The display is shown in Figures A through D. The exact appearance of printed display depends on the characters available on your printer.

A Prior probabilities

```
Prior Probabilities
   Group     Prior      Label
      1      0.58140    1ST WORLD
      2      0.13953    PETRO WORLD
      3      0.27907    3RD WORLD
   Total     1.00000
```

B The saved variables

```
These new variables will be created:
    Name       Label
    ----       -----
PRDCLAS   ---  PREDICTED GROUP FOR ANALYSIS    1
DISCSCR1  ---  FUNCTION   1 FOR ANALYSIS       1
DISCSCR2  ---  FUNCTION   2 FOR ANALYSIS       1
```

C Discriminant coefficients

```
Unstandardized Canonical Discriminant Function Coefficients

                 FUNC  1          FUNC  2
FOOD           -.7133619D-02    .6194062D-01
SERVICE         .8472984D-02   -.5365943D-01
BUS             .5255502D-01   -.2000084D-01
MECHANIC        .2805062D-01    .1326366D-01
CONSTRUC       -.4256104D-02   -.7536312D-02
COOK           -.1677760D-01    .2545888D-01
MANAGER        -.2570614D-01   -.2155895D-01
FSALES          .1637516D-01    .1486991D-01
(constant)    -1.852548        -.9620797
```

D Classification results

```
Classification Results -

                     No. of    Predicted Group Membership
    Actual Group     Cases       1         2         3
    ------------     ------    -----     -----     -----
Group       1         25         24        1         0
1ST WORLD                       96.0%     4.0%      0.0%

Group       2          6          0        5         1
PETRO WORLD                      0.0%     83.3%    16.7%

Group       3         12          1        0        11
3RD WORLD                        8.3%     0.0%     91.7%

Percent of "grouped" cases correctly classified:  93.02%

Classification Processing Summary
        45 Cases were processed.
         0 Cases were excluded for missing or out-of-range group codes.
         2 Cases had at least one missing discriminating variable.
        43 Cases were used for printed output.
        45 Cases were written into the active file.
```

FACTOR   This example uses six items from a 500-case sample from the 1980 General Social Survey. Respondents indicate whether they favor or oppose abortion in the following contexts:

- ABHLTH—if the woman's health is seriously endangered.
- ABRAPE—if the woman is pregnant as a result of rape.
- ABDEFECT—if there is a strong chance of a serious defect in the child.
- ABPOOR—if the woman has a low income and cannot afford more children.
- ABSINGLE—if the woman is not married and doesn't want the child.
- ABNOMORE—if the woman is married and wants no more children.

The data are in an external file named AFACTOR.DAT. The SPSS/PC+ commands in the command file named on the INCLUDE command are

```
DATA LIST FREE FILE='AFACTOR.DAT'
 /ABDEFECT ABNOMORE ABHLTH ABPOOR ABRAPE ABSINGLE.
RECODE  ABDEFECT TO ABSINGLE(1=1)(2=0)(ELSE=9).
MISSING VALUE ABDEFECT TO ABSINGLE (9).
VALUE LABELS  ABDEFECT TO ABSINGLE
 0 'NO' 1 'YES' 9 'MISSING'.
FACTOR  VARIABLES=ABDEFECT TO ABSINGLE
 /MISSING=MEANSUB
 /FORMAT=SORT BLANK(.3)
 /PLOT=ROTATION(1 2)
 /EXTRACTION=ULS
 /ROTATION=OBLIMIN.
FINISH.
```

- The DATA LIST command names the file that contains the data and assigns variable names. Keyword FREE indicates that the data are in freefield format.
- The RECODE and MISSING VALUE commands redefine the variables, and VALUE LABELS provides labels for the redefined responses.
- The VARIABLES subcommand on FACTOR names all the variables that are used in this FACTOR procedure.
- The MISSING subcommand forces mean substitution for missing data.
- The FORMAT subcommand displays the factor loadings in descending order of magnitude and suppresses the printing of factor loadings less than 0.3.
- The PLOT subcommand requests a plot of the variables in factor space, where 1 and 2 are the factor numbers to be plotted.
- The EXTRACTION subcommand specifies unweighted least squares as the method of extraction.
- The ROTATION subcommand specifies an oblimin rotation.

Portions of the output produced by this set of commands appear in Figures A through D. The exact appearance of printed output depends on the characters available on your printer.

- Figure A contains initial statistics, which are produced by default. Initial statistics are the initial communalities, eigenvalues of the correlation matrix, and percentage of variance explained.
- Figure B contains extraction statistics, which are produced by default. Extraction statistics are the communalities, eigenvalues, and unrotated factor loadings. Note the effect of specifying SORT and BLANK on the FORMAT subcommand.
- Figure C contains rotation statistics, which are produced by default if the model is rotated. These statistics are the rotated factor pattern and structure matrices (since this is an oblimin rotation) and the factor correlation matrix.
- Figure D contains a plot of the variables in rotated factor space. Although the rotation is oblimin, the axes are orthogonal.

A Initial statistics

```
Initial Statistics:

Variable      Communality  *  Factor   Eigenvalue   Pct of Var   Cum Pct
                           *
ABDEFECT        .44988     *    1        3.38153       56.4        56.4
ABNOMORE        .66747     *    2        1.19287       19.9        76.2
ABHLTH          .35555     *    3         .50823        8.5        84.7
ABPOOR          .66600     *    4         .40867        6.8        91.5
ABRAPE          .39760     *    5         .28847        4.8        96.3
ABSINGLE        .60394     *    6         .22024        3.7       100.0
```

B Extraction statistics

```
Factor Matrix:

              FACTOR  1      FACTOR  2

ABPOOR          .81970        -.32158
ABNOMORE        .81704        -.34273
ABSINGLE        .78051
ABDEFECT        .65764         .46888
ABRAPE          .62257         .33014
ABHLTH          .53469         .44445


Final Statistics:

Variable      Communality  *  Factor   Eigenvalue   Pct of Var   Cum Pct
                           *
ABDEFECT        .65233     *    1        3.05462       50.9        50.9
ABNOMORE        .78502     *    2         .81821       13.6        64.5
ABHLTH          .48344     *
ABPOOR          .77532     *
ABRAPE          .49658     *
ABSINGLE        .68014     *
```

C Rotation statistics

```
Pattern Matrix:

              FACTOR  1      FACTOR  2

ABNOMORE        .90007
ABPOOR          .88136
ABSINGLE        .80050

ABDEFECT                       .80734
ABHLTH                         .72675
ABRAPE                         .63777


Structure Matrix:

              FACTOR  1      FACTOR  2

ABNOMORE        .88574         .46583
ABPOOR          .88052         .48028
ABSINGLE        .82393         .48046

ABDEFECT        .44195         .80767
ABRAPE          .45976         .69852
ABHLTH          .33632         .69342


Factor Correlation Matrix:

              FACTOR  1      FACTOR  2

FACTOR  1      1.00000
FACTOR  2       .54667        1.00000
```

D Factor plot

```
Horizontal Factor  1   Vertical Factor  2          Symbol Variable    Coordinates
                                                      1    ABDEFECT    .001   .807
                                                      2    ABNOMORE    .900  -.026
                      3  1                             3    ABHLTH     -.061   .727
                           5                           4    ABPOOR      .881  -.002
                                                      5    ABRAPE      .111   .638
                                                      6    ABSINGLE    .801   .043



                                              6
        ──────────────────────────┼──────────────────
                                             4 2
```

HILOGLINEAR   In this example we will consider a market research analysis of laundry detergent preferences. Consumers in the survey prefer either Brand M or Brand X detergent. This analysis examines the relationship among brand preference and three other variables. The variables are

- BRANDPRF—preference for either BRAND M or BRAND X detergent.
- WATSOFT—water softness.
- PREVUSE—previous use of BRAND M.
- TEMP—washing temperature.

The data are in an external file named AHILOG.DAT. The SPSS/PC+ commands in the command file named on the INCLUDE command are

```
TITLE DETERGENT PREFERENCES RIES & SMITH(1963).
DATA LIST FREE FILE='AHILOG.DAT'
 / WATSOFT BRANDPRF PREVUSE TEMP FREQ.
VARIABLE LABELS WATSOFT   'WATER SOFTNESS'
                BRANDPRF 'BRAND PREFERENCE'
                PREVUSE  'PREVIOUS USE OF M'
                TEMP     'WATER TEMPERATURE'
                FREQ     'NUMBER IN CONDITION'.
VALUE LABELS WATSOFT 1 'SOFT' 2 'MEDIUM' 3 'HARD' /
             BRANDPRF 1 'BRAND X' 2 'BRAND M' /
             PREVUSE 1 'YES' 2 'NO' /
             TEMP 1 'HIGH' 2 'LOW'.
WEIGHT BY FREQ.
HILOGLINEAR WATSOFT (1,3) BRANDPRF PREVUSE TEMP (1,2)
 /PRINT=ALL
 /PLOT=DEFAULT
 /METHOD=BACKWARD
 /CRITERIA=MAXSTEPS(24)
 /DESIGN.
FINISH.
```

- The TITLE command puts the title "DETERGENT PREFERENCES RIES & SMITH (1963)" at the top of each page of output for this session.
- DATA LIST names the file that contains the data and defines the variables. Keyword FREE indicates that the data are in freefield format.
- The VARIABLE LABELS and VALUE LABELS commands complete the variable definition.
- The WEIGHT command weights the observations by FREQ, the variable containing the number of observations for each combination of values.
- HILOGLINEAR specifies four variables. The variable WATSOFT has three levels and the other three variables each have two.
- The PRINT subcommand requests all available displays: observed, expected, and residual values (display not shown); the result of the iterative proportional fitting algorithm and tests of effects for the saturated model and for each order (Figure A); measures of partial association for effects (Figure B); and parameter estimates (Figure C).
- The PLOT subcommand requests the default plots: residuals against observed and expected values, and a normal probability plot (partial display in Figure F).
- The METHOD subcommand requests backward elimination. The CRITERIA subcommand specifies a maximum of 24 steps, and the DESIGN subcommand successively eliminates terms from the default saturated model (partial display in Figure D). The observed and expected frequencies for the final model are also displayed (Figure E).

Portions of the display are shown in Figures A through F. The exact appearance of printed display depends on the characters available on your printer.

A Tests of effects for the saturated model and for each order

```
Tests that K-way and higher order effects are zero.

        K      DF    L.R. Chisq    Prob  Pearson Chisq    Prob   Iteration

        4       2         .738    .6915           .738   .6915           3
        3       9        9.846    .3631          9.871   .3611           3
        2      18       42.926    .0008         43.902   .0006           2
        1      23      118.626    .0000        115.714   .0000           0

Tests that K-way effects are zero.

        K      DF    L.R. Chisq    Prob  Pearson Chisq    Prob   Iteration

        1       5       75.701    .0000         71.812   .0000           0
        2       9       33.080    .0001         34.031   .0001           0
        3       7        9.108    .2450          9.133   .2433           0
        4       2         .738    .6915           .738   .6915           0
```

B Partial associations

```
Tests of PARTIAL associations.

Effect Name                               DF   Partial Chisq     Prob   Iter

WATSOFT*BRANDPRF*PREVUSE                    2           4.571    .1017      3
WATSOFT*BRANDPRF*TEMP                       2            .162    .9223      3
WATSOFT*PREVUSE*TEMP                        2           1.377    .5022      3
BRANDPRF*PREVUSE*TEMP                       1           2.222    .1361      3
WATSOFT*BRANDPRF                           2            .216    .8977      3
WATSOFT*PREVUSE                            2           1.005    .6051      3
BRANDPRF*PREVUSE                           1          19.892    .0000      3
WATSOFT*TEMP                               2           6.095    .0475      3
BRANDPRF*TEMP                              1           3.738    .0532      3
PREVUSE*TEMP                               1            .740    .3898      3
WATSOFT                                    2            .502    .7780      2
BRANDPRF                                   1            .064    .7996      2
PREVUSE                                    1           1.922    .1656      2
TEMP                                       1          73.211    .0000      2
```

C Partial display of parameter estimates for saturated model

```
Estimates for Parameters.

WATSOFT*BRANDPRF*PREVUSE*TEMP

Parameter     Coeff.       Std. Err.      Z-Value Lower 95 CI Upper 95 CI

        1   -.0086293293      .04833       -.17856     -.10335      .08609
        2   -.0296475092      .04734       -.62629     -.12243      .06313

WATSOFT*BRANDPRF*PREVUSE

Parameter     Coeff.       Std. Err.      Z-Value Lower 95 CI Upper 95 CI

        1    .0925171313      .04833      1.91437     -.00221      .18724
        2   -.0318024179      .04734       -.67182     -.12458      .06098

WATSOFT*BRANDPRF*TEMP

Parameter     Coeff.       Std. Err.      Z-Value Lower 95 CI Upper 95 CI

        1   -.0203612840      .04833       -.42132     -.11508      .07436
        2    .0048119005      .04734       .10165     -.08797      .09759

WATSOFT*PREVUSE*TEMP

Parameter     Coeff.       Std. Err.      Z-Value Lower 95 CI Upper 95 CI

        1   -.0474552194      .04833       -.98194     -.14218      .04727
        2    .0488797573      .04734      1.03257     -.04390      .14166

BRANDPRF*PREVUSE*TEMP

Parameter     Coeff.       Std. Err.      Z-Value Lower 95 CI Upper 95 CI

        1   -.0504586672      .03363     -1.50056     -.11637      .01545
```

D Partial display of final statistics

```
Backward Elimination for DESIGN 1 with generating class

   WATSOFT*BRANDPRF*PREVUSE*TEMP

Likelihood ratio chi square =      0.0       DF = 0  P = 1.000


Step 8

   The best model has generating class

        WATSOFT*TEMP
        BRANDPRF*TEMP
        BRANDPRF*PREVUSE

   Likelihood ratio chi square =    11.88633   DF = 14  P =  .615

If Deleted Simple Effect is            DF   L.R. Chisq Change   Prob  Iter

WATSOFT*TEMP                            2              6.098    .0474   2
BRANDPRF*TEMP                           1              4.361    .0368   2
BRANDPRF*PREVUSE                        1             20.578    .0000   2
Step 9

   The best model has generating class

        WATSOFT*TEMP
        BRANDPRF*TEMP
        BRANDPRF*PREVUSE

   Likelihood ratio chi square =    11.88633   DF = 14  P =  .615
The final model has generating class

        WATSOFT*TEMP
        BRANDPRF*TEMP
        BRANDPRF*PREVUSE

The Iterative Proportional Fitting converged at iteration 0.
```

E Observed and expected frequencies for selected model

```
Observed, Expected Frequencies and Residuals.
      Factor            Code        OBS count  EXP count  Residual  Std Resid


WATSOFT            SOFT
  BRANDPRF          BRAND X
    PREVUSE           YES
      TEMP              HIGH        19.0       19.5       -.52      -.12
      TEMP              LOW         57.0       47.8       9.15      1.32
    PREVUSE           NO
      TEMP              HIGH        29.0       28.4        .61       .11
      TEMP              LOW         63.0       69.6      -6.58      -.79
  BRANDPRF          BRAND M
    PREVUSE           YES
      TEMP              HIGH        29.0       30.8      -1.85      -.33
      TEMP              LOW         49.0       57.5      -8.52     -1.12
    PREVUSE           NO
      TEMP              HIGH        27.0       25.2       1.76       .35
      TEMP              LOW         53.0       47.1       5.94       .87

WATSOFT            MEDIUM
  BRANDPRF          BRAND X
    PREVUSE           YES
      TEMP              HIGH        23.0       23.7       -.65      -.13
      TEMP              LOW         47.0       47.0        .01       .00
    PREVUSE           NO
      TEMP              HIGH        33.0       34.4      -1.40      -.24
      TEMP              LOW         66.0       68.3      -2.32      -.28
  BRANDPRF          BRAND M
    PREVUSE           YES
      TEMP              HIGH        47.0       37.4       9.63      1.57
      TEMP              LOW         55.0       56.5      -1.48      -.20
    PREVUSE           NO
      TEMP              HIGH        23.0       30.6      -7.58     -1.37
      TEMP              LOW         50.0       46.2       3.79       .56

WATSOFT            HARD
  BRANDPRF          BRAND X
    PREVUSE           YES
      TEMP              HIGH        24.0       26.1      -2.09      -.41
      TEMP              LOW         37.0       42.9      -5.89      -.90
    PREVUSE           NO
      TEMP              HIGH        42.0       37.9       4.06       .66
      TEMP              LOW         68.0       62.4       5.63       .71
  BRANDPRF          BRAND M
    PREVUSE           YES
      TEMP              HIGH        43.0       41.2       1.77       .28
      TEMP              LOW         52.0       51.6        .44       .06
    PREVUSE           NO
      TEMP              HIGH        30.0       33.7      -3.73      -.64
      TEMP              LOW         42.0       42.2       -.18      -.03
Goodness-of-fit test statistics

   Likelihood ratio chi square =   11.88633   DF = 14  P =  .615
           Pearson chi square =    11.91780   DF = 14  P =  .613
```

F HILOGLINEAR residuals plots

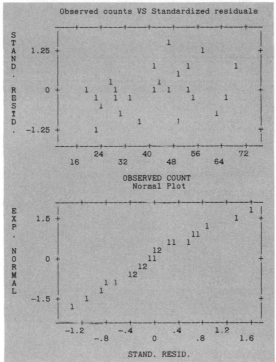

MANOVA

Example 1: Analysis of Covariance Designs

You can test different models with MANOVA through correct use of syntax. This example shows how to use MANOVA for analysis of variance and covariance. The example comes from Winer (1971).

The variables are

- A—a factor that represents three methods of training.
- X—a covariate that is a score on an aptitude test.
- Y—a dependent variable that contains the scores on an achievement test on material covered in the training course. The test is given to the subjects after the training is complete.

The data are in an external file named AMAN.DAT. The SPSS/PC+ commands in the command file named on the INCLUDE command are

```
SET WIDTH=WIDE.
DATA LIST FILE='AMAN.DAT' / A 1 X Y 2-5.
MANOVA Y BY A(1,3)
 /PRINT=PARAM(ESTIM)
 /DESIGN.
MANOVA Y BY A(1,3) WITH X
 /PMEANS=VARIABLES(Y)
 /PRINT=PARAM(ESTIM)
 /DESIGN
 /ANALYSIS=Y
 /METHOD=SSTYPE(SEQUENTIAL)
 /DESIGN=X, A, A BY X
 /DESIGN=X WITHIN A, A.
FINISH.
```

- The SET command sets the display width to 132 characters.
- The DATA LIST command reads variables A, X, and Y from the data included in the file AMAN.DAT.
- The first MANOVA command specifies the first analysis—a one-way analysis of variance—using the default DESIGN subcommand. The PRINT subcommand requests that parameter estimates be included in the display.
- The second MANOVA command specifies the second through fourth analyses. The second is an analysis of covariance using the default DESIGN subcommand. The default analysis fits covariates, factors, and factor-by-factor interactions if you specify more than one factor, and assumes homogeneous slopes.
- The PMEANS subcommand displays predicted means for the second through fourth models. The PRINT subcommand requests that parameter estimates be included in the display.
- The third analysis tests the assumption of homogeneous slopes. If the A by X interaction is significant, you must reject the hypothesis of parallel slopes. The ANALYSIS subcommand specifies the dependent variable. The METHOD subcommand asks for sequential sums of squares. The DESIGN subcommand specifies effects, including the factor-by-covariate interaction.
- The fourth analysis fits separate regression coefficients in each group of the factor. As in the third analysis, the ANALYSIS subcommand specifies the dependent variable for the analysis. The WITHIN keyword on the DESIGN subcommand fits separate regression models within each of the three groups of Factor A.

Portions of the display output are shown in Figures A through E. The exact appearance of printed display depends on the characters available on your printer.

- Figure A shows the display for the first analysis, including an analysis of variance table.
- Figure B shows the display for the second analysis, which includes the covariate X. MANOVA displays the analysis of variance table and regression statistics associated with X.

- Figure C shows the table of predicted means for the second analysis requested with the PMEANS subcommand. MANOVA displays the observed means, the adjusted means (which are adjusted for the covariate), and the estimated means (which are the cell means estimated with knowledge of A, not adjusted for the covariate).
- Figure D shows the analysis of variance table for the third analysis. Since the A by X interaction is not significant, the hypothesis of parallel slopes is not rejected. That is, we can assume that the effect of change in X on Y is the same across levels of A.
- Finally, Figure E shows the analysis of variance table for the fourth analysis. The X within A effect is the joint effect of the separate regressions. Since the third analysis shows the factor-by-covariate interaction is not significant, the second analysis (not the fourth) is the preferred solution.

A Results for first analysis

```
Tests of Significance for Y using UNIQUE sums of squares
Source of Variation          SS      DF        MS        F   Sig of F

WITHIN CELLS               26.86     18      1.49
CONSTANT                  817.19      1    817.19    547.69     .000
A                          36.95      2     18.48     12.38     .000


- - - - - - - - - -
Estimates for Y
CONSTANT

 Parameter      Coeff.   Std. Err.     t-Value    Sig. t  Lower -95% CL- Upper

        1    6.23809524    .26855    23.40281      0.0     5.67809    6.79810

A

 Parameter      Coeff.   Std. Err.     t-Value    Sig. t  Lower -95% CL- Upper

        2   -1.8095238    .37696     -4.80027      .000   -2.60149   -1.01755
        3    1.33333333   .37696      3.53704      .002     .54136    2.12530
```

B Results for second analysis

```
Tests of Significance for Y using UNIQUE sums of squares
Source of Variation          SS      DF        MS        F   Sig of F

WITHIN CELLS               10.30     17       .61
REGRESSION                 16.56      1     16.56     27.32     .000
CONSTANT                   58.05      1     58.05     95.80     .000
A                          16.93      2      8.47     13.97     .000


- - - - - - - - -
Estimates for Y adjusted for 1 covariate
CONSTANT

 Parameter      Coeff.   Std. Err.     t-Value    Sig. t  Lower -95% CL- Upper

        1    4.18639456    .42772     9.78766      .000    3.28398    5.08881

A

 Parameter      Coeff.   Std. Err.     t-Value    Sig. t  Lower -95% CL- Upper

        2   -1.3496599    .25584     -5.27535      .000   -1.88944    -.80988
        3     .838095238  .25825      3.24530      .005     .29324    1.38295

- - - - - - - - -
Regression analysis for WITHIN CELLS error term
Dependent variable .. Y

COVARIATE           B         Beta     Std. Err.     t-Value    Sig. of t   Lower -95%  CL- Upper

X           .7428571429  .7851199742    .14213      5.22671       .000       .44300     1.04272
```

C Adjusted means for second analysis

```
Adjusted and Estimated Means
Variable .. Y
  CELL      Obs. Mean   Adj. Mean   Est. Mean   Raw Resid.  Std. Resid.

     1        4.429       4.888       4.429        0.0         0.0
     2        7.571       7.076       7.571        0.0         0.0
     3        6.714       6.750       6.714        0.0         0.0
```

D Results for third analysis

```
Tests of Significance for Y using SEQUENTIAL Sums of Squares
Source of Variation        SS      DF       MS          F   Sig of F

WITHIN+RESIDUAL            9.63     15      .64
CONSTANT                 817.19      1   817.19    1272.24      .000
X                         36.58      1    36.58      56.94      .000
A                         16.93      2     8.47      13.18      .000
A BY X                      .67      2      .33        .52      .605
```

E Results for fourth analysis

```
Tests of Significance for Y using SEQUENTIAL Sums of Squares
Source of Variation        SS      DF       MS          F   Sig of F

WITHIN+RESIDUAL            9.63     15      .64
CONSTANT                 817.19      1   817.19    1272.24      .000
X WITHIN A                47.48      3    15.83      24.64      .000
A                          6.69      2     3.35       5.21      .019
```

Example 2: Multivariate Multiple Regression and Canonical Correlation

MANOVA produces multivariate results, individual regression results, and analysis of residuals, although residual analysis is not as extensive as in REGRESSION. Since there is no canonical correlation procedure in SPSS/PC+, MANOVA can be used for canonical correlation analysis.

This example uses MANOVA for multivariate multiple regression and canonical correlation analysis. The data for this example come from Finn (1974) and were obtained from tests administered to 60 eleventh-grade students in a western New York metropolitan school.

The dependent variables are

• SYNTH—a measurement of achievement.
• EVAL—another measurement of achievement.

There are three types of independent variables. The first is

• INTEL—general intelligence as measured by a standard test.

For the second type of independent variables, there are three measures of creativity:

• CONOBV—consequences obvious, which involves the ability of the subject to list direct consequences of a given hypothetical event.
• CONRMT—consequences remote, which involves identifying more remote or original consequences of similar situations.
• JOB—possible jobs, which involves the ability to list a quantity of occupations that might be represented by a given emblem or symbol.

The third type of independent variable is a set of multiplicative interactions of the three creativity measures with intelligence to assess whether creativity has a greater effect on the achievement of individuals having high intelligence than on individuals of low intelligence. These variables are created using the SPSS/PC+ transformation language. For all independent variables, standardized scores are used. The data are in an external file named AMAN.DAT.

The SPSS/PC+ commands in the command file named on the INCLUDE command are

```
SET WIDTH=WIDE.
DATA LIST FILE='AMAN.DAT'
 / SYNTH 1 EVAL 3 CONOBV 5-8(1) CONRMT 9-12(1)
   JOB 14-17(1) INTEL 19-23(1).
MISSING VALUE SYNTH TO INTEL(9.9).
DESCRIPTIVES INTEL CONOBV CONRMT JOB
 /OPTIONS=3 5.
COMPUTE CI1=ZCONOBV*ZINTEL.
COMPUTE CI2=ZCONRMT*ZINTEL.
COMPUTE CI3=ZJOB*ZINTEL.
MANOVA  SYNTH EVAL WITH ZINTEL ZCONOBV ZCONRMT ZJOB CI1 CI2 CI3
 /PRINT=ERROR(SSCP COV COR)
        SIGNIF(HYPOTH STEPDOWN DIMENR EIGEN)
 /DISCRIM=RAW,STAN,ESTIM,COR,ALPHA(1.0)
 /RESIDUALS=CASEWISE PLOT
 /DESIGN.
FINISH.
```

- The SET command sets the display width to 132 characters.

- The DATA LIST command names the file containing the data and defines six variables.

- The MISSING VALUE command declares the value 9.9 as user-missing for all the variables read from the data file.

- Option 3 on the DESCRIPTIVES procedure computes standardized scores for the intelligence and creativity measures. The new variables—ZINTEL, ZCONOBV, ZCONRMT, and ZJOB—are automatically added to the active file. Option 5 on DESCRIPTIVES specifies listwise deletion of missing values for the calculation.

- The COMPUTE commands compute three interaction variables—CI1, CI2, and CI3—from the standardized variables created with DESCRIPTIVES.

- The MANOVA specification names SYNTH and EVAL as joint dependent variables and specifies seven covariates—ZINTEL, ZCONOBV, ZCONRMT, ZJOB, CI1, CI2, and CI3.

- The PRINT subcommand requests several displays. The ERROR keyword prints the error sums-of-squares and cross-products (SSCP) matrix, the error variance-covariance matrix, and the error correlation matrix with standard deviations on the diagonal (Figure A).

- The SIGNIF keyword has four specifications. HYPOTH prints the hypothesis SSCP matrix (Figure A). STEPDOWN prints the Roy-Bargmann stepdown F tests for the dependent variables. DIMENR prints the dimension reduction analysis, and EIGEN prints the eigenvalues and canonical correlations (Figure B).

- The DISCRIM subcommand requests a canonical analysis. The results correspond to canonical correlation analysis since a set of continuous dependent variables are related to a set of continuous independent variables. The RAW keyword prints canonical function coefficients; the STAN keyword prints standardized canonical function coefficients; the ESTIM keyword produces effect estimates in canonical function space; the COR keyword prints correlations between the original variables and the canonical variables defined by the canonical functions; and the ALPHA keyword sets a generous cutoff value (1.0) for the significance of the canonical functions in the analysis, thereby ensuring that MANOVA calculates all possible canonical functions. Two is the maximum possible in this analysis (Figures C and D).

- The RESIDUALS subcommand with keyword CASEWISE prints four casewise results for each dependent variable: the observed value of the dependent variable, the predicted value of the dependent variable, the residual value, and the standardized residual, where standardization consists of dividing the residual by the error standard deviation (Figure F).

- The PLOT keyword on the RESIDUALS subcommand produces plots of the observed values, predicted values, and case number against standardized residuals, as well as normal and detrended normal probability plots for the standardized residuals (Figures G through I).
- Finally, the DESIGN subcommand specifies the model, which in this example is the default full factorial model.

Portions of the output are shown in Figures A through I. The exact appearance of printed display depends on the characters available on your printer.

- Figure A shows within-cells statistical results. The correlation of 0.380 is the partial correlation of SYNTH and EVAL, taking into account the independent variable set. The two standard deviations are adjusted. The Bartlett test of sphericity leads to rejection of the hypothesis that the partial correlation between SYNTH and EVAL is zero. Figure A also shows the adjusted variance-covariance matrix, the error SSCP matrix, and the hypothesis SSCP matrix for the regression effect.
- Figure B shows the default display and the stepdown display. Both the multivariate and univariate test results indicate that the predictor set has a statistically significant impact on the dependent variables. While two dimensions are fit, it appears that one dimension will suffice. Of the two eigenvalues, the first eigenvalue has most of the variance associated with it, while the second eigenvalue has relatively little variability associated with it. Likewise, the first canonical correlation is moderately sized, while the second canonical correlation is negligible in magnitude. Provided that you accept the order of the criterion variables—SYNTH, then EVAL—the stepdown F tests show that after taking SYNTH into account, EVAL does not contribute to the association with the predictors.
- Figure C shows canonical results for the two dependent variables. Recall that only the first canonical function is statistically significant. Correlations between the dependent variables and the first canonical variable are of similar magnitude. The part of the figure labeled "Variance explained by canonical variables of DEPEN-DENT variables" provides a *redundancy analysis* (Cooley & Lohnes, 1971).
- Figure D shows the analogous canonical results for the covariates. The correlations between covariates and the first canonical variable load most heavily on intelligence.
- Figure E shows the default display of the regression results for the two dependent variables.
- Figure F shows a portion of the casewise results for the synthesis variable produced by RESIDUALS=CASEWISE.
- Figure G shows two plots. The plot of observed versus predicted values for SYNTH reflects the multiple R for the model. The plot of observed values versus residuals shows how residuals vary in sign and magnitude across values of the dependent variable.
- Figure H shows two plots: the plot of predicted values versus residuals, and the plot of case number versus residuals. The latter plot is useful when there is some meaning to the order of cases in your file.
- Finally, Figure I shows the normal and detrended normal plots of the residuals.

A Within-cells results and hypothesis SSCP

```
Adjusted WITHIN CELLS Correlations with Std. Devs. on Diagonal

                SYNTH        EVAL

SYNTH          1.370
EVAL            .380       1.513

- - - - - - - - - -
Statistics for ADJUSTED WITHIN CELLS correlations

Determinant =                         .85577
Bartlett test of sphericity =      7.86554 with 1 D. F.
Significance =                        .005

F(max) criterion =                 1.21806 with (2,52) D. F.

- - - - - - - - - -
Adjusted WITHIN CELLS Variances and Covariances

                SYNTH        EVAL

SYNTH          1.878
EVAL            .787       2.288

- - - - - - - - - -
Adjusted WITHIN CELLS Sum-of-Squares and Cross-Products

                SYNTH        EVAL

SYNTH         97.669
EVAL          40.937     118.967

- - - - - - - - - -
Adjusted Hypothesis Sum-of-Squares and Cross-Products

                SYNTH        EVAL

SYNTH         81.181
EVAL          69.413      67.216
```

B Test results and dimensionality statistics

```
EFFECT .. WITHIN CELLS Regression
Multivariate Tests of Significance (S = 2, M = 2 , N = 24 1/2)

Test Name      Value   Approx. F  Hypoth. DF    Error DF   Sig. of F

Pillais       .55946   2.88501       14.00      104.00      .001
Hotellings   1.05995   3.78553       14.00      100.00      .000
Wilks         .47077   3.33286       14.00      102.00      .000
Roys          .49886

- - - - - - - - - -
Eigenvalues and Canonical Correlations

Root No.   Eigenvalue     Pct.     Cum. Pct.   Canon Cor.    Sq. Cor

       1       .995     93.914      93.914        .706        .499
       2       .065      6.086     100.000        .246        .061

- - - - - - - - - -
Dimension Reduction Analysis

Roots       Wilks L.        F  Hypoth. DF   Error DF  Sig. of F

1 TO 2       .47077    3.33286     14.00      102.00     .000
2 TO 2       .93940     .55910      6.00       52.00     .761

- - - - - - - - - -
Univariate F-tests with (7,52) D. F.

Variable   Sq. Mul. R    Mul. R  Adj. R-sq.  Hypoth. MS   Error MS        F    Sig. of F

SYNTH        .45390     .67372    .38039     11.59727    1.87825    6.17450     .000
EVAL         .36102     .60085    .27500      9.60230    2.28783    4.19712     .001

- - - - - - - - - -
Roy-Bargman Stepdown F - tests

Variable  Hypoth. MS  Error MS  StepDown F  Hypoth. DF   Error DF  Sig. of F

SYNTH      11.59727   1.87825    6.17450         7         52       .000
EVAL        2.32700   1.99625    1.16569         7         51       .339
```

C Canonical results for dependent variables

```
Raw canonical coefficients for DEPENDENT variables
        Function No.

Variable            1               2

SYNTH             .404            -.597
EVAL              .226             .670
- - - - - - - - - -
Standardized canonical coefficients for DEPENDENT variables
        Function No.

Variable            1               2

SYNTH             .704           -1.040
EVAL              .402            1.189
- - - - - - - - - -
Correlations between DEPENDENT and canonical variables
        Function No.

Variable            1               2

SYNTH             .947            -.320
EVAL              .828             .561
- - - - - - - - - -
Variance explained by canonical variables of DEPENDENT variables

CAN. VAR.   Pct Var DE Cum Pct DE Pct Var CO Cum Pct CO

        1       79.146      79.146     39.482     39.482
        2       20.854     100.000      1.264     40.746
```

D Canonical results for the covariates

```
Raw canonical coefficients for COVARIATES
        Function No.

COVARIATE           1               2

ZINTEL            .848            -.103
ZCONOBV           .265             .230
ZCONRMT           .193             .472
ZJOB             -.064            -.279
CI1              -.014            1.035
CI2              -.076            -.324
CI3               .207            -.047
- - - - - - - - - -
Standardized canonical coefficients for COVARIATES
        CAN. VAR.

COVARIATE           1               2

ZINTEL            .848            -.103
ZCONOBV           .265             .230
ZCONRMT           .193             .472
ZJOB             -.064            -.279
CI1              -.012             .887
CI2              -.101            -.431
CI3               .217            -.049
- - - - - - - - - -
Correlations between COVARIATES and canonical variables
        CAN. VAR.

Covariate           1               2

ZINTEL            .946            -.091
ZCONOBV           .303            -.061
ZCONRMT           .562             .418
ZJOB              .578            -.127
CI1               .180             .868
CI2               .494            -.010
CI3               .449             .063
- - - - - - - - - -
Variance explained by canonical variables of the COVARIATES

CAN. VAR.   Pct Var DE Cum Pct DE Pct Var CO Cum Pct CO

        1       15.074      15.074     30.217     30.217
        2         .832      15.906     13.728     43.945
```

E Regression results

```
Regression analysis for WITHIN CELLS error term
Dependent variable .. SYNTH

COVARIATE          B         Beta      Std. Err.      t-Value    Sig. of t   Lower -95%  CL- Upper

ZINTEL         1.00235     .57571       .217          4.617       .000         .567       1.438
ZCONOBV         .27761     .15945       .236          1.178       .244        -.195        .750
ZCONRMT         .16002     .09191       .238           .672       .504        -.318        .638
ZJOB           -.03625    -.02082       .267          -.136       .892        -.571        .499
CI1            -.15800    -.07779       .236          -.670       .506        -.631        .315
CI2            -.04376    -.03348       .215          -.204       .839        -.475        .387
CI3             .24763     .14904       .252           .982       .331        -.259        .754

Dependent variable .. EVAL

COVARIATE          B         Beta      Std. Err.      t-Value    Sig. of t   Lower -95%  CL- Upper

ZINTEL          .85582     .48177       .240          3.571       .001         .375       1.337
ZCONOBV         .33193     .18686       .260          1.277       .207        -.190        .854
ZCONRMT         .31633     .17807       .263          1.204       .234        -.211        .843
ZJOB           -.13500    -.07600       .294          -.459       .648        -.726        .456
CI1             .23964     .11563       .260           .921       .362        -.283        .762
CI2            -.15804    -.11852       .237          -.667       .508        -.634        .317
CI3             .20367     .12014       .278           .732       .468        -.355        .762
```

F Casewise output

```
Observed and Predicted Values for Each Case
Dependent Variable.. SYNTH

Case No.    Observed   Predicted Raw Resid.  Std Resid.

       1      5.000      2.824       2.176       1.588
       2      0.0        1.905      -1.905      -1.390
       4      4.000      3.648        .352        .257
       5      1.000      2.030      -1.030       -.752
       6      7.000      4.210       2.790       2.036
       7      1.000      1.950       -.950       -.694
       8      2.000      2.036       -.036       -.027
       9      1.000      1.763       -.763       -.557
      10      4.000      3.861        .139        .102
       .         .          .           .           .
       .         .          .           .           .
       .         .          .           .           .
```

G Observed values vs. predicted values and residuals

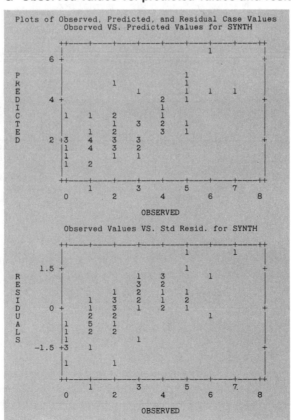

H Residuals vs. predicted values and case number

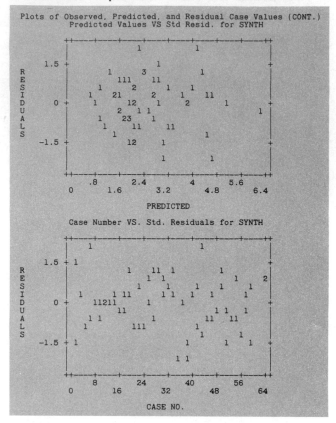

I Normal and detrended normal probability plots

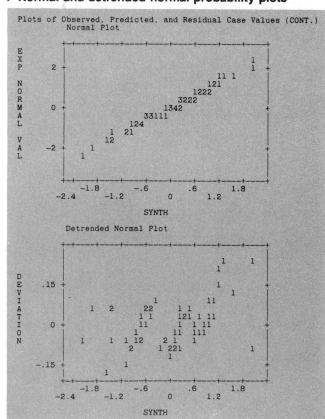

Example 3: Repeated Measures

This example is a repeated measures design using data from an experiment that studies the effects of four drugs on reaction time to a series of tasks (Winer, 1971). The subjects are trained in the tasks prior to the experiment so that the learning of the tasks does not confound the analysis. The experimenter observes each subject under each drug, and the order of administration of drugs is randomized. Since there are only five subjects in the analysis the data are included inline.

The SPSS/PC+ commands in the command file named on the INCLUDE command are

```
SET WIDTH=WIDE.
DATA LIST FREE/ DRUG1 DRUG2 DRUG3 DRUG4.
BEGIN DATA.
 30 28 16 34
 14 18 10 22
 24 20 18 30
 38 34 20 44
 26 28 14 30
END DATA.
MANOVA DRUG1 TO DRUG4
 /WSFACTORS=TRIAL(4)
 /CONTRAST(TRIAL)=SPECIAL(4*1, 1,-1,0,0,
                                1,1,0,-2, 1,1,-3,1)
 /PRINT=CELLINFO(MEANS)
  TRANSFORM
  SIGNIF(UNIV)
 /DESIGN.
FINISH.
```

- The SET command sets the width of the display to 132 characters.
- The DATA LIST command defines four variables that will be read in freefield format from the command file.
- The BEGIN DATA—END DATA commands surround the inline data.
- The MANOVA specification names DRUG1 to DRUG4 as four joint dependent variables. There are no between-subjects factors or covariates in the analysis.
- The WSFACTORS subcommand defines TRIAL as a within-subjects factor. The 4 in parentheses after the factor name indicates there are four drugs.
- The CONTRAST subcommand specifies a special set of contrasts for comparisons of the means across scores. The within-subjects factor requires *orthogonal* contrasts, which include difference, helmert, and polynomial contrasts. If you do not specify orthogonal contrasts for the within-subjects factor, MANOVA takes your specified contrasts and orthonormalizes them.
- The first row of the special matrix is always the contrast for the overall mean and is typically a set of 1's. The remaining rows of the matrix contain the special contrasts signifying the desired comparisons between levels of the factor. After inspection of the four means, the following comparisons are specified: (1) the mean of DRUG1 versus the mean of DRUG2; (2) the means of DRUG1 and DRUG2 versus the mean of DRUG4; and (3) the means of DRUG1, DRUG2, and DRUG4 versus DRUG3.
- The PRINT subcommand has three specifications. CELLINFO prints the means (Figure A). TRANSFORM prints the orthonormalized transformation matrix, which directly reflects the contrasts on the within-subjects factor (Figure B). SIGNIF(UNIV) prints the univariate F tests (Figure G).
- The DESIGN subcommand specifies the model for the between-subjects factor. Since there is no between-subjects factor in this model, the DESIGN subcommand simply triggers the analysis.

Portions of the display output are shown in Figures A through H.

- Figure A shows the cell means and standard deviations. Inspection of the cell means provides a rationale for the special contrast used in the analysis. Notice that the means for DRUG1 and DRUG2 have the smallest difference. Then, the mean for DRUG4 has a smaller difference from these two than does the mean for DRUG3. Finally, the mean for DRUG3 is most different from the others. Note: If the width is not set wide (132 characters), the confidence intervals are not included in the display.
- Figure B shows the within-subjects design. The orthonormalized transformation matrix shows the contrasts on the means. The original contrasts on the CONTRAST

subcommand are orthogonal. MANOVA normalizes the contrasts so that the sum of squares of any column of the matrix is 1.

- Figure C shows the beginning of the default display for multivariate repeated measures analysis. A message indicating that the variables are transformed is also displayed.
- Figure D shows the test of significance for the between-subjects effect, which in this example is just the overall constant.
- Figure E shows the next cycle of the analysis, which is the test for the trial within-subjects effect. MANOVA jointly tests the three transformed variables, making this a multivariate test.
- Figure F shows Mauchly's test of sphericity, which is printed by default. This tests the hypothesis that the covariance matrix of the transformed variables has a constant variance on the diagonal and zeros off the diagonal.
- Figure G shows the multivariate tests of significance of the trial within-subjects effect. The multivariate tests are significant at the 0.05 level. The univariate F tests, the result of specifying SIGNIF(UNIV), reveal more detailed aspects of the pattern. Recall that the T2 effect after transformation—the contrast between the means of DRUG1 and DRUG2—is the first contrast of interest. The F statistic for this effect is not significant, which leads to the conclusion that these two drugs do not produce differences in reaction time. On the other hand, the transformed T3 and T4 effects are significant at the 0.01 level.
- Finally, Figure H shows the averaged test of significance for the drug effect; these are the *univariate approach* statistics. There are twelve error degrees of freedom for this test, while there are two error degrees of freedom for the multivariate tests. Given the error correlation results above, the averaged test is appropriate. The observed level of significance of this test is less than 0.0005, so the averaged F test corroborates the multivariate test results.

A Cell means and standard deviations

```
Cell Means and Standard Deviations
Variable .. DRUG1
                                Mean   Std. Dev.     N   95 percent Conf. Interval

For entire sample              26.400    8.764       5    15.519     37.281

 - - - - - - - -
Variable .. DRUG2
                                Mean   Std. Dev.     N   95 percent Conf. Interval

For entire sample              25.600    6.542       5    17.477     33.723

 - - - - - - - -
Variable .. DRUG3
                                Mean   Std. Dev.     N   95 percent Conf. Interval

For entire sample              15.600    3.847       5    10.823     20.377

 - - - - - - - -
Variable .. DRUG4
                                Mean   Std. Dev.     N   95 percent Conf. Interval

For entire sample              32.000    8.000       5    22.067     41.933
```

B Within-subjects design

```
Orthonormalized Transformation Matrix (Transposed)

                    T1          T2          T3          T4

DRUG1             .50000      .70711      .40825      .28868
DRUG2             .50000     -.70711      .40825      .28868
DRUG3             .50000      0.0         0.0        -.86603
DRUG4             .50000      0.0        -.81650      .28868
```

C Constant within-subjects effect

```
Order of Variables for Analysis

   Variates      Covariates

   T1

   1 Dependent Variable
   0 Covariates

_ _ _ _ _ _ _ _ _
Note..  TRANSFORMED variables are in the variates column.
        These TRANSFORMED variables correspond to the
        Between-subject effects.
```

D Analysis of variance for CONSTANT

```
Tests of Between-Subjects Effects.

Tests of Significance for T1 using UNIQUE sums of squares
Source of Variation           SS      DF       MS            F   Sig of F

WITHIN CELLS               680.80      4     170.20
CONSTANT                 12400.20      1   12400.20       72.86      .001
```

E Trial within-subjects effect

```
Order of Variables for Analysis

   Variates      Covariates

   T2
   T3
   T4

   3 Dependent Variables
   0 Covariates

_ _ _ _ _ _ _ _ _
Note..  TRANSFORMED variables are in the variates column.
        These TRANSFORMED variables correspond to the
        'TRIAL' WITHIN-SUBJECT effect.
```

F Error correlation statistics

```
Tests involving 'TRIAL' Within-Subject Effect.

Mauchly sphericity test, W =        .18650
Chi-square approx. =               4.57156 with 5 D. F.
Significance =                      .470

Greenhouse-Geisser Epsilon =        .60487
Huynh-Feldt Epsilon =              1.00000
Lower-bound Epsilon =               .33333
```

D

Examples

G Multivariate tests of significance

```
EFFECT .. TRIAL
Multivariate Tests of Significance (S = 1, M = 1/2, N = 0)

Test Name           Value   Approx. F  Hypoth. DF   Error DF   Sig. of F

Pillais             .97707  28.41231       3.00        2.00       .034
Hotellings        42.61846  28.41231       3.00        2.00       .034
Wilks               .02293  28.41231       3.00        2.00       .034
Roys                .97707

- - - - - - - - - -
Univariate F-tests with (1,4) D. F.

Variable   Hypoth. SS   Error SS  Hypoth. MS   Error MS         F   Sig. of F

T2            1.60000    26.40000    1.60000    6.60000    .24242     .648
T3          120.00000    12.00000  120.00000    3.00000  40.00000     .003
T4          576.60000    74.40000  576.60000   18.60000  31.00000     .005
```

H Averaged test of significance

```
AVERAGED Tests of Significance for DRUG using UNIQUE sums of squares
Source of Variation          SS      DF        MS          F  Sig of F

WITHIN CELLS             112.80      12      9.40
TRIAL                    698.20       3    232.73      24.76      .000
```

References   Cooley, W. W., and P. R. Lohnes. *Multivariate Data Analysis*. New York: Wiley, 1971.

Finn, J. D. *A General Model for Multivariate Analysis*. New York: Holt, Rinehart, and Winston, 1974.

Winer, B. J. *Statistical Principles in Experimental Design*. New York: McGraw-Hill, 1971.

QUICK CLUSTER   This example uses Fisher's classic data on irises to group the irises into clusters. The clusters are then compared with the actual botanical classification. The variables used are

- SEPLEN—sepal length.
- SEPWID—sepal width.
- PETLEN—petal length.
- PETWID—petal width.
- IRISTYPE—type of iris.

The data are in an external file named AQCLUST.DAT. The SPSS/PC+ commands in the command file named on the INCLUDE command are

```
DATA LIST FILE='AQCLUST.DAT'
 / SEPLEN 1-2 SEPWID PETLEN PETWID 3-11 IRISTYPE 13.
VARIABLE LABELS    SEPLEN   'SEPAL LENGTH'
                   SEPWID   'SEPAL WIDTH'
                   PETLEN   'PETAL LENGTH'
                   PETWID   'PETAL WIDTH'
                   IRISTYPE 'TYPE OF IRIS'.
VALUE LABELS   IRISTYPE  1 'SETOSA' 2 'VERSICOLOR'  3 'VIRGINICA'.
QUICK CLUSTER   SEPLEN TO PETWID
 /CRITERIA=CLUSTERS(3)
 /PRINT=INITIAL ANOVA
 /SAVE=CLUSTER(CLUSTMEM).
VARIABLE LABELS CLUSTMEM 'CLUSTERS FROM DEFAULT METHOD'.
CROSSTABS TABLES=IRISTYPE BY CLUSTMEM
 /STATISTICS=1,4,5.
FINISH.
```

- The DATA LIST command names the file that contains the data and defines the five variables.
- The VARIABLE LABELS command assigns descriptive labels to the variables. The VALUE LABELS command assigns labels to the three values of variable IRISTYPE —three types of irises.
- The QUICK CLUSTER command bases clustering on the values of four variables: SEPLEN, SEPWID, PETLEN, and PETWID.
- The CRITERIA subcommand specifies three clusters.
- The PRINT subcommand requests the display of initial cluster centers and an analysis of variance table describing differences between clusters for each of the four clustering variables (Figure A).
- The SAVE subcommand saves the cluster membership of each case in a new variable, CLUSTMEM, on the SPSS/PC+ active file.
- The VARIABLE LABELS commands assigns a descriptive label to the new variable CLUSTEM.
- The CROSSTABS command crosstabulates the cluster membership variable with variable IRISTYPE, which identifies the actual type of iris. The STATISTICS subcommand requests a chi-square test of significance plus two measures of the predictability of iris types from the cluster types (Figure B). The CROSSTABS output shows that the clusters are strongly associated with the actual classifications.

The display is shown in Figures A and B. The exact appearance of printed display depends on the characters available on your printer.

A QUICK CLUSTER output for the iris data

```
Initial Cluster Centers.

    Cluster      SEPLEN        SEPWID        PETLEN        PETWID

       1        58.0000       40.0000       12.0000        2.0000
       2        77.0000       38.0000       67.0000       22.0000
       3        49.0000       25.0000       45.0000       17.0000

- - - - - - - - - - - - - - - - - - - - - - - - - - - - - - - - - - - - - - - -

Classification Cluster Centers.

    Cluster      SEPLEN        SEPWID        PETLEN        PETWID

       1        51.0091       35.5029       13.5981        2.3147
       2        72.7018       34.1981       63.3840       21.8201
       3        59.9192       27.5660       47.4896       16.9838

- - - - - - - - - - - - - - - - - - - - - - - - - - - - - - - - - - - - - - - -

Final Cluster Centers.

    Cluster      SEPLEN        SEPWID        PETLEN        PETWID

       1        50.0600       34.2800       14.6200        2.4600
       2        70.8696       31.2609       60.1304       21.4348
       3        60.1558       27.9610       45.7532       15.3636

- - - - - - - - - - - - - - - - - - - - - - - - - - - - - - - - - - - - - - - -

Analysis of Variance.

    Variable     Cluster MS    DF        Error MS       DF           F      Prob

    SEPLEN       3645.6374      2        19.9018      147.0    183.1817     0.0
    SEPWID        611.6477      2        10.9347      147.0     55.9365     .000
    PETLEN      21598.9198      2        22.0048      147.0    981.5565     0.0
    PETWID       3734.5515      2         8.0809      147.0    462.1462     0.0

- - - - - - - - - - - - - - - - - - - - - - - - - - - - - - - - - - - - - - - -

Number of Cases in each Cluster.

    Cluster     unweighted cases    weighted cases

       1              50.0                50.0
       2              23.0                23.0
       3              77.0                77.0

    Missing            0
    Total            150.0               150.0
```

B Comparing clusters to the actual botanical classifications

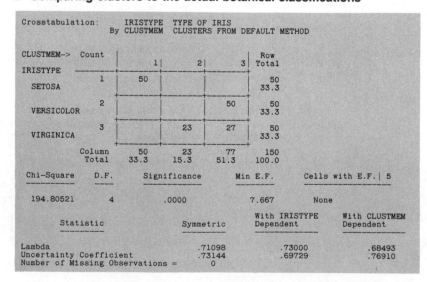

```
Crosstabulation:       IRISTYPE   TYPE OF IRIS
                 By CLUSTMEM   CLUSTERS FROM DEFAULT METHOD

CLUSTMEM->  Count
                          1|       2|       3|   Row
IRISTYPE    ---------+--------+--------+--------+  Total
                   1 |  50   |        |        |    50
  SETOSA           |        |        |        |  33.3
            ---------+--------+--------+--------+
                   2 |        |        |   50   |    50
  VERSICOLOR       |        |        |        |  33.3
            ---------+--------+--------+--------+
                   3 |        |   23   |   27   |    50
  VIRGINICA        |        |        |        |  33.3
            ---------+--------+--------+--------+
             Column    50       23       77      150
              Total   33.3     15.3     51.3    100.0

Chi-Square     D.F.     Significance       Min E.F.      Cells with E.F.| 5
          -----------   ------------      --------       ---------------

194.80521        4         .0000           7.667             None

                                                    With IRISTYPE    With CLUSTMEM
            Statistic                 Symmetric     Dependent        Dependent
          -----------                 ---------     ---------        ---------

Lambda                                 .71098        .73000           .68493
Uncertainty Coefficient                .73144        .69729           .76910
Number of Missing Observations =          0
```

RELIABILITY

The following example demonstrates the use of RELIABILITY to analyze an attitude scale of confidence in institutions in the United States. The data come from a 500-case sample of the 1980 General Social Survey. Respondents were asked how much confidence they have in the people running the following institutions: banks and financial institutions, major companies, organized religion, education, the executive branch of the federal government, organized labor, the press, medicine, television, the United States Supreme Court, the scientific community, Congress, and the military. The SPSS/PC+ commands are

```
GET FILE='GSS80.SYS'.
RELIABILITY VARIABLES=CONFINAN TO CONARMY
   /SCALE (CONSCALE)=ALL
   /MODEL=SPLIT
   /SUMMARY=TOTAL
   /STATISTICS=ANOVA TUKEY HOTELLING.
```

• The GET command makes the data from the system file named GSS80.SYS available for analysis.
• The RELIABILITY command analyzes the scale formed from the 13 confidence variables CONFINAN to CONARMY.
• The SCALE subcommand supplies a name (CONSCALE) for the scale.
• The MODEL subcommand specifies a split-half analysis.
• The SUMMARY subcommand produces item-total statistics.
• The STATISTICS subcommand produces the analysis of variance table, the Tukey test for additivity, and Hotelling's T^2.

Portions of the output produced by these commands appear in Figures A through D.

• Figure A contains the item-total statistics produced by the SUMMARY subcommand.
• Figure B contains the analysis of variance table. The F statistic for variation between measures is significant, indicating that the items have significantly different means. F for nonadditivity is not significant, so we can accept the hypothesis that the items are additive.
• Figure C contains Tukey's test for non-additivity and Hotelling's T^2. Tukey's test is close to 1, which again indicates that the items are additive. Hotelling's T^2 is significant, which indicates that we can reject the hypothesis that the items have equal means in the population.
• Figure D contains the split-half reliability coefficients.

A Item-total statistics

```
       # OF CASES =        415.0


ITEM-TOTAL STATISTICS

                 SCALE          SCALE        CORRECTED
                 MEAN         VARIANCE         ITEM-        SQUARED        ALPHA
               IF ITEM        IF ITEM          TOTAL       MULTIPLE       IF ITEM
               DELETED        DELETED       CORRELATION   CORRELATION     DELETED

CONFINAN       22.8361        17.8958          .4550         .2989         .7831
CONBUS         22.8410        18.6317          .3556         .2424         .7918
CONCLERG       22.8554        18.3172          .3693         .1671         .7912
CONEDUC        22.8458        18.0679          .4652         .2321         .7823
CONFED         22.4578        18.0459          .4692         .2961         .7820
CONLABOR       22.5181        18.4242          .3763         .2102         .7902
CONPRESS       22.7108        18.8147          .3215         .2220         .7947
CONMEDIC       23.1036        18.0158          .4962         .2740         .7798
CONTV          22.5518        18.5909          .3670         .1938         .7908
CONJUDGE       22.7446        17.5771          .5061         .3125         .7783
CONSCI         23.1036        18.6632          .3910         .2185         .7887
CONLEGIS       22.4145        18.0790          .5277         .3481         .7779
CONARMY        22.7952        17.7381          .4930         .2903         .7796
```

B ANOVA table

```
                         ANALYSIS OF VARIANCE

SOURCE OF VARIATION      SUM OF SQ.      DF      MEAN SQUARE      F        PROB.

BETWEEN PEOPLE            669.7412       414       1.6177
WITHIN PEOPLE           1858.9231      4980        .3733
  BETWEEN MEASURES        240.9631       12       20.0803      61.6571    .0000
  RESIDUAL              1617.9600      4968        .3257
    NONADDITIVITY            .0041        1         .0041       .0125     .9109
    BALANCE            1617.9559      4967        .3257
TOTAL                   2528.6643      5394        .4688

GRAND MEAN =               1.8960
```

C Tukey and Hotelling tests

```
TUKEY ESTIMATE OF POWER TO WHICH OBSERVATIONS
MUST BE RAISED TO ACHIEVE ADDITIVITY         =       0.9778


HOTELLINGS T-SQUARED =    694.5944          F =      56.3449       PROB. =    .0000
   DEGREES OF FREEDOM:            NUMERATOR =       12        DENOMINATOR =      403
```

D Split-half reliability estimates

```
RELIABILITY COEFFICIENTS    13 ITEMS

CORRELATION BETWEEN FORMS =    .6583     EQUAL LENGTH SPEARMAN-BROWN =     .7940

GUTTMAN SPLIT-HALF =           .7923     UNEQUAL-LENGTH SPEARMAN-BROWN =   .7948

ALPHA FOR PART 1 =             .6446     ALPHA FOR PART 2 =                .6955

  7 ITEMS IN PART 1                        6 ITEMS IN PART 2
```

Index

Contents

Installing SPSS/PC+ Advanced Statistics

Differences Between SPSS/PC and SPSS/PC+

Help for SPSS^x Users

Index